BOOM, BUST, EXODUS

BOOM, BUST, EXODUS

THE RUST BELT,
THE *MAQUILAS,* AND
A TALE OF TWO CITIES

CHAD BROUGHTON

OXFORD
UNIVERSITY PRESS

OXFORD
UNIVERSITY PRESS

Oxford University Press is a department of the University of Oxford.
It furthers the University's objective of excellence in research, scholarship,
and education by publishing worldwide.

Oxford   New York

Auckland   Cape Town   Dar es Salaam   Hong Kong   Karachi
Kuala Lumpur   Madrid   Melbourne   Mexico City   Nairobi
New Delhi   Shanghai   Taipei   Toronto

With offices in

Argentina   Austria   Brazil   Chile   Czech Republic   France   Greece
Guatemala   Hungary   Italy   Japan   Poland   Portugal   Singapore
South Korea   Switzerland   Thailand   Turkey   Ukraine   Vietnam

Oxford is a registered trademark of Oxford University Press
in the UK and certain other countries.

Published in the United States of America by
Oxford University Press
198 Madison Avenue, New York, NY 10016

Library of Congress Cataloging-in-Publication Data
Broughton, Chad.
Boom, bust, exodus : the Rust Belt, the maquilas, and a tale of two cities / Chad Broughton.
pages cm
Includes bibliographical references and index.
ISBN 978-0-19-976561-4 (hardback)
1. Galesburg (Ill.)—Economic conditions.   2. Reynosa (Tamaulipas, Mexico)—Economic conditions.
3. Working class—Illinois—Galesburg.   4. Working class—Mexico—Reynosa (Tamaulipas)
5. Maytag Corporation—Employees.   6. Offshore assembly industry—Mexico—Reynosa (Tamaulipas)
7. Globalization—Social aspects—Illinois—Galesburg.   8. Globalization—Social aspects—Mexico—Reynosa
(Tamaulipas)   9. Galesburg (Ill.)—Social conditions.   10. Reynosa (Tamaulipas, Mexico)—Social conditions.
I. Title.
HC108.G26B76 2015
330.9773'49—dc23
2014008029

1 3 5 7 9 8 6 4 2
Printed in the United States of America
on acid-free paper

To Mona

CONTENTS

PROLOGUE

ILLINOIS ROUTE 41 cuts straight through a flat landscape of corn and soy-bean fields that turn a lush myrtle-green in late summer. After you pass the last farmhouse on this southern approach to town, you may hear the metal-lic clang of rail cars being jostled into place in the switching yard. A modest wood sign proclaims, "Welcome to Galesburg."

Behind the welcome sign is a vacant parking lot scattered with con-crete blockades and rubble. And behind the parking lot rises a massive white-gray box of a building. A stylish cobalt-blue line wraps around its roof like a gigantic ribbon around a gift box. Several years ago you could have made out "MAYTAG," but the outlines of the letters have faded. Now there is only a pockmarked facade with spots of flaking paint, discolored exterior panels, and two big "Available" signs—one with an 1-800 number and another advertising what remains of the empty giant, "Plus or Minus 707,624 Square Feet."

Most Galesburg residents still remember this place as a source of pride and bustle. It went by many names—Coulter Disc, Midwest Manufacturing, Admiral, Galesburg Refrigeration Products—but "Appliance City" fit it best. That was the nickname of its heyday, when the factory itself had a population of 5,000. For over a century, men and women in the factory assembled farm equipment, kitchen cabinets, freezers, war munitions, military aircraft parts, microwaves, air conditioners, and millions—tens of millions—of refrigera-tors. If you bought a Maytag refrigerator in the 1990s or early 2000s, it was designed, manufactured, and trucked to your Sears or Home Depot from this spot.

Before Maytag, products from Admiral, Rockwell International, and Magic Chef emerged from Appliance City, which buzzed with continuous vitality in the heady postwar decades of heavy kitchen consumption. It drew in steel sheets, copper tubing, insulation, paint, and tar and converted this stew of raw materials and parts from across the globe into side-by-side refrigerators—an Appliance City specialty since 1960—by means of homegrown blueprints, concussive air guns, and lots of elbow grease. The Galesburg factory made this centerpiece of the American kitchen, in standard white, brushed chrome, and in colors that ranged from citron-yellow to turquoise.

Appliance City offered a fair deal. It was a place where for over half a century a worker just out of high school could exchange his or her best working years for economic security, health care for his or her family, and comfort in old age. This came to an end in 2004, and Appliance City went from workplace to empty shell, becoming over the course of a decade an object of both nostalgia and scorn. Former workers still admit to flipping off the factory or barking out an obscenity as they drive by. For many, the empty giant is a continual reminder of All That's Wrong with America: lost manufacturing, lost jobs, lost lives.

Much of it was demolished before I visited it for the last time in 2014. But my memory of the abandoned site before its demolition is indelible. The chain-link fence outside the factory's north side wouldn't have kept out an ambitious toddler. All one could see was a mix of gravel, broken bricks, and tall weeds pushing through cracks in the oil-stained concrete. Some doors were locked. Others weren't. Inside, an unidentifiable low-level electric hum still vibrated in chamber after chamber across 2.25 million square feet of emptiness—about the size of twenty-one Walmarts packed together. Birds nested in the high metal rafters and rodents scurried in the dark corners. In an old loading bay, the floor was layered so thick with birdshit that it was impossible to step around. Elsewhere, oddly, it had been swept clean, as if someone were expecting guests.

What happened there didn't happen overnight. Four years after the 2004 shutdown, remnants of one of the refrigerator assembly lines remained, with grimy conveyor belts draped over rust-splotched metal rollers. That year a water main spewed thousands of gallons into a pool sixty feet across that stretched into what had been the metal-cutting shop. It went unnoticed for weeks. At the northernmost end of the factory, some graffiti was still scrawled on the white brick wall. Written shortly after September 11, 2001, it read, "United We Stand."

It was a mile's walk from corner to dark corner of the hulk, whose vacuity was almost overbearing, and yet also spellbinding and even majestic.

Streaming down from the high skylights, natural light formed a checkerboard matrix of yellowish rectangles, softening the hard floor and shifting location as the day passed. Other sections were night-black. Noises from the outside echoed through this spacious wasteland. Little pattering sounds skipped across the roof—perhaps wind-scuttled twigs. Thunderous trains rumbled and whistled as they passed several times each hour. I remember being relieved that there was no one living there—no homeless, no feral predators, no meth lab. There were just random artifacts: an EZ-Go 822 electric cart, a collection of dusty red fire extinguishers, and a Toledo industrial scale.

Off the production floor, in the personnel area, was the former break room with an old Magic Chef refrigerator. Around the corner was the old union office, on the door of which was an FTAA (Free Trade Area of the Americas) sticker with a red slash crossing it out. There was also a "Solidarity Forever" sticker. Someone had tried to scratch out the "Surrender Never" bit.

I first visited the factory in the summer of 2002, having recently joined the faculty at Knox College, where I was teaching sociology. Appliance City was still in full operation. Hundreds of metal refrigerator shells dangled in endless lines and inched forward, like the climactic moment of "The Sorcerer's Apprentice," seeming to move in every direction. It was incredibly loud. I could make no sense at all of the frenetic activity of the place. Workers were melting thousands of white plastic pellets, delivered in big brown Dow Chemical boxes, into a wide but ultra-thin ribbon of milky plastic, which they then pressed into industrial molds. Once hardened, those working on the line set the noxious white liners into the thin steel shell of the side-by-sides. In a few weeks, in American homes from San Diego to Boston, jugs of orange juice and jars of mayonnaise would be pressed against those white liners. Few would know that their shiny, new refrigerator—along with a million others each year—was made in this little city in western Illinois.

Located about 200 miles southwest of Chicago and fifty miles northwest of Peoria, Galesburg is a hub of farm country. Nonetheless, the town's identity was rooted in the kind of work that got done on its southwestern edge, where the massive BNSF—which stands for Burlington Northern Santa Fe—classification yard, one of the largest in the United States, still feeds locomotives with long, beaded-necklace strings of rail cars. After Appliance City closed down, BNSF became Galesburg's largest employer.

Appliance City wasn't Galesburg's only loss. The remains of once-formidable Butler Manufacturing—a factory that made pre-engineered steel buildings such as grain bins, warehouses, and even factories like itself—are scattered on a razed site just west of the rail yard. Likewise, Outboard Marine made Lawn-Boy lawnmowers and engine components for boats in Galesburg until the early 1980s, when it was shuttered. Still, some businesses survive amid the wreckage of the town's southwest quadrant. As does a mobile home park, two cemeteries, a handful of street-side bars, and the 71-acre Henry C. Hill Correctional Center (where a few former refrigerator-makers found jobs). The Gates Rubber Company on the east side, downsized from nearly a thousand workers, holds on by a thread. On Main Street, Galesburg's peaceful downtown—home to Knox, a fine symphony, a rich abolitionist history, and antiquing tourists—endures.

The economic heart of the historic town, though, is gone. As I watched the empty giant gradually succumb to nature and demolition crews, I found it hard to imagine that this place had once meant so much to so many for so long. Indeed the site still exerts a residual force over the people and the region that surrounds it, a potent and enduring symbol of an abandoned middle- and working-class American Dream—as well as the necessity to find a new expression of it.

The summer before the closing announcement the workers inside seemed happy. Amid clanging metal and pneumatic pops, I remember a woman giving a friendly greeting from behind big plastic safety glasses and a brazing torch. Another looked intent as she trimmed the plastic lip off a water dispenser so it would seal tight. I remember seeing pictures of a forklift driver in a Santa costume and of men and women grinning as they worked the cabinets on the line. Working that line was a tradition that spanned generations for many area families.

Still, after 2004, life went on. There was bitterness and a lot of soul-searching, of course, but I quickly understood that former Maytag workers do not want to be viewed as victims. They went back to school, they scrambled from job to job, they scrimped and adapted. They went to yard sales. They found their niche working the rails, tending patients at the hospital, or coaching a junior high basketball team. For many this is a downsized existence, but a full-sized life nonetheless. Not everything had been exported out of Galesburg.

OVER A THOUSAND miles to the southwest of Galesburg, around the time Appliance City shuttered in 2004, workers began assembling side-by-side refrigerators in Planta Maytag III in Reynosa, Tamaulipas, Mexico. It was a newly built *maquiladora*—a foreign-owned, export-oriented factory. From the outside, it stood in contrast to the Galesburg plant. Indeed, the *maquila* suggested office park more than sweatshop or even industry. With narrow, dark windows, pleasing landscaping, and touches of Maytag blue, it would have looked at home in Silicon Valley. "The maquila is gorgeous," admitted Teresa Chávez, a longtime maquiladora worker and sharp-tongued critic of the industry. "It looks like the house of Walt Disney."

Assemblers' paychecks at the time showed they made $1.10 an hour, roughly what Galesburg workers made when they first started manufacturing refrigerators there in 1950. The pay did not nearly match people's needs, but there were basic benefits, lots of hours, and the occasional company barbecue. Refrigerator production in Planta Maytag III had been largely automated and most craft elements eliminated—to make each task as elementary as possible. Planta III required only a fraction of the workers needed in Galesburg, and the jobs, though taxing and incredibly tedious, required almost no skill. Each job could be learned in no time. Maytag refrigerator makers were now interchangeable—and they were cheaper.

As production grew, assemblers sometimes worked thirteen hours a day. One such refrigerator maker, Laura Flora Oliveros, needed the extra work but complained she had perpetually swollen feet and aching arms. She was far more concerned, though, about leaving her three elementary and middle-school-aged girls at home from dawn to dusk in Reynosa, which, since the manufacturing boom, had grown dangerous. Once a small petroleum city of 70,000 in the 1950s, Reynosa's population well exceeds one million today, according to leaders on both sides of the border. The city's haphazard urbanization has been fueled by the influx of more than 150 maquiladoras, promoted by savvy, bicultural capitalists in McAllen, Texas—Reynosa's sister city across the Rio Grande. Over 94,000 workers, wearing colorful outfits denoting rank, work in fourteen massive industrial campuses that dominate the sprawling outskirts of the city.

In Planta III the low-level line workers, the *obreros*, are almost entirely Veracruzanos who, for one reason or another, ended up here in the north in their pursuit of something better. The state of Veracruz stretches for hundreds of miles along the tropical Gulf coastline and into plains of corn, green pastures dotted with cattle, and, on its western border, into the cold, snow-capped mountains of the Sierra Madre Oriental. Life had been Spartan for most of these striving migrants, but not without its rewards and not lonely. At the border, the displaced newcomers become apprentices in this buzzing workshop of the global production system.

The southerners live among the maquilas, hidden away like unwanted guests on the city's edge. Their children ride colorful plastic tricycles and play with toy trucks, dolls, and stray kittens in slums built up on former ranchlands. Coca-Cola trucks with bagged snacks and bottled *refrescos* bounce through the rutted roads of their *colonias* (neighborhoods). In their midst are the three factions of the Reynosa theater of the Mexican Drug War—*El Cártel* (the Gulf Cartel), the ruthless Zetas, and the *federales* (federal police). The war, though, has not crimped production, cross-border trade, or foiled Reynosa's hardened migrants from eking out a living and raising their families. Factory managers and professionals and those in need of dental work or unregulated pharmaceuticals still cross the border each day from the southern tip of Texas. It may be a gritty, parochial backwater in some ways, but this border city throbs with the energy of commerce, legal and illegal. Reynosa sits at the boundary between two very different worlds—a place Gloria Anzaldúa, a poet and novelist from the area, described as "an open wound, where the third world grates against the first and bleeds."[1]

The contrast between Galesburg and Reynosa could not be greater. Galesburg struggles to provide a work life for its residents, one that matches what they had during the glory years of Appliance City. The maquila, on the other hand, has made Reynosa into one of the exploding "second-tier cities" of the developing world that often go unnoticed in the shadows of megacities such as Mexico City, Mumbai, and Karachi. But these cities will take in three-fourths of future world population growth as they absorb the displaced rural poor.[2] Just as African Americans trekked north in the two great migrations of the 20th century to find work and to escape sharecropping and Jim Crow, the rural poor of Mexico have migrated north to their industrial promised land in an era-defining rural exodus.

E. P. Thompson once warned of the incessant "attempt to provide simple models for one single, supposedly-neutral, technologically-determined, process known as industrialization . . . there has never been any single type of 'the transition.'"[3] The industrial revolution taking place in Mexico's north is not like England's in the late 1700s and early 1800s, or that of northern U.S. cities such as Chicago in the late 1800s, or that of China more recently. The "transition" in Mexico is unique in world history, shaped overwhelmingly by economic integration with its powerful neighbor to the north. As the saying goes, "Pobre México, tan lejos de Dios y tan cerca de los Estados Unidos" (Poor Mexico, so far from God and so close to the United States).

RECENTLY, MY THREE daughters and I explored the latest Maytag model at our local Home Depot in Evanston, just outside of Chicago. It looks like all Home Depots do, with wide aisles and factory-like height; there's the smell of mulch in the spring. The refrigerator immediately caught our eye. Inside its polished stainless steel casing was 24.8 cubic feet of room for food and drinks, and a freezer that could hold 120 pounds of Costco or Aldi plunder. The refrigerator had Foam-in-Place insulation, sealed FreshLock crispers, adjustable Spill-Catcher tempered-glass shelves, and the QuietSeries 200 sound package, featuring a muffler for the compressor.

When we got home, I looked at Home Depot's website, on which a search yielded 500 refrigerators, 83 of them Maytags. Every detail about the refrigerator we had admired was there: its assembled depth (34.4375 inches), its energy-efficiency rating (Tier 1), a description of its "Pick-off Gallon-Plus" door bins, and customer reviews. And to replace the Maytag retail salesman of yesteryear, there was a slick promotional video. In a game show-host voice and bright orange Home Depot apron, a salesman named Patrick promised that this refrigerator would make my life easier. It was hard not to believe him.

Nowhere, though, did Home Depot's or Maytag's website mention where the refrigerator had been manufactured. Probably it was simply not possible. First, you would need at minimum to include the several hundred steel-cutters, painters, silver brazers and metal-joiners, and assemblers who pieced together the refrigerator. You would also need to include supply-chain purchasers, shop-floor engineers, and those clever designers of the QuietSeries 200 sound package and that muffler. And if you included them, you would need to list steelworkers who fashioned the steel and subassembly workers who tinkered together various components, right down to the tiniest screw. There are also the warehouse workers, truckers, and logistics people who took the bulky appliance from the shop floor to the big-box retailer. You would also need the signatures of machine- and robot-makers, iron ore and copper miners, petroleum refiners, plastics workers, parts ship- pers, managers, VPs of this and that, and on and on. Very soon it is clear that an intricate worldwide, social division of labor must exist to make a single Maytag refrigerator—whether in Galesburg or Reynosa—right down to the adjustable Spill-Catcher tempered-glass shelves.

Karl Marx wrote that a commodity is a "social hieroglyphic," a mysterious thing filled with "magic and necromancy" and hidden meanings. What we do not see in a Maytag refrigerator, a green leather Fendi, or a Texas honeydew is that they are each, in their own way, a congelation of human labor. Every time a person buys something, he or she engages in a social exchange—a trade of money (your labor, abstracted and quantified) for the labor of others (objec- tified in the product). Marx argued that commodities conceal this inherently social nature. They appear therefore as "independent beings endowed with life" in our mind's eye.[4] Marx, of course, never owned a refrigerator. The rev- olution he observed was a revolution of steam engines and blast furnaces, of applied science and mass production, and of the factory and a new urban working class. It was a time when the origins of many of the things we con- sume—and their makers—faded from view.

If a refrigerator can be conceived to be magical, this beautiful side-by- side stainless steel Maytag was. It was as if it were born in that Home Depot. We admired the way the French doors opened and closed with a muted yet authoritative *wffft* and its pristine white interior (a contrast to our over- whelmed and less-than-spotless family refrigerator at home). When the door opened and the mild coolant breeze wafted toward us, it did seem like magic. The refrigerator makes modern life in the cities and suburbs—so far removed from where our food is grown, harvested, or made—possible. It's what teens forage through late at night, where parents hang spelling tests and family cal- endars, and where we put our Thanksgiving leftovers and Super Bowl beer.

Human labor produces just about everything we eat, wear, live in, and use, from Tupy blackberries to traditional *masa* tortillas, from garden gnomes to dialysis machines, from pseudoephedrine to elliptical machines. Even the products of almost entirely automated factories such as thin-film solar cells or computer keyboards are ultimately the products of human genius and toil. And yet all of consumer society seems designed to hide this simple fact and to fetishize the object itself—its high-tech wonder, its utilitarian uses, how it enhances the consumer's identity and distinctiveness. Our relationships with consumer goods such as smartphones or Smithfield bacon are immediate, visceral, and concrete. Our relationships to the human beings making our things, on the other hand, have only grown in distance and abstraction. But those relationships are still just as real.

IN A TALE of Two Cities, Charles Dickens—a contemporary of Marx's—reveals the dark underbelly of London and Paris. Dickens himself had been scarred by the despair he felt as a child laborer at age twelve in a London factory where he pasted labels onto pots of boot blacking. In his novels he shocked middle-class readers with stories of the forgotten and mistreated of the urban poor and working classes—many of whom had only recently come from the countryside. "We had everything before us, we had nothing before us," Dickens wrote at the opening of A Tale. Today, as then, we live in a time of paradoxes and extremes—a time of technological wonders, the amassing of great individual fortunes, and the dazzle of consumer culture—and, also, a time of anxiety, displacement, and lowered expectations.

Boom, Bust, Exodus is a book essentially about two places. It is about Galesburg, the place that used to make our refrigerators, and what happened there after it stopped making them a decade ago. And it is about Reynosa, the border boomtown on the fringes of American consciousness, and yet where much of the hemisphere's work—much of it once located in the Midwest Rust Belt—now gets done. At its heart, then, *Boom, Bust, Exodus* is a tale of two cities, a place that lost jobs and a place that gained jobs in the global contest to woo or retain fickle capital. Ultimately, it is also about the people who live in these places, and those drawn to these places: the displaced worker of the Rust Belt, the maquila worker of the borderlands, the farmers of the Mexican *campo*, and the migrant farmworkers harvesting for America's dinner tables. They have been bearing the burdens of the economic upheavals of the past three decades, so that we can buy and then fill our refrigerators.

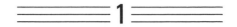

BOOM DAYS IN APPLIANCE CITY

Galesburg, Illinois

PACKING INSULATION WAS Mike Patrick's first job at Midwest Manufacturing.[1] He was one of 300 men, mostly young, hired in January 1959 to help Admiral, a Chicago-based company that owned the Galesburg factory, meet America's seemingly insatiable postwar appetite for appliances. He had failed an eye test during the nurse's exam at the factory and had to get glasses before he started. Patrick had suspected he needed glasses because he always had trouble seeing the chalkboard from the back of the room in high school. But because he was an athlete, he didn't want to tie glasses around his head during basketball games.

New hires got the nastiest, most grueling jobs, and stuffing insulation— which was like prickly cotton candy—into bare metal cabinets was one of them. The cabinets came from the metal-cutting area of the factory known as the "black line," because the steel, darkened with oil, hadn't yet been painted. The black line was the birthplace of these early Admiral refrigerators. Flatbed semis unloaded massive rolls of thick steel from Chicago—the plant used 10 rolls a day, 50 million pounds a year—that cutters and folding machines would shape into five sides.[2] Gun welders then joined what would become the back, the two sides, and the top and bottom of the refrigerator. They left the door for later.

The fused steel cabinet dangled from an overhead conveyor as it rode to the paint shop to be cleaned of its oily residue and painted. It would continue on the conveyor to a cabinet bank, where the empty cabinets gathered until they were needed on the line.

When the scheduler called for them, men would slide the cabinets to the line across a concrete floor, which had been treated with a smooth, protective coating to prevent damage. A young man then spread scalding, gooey tar into the corners and up and down the creases of the bare metal cabinets. He shot the tar out of a pistol-gripped nozzle attached to a long canvas hose that he snaked in and around the metal shell. A fuming tar tank fed the hose, and workers fed the tank big black globs of solid coal tar when it ran low. The tank belched benzene, naphthalene, and other polycyclic aromatic hydrocarbons (PAHs). Most of the PAHs that filled the factory's air are now recognized carcinogens, but Patrick and his co-workers didn't give the noxious gases a second thought.[3] Nobody, management included, had even an inkling that the stuff might be dangerous. The environmental movement was still over a decade away. The tar, the same as roofing tar, could saturate one's senses, even from a hundred feet away. But here it was just a stinky nuisance, part of the job, and none of them expected to be at the Admiral factory very long, anyway.

The tar-shooter then put the cabinet on its back on the wood-slat conveyor for the first assembler, and starting in January 1959 that was Mike Patrick. When the cabinet arrived at his station, Patrick matched five pieces of thick fiberglass to the cabinet's five interior walls: the rectangular back and two sides and the square top and bottom. The cabinet rested on six-inch wooden blocks on its back as it moved from station to station. An athletic eighteen-year-old, Patrick scrambled around the cabinet, contorting his body to place each piece as if in the throes of a frenetic toe-touching drill. The conveyor belt rattled along nearly continuously throughout the day: from 8 to 10 a.m., from 10:10 to noon, from 12:30 to 2 p.m., and finally from 2:10 to 4:28 p.m., leaving two minutes for clocking out. As the conveyor belt moved, Patrick had about forty seconds to open the giant tractor-wheel-sized rolls of fiberglass, cut the sheets to size, insert them, and repeat. A foreman watched over Patrick's shoulder to make sure the insulation was packed tight and covered every inch of the interior; otherwise the refrigerator would struggle to stay cool.

Admiral, an industrial powerhouse in the Midwest, churned out about 600 "standard" refrigerators a day in Galesburg, each of them hand-packed on Line 3 by Patrick. He was supposed to wear gloves, but to do the job right he really had to use his hands; the thick cotton work gloves of the time were too clumsy and imprecise. The fiberglass had to be forced into place in the corners and against the tar, which served as a sealant against leaks and as an adhesive for the insulation. Pressing against the tar, Patrick inevitably got hot tar on his fingers. And each time he tore off a fiberglass sheet, he launched thousands of glass slivers and particles into the air.

Four liner-setters, working in pairs, waited for Patrick's insulated cabinets at the third station. These were easier jobs, gained through seniority. They fastened plastic liners to each of the five sides, dressing the pink-furred, unkempt cabinets with clean and smooth white interiors. The liner-setters were allowed extra time; they had to set the liners just right to avoid cracking the plastic. Almost all refrigerators in 1959 still used porcelain liners. Admiral's "standard"—the refrigerator built for the poor and working class—featured some of the first plastic interiors. In the endless pursuit of lower prices, the plastic liner—molded right there in the Galesburg factory—was another win for postwar consumers.

Patrick provided good sport for the liner-setters. "Get yer ass in gear, Patrick!" they'd yell as he bounced around the cabinets leaving a trail of prickly fiberglass in the air behind him.[4] Dressed in a thick flannel shirt and Levi's, the fiberglass still managed to infiltrate every inch of his body. The industrial fans that hung from above blew the fiberglass around Patrick's station but could not keep him from sweating profusely in the intoxicating heat, even in the winter. As Dave Bevard, another veteran of the factory, put it, "Parts of that factory were 120 degrees in the winter; and then it got hot in the summer!"

After finishing a cabinet, liner-setters had a chance to puff a cigarette and make a wisecrack or two about Patrick. The factory was filled not just with tar vapors, but also the smoke of cigarettes, so pervasive that the factory floor was littered with them. Most of the cigarettes found their way into a pit at the end of the assembly line where the conveyor descended into an opening in the concrete floor. Cigarettes, coffee cups, and other trash accumulated so quickly in the pit that workers had to clean it out every few weeks.

When the line shut down at 4:28 p.m., Patrick's fingertips had been burned and scraped raw, and slivers of fiberglass had worked their way under his shirt and, worse, down his pants. Patrick had to learn to use the toilet without using his hands or suffer the consequences. He also quickly learned not to peel the tar off his fingers while it was still hot. If he did, it would cost him a layer of skin.

Patrick didn't have clean-up time at work so he would grab his jacket and lunch bucket and wait in line to clock out and clean up at home. First he would run a cool bath. A hot one would open his pores and make the maddening fiberglass itch run deeper. The cool bath also soothed his stiff back and sore hamstrings from the thousands of forward bends he had done that day. In the bath he would let cold water run over his hands and arms to rinse off some of the tenacious fiberglass. He had to resist the temptation to rub the fiberglass, which would only spread it around and push it in. After the bath, Patrick's fair-skinned body was splotched red with rashes but felt much better.

Patrick made $1.60 an hour on his first job and, with performance incentives, picked up a $70 paycheck each week (or about $3,500 a year)—not bad for a young man without family responsibilities in 1959, when the median annual income for men was $4,000.[5] The factory employed over 2,000 area residents in physically demanding line work, design and engineering jobs, and management with an annual payroll exceeding $8 million. In the early 1960s, Admiral paid roughly $55,000 for coal, $200,000 for electricity, and $2 million for freight each year. Eight miles of mechanized conveyors lined the shop floor, and it used enough paint to coat 17,000 houses.[6] The assembly-line jobs at Midwest Manufacturing had high turnover and were considered some of the worst of the plentiful industrial jobs in Galesburg. Nearly everyone on the line anticipated leaving assembly work, or at least leaving the hardscrabble appliance factory, for something better.

"I wasn't planning on staying there," Patrick said. "You know, I'm 18, and I certainly was going to be looking for other options for what to do with the rest of my life." He never dreamed he would spend the better part of five decades there.

AFTER SEVERAL WEEKS on the insulation hand-pack job, Patrick shifted to a newly added air-conditioner line, an even more disagreeable job. He spent all day lathering thick, strong-smelling glue onto pieces of insulation with a big paintbrush and then placing the pieces around the condensers of passing air conditioner units. It was another sweaty job that was fast-paced and incredibly tedious at the same time. The job came with its own uniform, which was passed to whoever had the job: a pair of coveralls and cloth gloves caked with dried glue.

That job paid a nickel more per hour, which was enough to draw the attention of Patrick's buddies. Workers in Appliance City were always jostling for a better position in the factory. So they asked him how he liked the job one day on their twenty-minute commute from nearby Monmouth, a nearby town of 10,000 where many Appliance City workers lived.

"Oh, I really like it over there," Patrick said, baiting the trap.

A couple of weeks later one of Patrick's carpool buddies came to the air-conditioning line and "bumped" him—he used his seniority to push Patrick out of the job. Patrick was then forced to find an opening in the plant, bump someone else with less seniority, or, if he could do neither, get laid off. That same day another buddy from the commute with even more seniority bumped the original bumper to get the nickel-more-an-hour job on the air-conditioning line. (Both had been bumped from their jobs earlier in the day. Young assemblers moved around a lot, often involuntarily. The seniority-based bumping system could create a domino effect that careened through the lower tier of jobs in the plant.) The two bumpers, though, soon learned that the air-conditioning insulation job was miserable. When they gathered in the car that afternoon, one of them said, "Patrick, you son of a bitch!" Patrick returned a sly smile.

Patrick worked nearly every area in the factory in his earlier years. He made the inexpensive, one-door "standard," the top-mount and bottom-mount "dual temp" with separate doors for the refrigerator and freezer, and Admiral freezers, air conditioners, and dehumidifiers. As he moved around the factory in his early twenties, his educational aspirations waned. He couldn't afford to go to school full-time, and Galesburg didn't have a community college yet that he could attend while he was working. Plus he had met someone and gotten married. Just as important, Patrick was becoming accustomed to the work and felt increasingly as if he belonged in the factory's rough-and-tumble community. Appliance City—now a 735,000-square-foot plant, the size of 175 high school basketball courts, in the early 1960s—was constantly expanding and producing more and more refrigerators, freezers, and air conditioners (see Figure 1.1). Along with other nearby factories, the Admiral plant had created a magnetic pull to Galesburg, which had grown by nearly 20 percent in the 1950s to its historic peak of 37,246 in 1960.[7]

In 1964, Patrick finally settled down for several years on the side-by-side refrigerator line, where he set porcelain liners on the new and immensely popular Admiral Duplex. The Duplex, which opened elegantly like French doors, was a leap forward in household technology. It had massive storage

FIGURE 1.1 DESIGNING APPLIANCE CITY

Admiral Corporation planners in Galesburg model an expanding Appliance City in the booming postwar years. The caption from this photograph from a 1953 issue of *Finish* magazine reads, "Production line changes and new plant construction first are planned on this scale model. Here, key men at Galesburg are inspecting the model before finalizing expansion plans. Use of the three-dimensional model has saved the company thousands of dollars during its expansion program, for errors were caught and corrected here." *Credit:* Finish *magazine, courtesy Galesburg Public Library Archive.*

on both sides and yet fit in the footprint of the refrigerators of the 1950s. In 1961, Admiral's engineers in Galesburg had developed Thinwall insulation, a seemingly mundane innovation that revolutionized the household-appliance industry. Instead of the hand-packed fiberglass, the injectable chemical foam took up much less space and doubled interior capacity in Admiral's higher-end refrigerators, as trumpeted by its advertisements at the time. The foam was also far more energy efficient. No longer would refrigerator compressors have to run constantly, heat up, and burn unsightly brown spots into the linoleum floors of America's kitchens.

One of Admiral's 1965 *Life* magazine advertisements read: "Never Before! A 19.1 cu. ft. freezer-refrigerator . . . side by side in one beautiful cabinet. Just 35 ¾" wide, 5'4" tall! Now, the big family with a small kitchen can shop once a week!" "No stooping! No stretching!" "Your food storage problems are over!" the ad declared. "Automatic ice maker and automatic defrosting in *both* freezer and refrigerator. In copper bronze, citron yellow, turquoise and white . . . *There's nothing finer at any price.*" A 1966 *Life* ad claimed that only the new 1967 Admiral Duplex "has the five features women want most!" There would be "No fumbling for frozen juice cans!" And one could "Now keep meat safely for a week!" (see Figure 1.2). A third ad made a grander claim: "Duplex living is a totally new concept developed for today's modern living."[8]

Consumers of the 1960s loved it. The company claimed that the Duplex was the best-selling refrigerator in the United States and the best-selling side-by-side in the world. Admiral started running three shifts a day at its Midwest Manufacturing plant. A photograph from the period shows a large sign hanging above a bustling shop floor that reads, "Remember . . . the next inspector will be the customer! HE *must* BE SATISFIED!" The factory even dedicated a workday to producing and donating a specially made, oversized Duplex to the Kennedy White House. Admiral was also selling Chicago-made color televisions as fast as they could make them. Money was pouring in as the company, like other manufacturers across the Midwest, attempted to manage rapid growth. Employment in Galesburg's Appliance City was up to 2,600 in 1966 and headed higher.[9]

AFTER THE LEAN years of the Depression and World War II, the American consumer was unleashed, and a new ethos was born. People constructed homes and bought cars like never before. Magazines and radios had planted the seeds of a new consumerism before the war, but the postwar television boom made it flourish. In 1948 there were a mere 172,000 American households with televisions. By 1952, it was 15.3 million. Along with the television, credit cards arrived, and indebtedness surged, more than doubling in the 1950s. Fast food emerged as well. The first modern McDonald's landed in Des Plaines, Illinois, in 1955, and by 1960 there were 228 franchises across the United States selling hamburgers for fifteen cents.[10]

Alongside the surging commodity economy, the U.S. population swelled from 152 to 181 million in the 1950s, the biggest increase in American history

FIGURE 1.2 ADVERTISING THE ADMIRAL DUPLEX

Actress Julia Meade displays the Admiral Duplex in a 1966 issue of *Life*. *Credit*: Life.

for any decade, either before or after. Between 1948 and 1958, 13 million new homes were built—11 million in the suburbs—as former soldiers settled and families expanded during the Baby Boom. And with the help of the federal government, most notably the GI Bill and the Federal Housing Administration, the home ownership rate rose to an unprecedented 62 percent in 1960, up from 55 percent in 1950 and 44 percent in 1940.[11]

At the heart of postwar household consumption was the kitchen. One of the biggest changes was the use of frozen food, as supermarkets replaced mom-and-pop stores. Until the 1930s American families stored their perishables in cellars and ice boxes (wooden pieces of furniture, insulated with sawdust or straw, which held a big block of ice inside for cooling). The first refrigerators, which appeared around that time, were small and boxy, like the ice boxes. The invention of Freon and other refrigerants in the 1930s fueled a manufacturing boom for early refrigerators, despite the Depression. From 1940 to 1950 American families owning a manufactured refrigerator jumped dramatically from 44 percent to 80 percent. The kitchen was being reborn across the newly minted suburban landscape, as a dazzling array of modern household appliances appeared, at least half of which were bought on credit.[12]

This postwar consumer boom was not simply a hedonistic free-for-all, but closely intertwined with Cold War patriotism. In the famous and impromptu "kitchen" debate between Vice President Richard Nixon and Soviet premier Nikita Khrushchev in 1959, Nixon pointed to consumer goods at the Moscow exhibition as evidence of capitalism's superiority for the average person. Walking through a model American suburban kitchen with the Soviet premier, Nixon said, "I want to show you this kitchen. It's like those of houses in California. See that built-in washing machine? What we want to do is make easier the life of our housewives." Khrushchev replied brusquely, "We do not have the capitalist attitude toward women." Nixon went on to argue that the kitchen appliances of the model home on exhibit in Moscow—along with the RCA, Pepsi, and other products on display—were available to every American. The variety of goods is symbolic of Americans' "right to choose" and what "freedom means to us," Nixon maintained. American mass consumption—centered on this ideal suburban home—provided evidence that the United States could win the Cold War by beating the Soviets at their own game of creating a classless, or at least more egalitarian, society.[13]

An expansive American middle class had indeed been born. At the end of the Depression nearly 50 percent of all white families and almost 90 percent of all black families lived in poverty. By 1960 the middle class swelled to include almost two-thirds of the nation. In the 1950s alone, U.S. household purchasing power rose by 30 percent. Economic growth in the 1950s was fitful but strong and characterized by wild surges, including four years with over 7 percent real GDP growth.[14]

Undergirding the glitz of the new consumer society—at its very foundation, making it all possible—was a juggernaut of production unparal-
leled in history. At the end of World War II, Americans owned two-thirds
of the world's gold stock and half of its monetary reserves, generated over
half of its electricity, and directed half of the entire planet's manufacturing
capacity.[15] Admiral in Chicago had used its radio know-how to manufacture
walkie-talkies for combat troops. In Galesburg, Midwest Manufacturing had
churned out refrigerators and powder canisters for the Army, 75-gallon disposable fuel drop tanks for the Air Force, and mines and parachute flares for
the Navy. The flares had lit wartime night skies to reveal Nazi submarines—
"America's Greatest Single Menace on the high seas," as a Midwest document
proudly proclaimed.[16] The energy behind the postwar American manufacturing juggernaut was an optimistic, unionized workforce. Union growth during
the war was unprecedented. In 1945, one out of every three workers—nearly
15 million—belonged to a union.[17]

The rosy prospects of this transformative period, however, were tempered
by an array of concerns. A generational divide began to emerge as the era of
postwar materialism drew in younger people enticed by the inflated expectations of the Good Life. An older generation that had learned the difficult lessons
of scarcity and thrift during the Depression looked on in astonishment as a new
generation dove headlong into a debt-driven consumer culture to attain modern household gadgets and air conditioning; big, flashy cars; and private swimming pools.[18] John Kenneth Galbraith, in the 1958 bestseller *The Affluent Society*,
warned that "wealth is the relentless enemy of understanding" in nations as it
is in individuals. Galbraith questioned the American preoccupation with the
production of private consumer products at the expense of investing in science,
research, and development. Production, he argued, had become a national
compulsion, when in the future, "the basic demand on America will be on its
resources of intelligence and education. The test will be less the effectiveness of
our material investment than the effectiveness of our investment in people."[19]

Others saw a promising future in the sprawling metropolitan landscapes—made possible by the mass produced automobile and the federal
highways—and the consumer revolution. In contemplating "The Future
City" at the conclusion of World War II, M. M. Samuels famously argued in
the prestigious *Annals of the American Academy of Political and Social Science*
that American society was threatened by a "forced collapse" of its most

important social unit, the family, due to rapid urbanization. To avoid this dystopic fate, it would need to call upon the kind of products being made in Galesburg. Samuels imagined that when automobiles came into general use, city dwellers could connect with faraway farmers to buy "perhaps a thousand pounds of fresh-killed frozen meat . . . [and] perhaps five hundred pounds of fresh-picked vegetables" to bring home to their refrigerators and freezers. No longer would it "be necessary to raise everything everywhere, struggling against forces of Nature." Refrigerators, freezers, "garbage grinders," "ironing machines," and other modern appliances would save not just time and labor, but the American family itself in the future American city.[20]

By the time teenager Patrick signed on with Admiral in 1959, American appliance makers were producing three million refrigerators a year. Fifty million homes had electric refrigerators; only one million did not. The future was now, and advances continued. By 1967, the year of the first Super Bowl, plastics had supplanted porcelain, defrosting had been perfected, and 4.5 million refrigerators were produced yearly, and by fewer and fewer manufacturers. Admiral's Galesburg plant was producing well over a half a million of those refrigerators each year.[21] An originally eclectic landscape of hundreds of small, independent manufacturers in the Midwest was already being flattened into oligopoly. Large manufacturers capitalized on economies of scale and beat out independent refrigerator makers, which frequently folded during recessions. In *Capital* Marx wrote, "One capitalist always kills many." The nimble and frugal Admiral, along with its bigger counterparts, General Electric and Whirlpool, was crushing smaller competitors. Meanwhile, Maytag was still exclusively focused on washers and dryers, as it had been for over fifty years, and was flourishing under the leadership of Frederick Louis Maytag II, the founder's grandson.[22]

ADMIRAL'S DUPLEX REFRIGERATOR—a distinctive, state-of-the-art item for discerning consumers—was produced in what amounted to a boy's locker room. Most of the production areas were male-only. Patrick said that when he started in 1959, "There were a few Rosie the Riveters from the Second World War and just a handful of younger women. I don't think they even made up 10 percent of the workforce."

Chain-smoking, lewd language, and practical jokes saturated shop-floor life at Midwest Manufacturing in the 1960s. Drinking was pretty well accepted, too, though one had to be discreet around certain foremen. Workers joked with, harassed, and threw screws at one another. If an assembler left his metal lunch bucket unattended, he might return to find it had been screwed to the wooden table beneath with an air gun. He would try to lift the bucket and it would not budge. The gags passed the time, and Patrick joined the fun.

But mainly it was hard work, and that is all you would have seen had you taken a tour of Appliance City in the 1960s and 1970s. "When you have less than one minute to do your job, that is your focus," longtime worker Dave Bevard said. "If someone went through the plant it was all assholes and elbows. It was a busy workforce that knew their jobs and did them with an alarming degree of precision given the environment." Some of the work was brutally tough. Some of it tedious. Some of it required great craftsmanship. Nearly all of it took its toll on workers in some way, and the suffering inspired a factory culture characterized by gallows humor and strong camaraderie.

It also inspired thirst. When their shift ended, many Admiral workers headed to the Suburban Inn, a Victorian home converted into a roadhouse restaurant and bar. The Suburban was essentially part of the plant, sitting at the intersection of Highway 41 and Monmouth Boulevard, a two-minute walk from the factory's guardhouse entrance. Workers could even take their 30-minute lunch there. Each day there was a special: a cheap meal of fried chicken, meatloaf, or the like. There was no cafeteria in the plant yet, so workers either went to the Suburban or sat next to the assembly line on a parts cabinet or a flattened cardboard box on the floor. The Suburban was hopping at breakfast, too, opening at 7 a.m. Some drank coffee, some drank beer, and some needed something stiffer before Midwest's opening buzzer rang at 8 a.m. and the line jerked into motion. And it wasn't just Admiral workers. The Suburban was a social center for the entire industrial corridor of southwestern Galesburg, including the bustling factories of Butler Manufacturing and Gale Products, where machinists made Lawn-Boy engines. As each respective shift ended, waves of thirsty, grubby workers came to the Suburban to unwind.

But it was Friday night when the Suburban truly came alive. Patrick, having moved to Galesburg, had been spending a lot of time at the Suburban, and Jack Burke, the owner, offered him a job. On Fridays Burke needed twenty-plus bartenders and servers. He was always recruiting more bodies. After initially declining, Patrick got to thinking, "Well, you know, if I was on the other side of the bar, instead of spending all my time on this side, I would be making money instead of spending it." He took the gig.

The bar was in the back of the old house. The bartenders worked nonstop on Fridays, serving a packed room. Patrons drank Budweiser, Miller High Life, and Falstaff, a "terrible beer" from St. Louis, as Patrick recalled. Aside from beer, there were only shot drinks since the bar didn't serve blended drinks. The most popular: Jim Beam and Coke, Jack Daniels on the rocks, and 7-and-7s, since at that time Seagram's 7 was made in a union shop down the road in Peoria. Grocery stores and gas stations didn't sell alcohol yet, so the Suburban Inn had a near monopoly on Friday night fun. In an area off to the side of the bar, Burke sold pints and half-pints of hard liquor and six packs of beer. Half-pints were perfect, Patrick noted, for slipping into a working-man's boot.

Patrick would start work at the bar after leaving the assembly line at 4:30 p.m. on Fridays. By 6 p.m. the co-owner, Burke's wife, or "Ma" as she was affectionately called, had to empty the cash registers because they were over-flowing with cash. Ma worked the entrance to the Suburban where the dining room was, greeting people as they came in. She also served as an informal bank, accepting paychecks to pay tabs that regulars had built up over the week and giving them change, if they had any coming. There was a second, private dining room for Midwest's management, with a big round table where they met for lunch and after hours to relax and conduct business.

An old-timer everyone called Sully had taken off the door to a closet in the hallway between the bar and the front dining room. Inside he set up a counter with bars across the front, just like bank tellers used to have. Sully cashed workers' Friday paychecks, keeping whatever was to the right of the decimal point. If the paycheck was $112.42, he would keep the 42 cents and front cash for the rest. Patrick once asked Sully how much he made on Fridays but he would only say, coyly, "Well, I do alright." It must have been three or four hundred dollars, Patrick calculated.

One afternoon in 1964, returning from a lunch of fried chicken and Pepsi at the Suburban, Patrick was met by some of his fellow Duplex line workers.

"Hey, we have a new department steward," he recalled them saying, refer-ring to the union leadership at the factory. Since 1957, production workers at Admiral's Midwest Manufacturing plant had been represented by the International Association of Machinists (IAM).[23]

"Great, who is it?" Patrick asked.

"You're the new line steward," they said, laughing, like it was another practical joke.

Patrick was surprised but agreed, not wanting to betray the trust that the vote conveyed.

This was the true start of Patrick's political education. At 18 he had eagerly followed the rise of John F. Kennedy in 1960. He remembered the first televised presidential debates from that year. "Let's just say that it helped Kennedy more than it did Nixon." The charismatic Kennedy appealed to him, and it didn't hurt that Kennedy promised and delivered on an unemployment benefit extension when he first came into office. At the low end of seniority, Patrick cycled in and out of work at Midwest as production ebbed and flowed. He saw that unemployment insurance was a reasonable benefit for people like him who, through no fault of their own, found themselves out of work when production waned, as it typically did in the summer. Patrick was predisposed to think that way, though, since his parents were big supporters of Presidents Roosevelt and Truman, having been factory workers in FDR's "Arsenal of Democracy." Patrick still remembers being on his uncle's shoulders and seeing Truman on the president's famous whistle-stop campaign visit to Mattoon, Illinois, in 1948.

Nonetheless, Patrick had not given much thought to unions. He had been more focused on Midwest and the Suburban Inn, playing basketball, and going out at night with his friends. The union was just another deduction on his paycheck.

But that changed after his election as steward. He checked out every book the Galesburg Public Library had about unions and union leaders like AFL-CIO president George Meany, John L. Lewis of the mineworkers, and Walter Reuther of the United Auto Workers. He also began to meet labor veterans who endured the "rough days of organizing" across the industrial heartland. Some had been accused of being communists and forced to testify in front of Congress during the Red Scare. He started to embrace his new role and see the factory differently. "I guess it gets in your blood."

Patrick began to wonder about the old men still working the line. Their bodies contorted from decades of grueling physical labor, many of them could hardly walk or straighten their back. All they had to fall back on was Social Security—there was no employer-provided medical insurance, no Medicare, no company pension, no IRA, no 401k. Only the most penny-pinching had personal savings of any consequence.

"They had to work," Patrick said. "And back then factories were not automated; these were tough jobs. And the problem is, when you get older you start to have medical problems, you and your spouse. A lot of them did manage to pay for their home over the years. But due to their medical bills, and goin' into debt, they'd end up losing their homes just because they got sick. It was a sad situation."

Patrick and his union, Machinists Local 2063, fought locally for Medicare in 1964. His and other unions in the area put their support behind Gale Schisler, an Air Force veteran and teacher from nearby London Mills, who agreed to vote for Medicare and the Civil Rights Act to earn union support. He won and joined others in Congress in a bitter fight against large insurance companies and the American Medical Association, both of which were opposed to Medicare.

Patrick was reminded of the Medicare fight decades later in the nasty battles in the summer of 2009 over Obamacare. "The AMA came out and swore to us that any congressman who got elected and voted for Medicare, we're goin' to make sure that they're only in office one term," Patrick said. "They poured the money in." And the AMA was right. Republican Thomas Railsback beat Schisler in Lyndon Johnson's midterm election in 1966. But Schisler and Local 2063 had already done their part in getting Medicare and the Civil Rights Act passed, two changes that would serve Admiral workers well.

DURING THE EARLY 1960s there were occasional and brief wildcat strikes when key workers would force a line shutdown at the plant—either to protest a real injustice such as an unfair dismissal or simply out of a strong urge to drink beer and go fishing for the day. These strikes were breaches of contract, so the union did what it could to remedy the disruptions as quickly as possible. More significant were the strikes that happened when a yearly contract ended. The union would rally the workers, hold out for incremental improvements, and stop work for a few days almost out of routine.

The Admiral factory in Galesburg was slowly transforming from a rowdy, bottom-of-the-barrel place to work to a respectable and even attractive workplace. Each contract nudged forward health and dental insurance, health and safety conditions, holiday and vacation days, and the company's pension plan for retirement. Benefits that were unheard of in the 1930s, such as annual paid vacations, were now on the table during negotiations. The question back then, Patrick recalled, was, "How much are we going to get?" In the mid- to late 1960s, there were few layoffs, and three shifts kept the factory under nearly continuous operation. The factory was adding jobs even as it was becoming more and more automated and streamlined. Jobs at Midwest and the other factories in town were increasingly seen as regular ones rather than seasonal or a last-ditch option.

Admiral founder and president Ross D. Siragusa started with radios and phonographs in 1934. His business philosophy, according to Ross Jr., his son, was to "sell a lot at low-profit margins and low overhead. Make your profit on volume."[24] Siragusa's expansionist strategy required more space. In 1965 Admiral bought out the Suburban Inn and knocked it down. In the place of greasy lunch specials, tight-knit social bonds, and the occasional drunken factory worker dancing on a table, Admiral built a personnel department at the southern tip of the plant. Working with nearby farmers and business leaders Admiral blocked the Burkes from building a second Suburban Inn across the highway from the plant, as Jack and Ma had planned. The Burkes (and many of the workers, including Patrick) were heartbroken when the company chased them off. The factory was becoming a different place.

In 1966 Local 2063 went on a ten-day strike. Admiral ran on a shoestring and was stingy with yearly concessions. Siragusa had not wanted production stopped for even a few days each year so he pushed for a longer deal with the union and offered a three-year contract, which the union signed. The factory had seemingly unlimited demand to meet, including huge contracts with Montgomery Ward to make appliances under Ward's brand name. There was tremendous pressure to produce inside the plant, which was running day and night.

In 1969, as the three-year deal approached its end on November 1, management and labor dug in for a major battle for the spoils of the plant's success. The main point of contention involved time-study rules. As a low-base-pay, high-incentive shop, the calculations that went into production bonuses factored significantly into workers' earnings. Patrick said that management had a technique to take back increases in wages by shortening the amount of time a job should take, thus trimming incentive pay. Over forty years after the fact,

Patrick could still recount the arcane details of the complicated formulas used in time-study calculations and the tensions they led to that year.

The negotiations started in September. Admiral assumed a short, routine strike was coming to "get it out of their system," according to Patrick, who was fully immersed in the drama as union negotiator—and as a barkeep at the Labor Temple, a gathering place for union workers in the area. The Siragusas were widely known as tough negotiators. And the refrigerator business, even in this prosperous era, had slim profit margins. Siragusa sent his brother-in-law, Paul D'Arco, an attorney with reputed ties to the Chicago mafia and in charge of the corporation's labor relations, to hammer out a deal.

Neither side conceded much before the contract expired, and November 1 came and went. The work stoppage continued into early January 1970, when the negotiating team took a tentative contract offer to the workers. Hardened by an austere holiday season, the membership voted the contract down and sent Patrick and the others back to the negotiating table. "To me the strike wasn't the way to go," Patrick said. "Strikes are rough. Withholding your work was an important thing in the labor movement but if you can sit down and get an agreement that both parties can live with, then you go from there." Union democracy, like any democracy, is messy and imperfect.

At the end of January, Admiral conceded on some key points, and Local 2063's membership accepted the new contract offer. Admiral workers landed on the other side of the painful three-month strike with a thick contract book full of time-study regulations to ensure fairness in compensation. Health insurance premiums for their 80/20 plan became free for workers and their dependents. The pension plan, established in 1966, was doubled, and qualification criteria eased. The contract came with improvements to holiday and vacation days and added dental insurance and a limited cost-of-living clause as well. Patrick described the cost-of-living clause as a "foot in the door" to use later. And finally, because the plant had grown so large, the union bargained successfully for Local 2063's president and vice president positions to be full-time, paid positions fully devoted to union business in the plant.

Despite the gains Patrick recalled the strike with ambivalence and sadness. "That contract was important to the whole community," he said. "The strike hurt not just the employees and the company, it hurt the whole area, for a fifty-mile radius around here. It hurt the office and management people and their families—there were hundreds of them too. And local businesses.

There's a lot on your shoulders. You wanted to get that contract. You didn't want people to go through tough times.. . ." Patrick trailed off and went silent for a moment; what had happened over four decades earlier still felt close.

The 1969 strike was the last strike or major work stoppage until the plant's 2004 closing. In the 1969 fight, capital and labor came to the negotiations roughly as equals. Both sides had leverage and could cut deeply into the other side's bottom line. U.S. companies needed the elbow grease, skills, expertise, and expanding productivity of American workers and were not yet leaving for foreign countries and announcing major layoffs. Perhaps most importantly, blue-collar workers had other options to get by in the event of a work stoppage. "What got us by in 1969 was that most of our workforce was working somewhere else," Patrick said. "The women would get jobs working in the restaurants as waitresses or in retail or sales. Our men went to work in construction. Our tool-and-die makers worked in a machine shop in Chicago."

At the dawn of the 1970s, after two decades of expansion, struggle, and toil, the jobs inside Appliance City had become good, decent jobs. "The 60s and the early 70s," Patrick said, "those were the good times."

AS THE FACTORY grew, it changed. In the early 1960s Patrick could go weeks without seeing a woman on the shop floor. Men and women mixed in the bustle of shift changes, but when the line ran there was nearly complete segregation across the departments inside. Women were flooding the labor market in the second half of the 20th century, ultimately increasing their labor force participation rate from 34 percent in 1950 to 60 percent in 2000, as men's rates declined.[25] In the 1960s and early 1970s, popular thinking about women's roles shifted dramatically as activists took on job and wage discrimination and other workplace injustices.

At Appliance City, the escalation of the Vietnam War propelled social change. Instead of starting their adult lives inside the factory, many young men from western Illinois were drafted into military service. Women replaced the departing soldiers just as production of the Duplex and other Admiral products ramped up. Of the 3,000 workers at Midwest, 40 percent were women by 1970.

Sue Wilson was hired while she was still in high school on April 23, 1970, three days after she turned 18. She started at $1.61, a penny more than Patrick's starting rate in 1959.[26] Admiral automatically classified women as "Class 3," which meant they earned ten cents less than men, about fifteen cents less once production bonuses were included. Admiral argued that women could not do "men's work" and cost more in medical expenses, especially those with the audacity to have children. The company argued the equal-pay provision of the Civil Rights Act should not apply to wages in the factory.

The foremen on the shop floor reflected the company's official discrimination, enforcing what most saw as a natural distinction between "men's jobs" and "women's jobs." As women grew in numbers and in their aspirations, they sought to move from light door-assembly work, silver brazing, and working with smaller parts to higher-paying and more demanding jobs. Foremen resisted and tried to subvert the process, such as by putting a new female employee on the heaviest job in their department, a job that many men couldn't do. The job might be lifting and installing heavy compressors or standing up half-finished refrigerator cabinets all day long. If the woman survived the day, a foreman could disqualify her on a whim after the three-day qualifying period.

Wilson found herself on the forefront of these local battles. Though Second Wave Feminism was cresting and focusing on just this sort of discrimination, Wilson was not thinking big picture. An introverted teenager, she was just trying to survive. In February 1971 she went to the doctor because of abdominal pain and excessive bleeding. She was pregnant and on the verge of a miscarriage and instructed to go on immediate bed rest. She couldn't afford it, she told her doctor. Her husband—she had married right out of high school—was mostly absent and "drank up his paycheck," as Wilson put it. When he was around, he was physically abusive. And asking for family help or applying for welfare didn't cross her mind. She had to work. The doctor relented and wrote a note that Admiral had to find her a job that required only light lifting.

Wilson's foreman on the air-conditioner line, where she fastened fan blades, was notorious for despising anyone with a "restriction," especially women. He looked at the doctor's slip, told her, "Absolutely not!" and sent her to personnel. Personnel was just as dismissive. "There wasn't even any talking to them," Wilson recalled. She was laid off without pay and couldn't even collect the couple hundred dollars' lump sum that constituted maternity leave (meant to cover five or six weeks off after the baby was born). Several months pregnant and desperate for income, Wilson went downtown and filed for unemployment at the local State of Illinois unemployment office. She didn't realize that no woman from Midwest Manufacturing had ever done that before.

The filing created a stir in the factory and among local management in the little industrial city. Admiral challenged her claim, which made Wilson's blood boil. The teenager already had enough seniority, after all, to qualify for several "light-lifting" jobs. She could work, she needed to work, and they wouldn't let her. So a reluctant Wilson overcame her fear of confrontation and went to union vice president Michael Patrick. Wilson and Patrick strategized for a few days and then asked for a hearing in front of a State of Illinois arbitrator. In a thirty-minute hearing that took place in April 1971, Patrick argued that Admiral had acted illegally and that it had to decide either to lay Wilson off for medical reasons or find her a doable job because seniority ruled in job allocation. The company countered that the medical problem, Wilson's pregnancy, was "self-inflicted"—a term they used repeatedly—and was not a legitimate claim for sick leave. Wilson won.

The company did not appeal the ruling and instead decided to lay Wilson off, entitling her to sick leave pay for the rest of her pregnancy and maternity pay after she delivered. Wilson set a precedent. Until then, pregnant women often worked until the day they went into labor. Sometimes a sympathetic foreman would put the pregnant woman on a lighter job, but often they would not. Wilson did not realize that similar battles were being fought across the country in factories and in courtrooms, eventually leading to the Pregnancy Discrimination Act of 1978, an amendment to the Civil Rights Act.

When Wilson returned, she continued to blaze trails in the factory, pushing into higher-paying, higher-skill jobs. Supervisors said things like, "No woman will walk through these doors as long as I run this paint shop." Some fellow workers badmouthed her, saying she was stealing a breadwinner's income. Wilson was unwelcome in the lunch or break rooms when these shop-floor controversies flared. There was usually some fair-minded worker willing to teach Wilson a new job and not raise a fuss. And when there was a problem, Wilson knew Patrick had her back, even if she was, as she put it, a constant "pain in his ass." Wilson did not think of herself as a feminist or even an avid union member at first. "I was just trying to sustain my family." She waitressed evenings at the Kozy Inn, a roadside restaurant and bar a few miles north of town, to make ends meet.

As time passed, though, her personal struggles as a single mother of two—her husband had virtually disappeared by this point—became political. In the 1970s Local 2063 finally won pay equity for women. In the 1980s Wilson and other women joined the all-male, highly remunerated world of over-time. In the 1990s, women broke into highly skilled tool-and-die work, the last all-male enclave in Appliance City. In the 2000s Wilson would face her most demoralizing battle. Having ascended to the Machinists' International office, she ran into gender discrimination, sexual harassment, and "an old boys network" that had "lost sight of what the labor movement is all about." Patrick had always told her to, "never forget where you came from." At the International, Wilson said, many had.

From the loud, dirty work as a teenager on the assembly line in the early 1970s, Wilson had worked her way into increasingly better jobs and elected leadership in Local 2063. She faced some chauvinism inside the union and had to press its leaders for change. But the Local fought by her side and even put her through Marycrest College, where she graduated Magna Cum Laude at age 38. They supported her ascent to regional business representative, where she handled grievances at factories on either side of the Mississippi. They supported Wilson as she became a representative for the International Association of Machinists and Aerospace Workers, a prestigious appointment that "overwhelmed" her proud father. As Wilson carved out her American Dream, Local 2063 had been there at each step to amplify her voice, fight for fairness and justice, and break a few glass ceilings.

THE POSTWAR BOOM was a period of shared prosperity, one in which wages moved up with productivity gains. From 1950 to 1980, Americans across the income-distribution scale experienced a doubling of their inflation-adjusted incomes. Each quintile of the distribution grew at nearly the same rate. Those families in the lower-middle quintile (20 percent to 40 percent), which included factory workers in Appliance City, saw their incomes increase 94 percent from $18,668 to $36,268 (in 2011 dollars). The average family in the top fifth experienced a 93 percent increase from $66,428 in 1950 to $127,984 in 1980. The rising economic tide, as President Kennedy had said, lifted all boats. Nixon seemed prophetic in his assertion to Khrushchev that the United States would beat the Soviets at their own game, creating a class-less society. By 1973—when Nixon was inaugurated for his second term as president—nearly every American household had a television, and about half had swapped their black-and-white sets for color ones. Nearly every American household had a refrigerator as well, so the appliance binge turned to freezers and microwaves.[27]

In 1973, the New York Times wrote about a massive backlog of Admiral freezer orders caused by the "greatest home-freezer buying splurge in history." "They couldn't hire enough people," Patrick remembered. "They'd even give you $50 if you brought someone to personnel." The Vietnam War, racial tensions, and cultural wars had divided the country, but America—and with it this little industrial city in western Illinois—remained atop the world. In the summer of 1973, the population of the factory known as Appliance City exceeded 5,000 people for its first and only time. There were 4,000 assemblers on seven product lines; about 1,000 office workers, managers, and engineers; and maybe 100 Teamsters truckers to haul the finished products away. Appliance City was humming.[28]

That's when 22-year-old college student Dave Bevard needed a job. In March 1973, having barely escaped the draft—he had a draft physical scheduled when he heard the draft had ended—and out of tuition money, Bevard went where he knew you could get a job right away. He remembers his introduction to Appliance City well. After some paperwork, Bevard was escorted into a disorienting buzz of activity—speeding forklifts, people lugging parts, and row upon row of busy people doing God knows what—to a small desk in the middle of the plant. A supervisor zipped up on a golf cart, reviewed some papers, and sent Bevard into the clatter. At day's end he had no clue where he was or how to get out. "Just follow the crowd," someone told him.

Bevard bounced around in the weeks that followed. He worked with men in metal-pressing on the black line, the paint shop, and in the noxious inferno that was plastics. And he worked among the armies of women doing nimble-fingered piecework at the parts tables. One of Bevard's first jobs was at the beginning of the standard line, right next to where Patrick had started, a place that could always use a young body. He stood astride the conveyor, with cabinets moving by at chest height. All day he would bend into the cabinet, pressing his bare torso—the heat was intense—against the fiberglass to thread a long copper tube through a hole in the plastic liner as a pair of guys set the liner into the steel cabinet. Bevard breathed in tiny glass shards suspended in the air, just as Patrick had fourteen years earlier. "It was a joy," he reflected with a mixture of nostalgia and sarcasm. Like Patrick, Bevard did not expect to be there long before going back to college. But his eyes bulged when he cleared $112 in his first week.

In 1974 manufacturing jobs in Galesburg, population 36,000, were at a whopping 10,275, having increased 62 percent in the previous ten years. Beyond Admiral appliances, Galesburg's southwest edge produced something for just about everyone and every use: railroad ties, prefabricated metal buildings, rubber hoses for hydraulics, landfill liners, swimming pool products, toilets and vitreous china, and Lawn-Boy mowers and garage doors for the growing suburbs. A 1976 report, ominously titled *Industrial Invasion of Nonmetropolitan America*, warned that, by taking farmers off their farms, rural manufacturing constituted a "process of societal realignment with a scope and magnitude rivaling the emergence of industry in the last century." Patrick put it more calmly and succinctly. "Everybody in town was going good." Another local said that well-paying jobs were so plentiful in Galesburg that you could leave one in the morning and walk down the street and start another that same day. There were 18 million manufacturing jobs in the United States at the time, a shade off its coming historic peak in 1979. And while big Midwestern cities, including Chicago, were being hit by deindustrialization, suburban and rural areas of the Midwest continued to flourish in the 1970s. Downtown, along Main Street, retail thrived. There was still a Sear's, a Carson's, and other big stores that drew people from across the region.[29]

A *Chicago Tribune* writer described an "industrial Eden" in his 1974 article, "Galesburg: Rockwell's America."

Galesburg looks like the scale-model village adorning an electric-train layout. Neat as a pin and clean as a whistle . . . a main street lined with prosperous stores, a railroad station with passenger service . . . a miniature college, and . . . a cute little airport. . . . It looks almost real except that, like most toy cities, it has virtually no slums, no traffic jams, and no crime. . . . They are, for the most part, mid-Americans straight out of a Norman Rockwell *Saturday Evening Post* cover: thrifty, competent, polite to strangers, struggling to give their kids the college education they never had.

The article's subtitle was "Stability in heartlands."[30]

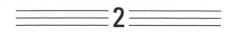

2

UNREST IN THE MAGIC VALLEY

Empezar con la gente.
("Begin with the people.")

—Reverend Edgar Krueger

ONE EVENING IN May 1967, in the parched border city of Mission, Texas, Ed
Krueger had worked into the early evening on a painting and was late to the
demonstration at the railroad crossing. He arrived there at 8:45 p.m. with his
wife, Tina; his 18-year-old son, David; and Doug Adair, a young journalist
writing for the magazine *El Malcriado: The Voice of the Farm Worker*. Just a
few union members and bystanders were at the crossing when they arrived.
Krueger, 36, a lanky and clean-cut minister, had been working with Local 2 of
the United Farm Workers Organizing Committee (UFW) and had expected
to see thirty or forty striking farmworkers and activists protesting the "scab
melons" passing by on the next train. But they weren't there, and Krueger was
worried.[1]

They parked 75 feet south of the railroad crossing, on the west side of
Conway Street. Krueger and his wife grabbed some hamburgers and sodas
and leaned on their bumper to eat with their son. Adair went to talk to a
reporter on the north side of the crossing. Joining Krueger was Magdaleno
Dimas, an itinerant 29-year-old farmworker. A Mexico-born U.S. citizen,
Dimas had a dragon tattoo on his right arm, a rose on his left, and an edgy
zeal for the strike. They were waiting for a freight train carrying tens of thousands of recently harvested cantaloupes and honeydews loaded into thirty or
so refrigerated cars.

The melons had just been cut at La Casita ranch in Rio Grande City, thirty miles west of Mission. After a switch down-valley in Harlingen, the ranch's melons would head north to San Antonio. La Casita, owned by a California company, operated nearly year round and employed 300 to 500 laborers on 2,700 acres of melons, peppers, carrots, cabbage, celery, and lettuce.[2] The southern boundary of its well-ordered fruit and vegetable fields was the snaking Rio Grande River. All that separated La Casita from Mexico was a short swim across the slow-moving, greenish river that irrigated its fields.

Few, if any, in the Rio Grande Valley gave the protesters much of a chance. But the very fact that late-1960s radicalism had reached Starr and Hidalgo counties at the southern tip of Texas was in itself astonishing. Starr County, home of La Casita, was the poorest county in the state and may well have been the poorest and most remote place in the United States. Nineteen of twenty residents were of Mexican origin. In 1967, the typical resident was uneducated, living in ramshackle housing, and scraping by on around $1,200 a year. A newly hired high school dropout could earn five times that in Galesburg— not to mention the benefits and protections—hand-packing insulation or hanging doors at Admiral. Farm work was the poorest-paid occupation in the country, and wages got lower the closer one was to Mexico. The typical farmworker in Starr County made about 75 cents an hour.[3]

The strikers were demanding $1.25 an hour and the right to bargain collectively. The New Deal had left out farmworkers (mostly Mexican) and sharecroppers (almost entirely black) in Roosevelt's bargain with southern Democrats. According to the 1935 National Labor Relations Act, "employees" had "the right to self-organization. . . and to engage in other concerted activities for the purpose of collective bargaining or other mutual aid and protection." Farmworkers, though, were not employees. The term "employee," the act read, "shall not include any individual employed as an agricultural laborer."[4]

The strike had started on June 1, 1966, and the reaction in Starr County was swift. The governor, the county prosecutor (who moonlighted as an attorney for an area grower), the county sheriff's office, and the powerful growers acted in concert against the protesters. There were arrests and jailings, beatings, and a report that a county jeep—on official county business—plowed through a protest spraying strikers and their allies with a mosquito insecticide. One grower reportedly said that he "would rather see his crops rot and the workers starve, than recognize the union."[5]

The sunny lower Rio Grande Valley, called the "Magic Valley" by some for its year-round fecundity, amounted to an internal colony of the United States. This feudal, isolated realm was hardly fertile ground for organizing. In November a Starr County grand jury called the strike "unlawful and un-American" and recommended that President Johnson, a rural Texan himself, send help to restore order. Local press coverage labeled the activists "outside agitators," "criminal elements," and communists—unfair generalizations, though not without a grain of truth. Cesar Chavez had sent Eugene Nelson to Houston in May 1966, seeking to build upon the grape boycott in California. Nelson soon targeted the far-flung border valley and was, within days, speaking in front of hundreds of farmworkers in San Juan Plaza in Rio Grande City.

"They had guns and they tried to run us down with cars," Nelson said to the crowd, waving a magazine from the California strike with a cover photograph of Mexican revolutionary Emiliano Zapata. "You are the sons of Zapata! You must be brave!" The fruit and vegetable workers waved red *huelga* (strike) flags emblazoned with black thunderbirds. A protest sign listed, in Spanish, workers' wages: electricians at $6.00 an hour; plumbers at $5.50 an hour; mechanics at $4.50 an hour; carpenters at $3.50 an hour; truck drivers at $2.95 an hour; waiters at $2.00 an hour; and farmworkers at $.50 an hour. "*¿POR QUÉ?*" read the sign.[6]

A few months later, "La Marcha," a 380-mile pilgrimage of farmworkers from Rio Grande City to Austin, ending on Labor Day 1966, gained sympathizers for the grassroots movement. Mostly, though, the fight was contained to the borderlands where the Anglo power structure had reigned supreme since Mexico ceded the land in 1848 at the end of the Mexican-American War. The upstart farmworkers plotted their strategy in a sparse little office in the corner of an old Mexican theater in Rio Grande City. Two portraits hung on the headquarter's walls: John F. Kennedy and the Virgin Mary.

The biggest problem for the strikers was that they simply could not stem the limitless flow of "green carders" streaming through the porous border from Reynosa—McAllen's sister city across the Rio Grande—and elsewhere on the Mexican side. Initially the UFW coordinated a picket line on both sides of the border with the Confederation of Mexican Workers (CTM). Mexican authorities soon broke up the Mexico-side picket and, after some tense standoffs with authorities at the bridge, the flow of replacement workers resumed. The UFW, grasping for a new strategy in late May 1967, set

FIGURE 2.1 DISSENT IN CARTOONS

The underground newspaper *El Malcriado*—meaning A "poorly raised" child who talks back to his parents— was founded by Dolores Huerta and Cesar Chavez in 1964 in Delano, California. The mailed-out newspaper used art, humor, and reporting to criticize growers and to promote the work of the United Farm Workers Organizing Committee (UFW). After its successful grape strike and boycott in California, UFW sent organizers to South Texas, where its efforts ran into stiff opposition from large growers and the Texas Rangers. *Credit*: El Malcriado.

its sights on melons instead of the ubiquitous replacement workers.[7] The new strategy would reach its climax on this night.

On the north side of the tracks, across from Krueger, Dimas, and the others, stood several Texas Rangers, led by Captain A. Y. Allee. Growers and the Starr County sheriff had called in the Rangers to break the strike, and Allee, something of a legend in the region, relished the opportunity to defend Texas from outside meddlers. A picture from the time shows him standing, arms crossed, masticating a cigar, and scowling beneath a Stetson drawn tight to his brow. He especially liked to pose with his hand resting on his early model Colt .45, its stock decorated with Aztec designs of silver and gold.[8]

Krueger learned from a bystander that twelve protesters had been arrested earlier. Allee told Krueger that they had been trespassing on private property and launched into a windy lecture about Indians, the history of the railroads, and private property, as Krueger recalled. Krueger, a kind but persistent man, pestered Allee on where exactly the boundary between public and private property was at the crossing.

"Krueger, you're masterminding this whole thing!" Allee said accusingly. Ending their tense standoff, Allee turned his back and went to the north side of the tracks, where he waited for the train.[9]

Krueger by this time was a well-known religious activist in the Valley, but he insists he didn't deserve much of the credit or blame for the demonstration. He had worked with Migrant Ministries since returning in 1961 from three years of missionary work in Honduras. Between 1961 and 1967 he had become a steadfast advocate of the rights of marginal groups. *Empezar con la gente* (begin with the people) was his guiding refrain. Krueger had joined as a church liaison to the conflict in March 1967 at the request of the Texas Council of Churches.

Just after 9:30 p.m., with a humid darkness fully set in, the train approached. The Rangers and the growers suspected that the strikers had sabotaged the tracks so the train passed slowly. Earlier that month, a *Texas Observer* reporter had seen a pair of Rangers in a Plymouth Fury tracking the engine, another pair driving alongside its midpoint, and yet another pair tailing the caboose.[10] As the train approached on this night, the Rangers moved from their parked cars. Standing on the track, a couple of them flashed an "all clear" signal to the conductor with their flashlights. They then crossed the tracks, leaving Adair, another reporter, and a photographer on the north side as the train moved into the crossing.

With the Rangers foregrounding the train, Krueger and his wife took pictures while Dimas finished his hamburger. They wanted to get photographs of these public law men guarding La Casita's private shipment like Pinkertons. The picture-taking, though, set the Rangers off. They scrambled toward the protesters. Captain Allee snatched Krueger by his belt and said, "You've been wanting to get arrested for a long time, Krueger!"

Tina Krueger, standing at a good distance, saw this and started taking pictures. Allee handed Krueger off to another Ranger, Jack Van Cleve, and chased her down and twisted her arm to get the camera. "So you're a trouble-seeker, too?" he said. Allee opened her camera, exposed the film with his flashlight, pushed her toward their car, and ordered another pair of Rangers to get Dimas.

"Get rid of that hamburger," said a Ranger as he slapped it from Dimas' hand. He then cocked his arm and hit Dimas in the face and dragged him toward the passing train. As they waited for the train to pass, Van Cleve and another Ranger held Krueger's and Dimas' faces to the passing train, just inches from the protruding side ladders that passed with each car. To Krueger, the scary part was not the hard metal of the passing ladders but that he was at Van Cleve's mercy. Van Cleve was a volatile hater of the strike who had hit him before without provocation.

Adair struggled to see the scuffle on the other side of the train. He and Gary Garrison, an Associated Press reporter, and Felix Ramirez, a photographer, moved closer to the train. As the train caboose passed, Ramirez took a picture of Dimas and Krueger being held close to the train. As Ramirez went to take a shot of the manhandling, Allee told him he'd bust his camera and throw him in the car, too, if he didn't lower his camera. Ramirez backed away; he had expensive gear to protect and two weddings to shoot the next day. His was the one picture to survive the night.[11]

The train and the melons were gone. Van Cleve shoved Krueger against the Plymouth Fury and frisked him. Another banged Dimas' chest into the car. Reporter Adair watched in disbelief and let out a nervous, befuddled laugh. In his testimony to Congress, he would say the Rangers "appeared ludicrous as they roughly handled Mrs. Krueger (under five feet tall) and searched the minister for weapons." Captain Allee recognized Adair and shoved him into the back of the Fury with the Kruegers and Dimas. Krueger reached to the front seat to grab Adair's pipe, which had been lost in the frisking. Van Cleve, now getting into the passenger seat, slapped Krueger with an open hand.[12]

"Krueger, you better behave and be quiet," Van Cleve said. "If you were a good preacher, you would already have tried to stop these people. You are no preacher. You are just a damn troublemaker." Shaken, it took a few moments for Krueger to reply. When he did, he said, "May God bless you."

This infuriated Van Cleve. "If you don't shut your mouth, I'll knock your head off," he said. With a year to calm down and put together a plausible story, Van Cleve would claim he "nearly" slapped Krueger because the minister got too close to him and had "bad breath."[13]

The rest of the trip the Rangers and the protesters sat in silence, trying to take in what had just happened. Ranger Frank Horger sped at 80 or 90 miles per hour, and through some red lights, toward the Hidalgo County seat in Edinburg. In his testimony Adair claimed that Horger and Van Cleve were shaking with rage during the 16-mile trip.

In the Hidalgo County jail the four met up with the twelve other demonstrators arrested earlier, including a 15-year-old who was still spitting up blood. The jail cell was medieval. Eugene Nelson said he had killed 212 cockroaches in a night there earlier in the campaign.[14] Krueger and the others knew that this night was a turning point for the Magic Valley—for better or for worse. In jail the young minister took notes of the night's events on a paper towel.

BEFORE SUNDOWN ON that infamous night, Pancho Medrano, a United Auto Workers (UAW) national staffer, had been arrested at the railroad crossing before Krueger and the others showed. He had been taking pictures of Captain Allee and eight or so Rangers rounding up four young women pickets, including the fiery, four-foot eleven, 100-pound Kathy Baker. As Allee wrestled away her picket signs, Medrano recalled Baker yelling, "Viva La Huelga!" and "Turn me loose!"[15]

A Ranger confiscated Medrano's camera and smashed the camera's base into the organizer's mouth and nose. He snapped Medrano's other camera off his neck, breaking the strap as he took it. The Rangers told Medrano he was under arrest for trespassing on private property. When he protested that he was in the middle of a city street, they changed it to "obstructing traffic." When Medrano, Baker, and the others were taken to jail, the charges were changed again to "unlawful assembly." A few days later the charge would change again to "secondary picketing" of the railroad company.

After being denied a phone call until after midnight, Medrano called a UAW official who got in touch with UAW chief Walter Reuther who called President Johnson. The White House called Governor John Connally and a Texas congressman. The next morning Medrano got special treatment by his Hidalgo County jailers. "I didn't know you knew President Johnson," one of them said, clearly star-struck. Medrano had breakfast with coffee and cream in the sheriff's office.[16]

A few days after the standoff at the railroad crossing, Captain Allee and a carload of Rangers stormed a UFW dinner at Baker's house. They had been tracking Krueger's friend, Magdaleno Dimas, and he was there. Allee, who thought Dimas was a violent criminal, and some other Rangers beat him and fellow striker Benjamin Rodriguez until, according to an X-ray, Dimas's spine was bent out of shape. Dimas needed four days in a hospital to recover from what would come to be known as "the Dimas incident." Allee would later admit that he hit Dimas in the head with the butt of his shotgun. But Dimas' and Rodriguez's injuries came, he said in an interview, when they fell on some furniture. Later, in court testimony, Allee said they were injured when they ran into each other and a door at the same time. Another Ranger told a reporter that Dimas was in a car wreck.

The climatic events in the Magic Valley in late May 1967 finally drew a federal response. On June 28, 1967, in an overflowing, decrepit courthouse, three perspiring senators, including a young Ted Kennedy, listened all day to eyewitness testimony. Senator Harrison Williams, chairman of the Subcommittee on Migratory Labor, called the day's testimony "the most powerful the subcommittee had ever received"—and it had received a lot.[17] In one exchange, Medrano said that he was cussed at and challenged to a fight by La Casita's manager, also a special deputy of Starr County, Ray Rochester. Medrano, a professional boxer, said he could hit hard with either hand but that there wasn't a fight. "You don't think you can hit harder than pistols, do you, Mr. Medrano?" Senator Ralph Yarborough quipped. Later in his congressional testimony Medrano said, "Now, I tell you that never in my life have I seen . . . the hatred, through a human being, that these Rangers had. You should have seen the hatred they had toward us."[18]

After Medrano, Krueger testified to the senators that Dimas, on the night of May 26, 1967, was "a beautiful example of non-violence." "Dimas," Krueger said, "did not try to retaliate or give evil for evil, but took all of the bitterness, and hatred, it seems, that the Rangers had to offer, without a word." Krueger continued, "Being interested in the development of people and human relationships . . . I am encouraged when I see this growth in positive leadership."

The subcommittee was sympathetic and eager to legislate for the disenfranchised, reflecting the politics of the Great Society era. "No other group of workers labor so hard, produce so much, and get so little for their labor," Senator Harrison Williams said of the farmworkers. Farmworker impoverishment was, the senator said, the result of an oversupply of labor, an imbalance of power, and "government intervention against his side of the equation."[19] Finally, this remote growers' fiefdom—and its hidden field hands, who endured scorching heat and long hours to fill America's refrigerators—was in the national spotlight.

The subcommittee, which included the farmworkers' biggest advocate in Washington, Robert F. Kennedy, had eliminated Public Law 78, better known as the Bracero Program, three years earlier in 1964. The progressive Senate subcommittee now sought to amend the National Labor Relations Act (NLRA) to "make its provisions applicable to agriculture" in order to provide federal protection for collective bargaining and against unfair labor practices.[20] Two years later, after Robert Kennedy was assassinated, the subcommittee again filled thousands of pages with its hearings on "Migrant and Seasonal Worker Powerlessness" in 1969. Ed Krueger testified again, telling Chairman Walter Mondale of "a radical surplus of labor" in the Magic Valley. "The oversupply of labor I think enhances, if you might call it that, the callousness or the sense of cruelty on the part of some of the employers."[21]

Five years later a federal district court in Brownsville ruled against the Texas Rangers in *Medrano v. Allee*. It held five Texas statutes unconstitutional, admonished the Texas Rangers for violating free speech and lawful assembly protections, and detailed the Rangers' abuses on these nights and others. Of the Dimas incident, the court stated, "It is difficult indeed for this Court to visualize two grown men colliding with each other so as to cause such injuries."[22] In 1974, in *Allee v. Medrano*, the U.S. Supreme Court upheld the ruling with some modifications. The one picture that survived the night—that of wedding photographer Felix Ramirez—provided critical visual evidence of the Rangers' excesses.

The 1974 decision was a landmark civil rights victory for farmworkers. The Rangers' vigilante—and one-sided—independence was reined in and they withdrew from the Valley. Captain Allee's reputation, and that of the Texas Rangers, was tarnished. State Senator Joe J. Bernal called the Rangers, "the Mexican-Americans' Ku Klux Klan." Allee himself was mystified by the fallout and insisted he wasn't a "hoodlum" or "cutthroat," but rather "a human being just like anyone else."[23] Sure, he was prone to pontificate, but he swore he wasn't a "damn strikebreaker"; he was administering justice as he saw fit, and according to local custom. "We are not instructed in any way [about the use of force]," Allee testified in 1968 to a panel of civil rights commissioners. "We use what force we deem necessary to make any kind of arrest."[24] For Allee, enforcing the law in South Texas meant getting fruit and vegetables to market and keeping the local economy rolling. If some bad guy outsiders wanted to gum it up, well, that's what the Rangers were for. The rule of law was especially critical come harvest time, when the money was made. Allee's testimony revealed his detailed under-standing of the agricultural economy. Each refrigerator train car, he said, cost $400,000. Protecting the cargo from meddlers was best for everyone in Starr County, including the workers.[25]

Despite the eventual civil rights victory against Allee and the Rangers, the labor rights struggle was lost. The UFW did have one success. One big Starr County grower, Virgilio Guerra, grew weary of the strife and signed a union recognition agreement in mid-May 1967. "Any course of action which is advocated by the ten bishops of Texas can't be far wrong." At the signing, the union pickets tore up their signs and threw the pieces in the air. They then threw a gala and said the "historic document" was surely the beginning of "a chain of union victories." The other growers promptly visited a local bank that Guerra's family partly owned and threatened to withdraw their money. Guerra's family also received threats and suddenly found it difficult to buy vegetable crates and supplies, according to their lawyer. The Anglo elite was sending a clear signal to other growers contemplating negotiations with the strikers.[26]

And indeed the UFW's strike withered shortly after the Dimas incident. After its hopeful beginnings in 1966, the South Texas movement had gotten ugly, Krueger told the senators during his testimony before the committee. Cesar Chavez also withdrew his support as the militancy grew. "I sent you to Texas to organize workers, not inmates," Chavez told Antonio Orendain, an organizer. "You're in jail all the time." A strike that once had workers sing-ing, "We shall overcome," on the international bridge had devolved under the repressive grip of the Rangers and cannibalized itself. Krueger himself was fired by the Texas Council of Churches. "He got too militant," a council spokesman maintained. Krueger's offense? He refused to sign an agreement exonerating the Rangers.[27]

The UFW's unionization effort in 1966 and 1967 shattered against an implacable Anglo power structure and an endless supply of impoverished Mexicans from Reynosa and farther south seeking work in the post-Bracero years. In 1967 northern industrial unions in the United States were strong. Over a quarter of American workers, over 28 percent, belonged to unions.[28] And in places like Galesburg, where Local 2063 was in its heyday, withholding work was a very real threat to place-based industrial employers. The UFW, on the other hand, could not control the flow of strikebreaking "green carders" to gain leverage in their effort. To this day farmworkers in Texas still have no union, and wages in the Magic Valley remain dirt low.[29] And according to the NLRA, a farmworker is still not an "employee." To say work in Texas' fields and other low-wage jobs is "at will" understates the utter flexibility of a labor pool, on both the McAllen and Reynosa sides, that is at once limitless, desperate, and transient—just the way employers like it. Such is the enduring legacy of the Magic Valley.

OTHAL BRAND CLAIMED he produced more onions than anyone in the world. The multimillionaire was based in the Valley, but his 40,000 acres spread across Colorado, Idaho, and California, and his company had offices in Mexico, Europe, and the Far East. He was one of the eight or nine growers targeted by the 1966–1967 strike.[30]

In 1977 Brand, a veteran of the Pacific War, became mayor of McAllen, Texas, the largest city in Hidalgo County and would reign for two decades in the majority-Hispanic area. He called himself a "conservative visionary," and because of the growers' victory in 1967, relished his role as the biggest obstacle to a farmworkers union in the Magic Valley. In 1975 he was caught by a television crew jumping out of a pickup truck and waving his pistol at strikers. In 1979 he crippled a strike by marching his own workers past strikers to harvest his onions on someone else's farm. In 1981, as Brand campaigned for a second term as mayor, national news outlets aired videos of McAllen police officers beating and torturing Mexican American inmates. With Brand's knowledge, his late-night police force had thrown prisoners against the wall and smashed their heads onto booking tables. The officers called themselves the "C-shift Animals" and wore T-shirts advertising as much.[31]

In the midst of the controversy, Ramiro Casso challenged Brand for the mayor's seat. Casso, 58, was the doctor who examined Dimas the night of his beating by the Rangers. He had remained a steadfast advocate of the poor, running a free medical clinic in McAllen. During the campaign, Casso, an accomplished man with degrees in chemistry, engineering, and medicine, called Brand a "barbarian" and a "dictator" who sanctioned "the beating of our sons." The election gained national attention, and Ted Kennedy, another veteran of the 1967 affair, made a highly publicized endorsement of Casso. For its part, the Brand campaign passed out pictures of Casso standing with Cesar Chavez and warned, as they had done successfully for decades, of diabolical "outside influences trying to take over our city." After Casso won a three-way contest, Brand won the run-off, sustaining the Anglos' undefeated run in McAllen mayoral elections. McAllen remained the only city in the Valley not to have elected a Hispanic mayor. The night of his defeat, an exasperated Casso stood in front of his supporters and called his opponent "the scum of the earth."[32]

Brand insisted that city hall needed to be run like a business. For him that meant ignoring procedure, making backroom deals, and stacking political offices with allies in order to get things done. Critics said he bullied enemies, illegally rewarded friends, and governed by temper tantrum. And yet nobody can dispute that Brand grew and modernized McAllen aggressively. After his five-term, twenty-year reign, the physical infrastructure of McAllen was breathtaking: an attractive airport, wide and smooth streets, and the most successful mall per square foot in the country. In 1970 McAllen, population 37,636, was Galesburg's size. By 2000 its population nearly tripled to 106,414 as Galesburg's slowly declined.[33] Under Brand, McAllen became the unofficial capital of South Texas, sitting at the geographic and economic center of the vital, interconnected sprawl that includes Edinburg, Pharr, Mission, and a smattering of smaller cities in Hidalgo County.

It was in 1987 that Brand made a decision that would change the Magic Valley forever. That year he created the McAllen Economic Development Corporation (MEDC). As the negotiations for what would become NAFTA began between the United States, Canada, and Mexico, Brand envisioned a new role for the burgeoning Rio Grande Valley. With trade constraints ready to loosen, Brand wanted the MEDC to cultivate ties with the Mexican side and recruit companies to build maquiladoras across the river in Reynosa.[34] Mike Allen, his choice to lead the agency, would become binational wheeler-dealer-in-chief and eventually eclipse mere mayors like Brand as he crafted McAllen-Reynosa's synergetic niche in the emergent transnational economy. It would soon seem appropriate that Mike Allen would become synonymous with McAllen, an inchoate node of exchange (of people, products, contraband, and more) between the United States and its southern neighbor.

3

AN AMERICAN CLASSIC IN
THE GLOBAL ERA

Galesburg, Illinois

IN APRIL 1974, Admiral was absorbed into Rockwell International's growing empire. The Vietnam War contractor was, according to the *New York Times*, on a "debt-financed acquisition binge that lasted almost a decade" as it spread its reach into aircraft, defense, aerospace, electronics, and appliances.[1] Admiral, meanwhile, was still churning out televisions, radios, and home appliances at factories across the Midwest. Productive as it was, the little company couldn't afford the massive capital outlays required to modernize, market, and survive in the increasingly brutal electronics and appliance businesses.[2]

Accustomed to the massive revenues and fat profits of big government contracts, Rockwell International trimmed employment at the plant, investing $25 million to automate the chest-freezer line. In 1975 Rockwell added a 60,000-square-foot microwave oven facility, and in 1978 it spent $12 million to retool the top-mount refrigerator line and erect the "Blue Goose," a massive machine the length of a football field that spat out finished metal cabinets. In earlier times, investment meant more jobs. Under Rockwell's rigorous ethic of scientific management, it usually meant fewer. Admiral accounted for about an eighth of Rockwell's revenues. "We weren't even peanuts to Rockwell," Michael Patrick said. It was a new era for Appliance City.

One afternoon in the mid-1970s, Dave Bevard was let out of work an hour and a half early. Production workers were instructed to gather in the vast parking lot across the street from the factory. Under a circus tent, a Rockwell representative and the Admiral plant manager told workers about the importance of the B-1 bomber to the nation's defense, to Rockwell's

future, and, consequently, to Galesburg jobs. By this time Rockwell had production of the B-1 in over forty states, making itself the model practitioner of
military-industrial growth. The plan was to use its nonmilitary production
facilities in a lobbying campaign to maintain one of the most lucrative military
contracts in history—around $10 billion at the time. Workers signed premade
postcards for their congressman and went home early that day. Not everyone was on board with the B-1. Bevard and his troublemaking buddies made
unflattering posters about the bomber, already considered one of the greatest
boondoggles in military history, and hung them in the plant. Management
tore them down the next day. When Bevard protested about "equal time" to
present criticism of the B-1, he was told—correctly, he admitted—that the
privately owned facility was not required to provide equal time. "Do it again,
and you'll be fired for insubordination," he was told.

Rockwell's strategy might have been good for propaganda, but it was not
good for its bottom line. After its buying binge, the corporation suffered financial
setbacks as Admiral was ravaged in the 1970s by big Japanese competitors, which
aggressively dumped low-cost televisions to capture the U.S. market. Rockwell
never made a profit with Admiral, discontinued Admiral televisions, and closed
all their Midwest factories—except Galesburg's. Rockwell looked to unload the
remnants of Admiral in any way it could and to get back to the more profitable
business of building rockets, space shuttles, and $200 million bombers.[3]

Michael Patrick, now Local 2063's president, fretted about Rockwell's
crazed job-shedding. He also fretted when the big shots from corporate
came to Galesburg, insisting that Local 2063 renegotiate its labor contract
a year before it expired to facilitate a sale to Magic Chef, a Tennessee company privately owned by S. B. "Skeet" Rymer, Jr. Rockwell's lead negotiator,
a tough-as-nails Southerner named Robert Sutherland, came to Galesburg
and said to Patrick, "My job is to go across the country and shut down plants.
I negotiate closing agreements." After a long pause Sutherland added, "But
let's see what we can work out."

Sutherland and Local 2063 worked out a good deal. Nonetheless, something had changed. Instead of going into negotiations asking, "How much are
we going to get?" Patrick and union leaders across the Midwest were starting to ask, "How much will we have to give up?" The tables were turning.
Labor's leverage at the bargaining table had begun to wane. Some in Local
2063 wanted bigger gains and refused to see the plant's position as vulnerable.

"That's bullshit; they're not going to shut down the plant," Patrick recalled people saying. "The company has you in their back pocket."

In Appliance City, amid the sounds of metal presses shearing and pneumatic air guns popping, it was not yet apparent that the crest of the wave they had been riding for three decades had just broken. Life was still good. *Focus,* a company magazine from the time, reported scores from the softball league, announced engagements and retirements, and featured an Admiral worker who was building an airplane in his garage. On the cover was a photograph of an exultant man holding up a 17-pound trout.[4]

Things were now different, though, and it would be a hard lesson to learn. "The plant was just an eyelash from shutting down that year," Patrick said. "I'd rather take shit from some of the people than be proven right about the seriousness of the situation." Patrick said he still had the "silent majority" with him, though, and the plant marched on.

In 1979 Magic Chef purchased what was left of Admiral's appliance division from Rockwell. Stoves specialists, Magic Chef had to get bigger to survive the intensifying crush of consolidation in appliances. By the end of the 1970s, only about a dozen appliance manufacturers were left.[5] Magic Chef was thoroughly anti-union, and Rymer was dead-set on taking away the "30 and out" retirement plan that the union negotiated in 1966 and expanded in the 1969 strike. Local 2063 members would be damned if they would give up their pensions. It was what made working at the grueling factory year after year bearable. In 1983 contract negotiations between Magic Chef and Local 2063 were not going well, and the entire region seemed to be sinking into gloom.

Rust Belt counties ebbed and flowed with automobile and steel production. When the auto industry shed 500,000 jobs and the steel industry lost 350,000 jobs between 1977 and 1987, shockwaves crashed through the Midwest in places like Rockford, Illinois, Youngstown, Ohio, and Flint, Michigan. They also crashed through the "industrial Eden" of western Illinois.[6] Layoffs cost Galesburg 3,000 jobs, or 11 percent of Knox County's entire workforce in the early 1980s. Outboard Marine Corporation, maker of Lawn-Boy lawnmowers, sent production to Mississippi, Ciudad Juárez, and Hong Kong. A big community mental health hospital closed. Other local manufacturers thinned their ranks. Home values sank by a quarter, and unemployment hovered at 15 percent during much of the 1980s. The local U-Haul guy said his moving trucks were headed one-way—out. A *Wall Street Journal* article reported that personal bankruptcies and child and spouse abuse shot up in Galesburg. Eight years after being cast as "[Norman] Rockwell's America," Galesburg was now the prototypical "Troubled Town" of the Reagan recession of the early 1980s. The *Journal* reporter noted a hand-scribbled sign on State Route 34 outside the town that read, "The last one out of Galesburg, turn off the lights." The future of the town hinged on Appliance City.[7]

Fate intervened during contract negotiations. Magic Chef faced a dogged unionization drive in Cleveland, Tennessee, its hometown. Tennessee workers got hold of the union contracts from Magic Chef's factories up north—Admiral in Galesburg and Norge in Herrin, Illinois—and found a lot to like. The subsequent strike in Tennessee—and Magic Chef's crackdown—became violent, resulting in broken car windows, police using tear gas, and accusations that Cleveland's police chief—a family relation of Rymer's (as was the town's mayor)—planted marijuana in the truck of the union organizer's car.[8] Up north, Patrick was sweating bullets. He was about to present Magic Chef's offer, which gutted the pension plan, to a few thousand workers in Galesburg High School's auditorium. Just before taking the stage, Patrick learned that Rymer would relent on the "30 and out" clause, averting a certain strike and earning Patrick and Appliance City a few years' respite. Despite continued battles with Rymer's lawyers, Patrick always felt gratitude toward Magic Chef, which had rescued the Galesburg factory from the cost-cutting giant Rockwell. By the mid-1980s, though, an aging Rymer was looking to trim back his operations, and the plant's future was again uncertain.

In stepped Maytag, which acquired Magic Chef in 1986. The company, renowned for being thrifty and conservative, had carried zero debt until it bought premium appliance maker Jenn-Air in 1982 but now had to hunt or be hunted. Whirlpool had just acquired KitchenAid, and in Europe, Electrolux of Sweden purchased White Consolidated, which in 1979 had gobbled up Frigidaire. One capitalist continued to kill many, and those still standing were the appliance giants of the new global era. Like Magic Chef before it, Maytag was desperate for a full line of kitchen and laundry appliances. It now sold personal and commercial washers and dryers, stoves, refrigerators, microwaves, freezers, and more under the brand names of Maytag, Magic Chef, Hardwick, Jenn-Air, Toastmaster, Dixie-Narco, Norge, Warwick, and others. It added Hoover (in a billion-dollar merger with Chicago Pacific Corporation) in 1989 and dishwasher production in 1992 in Tennessee. Maytag brought

Admiral's headquarters from Schaumburg to Galesburg in 1987 with the help of low-interest loans and tax breaks and invested tens of millions each year in venerable Appliance City.[9]

Maytag now had twenty-six manufacturing operations in eight countries and 26,000 employees. Three thousand of them worked the ten miles of conveyor lines in Galesburg's factory, now measuring 2.25 million square feet. Those workers spent a $70 million payroll in town and across Knox County and the region. Despite its swelling size, Maytag still considered itself the little guy, battling industry giants such as Electrolux and General Electric. Its archrival, however, was Whirlpool, the company from Benton Harbor, Michigan, and the only other remaining independent Midwest appliance maker. Almost a century earlier, some of the raw stuff of appliances—the railroads, oil, and steel—had consolidated into powerful trusts. Now it was the turn of the appliance makers. In 1986 Maytag and its three competitors emerged from the feeding frenzy with control of over 80 percent of the appliance industry.[10]

Local 2063 president Patrick was relieved when Maytag arrived in 1986, and a leaner Appliance City seemed poised to survive a rocky decade of mergers, deindustrialization, and downsizing. "It wasn't easy to keep the thing going," Patrick recalled. "It was touch and go all along, and I'm not sure how much our people realized that." With unemployment all around, though, decent jobs, especially for the less educated, were suddenly at a premium. Now the town, proud of its abolitionist history, its symphony, and its college, was campaigning frantically to be the site of the next state prison—an idea residents had soundly rejected a few years earlier. In 1986 Galesburg, with unemployment at 14 percent, welcomed the medium-security Henry C. Hill Correctional Center, just across the railroad tracks from Appliance City, with a band, balloons, schoolchildren, and cheerful speeches from local dignitaries.[11]

Dave Bevard stuck around. He had a family, the money was still good, and there weren't many other options. After a decade at the factory, he ran for union steward and won. The union work fit his combative personality and sense of justice. "The more I did it, the more I realized that this was all the stuff we were going for in the 1960s," Bevard said. "But it was a little more structured than [Yippie agitator] Abbie Hoffman!" Bevard agitated for the little guy as union steward but was proud to build an "American Classic" for the Maytag Corporation, a demanding, but fair red, white, and blue company with a sterling reputation. "We were tickled to death when Maytag stepped in," he said. "We saw that as security."

GALESBURG WAS HAPPY but the acquisition of Magic Chef left loyal Maytaggers in Iowa in "utter shock." The Magic Chef lineup "didn't belong in the same ballpark" as Maytag, which dominated the upper end of the market.[12] Expanding to a full array of premium household appliances made sense, but competing toe-to-toe with Whirlpool and the others on price and volume seemed like madness. Aging Appliance City in particular needed some work after the Rockwell and Magic Chef years. "We were Maytag's red-headed stepchild," Bevard said. Galesburg and Newton were a good match culturally, but it would take some time to be accepted into the Maytag family.

For Joe Krejci, who joined Maytag management from Whirlpool in 1993, the acquisition was the beginning of the end. "When I was at Whirlpool in the 1980s, we were always amazed at Maytag because they made as much money as we did with about a quarter of the sales. They were getting the premium price. But then they stepped on the gorilla's foot and the gorilla didn't like that." The "gorilla" was Whirlpool. Some Maytaggers were concerned about the transition from an old-school company to a corporate governing structure, as the Maytag Company became the Maytag Corporation. The Maytag Company had been composed of lifelong, devoted managers, engineers, and line workers. They were neighbors, friends, teammates. And they remained fiercely loyal to Newton, population of 16,000, Maytag's rural Iowa headquarters, and to the Maytag legacy, which began with a character still known locally as "F. L."

According to legend, "the central Iowa plains were littered with the broken-down remnants of Frederick L. Maytag's handiwork," a result of F. L.'s early beginnings with farm machinery.[13] A high school dropout, F. L. tried just about everything to make a buck in the frontier farming economy. In 1907, the young entrepreneur started a small company and introduced the Pastime, a hand-cranked washing machine that pushed clothing along the corrugated inner side of a water-filled cypress basin. It was a hit, and Maytag went on to revolutionize the washing machine further with electric- and gas-powered engines.[14]

F. L. may have been an also-ran among the hundreds of small, independent manufacturers, however, if it hadn't been for Howard Snyder, the mechanical genius of F. L.'s company and inventor of the Gyrafoam in 1922. The Gyrafoam used an agitator and didn't need the friction of a washboard to clean clothes. After some disastrous missteps, bopping around the Midwest losing money making cars and building railroads, F. L. had now focused the company exclusively on washing machines and, at an energetic 64, went on the road himself to sell the Gyrafoam. Maytag went public in 1925 and by 1927 had sold five million washers, vaulting from 38th-largest U.S. washing machine producer to the very top of the nascent industry in the booming 1920s. F. L.'s lawyers were ruthless, extracting royalties from competitors under threat of lawsuit if they stole the Gyrafoam agitator technology.[15]

F. L. entered old age as a hero of frontier, bootstrap capitalism—a successful and scrupulous patriarch absolutely devoted to those who lived in his Iowa fiefdom, including his "best friend" Snyder. He was uneducated, but prioritized education as a state senator.[16] He was a farm boy, but committed to modernizing Newton's roads and its civic and religious institutions. He wasn't an engineer, but always seemed to find the right people for the task. He gambled (and often lost) on risky innovations and investments. His sons, who ran the company for much of the early run, were worried and skeptical of their father's irrepressible optimism. In the end, with a little luck, enthusiasm, charisma, and vision, he carried the company to the top.

To mark his seventieth birthday, and without previous fanfare, F. L. bought a $15,000 pipe organ for a local church, built a $250,000 swimming pool and public park in Newton, and handed out an extraordinary $130,000 to employees who had been in his service for three years or more—the amount based on their tenure. Anna Griebel, a devoted worker at the Maytag Company for thirty years (since 1897), received a gift of $1,650.[17] As with Henry Ford's paternalism, F. L. Maytag believed that good business could not be separated from community-oriented morality. As his friend and swooning biographer, A. B. Funk, wrote in 1936, "The dirty dollars of intrigue and chicanery do not pollute his possessions. He has never sought to reap in riches where he has not sown in service."[18]

F. L. spent time with salesmen, retail dealers, and factory workers, purportedly beginning conversations with the question, "Is everybody happy?" Funk wrote that the tribute these men would pay F. L. when he strode into a room "would bring a lump to the throat of a man of stone." Workers would flock to hear him speak, "compose songs and sing them to him," and "write poems and dedicate them to him." He was called upon to settle controversies and with the "wisdom of Solomon"—Funk again—provided a fair hearing. His greatest joy, though, was providing a livelihood to others. The company claimed Maytag paid the highest wages west of the Mississippi River. W. I. Sparks, longtime secretary in the Maytag Company at the time, wrote, "This organization is an outstanding exception to the rule that there is no sentiment in business."[19]

F. L. fully expected his loyalty and trust to be reciprocated. The saddest days of his life, according to Funk, were when a colleague had "broken a trust that I held no less sacred." According to *An American Quality Legend: How Maytag Saved Our Moms, Vexed the Competition, and Presaged America's Quality Revolution*, a loving portrait of the company published in 1993, F. L. treated "his boys" well, but "he also decided what was best for them as a proper German patriarch always did." In addition to hard work and loyalty, F. L. expected his people to attend the Jasper County Fair, church organ recitals, company picnics, and Maytag Night at the tabernacle revival series.[20]

F. L. left an indelible mark on the company he founded. Looking back on his life in a speech he made in 1933, when he was 75, F. L. said this to sales and company executives:

> I have given my life to the building of a monument to a name, to an ideal, and to a purpose—one that I hope will be perpetuated down through the years. . . . There are responsibilities which leaders must accept, once they have attained leadership. I hope that you, as part of this organization, will share in your responsibility to the public, to the thousands of Maytag employees and Maytag stockholders, and to the millions of Maytag users around the world. . . . I feel proud of the men who have grown up with me—my boys who have helped to make this business what it is today—an institution with a world-wide reputation for achievement. I owe much to them, because without their loyal support and trust I could have done little. An institution does not consist of so much brick, stone, and machinery, but its greatest assets are personalities.[21]

F. L. died in 1937, and a younger generation took control. In the largest probated estate in Iowa's history, he left between $1,000 and $50,000 to 200 of

Newton's residents and $1,000 to selected Maytag employees. But he shocked his production workers, to whom he didn't leave a penny. This uncharacteristic slight, along with new, more autocratic management, had workers worried. It didn't help that Elmer Henry Maytag, who ran the company from 1926 to 1940, was not charismatic like his father and had an authoritarian streak. He didn't ask whether people were happy.[22]

In the 1920s Maytag advertisements claimed it had "the best cared-for factory workers of the middle-west" and was a model of welfare capitalism. But in the 1930s, a trade unionist movement swept through the Midwest, led by the Council of Industrial Organizations (CIO). Maytag workers sought to make Newton a "model CIO town" by organizing everything from the factory to the Woolworth's to the local cafés. A battle ensued in the placid prairie town. Maytag brought in Art Taylor, a veteran union-buster from the East. The CIO sent William Sentner—an equally experienced organizer—to help the workers. Tension erupted, and Iowa governor Nelson Kraschel declared martial law, mobilizing 250 troops from the National Guard to Newton in the summer of 1938. Newton police arrested union leaders and held them without bail. Some workers were charged with kidnapping because they had kept foremen and company officials from leaving the factory during the sit-down strike. On August 4, 1938, workers walked single file back into the factory between the bayonets of the National Guardsmen with a 10 percent pay cut but with the union intact.[23]

Fred Maytag II, F. L.'s grandson, assumed control of the company in 1940. Fred's approach was forged in the hard lessons of the 1938 strike, where, at the age of 27, he played a central role in negotiations as Elmer, his father, lay ill in Florida. Looking back at the strike, Maytag wrote, "The managers and owners adopted a paternalistic attitude towards their employees . . . It was assumed that our employees were completely happy and it was a source of great pride that no serious attempt had ever been made to organize a labor union. . . . Apparently, our employees weren't so happy as we thought!"[24] A devout capitalist, duck hunter, and Republican—serving as state senator, like his grandfather before him—Fred Maytag was ambivalent about unions. But he was worldlier than the previous two generations of Maytag men. He was an airplane pilot, scuba diver, and Leica enthusiast. In the end, he endorsed the union and modified the austere paternalism of his father into a new regime in Newton. He stuck close to tradition, but updated it.

There is a picture of Fred Maytag II in a 1949 *Life* article, "Mr. Maytag: The Big Man of Newton Faces up to his Responsibilities." In the photograph he sits under the portrait of the grandfather he revered, looking appropriately businesslike. But there are also pictures of him lighting the cigarette of a union leader and sitting cross-legged while eating Japanese food at a San Francisco restaurant. There is yet another in which he is throwing lingerie to Maytag dealers at a West Coast convention to demonstrate the quality of Maytag's new automatic dryer. Maytag said that over time he had learned that a strong union helps to enforce contracts, avoid wildcat strikes, and pursue the win-win goals of quality and dependability. After peace was restored in 1938, a union leader said of him, "We never would have had this trouble if he'd been here all along."[25]

As chief executive of Maytag for twenty-two years, F. L.'s grandson defined what "Maytag" would mean for millions in the second half of the 20th century. He shunned built-in obsolescence and was obsessed with giving the public its money's worth. He preached "enlightened self-interest" and was like his grandfather in more than name. In keeping with family custom, Fred Maytag had worked on the factory floor and in sales during college. Once in charge, he continued to eat lunch with workers and insisted they call him "Fred." Promotion from within was the norm, but it had to be earned.[26]

In that 1949 *Life* article "Fred" is portrayed as humbly carrying his own groceries, making his son sign interest-bearing promissory notes (even for as little as 15 cents), and taking *noblesse oblige* with the utmost seriousness. When he built a new factory on the outskirts of Newton during the postwar boom he stipulated that the area be incorporated within Newton city limits so that it could pay its fair share of taxes. In the lobby of Maytag headquarters, at One Dependability Square, Fred had inscribed, "Our management must maintain a just balance among the interests of customers, employees, shareowners and the public. Although these groups may apparently compete in their short-term goals, their long-range interests coincide, for none can long benefit unless the needs of all are served."[27]

According to the *New York Times*, by the time of his early death at age 51 in 1962, Fred Maytag had taken a "feudal Midwestern firm" and transformed it into a model corporation with national reach.[28] Under his guidance, the word itself, "Maytag," became synonymous with quality and dependability. The name symbolized what many small-town Midwesterners cared about profoundly: a moral commitment to work, craftsmanship, and community. Newton's Maytag—like other icons of the prairie such as John Deere in the Quad Cities, Caterpillar in Peoria, and Appliance City in Galesburg—had their beginnings in the production of the machines of agriculture. These companies matured in a rugged farm culture devoted to frugality, fierce self-reliance, but also a sense of duty to others. These were not just companies located in the Midwest; they were Midwestern companies.

AFTER FRED II'S death in 1962, successive chief executives, all lifetime Maytaggers, paid homage to both him and his grandfather's leadership style, as well as to their traditionalist ethos of social responsibility. CEOs Daniel Krumm (1974–1992) and Leonard Hadley (1993–1999, 2000–2001) clung to the organization's traditions and connection to place even as Maytag moved into an era of cutthroat takeovers and intensified global competition. Hadley, Maytag's president in 1986, was "tough, but fair" with the newly acquired Galesburg facility, according to Dave Bevard. Magic Chef had invested enough for the appliance factory to remain viable and productive. But Maytag's brand, reputation, and entire business model was predicated not on viability, but on excellence. On one of Hadley's first visits to the factory, a labor leader jokingly asked Hadley when he would replace the old "Admiral" lettering on the water tower with "Maytag." Hadley shot back without a trace of humor: "When you earn it!"[29]

By this point Appliance City—named Galesburg Refrigeration Products after the purchase—needed Maytag. But Maytag needed Galesburg just as badly. Laurence D. Ackerman, a Hadley consultant, wrote that the Galesburg acquisition brought not just the desperately needed refrigerator line, but also "engineer and design know-how, which could perhaps be translated into areas beyond refrigeration."[30] The first refrigerator with a "Maytag" logo did not arrive in stores until 1989 after three years and several painstaking rounds of redesign of the prototype—a process involving over 1,100 separate engineering changes and $60 million in new investment.[31] "They were incredibly picky," Bevard said. "A refrigerator is much more complicated than a washer or dryer. Frankly they didn't know what they were doing at first." But the long-awaited refrigerator was a hit. Maytag had to ration its supply.

When he became CEO, Hadley seemed to have the magic touch. He put Maytag's disastrous European operation in the profit column and then dumped it. The board of directors had been pushing globalization, but Hadley trimmed back to focus on innovation, product quality, and other core functions. "Our future lies with the past," he liked to say.[32] And observers applauded his old-school style. "Maytag Corporation may not be the biggest player in its field or the most global," Ackerman wrote. "What Maytag has in abundance as an organization, however, is integrity; it is whole, complete, and confident in who it is . . . it is this integrity that yields a strong reputation and steady, profitable growth over time. Maytag, the corporate being, knows itself."[33]

Hadley, a Maytagger since he graduated college in 1959, lived and breathed the company, just as the CEOs before him had. "There is nothing more dear to me than Maytag," he declared. "It's my life." Decades later Hadley could still "recite numbers of washing-machine parts he memorized as a young accountant in the 1960s," according to a *Wall Street Journal* account.[34] His ascendance to CEO had been unlikely in a 1990s business culture increasingly focused on global expansion, dazzling top managers, and short-term gains. A business school textbook put it like this: "No one thought that major change could come to an organization from someone who had spent his whole life there, who was a clone, so to speak, and an accountant to boot. Everyone thought that changemakers had to come from the outside. Well, he had shown them, and given hope to all number-two executives who resented Wall Street's love affair with outsiders."[35]

Maytag was humming along in the second half of the 1990s under Hadley. The "Lonely Repairman" marketing campaign, which it launched in 1967, was still one of the most successful and durable in advertising history. In the original commercial, actor Jesse White, playing the head repairman, feigns melancholy and tells his handymen they'll be the "loneliest guy[s] in town" because of Maytag's legendary dependability. Instead of tools, the Lonely Repairman offered them a "survival kit" with crossword puzzles, cards for solitaire, and beads for beadwork. (Gordon Jump, who played the goofy Arthur "Big Guy" Carlson on WKRP in Cincinnati, assumed the famed role from White in 1989.) In the late 1990s, Maytag was making remarkable gains in market share on its competitors, in part because of its redesigned refrigerator.[36]

Tradition not only survived, but actually seemed to thrive in the relentless onslaught of domestic and global competition. At the root of Maytag's strength were enduring relationships and a strong sense of place. There was the longtime, reciprocal connection between Maytag and the people of Newton. Also, Maytag's fanatical devotion to quality and customer service bound together Maytag and its loyal customers and value-oriented share-holders. And, though it could be contentious, there was genuine engagement between the Newton corporate office and the Galesburg union. "There was always give and take," Bevard said.

Mike Patrick spent forty years in contract negotiations. Like Fred Maytag, Patrick and his longtime vice president, Chuck Unger, thought not just in terms of their side's narrow interest, Bevard argued. They considered the broader interests of the community, the shareholders, and factory productivity when working with corporate. "I can't think of anyone in management that sat across from us that didn't respect Mike and Chuck," Bevard said. "They all did."[37]

The same went for the day-to-day relationships between local managers and labor leaders in Galesburg. Fred Pickard, who started at Midwest Manufacturing in 1952, was a Galesburg superintendent for thirty-three years of the nearly fifty that he spent at the plant. Five superintendents oversaw the five divisions of the factory: the black line, plastics, the paint shop, parts and supplies, and Pickard's domain—the assembly. As superintendent, Pickard battled Patrick on the minutiae of shop-floor disputes and contract interpretation. But they trusted and listened to each other. They knew they had to work within a set of mutually understood values and expectations about fairness and the common good. "The union and I worked together almost every day of our lives," Pickard, a registered Republican and energetic, garrulous 76-year-old recalled in 2011. "You win a few and you lose a few. You give and take." As he reflected on the past, Pickard's voice cracked. "The hourly people out there were very, *very* good people. You could work with them."

In 1994, just as the North American Free Trade Agreement (NAFTA) was implemented and rumors swirled again about a plant shutdown, the State of Illinois chipped in $7.5 million in grants and loans for training and improvements, and Galesburg increased its sales tax one-quarter percent to raise $3 million for the company. Hadley's Maytag, in turn, invested in a massive $190 million retooling of the old factory. Appliance City, still the largest employer in this part of western Illinois, anchored a startling comeback. After the disastrous 1980s, Galesburg's housing market recovered and even grew. Unemployment, which had been at 16 percent when Maytag bought the plant in 1986, dropped to 4 percent in 1999 in the late 1990s boom. In 1999, 2,475 people worked at Galesburg Refrigeration Products, 889 had jobs supplying it, and another 2,253 jobs were supported by the big factory.[38]

Maytag Corporation's success was reflected in the company's bottom line, in top accolades from *Consumer Reports* for Galesburg's refrigerators, in awards for the Galesburg plant, and in the business press. At the annual shareholders' meeting in May 1999, Hadley boasted, with some justification, "For Maytag, last year was a grand slam home run, wind-aided by the strong economy and industry environment." On July 30, 1999, with its share price at over $70, *BusinessWeek* posed the question, "How can you fault a company that has engineered a successful turnaround and has hot new products, expanding profit margins, and surging earnings? Often, there's just one nagging doubt in such a case: Can the company do even better?"[39]

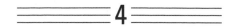

4

THE RED-HEADED STEPCHILD

Galesburg, Illinois

TWO WEEKS AFTER *BusinessWeek* lauded Maytag's remarkable success, the company broke clean from a century-old tradition. On August 12, 1999, Lloyd Ward replaced Leonard Hadley by a vote of the board of directors. Ward was the first executive never to have worked for Maytag. He had not been raised in the idiosyncratic Maytag culture. He was not even an appliance guy. Hadley had been grooming Ward for the CEO's position since Ward came to the company as president of the home appliance division in 1996. Two internal candidates had been groomed and judged unfit for the CEO's job; Ward was their last hope. Still, the board's choice shocked many.

Ward was anything but short on confidence though. He had wrestled a childhood of poverty and a career touched often by racism and had won. He had captained the Michigan State basketball team. He had earned a black belt in karate. He was now a star of business on the rise. When Ward became only the second African American to become a CEO at a Fortune 500 company, *Black Enterprise* declared it a "watershed moment." It was easy to see why Hadley liked Ward: he brought Maytag a magnetic personality, inspirational leadership, and some badly needed diversity. Hadley said he "drooled" when he saw Ward's resume and relished bringing in this bold, extroverted marketing man.[1]

Even before he became CEO, Ward began to revamp Maytag's old-fashioned culture with an "unapologetically macho" leadership style. He began to shift Maytag's focus to brand management, lower-end products, and sophisticated consumer research. Ward also brought in people from outside the appliance industry, from P&G and PepsiCo mainly. Ward's ascendance won praise, including a fawning cover story in *BusinessWeek*.[2] Joe Krejci, a Galesburg logistics manager who reported directly to Newton, was taken by Ward's irresistible charm. Ward, still a diehard Michigan State Spartan, once came into Krejci's office and stomped on his University of Michigan doormat with a theatrical smile. They then "shot the shit" about Big Ten football and basketball. "He could make you feel like he was really talking to you, like he wanted to connect," Krejci recalled. "And he was like a reverend when he gave a presentation. You'd rise up, clap and sing—you'd be speaking in tongues by the end. I see how he got the job. I mean, he could sell *anything*."

Ward always put on a good show, as he had hawking Doritos for Frito-Lay and Crest and Tide for Proctor and Gamble. As Hadley's sidekick in the wide-eyed days of the late 1990s stock boom, he mesmerized Wall Street analysts with visions of Maytag's future earnings. Maytaggers, those both in high and low places—board rooms and on the production lines—felt a tectonic shift as Ward's influence increased. "It was all stock price, stock price, stock price," Krejci said. This was a notion antithetical to the company's blue-chip heritage, but one that fit the heady moment. As John S. Reed, former Chairman of CitiGroup and former chairman of the New York Stock Exchange, said, "In the '90s, the investors took over . . . managers started being scared of their stockholders and this idea of shareholder value came into being. . . . [Before] it was customers, customers, customers."[3] Even tucked away in little Newton, the assault of Wall Street proved impossible to resist, and Ward—the heir apparent, the modernizer—was leading the charge. Internal memos would later show that Ward, who owned nearly 200,000 shares of Maytag stock, was obsessed with "shareholder value."[4]

Perhaps predictably, things went horribly wrong. It became apparent that Maytag's share price had been inflated beyond what the fundamentals merited. As that realization hit, the price tumbled. In May 1999, shares of the Wall Street darling had peaked at just under $75. In September, a month into Ward's tenure, the share price had sunk to around $40.[5] The steep drop reflected internal turmoil throughout Maytag's kingdom. Rumors swirled that Ward was out to sell not just appliances, but the company itself—possibly at the behest of key investors and board members. As a result, his critics said, salesman-in-chief Ward did not attend to the nuts-and-bolts of the business. Concern mounted that the venerable company was losing its laser-like focus on product quality, business fundamentals, and customer service. Looking back, Dave Bevard likened Ward to a "cheap snake oil salesman" who "didn't have a clue" about appliances and how to run a company like Maytag. Apparently some on the board didn't trust him either. They hired a woman—nicknamed, in misogynistic fashion, "Cruella de Vil" for the prominent white streaks in her hair—to shadow his every move.

To add to the problems for the new CEO, not everyone in 98-percent-white Newton was entirely enthusiastic about this "watershed" moment. On an early trip to town, Ward was approached and told, "We don't need your kind here." And when his wife, Lita, attempted to buy a home in the area, they discovered a restrictive covenant in the deed prohibiting the sale to those of "Negro Blood." Both incidents were roundly denounced by townsfolk in Newton, Hadley, and by a mayoral proclamation and front-page letter in the Newton paper. Ward's wife was reluctant to move to the small town for other reasons as well. Fearing she would have no place to shop in Newton, she bought a year's worth of panty hose in anticipation of the move. Ultimately, the Wards chose to live forty miles away in a Des Moines suburb. It was not an auspicious beginning.[6]

Nonetheless, Ward hard-charged into the corporate offices with a zealous righteousness for swift change. He cleaned out several top executive positions, replacing five or six vice presidents with old buddies. They were mostly from PepsiCo, and none had knowledge of appliances. It was a kind of shock therapy for the staid small-town company, and it did not go over well. "All appliance companies have Midwest roots, and Midwest values. Newton, St. Joseph's, they're small towns. He hired all these big city types," Krejci said. "And [it wasn't] that that was wrong or that they were unqualified people. You could have done that at Whirlpool and it would have been fine. But it was too much change, too fast. I mean, when I joined Maytag in 1993 there was one black person in Newton in the corporate office out of 700 or 800 people."

The souring mood in Newton could be felt three hours away in Galesburg. The union complained about corporate micromanaging and finicky new policies. Local management felt it, too. Resources dwindled, work hours and stress increased, and the corporate culture became—as Krejci put it— "terrible" and "Gestapo-ish." There were "no compromises" and "no dissent."

That year assembly superintendent Fred Pickard left the factory he loved and was not coy about where to cast blame. "We'd still be here today if people hadn't got too educated," he said. "We hire [Ward] and the first thing he does is hire a bunch of consultants to tell us how to run this plant. I couldn't live with myself trying to agree with people when I didn't. It came to the point where you either agreed with senior management or they got rid of you. I always operated on the idea that you lose one minute, you cost the company $10,000. Then these guys come in and say, if you got a problem, shut the line down and bring the people together to talk about it. They were full of shit!"

Ward met unfortunate timing. From 1998 to 2003 the nation would lose three million manufacturing jobs, the trade deficit would balloon (our deficit with China more than doubled), and the stock market would peak and then free fall.[7] For appliance makers, it was especially tough. Foreign producers like China's Haier and Germany's Bosch and Siemens not only gained footholds in the domestic market, but actually built sparkling new nonunion factories in the South. Those factories employed a fraction of the people at a fraction of the cost. Maytag's biggest challenge, though, came from big-box retailers like Sears, Lowe's, and Home Depot. Mom-and-pop appliance stores had closed. Circuit City stopped selling appliances. Heilig-Meyers, another big Maytag carrier, went bankrupt. In the new retail environment, a handful of giant retailers had all the power and they used it to squeeze Maytag, the littlest of the giant appliance makers still standing.[8] "The big guys with the hammers, they drive so hard on price," Kirk King, a number-crunching veteran manager with twenty-three years at the Galesburg plant, said. "We used to deal with the local mom-and-pop dealers on the corner but now most of our business goes through these jumbo retailers, and they have an awful lot of clout."

Ward lasted only fifteen months, resigning on November 9, 2000. Maytag's board bought him out of his contract for $1.7 million.[9] He had failed to sell off the company, misfired on several initiatives, and led Maytag into a precarious financial situation. And, in a final irony, Maytag's share price sat at $28 upon his departure, down 60 percent since he had taken charge. In the end, one analyst said that Ward's marketing brilliance and salesmanship could only go so far. "I don't think Lloyd ever fully understood Wall Street," the analyst said.[10] And, clearly, Ward did not understand how to lead Newton's old-fashioned company in a global age. As Leonard Hadley conceded in a phone conversation, "Sometimes you don't know until you actually put someone in the chair." In a tone that suggested a touch of bitterness, he added: "He was a better talker than an executer."[11]

Ward was gone, and Newton and Galesburg sighed in relief, thinking the storm had passed. "It's like coming out of the root cellar and the wind quit blowing," one Newton worker said. Another said there was a "collective roar" that swept across the assembly lines in Newton when the resignation was announced. Before the announcement, corporate headquarters even leaked a warning to local bars to prepare for a night of heavy celebration. With Ward gone, people didn't have to worry about job cuts, the company being sold to Sweden's Electrolux, or corporate headquarters moving to Chicago or Dallas. Recent newspaper rumors had whispered as much, and Ward had intimated dramatic changes were in the works. Hadley, the hard-nosed, sensible Quaker, was dragged out of retirement to correct his and the board's devastating mistake. He immediately asserted that any plans to move the company were dead as long as he was at the helm.[12]

A couple of years later, after failure and scandal in running the U.S. Olympic Committee, the once-heralded business superstar faded into disgrace.[13] *New York Times* writer Selena Roberts called Ward "a Mini-Me entrant into America's exclusive club of tainted chief executives." He delivered "cavity-causing" speeches and embodied "the C.E.O. culture he came of age in by leaning on his charismatic image as a substitute for substance, by offering up fortune-cookie phrases instead of hard truths about the future."[14]

IN SEVEN MONTHS Hadley had replaced Ward's people, bought Amana to solidify their position in refrigeration, and went about "fixing up" the business. In June 2001, the board hired "Successor #2," as Hadley called him: Ralph Hake. Hake was an appliance man, having spent twelve years at Whirlpool, most recently as chief financial officer. But he had been passed over for the CEO position at Whirlpool and also at Fluor Corporation, where he was executive vice president and CFO when Maytag recruited him. Hake was a socially awkward number cruncher with an MBA from the University of Chicago—quite the opposite of the charismatic Ward. The business press loved the move, and Newton welcomed Hake—even if his mansion, once built, would be the biggest in town. Hake's new neighbor, Lori Yoder, met the Hakes while doing fall yard work. "They seemed like wonderful, very down-to-earth people," she said.[15]

BusinessWeek approved as well, lauding Hake's "no-nonsense management style" and aggressive "paring down" of costs. The same magazine that had lionized Ward three years earlier now praised Hake's valiant effort to recover from "costly misfires under Ward." In his first year, Hake opened two subassembly plants in Reynosa and completed Hadley's takeover of nearby Amana in eastern Iowa. Maytag was now the third-largest company in the core-appliance market, holding a 22 percent combined market share. The little town's company was now earning over $1 billion a quarter. Yet it was still a little giant compared to its rivals. Whirlpool had 36 percent market share, and General Electric was at 29 percent.[16]

It was a pivotal moment for the company and their new CEO, and despite Hadley's steadying influence, Maytag had changed for good. The old days of Fred Maytag's "just balance among the interests of customers, employees, shareowners and the public" was little more than folklore. Looking at the "long-term" now meant a focus on quarterly earnings reports instead of daily ticks in the stock market. Maytag's brand, perhaps its most prized—and proudly parochial—possession, had been compromised. Newton workers saw it. Mike Patrick, Sue Wilson, Dave Bevard, Fred Pickard, and Joe Krejci in Galesburg all saw it. Once beholden, perhaps to a fault, to traditional values, Maytag now lacked a motivating vision. Morale was on the decline despite the fresh start with Hake. People trusted Hadley, but it would be hard to trust another outsider CEO now.

Kirk King was worried, too. As a high-ranking Galesburg manager with access to performance numbers, he could see that things were coming apart. "It's kind of like the Cubs. They just keep trying to win. We're fighting a hell of a battle while the laundry people are making money and cruising. Refrigeration is a tough business. I'm kinda in the wrong spot here." As a cost-cutter himself, King was happy, though, with Hake's aggressive focus on trimming the fat. Indeed, each decade at Appliance City, managers, engineers, and workers had to figure out how to produce more with less. And they had. In 1952, when Fred Pickard started, each job was already subject to scientific management and time studies. In 1960, the factory was enormously productive for the time, producing 250,000 appliances a year.[17] Now, at the turn of the millennium, the Galesburg factory made more than a million refrigerators a year, and every aspect of production was continuously scrutinized for efficiencies. Echoing Pickard's rule about accounting for every last second on the shop floor, King said that every penny he pinched in the material costs of a refrigerator saved the corporation $10,000. "It's high stakes," King said.

Under Hadley, Local 2063, local managers and engineers, and corporate worked together to drive efficiency gains. Reflecting back, Hadley called the Local "very professional." "We worked very hard together to design a product so we could compete in the marketplace. They knew that was their job security. And they got there too. We put 'Maytag' on the water tower." Hadley still has an 18-inch replica of the water tower with the name "Maytag" on it, done by a model shop, given to him by Local 2063, the only union that said good-bye to him in 1999. They requested a special meeting to give the gift. "It meant more to me than they probably knew," the former CEO said with feeling. "It was a nice gesture."[18]

After 1999, shop-floor collaboration and management–labor compromise began to disappear. Ward, and especially Hake, brought in top-down, cost-cutting initiatives under the various headings of Gatyam ("Maytag" spelled backwards), Kaizan, and Six Sigma. Production workers were upset about the relentless cost-cutting. It had gone too far, workers began to say. It was showing up in the appliances they made. It was especially galling when the orders came from outsiders unfamiliar with appliance making and the idiosyncrasies of the factory. Bevard criticized the "flavor of the month" programs imported by $10,000-a-day consultants that forced them to speed up the line, cut corners, and compromise quality. On top of that, the subassembly plants from Reynosa were sending chilled water and ice dispensers and other components that were 50 percent scrap—meaning useless—on arrival, Bevard said. Management called it "start-up problems" and implied that 50 percent scrap was still acceptable since Mexican labor was so inexpensive.

Where was the vision, Bevard, Pickard, and others wondered? Where was the leadership beyond the cost-cutting? Workers soon realized that, like salesman-in-chief Ward, their new bean-counter-in-chief was leading the company astray. "Hake," Bevard said, "was a one-trick pony." With Hake determined to cut Maytag's way back to prosperity, what would Maytag become? And where, in the tumultuous early 2000s, did Galesburg fit into this plan? Galesburg Refrigeration Products workers were about to find out.

ON APRIL 7, 2002, Local 2063's negotiating team took the stage in the packed, tension-filled 2,340-seat auditorium at Galesburg High School. Following custom, the proposed three-year contract was printed and distributed to the 1,900 Machinists on Saturday to preview. The contract presentation and vote took place on Sunday afternoon after church let out. At stake were 2,300 jobs at the Maytag facility—one of every twelve jobs in the entire county.[19] All eyes in the region were on the vote.

"You're a bunch of dogs!" screamed someone from the audience. "Shills!" "Suck-asses!" "This contract is a crock of shit," several screamed. "What are we paying dues for?" Many threw their contract papers into the air, and some left the auditorium.[20]

The membership had broken into warring factions, and a few pockets in the audience seemed more interested in instigating violence than in hearing a presentation and casting a vote. Paranoia had infected Maytag facilities across the country less than a year into Hake's tenure. By contrast, the 1999 contract presentation had been a cheerful affair. That contract was accepted by a vote of 1,400 to 235.[21]

Doug Dennison, a younger member of the negotiating team, remembered that day in 2002 vividly. "If words could kill, I'm not sitting here today." Dennison's wife, Annette, a thirteen-year veteran of the factory, sat in the auditorium, enduring the insults being hurled at her husband. On the stage sat Don LeFebvre, president of Local 2063; Bevard, vice president; Dennison, recording secretary; Kevin "Fuzzy" Robinson, second-shift chief steward; and John Ester and Tony Scislowicz, negotiating team members. Mike Patrick and Sue Wilson, who were both working regionally across the Midwest for the Machinists, were also on stage. Two muscular guys stood in front of the stage for security.

"Well, I'm glad you're here!" Bevard recalled saying to the men.

"What makes you think we'll do you any good if they turn on you?" they replied.

"Well, it may be a false sense of security," Bevard said, "but don't take that away from me!"

Bevard went to sit at one of the two rectangular tables on either side of the lectern. He looked out at the audience and leaned toward the other members. "Man, it is a good thing that we like each other because there isn't anybody else in this room that likes us!"

The auditorium continued to ring with boos and catcalls when President LeFebvre took the microphone. "We hear you, we know it's a crappy proposal. We've had time to get used to it. Now get it out of your systems. After you're done, we'll explain it the best we can."

Michael Patrick had been through forty years of contract negotiations in Galesburg. He had seen plenty of tension, dissent, and disagreement, but he had never seen anything like this. There were always malcontents, even when they brought good contract offers. Some of Patrick's harshest critics, in fact, were his closest friends. But, usually, the Monday after a contract was voted in, Patrick would get back slaps and "attaboys!" shouted at him on the shop floor.

A politicking contender for union leadership had stirred up some of the nastiest dissent. But the main problem was the contract itself. Unlike the 1999 contract, this proposal was "all takeaways." The most controversial was the points-based attendance system that seemed designed to get people with children or health problems fired within months. Wages under the contract did not nearly keep up with inflation, and health-insurance contributions shot up. If this was the best the union could do, they must be weak, incompetent, or on the take, many insisted.[22]

"Let's hear what they have to say," someone finally yelled. A quiet majority, Patrick said, still stood by the union. LeFebvre was obligated to present the contract and did so. It was a rocky hour and a half.

The negotiators from Newton had been uncharacteristically inflexible in the contract talks over the preceding month. A federal mediator was brought in, but even he could not help move the company. Pickard, who sat across the table for many years, was gone. The collegial, if sometimes heated, back-and-forth was gone. Union leaders suspected something was amiss. There was something the other side was not telling them.

As time ran out on Saturday's negotiations, the day before the contract had to be presented, the union negotiators were baffled. "You guys have always worked with us before," one negotiator said to the Maytag representatives. "What's going on?" In 1999, for instance, management adopted wholesale union-written contract language on collaborative, lean workstation design. They praised the union for their forward thinking. This year it was not just that wages, benefits, and new rules were punitive. It was that anything the union proposed was rejected out of hand.

Before the Local's negotiating team left Saturday's tense session, each took a turn venting his frustration. Maytag's negotiators, a couple with long-standing ties to the Galesburg plant, absorbed the abuse with their eyes averted. The only time they interjected was at the very end. "Will you recommend this to the membership?" they asked.

"We're the messengers," Bevard replied. "We don't make recommenda-tions." Everyone in the room knew the threat of a strike loomed with the con-tract as it was.

After President LeFebvre finished the contract reading, people lined up to cast their votes. The negotiating team could see fire in the membership's eyes as they came on stage to vote. "Where do I sign up for strike committee?" one person asked. "Where can we sign up for picket duty?" asked another. "I can bring the axe handles!" joked one. Tellers in the trap room beneath the stage tallied the vote. Seventy percent voted to reject the contract.[23]

Next was a vote on whether to strike. Two-thirds needed to vote for the strike; otherwise, the membership would have to accept the contract despite having rejected it in principle. For some it was an easy decision. Take a stand, damn the consequences. Others agreed that the contract stunk, but made a stra-tegic call to vote for it. Many could not afford a work stoppage. Others were afraid the company would downsize or even leave if they struck. "Nobody wins in a strike," one worker said.[24] Well over a thousand women and men lined up single-file, grabbed their ballot, and walked again to the auditorium stage to vote. The tellers counted the votes as they came in. When they finished, Bevard heard someone utter, "Uh oh." The vote was too close to call.

Some in the membership, now more critical of the union than ever, won-dered if the vote was rigged. There were several tellers and witnesses working to get an accurate count, which took a few recounts to verify. In the end, over 65 percent voted to strike, just eleven votes shy of authorizing Local 2063's first strike since 1969.[25] To this day, many are unwilling to reveal their vote from that afternoon, even those who would talk openly about depression, family troubles, and struggles in returning to school. The day left an unhealed wound in Galesburg's collective psyche. It would turn out, however, that those eleven votes would shape the next several years to the workers' advan-tage. They had avoided a trap set by the company.[26]

Later that week, union leaders met with Kevin Bradley, human resources director at the Galesburg plant. Together they reviewed and finalized the newly approved contract. Mike Patrick and Sue Wilson attended the meet-ing along with Bevard, LeFebvre, Dennison, and a couple others. With the contract booklet ready for printing, Bradley, following local tradition, asked, "What color do you want this book?

"Black," one of the Machinists said.

"Come on guys, you can't have it black," Bradley responded.

"Yeah, it's like a funeral. Black is appropriate."

"Come on guys," Bradley pleaded.

"Brown, then, we know you can do brown," someone else proposed.

"Brown?"

"Yeah, because it's the color of shit and that's what the contract's worth." The union leaders refused to budge on brown. Bradley conceded, and the union had its sole victory of the 2002 contract talks. Or so they thought. When the contract booklet was bound in the factory's printing press in mid-April 2002, it was an attractive tan.

SIX MONTHS LATER, on the afternoon of October 11, 2002, a *Forbes.com* article announced, "Investors finally got news from Maytag they could cheer today: The home-appliance maker said it was going to close a facility in Galesburg, Ill., and lay off 1,600 workers, or about 8% of its total staff. The announcement sent shares of the Newton, Iowa-based firm soaring by more than 7%."[27]

That morning first-shifters in the Galesburg plant had been pulled into four sprawling groups on the shop floor and read a letter from Jim Little, Galesburg Refrigeration Products operations manager. "The organization believes," the letter read, "that it is not possible for the production of side-by-side and top-mount refrigerator models here in Galesburg to become competitively viable."[28]

As the news hit, first there were grumblings, then expletives. "Why didn't that fucker Hake have the nerve to come here to tell us himself," shouted one worker. "A chicken shit like Hake would know better than to show his face in this town ever again," answered another.[29] After the reading of the announcement, workers were handed a FAQ sheet, a packet of information, and sent home for the day as a pall fell over the small city.

The night before Dave Bevard and other leaders had been receiving disconcerting phone calls. Rumors were once again circulating about the factory after the evening news on WQAD TV-8 Moline reported that a big announcement was in the offing for the next day. The good money was on a buyout of Maytag by global appliance giant Electrolux of Sweden, producer in the United States of Eureka vacuum cleaners and Frigidaire appliances.

When Bevard and the others arrived for the early morning meeting, Bill Beer, president of Maytag Appliances, was there. They were ushered inside, and Beer gave the closing presentation. Bevard and the others, stunned, managed a few questions and then, like that, it was over. Bevard walked into an already evacuated factory and then out into the emptying parking lot. Monmouth Boulevard was lined with police cars in case of trouble, an insult, Bevard said, that added to the morning's injury.

Maytag said it would shutter the old Appliance City in two years. Workers who a generation earlier were naive to the cost-cutting machination of global corporations were by 2002 all too aware of the decline in manufacturing jobs region-wide—even if some, according to one labor leader, still lived in a "fool's paradise." Still, the Maytag announcement shocked and numbed the region for weeks to come.

Kirk King had expected the announcement, but it nonetheless floored the local manager. "I characterize this like a terminal illness situation. You always knew it was going to happen. But when it did, it just hits you in the heart. It was like somebody telling you that your father's dead. It just knocked me out.

FIGURE 4.1 THE ANNOUNCEMENT
Headline from Galesburg's newspaper, *The Register-Mail,* October 11, 2002. *Credit:* The Register-Mail.

There are so many stories. All the exchange. The gifts. The relationships. The whole deal."

As the day wore on, workers wept, called family members, and hit the bars in record numbers to commiserate. Some in town forecasted economic ruin and utter social devastation. Some plotted vengeance. Some lashed out at the union. "I am tired of paying union dues every month for nothing," appliance maker R. J. West said. "If [the union] is going to allow the company to beat me down, why are they even here?"[30]

What really stuck in the town's collective craw was the phrase, "competitively viable." It felt like an insult. The hard work, physicality, and monotony of the jobs took their toll on the body and, for some, the soul. Some just put in their time and dreamt about doing something else. But for most Maytag workers, Fred Maytag's evocation of "the spirit of love which the true craftsman holds for his job" meant something. They were proud of what they made. They all owned Maytag appliances and were proud to see them in a Sears showroom, in on-line advertisements, or in someone's home.

And in their minds they were partners to a deal with their employer. They would show up on time, work hard, and sacrifice their bodies for a thirty-plus-year span, one that left nearly all lifers injured in one way or another. Maytag's end of the bargain was to offer a decent wage ($15.14 was the average in 2002), steady and secure work, affordable health care, and a modest retirement program. That was the deal. It was what they had earned through their union, it was Appliance City's legacy, and what generations of Maytag leaders—going back to the founder himself—had supported. They were owed a better explanation. Four days later Maytag would announce a $55.6 million third-quarter profit (up 48 percent over the previous year) on $1.2 billion in revenue.[31]

As a public debate escalated, Maytag offered vague justifications for the closure, citing labor flexibility needs and quality problems. Maytag's top brass rejected meeting requests by Galesburg officials, local congressional representatives, and even the Illinois governor. It became clear that Newton had been strategizing about how to pull the plug since Hake's arrival sixteen month earlier. Maytag's Wall Street-driven management wanted to close a strong union plant and use it as a bludgeon on its other union shops. It also left little doubt that Hake's team had tried to instigate a strike that previous April as a pretext for shuttering the factory. A strike would have given Maytag the upper hand in the inevitable public-relations battle. They could pin blame on the recalcitrant union. Instead, the new management would become a punching bag for the next two years.

After all its near disasters—the sudden shifts and last-minute saves—Appliance City, a mainstay of western Illinois' economy seemed destined to buck the Rust Belt trend, just as Caterpillar in nearby Peoria and John Deere in Moline had. After all, engineers, craftsmen, and assemblers had been manufacturing things nearly continuously on that spot since 1905, when the Ingersoll family began producing its steel plow blades there.[32] As it had with Chicago's Admiral in its postwar heyday, Appliance City forged a strong and successful relationship with Newton's Maytag—even as the appliance industry entered the global era and moved toward oligopoly. But in the last years of its sixteen-year partnership, Galesburg workers saw first-hand how slash-and-burn cost-cutting had hollowed out the venerated brand that F. L. and Fred Maytag had built.

October 11, 2002, became a marker of changed lives and altered trajectories. Men and women added the date to their biographies and started to speak about their lives before and after "the announcement." Some would fight back at rallies and in the press. Others began the unsettling process of midlife reinvention. Most struggled to shake their resentment and newfound worries. Everyone faced change.

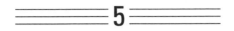

5

PADRE MIKE AND NAFTA MAN

The Magic Valley

MIKE ALLEN'S PATH to global dealmaker was a strange one. He graduated from Oblate College in San Antonio and was ordained a Catholic priest in 1964. As an oblate in the church, Allen committed his early adult years to the lives of migrant workers and others on the margins, and he considered himself a socialist. He lived in a grungy trailer near the impoverished members of his McAllen parish, where he was known as "Padre Mike." Not unlike Ed Krueger, Allen worked with the United Farm Workers, taught his parishioners how to work the welfare system, and railed against the injustices of capitalism. He had a friendly relationship with Krueger during those years. When Krueger needed something mimeographed, for example, he would go to the office where Allen worked to use his machine.[1]

In 1974 Mike Allen left the priesthood and became that most diehard of capitalists: the convert. As he tells it, he evolved, realizing that handouts cannot offer the dignity of work. He took a job working with the Texas Office of Economic Opportunity, where he lobbied in D.C. to get money for Texas and handled economic development grants for Texas businesses. In the mid-1980s he started a company that sold corrugated cardboard to Mexico, invested in a shoe-making maquiladora, and did various consultancies. Then in 1987 Allen moved back to the Magic Valley to lead the McAllen Economic Development Corporation (MEDC) at Mayor Brand's invitation. He was the perfect choice; he felt as comfortable with a Mexican developer or impoverished *colonia* (neighborhood) dweller as he did with corporate executives or Austin politicos. He wasn't only bilingual, he was bicultural—and persuasive to boot.

In 1988, a year into his tenure at MEDC, Allen met with the mayor of Reynosa, Tamaulipas. A gritty border city of a few hundred thousand, Reynosa lagged behind Tijuana, Ciudad Juárez, and Matamoros, but had been relatively self-sufficient—supported for several decades by its petroleum and natural gas reserves. Allen promised the mayor, a wealthy Mexican rancher named Ernesto Gómez Lira, to bring name-brand American, European, and Asian manufacturers to Reynosa. "We'll put them there," Allen told the mayor. "You take care of the infrastructure." During their conversation, Allen noticed an AK-47 on the back seat of the mayor's Chevrolet Suburban. "What do I do with this?" Allen quipped awkwardly. They laughed and shook hands to affirm a gentleman's deal that would change their part of the world forever.[2]

Reynosa accounted for merely 5 percent of all maquiladora employment in Mexico at the time. (Workers in Juárez and Tijuana together accounted for 40 percent.) There were already factories scattered across Reynosa, though, employing about 16,000 workers, mostly young women between 16 and 22. Half labored in the six large maquiladoras owned by Zenith, the last of the American-owned television makers. Zenith, knocked on its heels by Japanese competition in the 1970s, was nearly finished moving over 13,000 American jobs to its plants in Reynosa, as well as in Matamoros and Juárez. The Chicago-based manufacturer wasn't coy about why it shifted production to Mexico; there were no euphemistic phrases, such as Maytag's "competitive viability," or distracting canards about "challenges" around quality and safety. A Zenith spokesperson said bluntly: "It is a foreign country, and the wages are lower. That is why we're there." The wages were indeed lower. A Reynosa newspaper in 1988 calculated that a Zenith worker would have to work 45 minutes to buy a potato, 1.5 hours to buy a can of corn, 3.4 hours to buy a liter of shampoo, and nearly two weeks to buy a new pair of shoes.[3]

By the mid-1980s, the maquiladora program, called the Border Industrialization Program, had already been around for two decades, having been initiated in 1965 to address the growing unemployment crisis at the U.S.-Mexico border. After the mass deportation of Mexicans during the Great Depression in the 1930s, the United States faced monumental labor shortages during World War II. In 1942, President Roosevelt and Mexican president Manuel Ávila Camacho agreed to a temporary guest worker program that would bring in Mexican railroad and agricultural workers. The next year Roosevelt visited Ávila Camacho in Monterrey to solidify bilateral wartime relations as part of his Good Neighbor policy. At a banquet,

Roosevelt assured Mexicans that, "The day of exploitation of the resources and the people of one country for the benefit of any group in another country is definitely over."[4] After World War II, U.S. growers insisted that they still faced a labor shortage and urged that the Bracero Program be continued for seasonal agricultural workers. The controversial program, decried as a system of indentured servitude by its critics, lasted until 1964, when religious and labor organizations pressured Congress, including their allies in the Senate Subcommittee on Migratory Labor, to let it expire. Despite its end, the Bracero Program—which brought in over 400,000 Mexican workers a year at its peak—had established well-worn northward migration pathways in Mexico for the poor. Its end also left hundreds of thousands at the border looking for work and set the stage for the battle between South Texas farmworkers and Allee's Rangers in 1966–1967.[5]

The Border Industrialization Program allowed American and other multinational corporations to import parts and raw materials duty-free and then assemble color televisions and whatever else with Mexican labor, paying duties only on the value added in Mexico. Thus was born the maquiladora, from maquila, of Spanish origin, referring to the act of a miller converting a farmer's wheat into flour. Though meant to sop up a reserve army of dislocated men, maquiladora operators preferred young women for their supposed docility and nimble fingers in working with the electrical components of televisions and auto parts.[6]

Reynosa was poised to boom. MEDC's staff was by now thirty-strong, and they put together a slick, ten-minute video promoting the transnational twin cities as a high-tech manufacturing center. They dubbed the video into seven languages and took their sales show around the world. In Mike Allen's first six years, the MEDC attracted seventy companies to the McAllen area and about one hundred to Reynosa. By 1994, those companies employed 50,000 workers directly in the region and drew many other suppliers, retailers, and other employers in their wake. The MEDC claimed the Reynosa maquilas were injecting over $136 million a year into the McAllen-area economy by 1991.[7]

In order to realize his vision for the borderlands, Allen had to crack the whip from time to time. When a strike closed fifteen Reynosa factories in 1989, the maquila sector descended into turmoil. Allen called the governor of Tamaulipas and warned him that if he didn't fix the problem the MEDC would buy a full-page ad in the *Wall Street Journal* saying companies should no longer locate in his Mexican border state. The tactic worked. Mexican president Carlos Salinas de Gotari himself intervened on the side of foreign, mostly American, owners in Reynosa. "Salinas has made clear he will not let unions stand in the way of his goal of modernizing the Mexican economy and attracting more foreign investors," the Associated Press reported. Maquiladora operators praised the intervention, which inaugurated an era of flexible labor relations. "We blazed a new trail," boasted a local manager. In just his second year on the job, Allen made it clear who was in charge in Reynosa.[8]

Labor bosses in Mexico, *caciques* (chieftains), had dominated labor relations for some time. Like the drug lords that would follow them, caciques often had curious nicknames (one was "The Professor"), wielded unchecked power at the local level, and fought with each other over turf. As U.S. corporations began to dominate the border landscape, things changed. "In truth," two labor analysts wrote, "the U.S. maquiladora managers are the only force on the scene capable of challenging the hegemony of the labor leaders." From the unrest of 1989 in Reynosa emerged the *sindicatos blancos*. In these business-controlled "white unions," one dubious representative of the common worker (the cacique) was replaced by another (the company). After the Tamaulipas governor negotiated the resolution, Mike Allen rewarded him publicly for his efforts: "The [strike] flags are coming down right at this moment," Allen was quoted in the *Houston Chronicle* in August 1989. "The governor of the state of Tamaulipas deserves a lot of credit."[9]

McAllen-Reynosa was becoming a unique place, and Othal Brand and Allen let everyone know. "We are what we are because we have worked at it," Brand said in 1992. "We are not a rail head. We are not a seaport. We are not a county seat. We are not a crossroads. But of the cities surrounding us, none approach us in size, vigor, or vitality." The 73-year-old mayor bragged that he still put in fourteen- and sixteen-hour days, seven days a week. Allen and Brand helped to wrangle a deal to have the three-mile Anzalduas International Bridge built. When it opened seventeen years later, in 2009, the bridge connected Mission, Texas, to a newly built superhighway to Monterrey. Brand and Allen knew even before NAFTA that it would be integral to the region's long-term binational transportation and just-in-time manufacturing strategy.[10]

The massive private and public investments Allen was bringing to Reynosa fed the McAllen economy through the co-production, or "twin plants," model. To complement the labor-intensive factories just a few miles south in Reynosa, suppliers, logistics and technical support, and distribution operations located in McAllen. Quality Screw & Nut, to take one example, supplied bolts, washers, and other fasteners to the Reynosa-side operations for Johnson Controls, General Electric, and—to hold together their air conditioners—York International and Carrier Corporation. A bilingual call center was set up in McAllen. American and Mexican managers converged on the area as McAllen-Reynosa became the hotspot for economic integration between the United States and Mexico.[11]

Critical to Allen's co-production scheme was the MEDC-run McAllen Foreign Trade Zone—the first and still largest inland zone in the country—where products imported from Reynosa's maquilas could be further assembled, processed, packaged, or stored on the American side. General Electric, Zenith, as well as Chinese, Taiwanese, and Japanese companies, including Sony, crammed into the zone in the early 1990s, supporting 2,200 jobs on the eighty-acre, U.S. Customs Service monitored zone. Here the MEDC worked daily with companies from twenty-five countries to give them everything they wanted: a cheap and flexible labor force, a fluid border, low transaction costs, efficient logistics, and access to the largest consumer market in the world.[12] The MEDC *was* economic globalization.

Allen and Brand pushed hard for NAFTA. They knew that the fermenting free trade deal was a golden opportunity for the Texas side and enlisted Mission native, Lloyd Bentsen, an influential Democrat and 1988 running mate of presidential candidate Michael Dukakis, in their effort. They pushed hard, framing it as a win-win-win for the area and for both countries. In a *New York Times* article a month before the 1993 NAFTA vote in Congress, Allen said, "I talk to people in Reynosa all the time, and I can tell you, it's bordering on a tremendous insult to Mexico if NAFTA is voted down."[13] President Clinton signed NAFTA on December 8, 1993, after contentious debates and votes that revealed stark divisions on trade within both major political parties.

NAFTA hastened the boom in the Valley; it was full steam ahead for Mike Allen, or "NAFTA Man," as *Time* dubbed the former priest.[14] The big-thinking Texan had no trouble squaring his previous and current vocations. Arguably the region's most powerful man, Allen shaped the lives of hundreds of thousands of people. The maquilas and unrestricted free trade were good for everyone, he argued, including the impoverished parishioners he used to serve out of his humble trailer. Out of a slick McAllen office, he served South Texas in visits to Reynosa, Washington, D.C., Austin, Germany, and China—and in recruiting trips to the Rust Belt. Allen had enlarged upon Brand's legacy, becoming a "conservative visionary" on the global stage. He could do much more for the Magic Valley as "NAFTA Man" than he could as "Padre Mike." As Allen liked to say, "It's hard to tell people about Jesus when they don't have a job and are hungry."[15]

ON JUNE 27, 2003, in the offices of the McAllen Economic Development Corporation, Mike Allen and his partner, Keith Patridge, seemed ready for battle. They always were. The economic development game—in which an uncountable number of desperate places vie for jobs—is a kind of unrelenting war. And despite their success, and perhaps even because of it, Hidalgo County, Texas, remained among the most desperate of those places.

Allen—balding, lively, and dressed in a sharp black suit—was feeling particularly quarrelsome that morning in June when we first met him. He had been taking heat for his role in Maytag's Galesburg closing announcement the previous October. He and Patridge had even been picketed on a recent trip to Chicago. But he was also in trouble with Maytag. In April he had inadvertently revealed their plans to expand in Reynosa and outsource more American jobs. "By the time [Maytag] is finished," he was quoted in a newspaper article, "we're talking about 3,000, 4,000, maybe even 5,000 workers."[16]

"Do you mind if we record our discussion?" I asked at the outset. Josh Walsman—my friend, colleague, and translator for the border-area research—sat next to me.

"I'm not apologizing for anything I say anyway," he replied, leaning in. "Listen, this whole organization here, what we try to do is provide jobs for our community. In the process of that we've created 60,000 jobs in Mexico. So when Keith and I went to Chicago, we got picketed there because they said that we're taking jobs from Illinois. Yeah, we were! There was no question that we were trying to bring them down here to McAllen, Texas. But that's free enterprise."

"Nobody gave a damn about our people," he continued. "There was no outcry in Galesburg, Illinois, about how the people in our community were being treated. And I've read some of this crap in your Galesburg newspaper. All the moaning and groaning does no good. And you can tell Galesburg and anybody else in Illinois we're coming back!" If Allen saw us as Rust Belt diplomats or partisans, he clearly wasn't interested in making peace. In the world of bare-knuckle capitalism Allen punched first and asked questions later.

Patridge, Allen's right-hand man of a more traditional corporate pedigree, took his turn lecturing. He pronounced himself bewildered that people in

Galesburg apparently didn't get what was happening. "If a person thinks that they should get $20 or $30 an hour to put something together with screws when someone else is willing to do it for 50 cents an hour, guess where it's going to go? I mean, that's economics. The problem is that we get too many people that are too lazy. They think they're owed something."

"You can rail against capitalism," Allen added. "I was probably more of a socialist when I got out of school. I had to live every day with people that didn't have enough food to eat, that didn't have jobs, that were working in the fields. My point is that you can't change this capitalistic system."

Allen saw himself as a warrior, fighting to take Rust Belt jobs and to stop China from stealing low-wage work from the maquilas. Even other border cities were his enemies. He dismissed Brownsville-Matamoros as pathetically low-tech and low-value-added—meaning that the local contribution to the product was less meaningful, just assemblage. Allen derided Laredo-Nuevo Laredo as a mere "truck stop."

And yet for all his combativeness it was easy to see how his outsized personality had won over Maytag and other corporations that came to his kingdom. He spoke their language, and dispensed with the bullshit. The larger question of whether the growth-machine game was ultimately zero-sum— that all the intensive recruitment merely shifted capital and jobs around rather than adding aggregate value to the broader American economy—was utterly irrelevant to Allen. This was high stakes poker, and he needed to win for the Magic Valley.

"Corporations want hard numbers and information," Allen told the *San Antonio Express-News*. "They are not interested in chamber-of-commerce-type tours. They don't want to look at all the beautiful churches we have. They want to know how they can make money."[17] Like Captain Allee and Mayor Brand before him, dealmaker Allen was persuaded about the rightful power of economic elites. As long as they were unrestrained, their pro-business, pro-growth model would lift the lives of the poor in the area. The benefits of growth would, to use the infamous expression, "trickle down."

But where Allee and Brand had propped up local and regional Anglo elites, Allen was cosmopolitan—a global thinker of the next generation. He had visited Europe and China and met with corporate leaders of multinational firms. And he had become wealthy as a broker of international business deals at the MEDC. Allen insisted, though, that he never forgot his former parishioners. A 1960s photograph of them in front of his old trailer sat in a

prominent place on his desk. The MEDC website reflected this socially progressive, laissez-faire conservative ethos in its tagline: "McAllen is the New
Texas. Bilingual, Bicultural and Pro Business."

"I guess the antagonism that you might be feeling for me right now is
based on the fact that so many people don't understand Mexico," Allen said.
"We haven't thought of ourselves as *gringos* on one side and *Mexicanos* on the
other. We believe we're a totally integrated community. People ask me, 'Why
do I have a Mexican flag in front of my office?' Well, you go across Texas, and
every single stream, river, town has a Mexican or Spanish name to it. And they
say, 'Well, why don't they go back to Mexico?' We got to realize that we stole
all of their land in 1848. We stole it from them!"

"We don't believe that anybody likes us," Allen continued. "They come
down here because they're going to make money. Everything boils down to
economics. And you can't fault that. You have to look at everything from the
standpoint of what can I do to help a company reduce or minimize their cost.
The minute they can make more money somewhere else, they'll move. They're
not bad people. They're not evil organizations. It's just bottom-line economics."

After a couple of hours, the interview ended with Allen and Patridge
softening. Allen, in particular, was hard not to like, or at least admire. As we
walked out of the meeting room, a young woman in shorts and a tank top,
jumped out of her chair when she saw Allen. "I wanted to thank you for finding me that job. I got it and I really like it!" she said, making Allen's closing
argument for him. "Oh, good!" Allen said with genuine affection.

By 2003, sixteen years into his reign, Allen had made McAllen-Reynosa
into a global magnet for capital, regional tourists, the wealthy, and impoverished laborers from Veracruz and other southern states. The middle class
and wealthy of northern Mexico spoke of "McAllenando," literally to go
"McAllening." Many came two or three hours from Monterrey, home to the
highest per-capita concentration of millionaires in Mexico. They came to visit
the upscale La Plaza Mall, for the safe and well-maintained streets, to buy
Jaguars and Range Rovers, to find marble imported from Turkey—all the
while never having to switch out of Spanish.[18] Nancy Millar of the McAllen
Chamber of Commerce told us that McAllen had fixed itself solidly in the
Mexican imagination. In *telenovelas*, McAllen was mentioned as a sign of
prestige. "Oh, you remember, I was wearing that dress I bought in McAllen,"
Millar said, acting out a scene in a Mexican soap opera. "I mean we're part

of the culture! I've been to trade shows in Mexico City. Everyone knows McAllen. Everyone!"

Managers, professionals, and the wealthy built vacation homes and moved to Hidalgo County. The palm tree-lined, upper-class homes of Sharyland Plantation in Mission—not far from where Krueger and Allee had their late night standoff in 1967—became a concrete expression of the moneyed part of the area's big boom. As the Sharyland website proclaims, the development, once a home to golden-skinned grapefruit and navel orange trees, is "largely a result of the economic changes spawned by the North American Free Trade Agreement."[19] Driving around Sharyland, you wouldn't know the climate of South Texas is semi-arid. The lush green grasses and golf courses of these walled-off and gated communities provide an oasis to Mexicans and Americans who can afford the McMansions or gorgeous Spanish colonial style homes there.

Mike Allen had convinced the Dallas oil and real estate tycoon Ray Lee Hunt to develop a 6,000-acre master plan in the McAllen area. Hunt Valley Development Ltd. was created to develop Sharyland, which includes both luxurious and moderately priced housing, a fifty-seven-acre sports complex, schools, shopping centers, and hiking and biking trails—a massive development that could be home for up to 40,000 border-dwellers. Sharyland Business Park, which is in MEDC's Foreign Trade Zone, was also part of the plan, undertaken with Ramiro Garza, a real-estate magnate on the Mexico side who began developing 16,000 acres in Reynosa. Together the developers had 22,000 acres and pushed hard for the Anzalduas International Bridge to connect their developments. "In our eyes we don't see a river, we see 22,000 acres," said Hunt's marketing manager back in 1998.[20]

In the booming 1990s, only Las Vegas (86 percent) had a higher decade growth rate than McAllen-Edinburg-Mission (49 percent) among the 100 largest metropolitan areas in the United States. This sprawling border node had even outpaced high-tech Austin (48 percent), number 3 on the list. The McAllen MSA (Metropolitan Statistical Area), with little fanfare outside of South Texas, had doubled from 283,229 in 1980 to 569,463 in 2000.[21] Metropolitan areas in the Rust Belt—Youngstown, Scranton, Buffalo, Pittsburgh—experienced the highest rates of population decline. Even in the American economy's post-9/11 hangover, Hidalgo County was humming along, leading Texas in job growth.[22] John Sargent, an economist and maquila expert at the University of Texas-Pan American, gave credit to Allen and Patridge. They had "the perfect partnership," wherein Allen handled the politics on both sides of the border and Patridge "put things together." Other border development organizations had high turnover, inconsistent planning, and succumbed to a cultural "line in the sand" at the border.

Rumors in the early 2000s had it that a Mexican pop star and President Vicente Fox's brother had vacation homes in the area. In McAllen the wealthy's assets were out of reach of Mexican taxing authorities but injected into McAllen's local economy. About 30 percent of the city's sales tax receipts came from sales to Mexicans, allowing the area to maintain a low property tax rate and provide ample city services. A reliable influx of "Winter Texans," most of them from the Midwest, swelled city and local business coffers as well.[23]

Even in the wealthiest areas of Hidalgo County, most people identified themselves as "Hispanic."[24] This was indeed the new Texas. In 2003, the Chamber of Commerce in McAllen said that as many as 80 percent of new businesses were owned by Mexican citizens, a reversal of the proportions from five years earlier. The Rio Grande Valley, a Democratic stronghold in Republican Texas, had become more tolerant of women and minorities, all the way up to the top, Millar said. In 1997 McAllen, a city that was 80 percent Hispanic, elected its first Hispanic mayor.[25] "Leo Montalvo is very different from Othal Brand," Millar said carefully, "a real consensus builder, which is a refreshing change."

Despite its wealthy, bicultural sparkle in the NAFTA era, the Magic Valley had one of the highest unemployment rates in the nation, ranked near the bottom in per capita income and near the top in drug seizures. In the 2000 census the McAllen MSA ranked highest in percent living in poverty at 36 percent and percentage of children living in poverty at 46 percent. Neighboring Starr County mimicked McAllen's statistics and ranking among rural counties.[26] Regarding the area's boom, Stephen Spivey, a business writer for *The Monitor*, remarked, "It's good, but it's not channeled in a way that really lifts people up."

Approximately 400,000 Texans live in colonias, mostly in southern Texas. In these improvised settlements, residents live in used trailers and ramshackle homes of plywood and scrap metal. Texas, with 2,333 colonias, has by far the largest concentration of any state, followed by New Mexico, Arizona, and California. These neighborhoods, which typically lack basic services, dot the southernmost tip of South Texas, mainly in Hidalgo County. In 2002 an astonishing one out of every three residents, or 160,000 people, in Hidalgo County lived in a colonia. According to border public health scholars, the worst-off face conditions not unlike those in sub-Saharan Africa. HIV/AIDS, tuberculosis, and diabetes approach crisis levels. At the same time, the border colonias buzz with microbusiness activity, children playing, residents improving their homes, and people heading to work early in the mornings.[27]

Some in the U.S.-side colonias are migrant farmworkers, here one season, gone the next. Many, though, are longtime residents, and 85 percent are U.S. citizens, according to one study.[28] They find work, usually making poverty wages, in the fields and packing houses, at temporary construction jobs, or as janitors or warehouse workers.[29] The informal economy thrives here. People exchange items at *la pulga* (local flea markets) and do odd jobs where they can find them. In the face of a policy that has freed capital and goods to move fluidly across the border, but simultaneously restricted the cross-border movement of people, these U.S.-side colonias serve important needs for Mexicans and Mexican Americans. Housing in the colonias is inexpensive, and there are fewer checkpoints to get through for those without documentation. Being near the border, colonias also offer access to cheaper medical services and medicines in Mexico, as well as a wide range of Spanish-language television, radio, film, and entertainment options.[30] NAFTA was indeed, in its way, working in the Magic Valley. Here it was economic globalization on steroids, with its frentic intensity of growth and the attendant extremes of wealth, income, and housing.

When we visited Mike Allen and Keith Patridge again later in 2003, they kept hammering away at their message. Patridge, apparently believing we hadn't gotten it the first time, said, "The fact that someone sits on their rear end, doesn't try to better themselves, doesn't try to get any education, doesn't try to gain in skills, but still says, 'I'm not making enough money.' How can you feel sorry for them? I mean there is a personal responsibility in this. Just as there is a personal responsibility in Galesburg. I mean there is no right to a job. There is no right to a living wage."

Allen and Patridge understood the free-wheeling ethos of this new world better than Rust Belt laggards and other border leaders. They embraced cutthroat competition and the impulse to disorienting change. Like Karl Marx, they recognized the revolutionary power of this raw form of capitalism, in which, "All fixed, fast frozen relations. . . are swept away," in which "All that is solid melts into air, all that is holy is profaned."[31] In soon-to-be-shuttered Appliance City, what was once holy—the regularity and security of factory life, the loud collective voice of local union democracy, the bonds of loyalty and mutual obligation of traditional Midwestern capitalism—had, in this new era, become profane.

The dissent that was bubbling in western Illinois found no audience at the booming border, where critical voices were hard to find. Ed Krueger and a smattering of others continued to work quietly in the Mexico-side colonias, but they were a mere annoyance to Allen. U.S.-side unions in the area were weak as well. "There is, like the rest of Texas, a hole when it comes to unions," *Monitor* reporter Stephen Spivey said. *The Monitor* itself, like other newspapers in the area, was until 2012 owned by Freedom Communications, a California corporation with a strong libertarian bent. There was little interest, Spivey told us, in covering the colonias or the maquilas at the Freedom newspapers. With Maytag set to join Nokia, Halliburton, Panasonic, Whirlpool, Delco, and other multinational corporations, Allen and Patridge saw the sky as the limit. In the global era, McAllen-Reynosa not only remained a capitalist's paradise but was now the new global world incarnate.

In 2003, on the southern side of the meandering Rio Grande, rose another of Mike Allen's creations. It emerged in the summer heat out of a corn field ten miles southeast of downtown Reynosa's Plaza Principal. About ten maquiladoras occupied the otherwise barren farmland on the edge of the city in Parque Industrial Colonial. Across the street from Maytag's site, men and women in blue coats sat at tables in a cool and bright cavern of a building, working on computer hard drives at the Jabil factory. Old Appliance City, a mash-up of structures representing nearly every decade in the 20th century, would have been out of place here. Under endless sky stretching in all directions, tall concrete slabs formed the gray husk of the new refrigerator factory. Cranes put the slabs in their upright position, and enormous wood planks held them in place. A tastefully landscaped Maytag sign on raised stone welcomed people to the half-finished Maytag facility: Planta Maytag III. Soon it would need workers.

LAURA FLORA OLIVEROS was one of the hundreds of thousands, probably millions, of Veracruzanos contemplating the long voyage to the border at the dawn of the NAFTA era. Flora's intrepid sister, Beatriz, had been the first to leave their home in Tierra Blanca, Veracruz, a city 550 miles south of Reynosa. After crossing the Rio Grande and walking to a small town, Beatriz hid in a garbage can as *la migra* (border patrol) appeared. As the family story goes, a sympathetic local sheriff pretended he didn't see the migrants and a local woman who saw them from her apartment balcony waved them up and hid them away until it was safe. Beatriz has lived in the United States ever since; it has been over twenty years since Flora has seen her older sister. Flora's youngest sister, her brother, and then her mother each followed Beatriz north in the 1990s.

Economic conditions in Veracruz had worsened, but Flora didn't want to leave home like the others. She just wanted to be "a mother hen with lots of chicks running around." She was in her mid-30s and made *pasteles* (sweets), *panes* (breads), and curiosities and keepsakes to sell in the marketplace in downtown Tierra Blanca. She also taught classes on how to make the handicrafts. Flora's father had been a jewelry maker who made gold chains and rings in town, but drank away a good portion of his earnings. The father of Flora's two older children helped when he could, but the father of the three younger girls, a wholesale fruit and vegetable vender, did not. With an alcoholic father and two spoiled marriages, Flora had come to think of marriage as "a chain." "I'm bad because I think this way," she said, recalling the shame she had felt as a single parent in traditional southern Veracruz.

When Flora's mother returned to Tierra Blanca in 2001, she told Flora that the only way to get ahead was to go north. It was a wrenching moment, one that she knew had been coming. Perhaps she could get by in Tierra Blanca, but there was nothing there for her children. The local economy, based largely on basic grains and livestock, had suffered in recent years for reasons she didn't understand. She would have to leave her three youngest, all vulnerable girls under ten, with her parents and head north with her two teenagers. The thought of leaving them behind, of not seeing them for years, was agonizing. Plus, as much as Flora hated to admit it, she was scared of the north. She had never traveled before. And though Flora could read and write, she didn't know any English. She would have never dreamed that in just a few years she would be a foul-mouthed factory worker assembling Maytag refrigerators at a sparkling new factory on the U.S.-Mexico border.

In August of 2001, Flora paid a *coyote* (smuggler or middleman) her entire savings, $1,500, to guide her and her two teenagers—along with twenty or so others—through the Sonoran Desert and into the north. After making it through a few strands of barbed wire at the border and into the Tohono O'odham Indian Reservation, the coyote forged ahead while Flora lay hidden in the dusty brush. Their guide staggered water and food stops and permitted travel only in the darkness of night. The memories were still vivid to Flora years later. The biting red ants climbing inside her pants. The silent waiting for nearby border agents to pass. Flora said that the empty skulls and skeletons of less fortunate migrants served as macabre reminders of the perils of their trip. In the mid-1990s, the U.S. had tightened border controls in urban areas like San Diego and El Paso, forcing migrants to attempt more dangerous and circuitous pathways north. "People were scraped up, tired," Flora said. "Their shoes were ragged by the end of the week in the hills and brush."

The coyote eventually collected the weary travelers along a remote section of highway in southern Arizona. Flora, her teenagers, and the others were then packed into a windowless van. Flora's two-week trek from southern Veracruz ended near Orlando, where she began her time in the United States harvesting tomatoes and oranges. When she looks back, Flora pinpoints the time of her first voyage north not with a specific date, but as "la mes antes el atentado a las Torres Gemelas," the month before the attack on the Twin Towers.

It would be three years until she would see her three youngest girls again.

6

RESIST OR REINVENT

Galesburg, Illinois

ANNETTE DENNISON WAS asleep when a girlfriend called her with the news. It was mid-morning on October 11, 2002, her thirty-fifth birthday. Annette, a self-proclaimed "night owl," had worked the second shift the night before and pulled into her driveway in Monmouth at 1 a.m. after the sixteen-mile trip from the warehouse in Galesburg. Monmouth, over forty years after Michael Patrick made his first commute to Appliance City in 1959, was still a town of about 10,000. Home to a hog slaughterhouse on one side and little Monmouth College on the other, Monmouth claimed to be the hometown of gambler, gunfighter, and lawman Wyatt Earp.

"No way!" She sat alone, dazed. Her boys were at school. Her husband, Doug, was at the factory getting briefed by managers from Newton. *Happy birthday, Annette,* she thought. *Now find something else to do with your life.*

A flood of emotions overwhelmed her that morning. She had been stuck in the factory since she was 22 and didn't care for the mind-numbing work. Recently she had spent her evenings on an electric forklift in the Regional Distribution Center zipping through a landscape of brown cardboard boxes. She loaded and unloaded washers, dryers, microwaves, stoves, and refrigerators in and out of semis, one after the other, all night long. Most Maytag appliances built in Iowa, Illinois, and Ohio came to the cavernous warehouse across the street from Appliance City.

On the forklift Annette would sometimes daydream about getting out, but the work had become comfortable. She had spent nearly her entire adulthood in the factory. She had girlfriends, drinking buddies, and an assortment of familiar and friendly faces she would miss. It was through them that Annette had developed strong loyalty to the factory and even to the brand itself since she started in 1989, the year of the first Maytag refrigerator.

A million questions popped into her head. She had always been a Type A personality and planner, and this was so sudden. She had no idea what to do. With a mortgage and debts to pay, her daydreams of getting out had never taken a concrete form. Her boys, Dylan and Dalton, were in elementary school. Like Mike Patrick a generation earlier, Annette never intended to stay at Maytag but had made her peace with being a factory worker.

Doug called her a few minutes later. The warehouse would remain open until February 2005. Annette would have sixteen years' seniority at that point—not enough to stay until the very end. Instead she would be laid off in September 2004. Doug told her she had the day off.

Annette had a spotty college record. She graduated in 1984 from Union High School, a small rural school just east of the Mississippi River. The next year, liberated from her parents, she rented an apartment in Galesburg with some friends. She was registered at the local community college, but she attended parties more often than classes. "I had other interests when I went right out of high school," she confessed with a grin.

This was her second chance. The Maytag layoffs were unusual—strange even—in that there would be nearly two years until her layoff. After that, if the shuttering was deemed the result of foreign competition, Maytag workers were eligible to receive federal Trade Adjustment Assistance (TAA) for two years. There was time to chart out of a new life, even with a lousy transcript. The end was coming, but there was time. The transition would be drawn out.

In January 2003, three months after the closing announcement, Annette started at the community college again, this time with a vengeance. Indeed Carl Sandburg College—a 1,400-student school named after the populist poet and socialist who was born in a cottage near the Galesburg rail yards where his father worked—was filled with transitioning Maytag workers. In the morning Annette began hammering away at prerequisites such as algebra, biology, chemistry, geometry, and freshman composition at Sandburg. At 4 p.m. she would hop on the forklift on the southwestern edge of town, stealing study breaks when she didn't have an order to fill. Most of the other students at Sandburg were far younger, and she hadn't thought one bit about algebra in fifteen years. It all intimidated her. Soon enough, though, Annette was replacing F's with A's.

Annette knew an associate's degree would do nothing for her. She needed a marketable skill, something directly connected to a profession. Annette never had a particular interest in health care, but western Illinois needed health-care workers. It was *the* growth field, and everyone knew it. All the Maytag women were headed that way, it seemed, and there were hundreds like her. In fact, there would be nearly as many women as men in each round of layoffs.[1] With a wave of desperate women knocking at the gate, the professional programs in health care would turn away most comers. She would need to finish the prerequisites and get stellar grades.

Annette set her sights on radiology. There were eighteen slots each year at Sandburg and five times as many applicants. Any program that led to a wage comparable to Maytag's was that competitive. She would need to be ready to apply for the program after her layoff. That way she could match her two years of unemployment benefits to the two-year radiology program. Like others, Annette would have to start a job the first week after she graduated or go without income. The timing was tight. Plus Annette would be 40-years-old by the time she finished all this. "Will anyone want to hire me?" she wondered.

A LITTLE AFTER 6 a.m. on May 8, 2003, George Carney, Mike "Smitty" Smith, and Samuel "Rooster" Fouts mounted their Harley-Davidsons to ride around the Sodexho Marriott in Newton, Iowa. The little town had served as Maytag's headquarters for over 100 years, most of them rather idyllic ones of prosperity and productivity. But today's annual shareholder meeting, on a chilly Iowa morning, would be different. The motorcycles with their characteristic Harley staccato punctuated the air as Carney and his friends rode in circles around the growing encampment of Galesburg workers.

A white banner waved and cracked off the back of Carney's bike. It read, "MAYTAG: MADE IN THE USA," in blue lettering. A red circle ringed the lettering and a red line slashed diagonally across the words. Smitty and Rooster, both muscular and heavily tattooed, flew large American flags off the back of their bikes. They revved their engines when they passed, drawing cheers from the huddled workers. They had all awakened around 3 a.m. to make the three-hour trip to Newton.

The sun had just peered above the hotel parking lot. Workers and their supporters picked out signs and drank hot coffee. They put on white or bright orange T-shirts over their clothes that read, "MAYTAG: MAKE IT IN THE

U.S.A" above a waving American flag. Below the flag the T-shirts read, "OR THE U.S.A. WON'T MAKE IT." One man didn't need the T-shirt. The American flag on the back of his leather jacket stretched from shoulder to shoulder and nearly down to his belt. As the workers gathered, Maytag executives, members of the board, and other shareholders alerted to the rally snuck in the back door of the Marriott.

From a makeshift PA system set up on the beds of two pickup trucks, the Machinists blasted Bruce Springsteen from two tall black Peavey speakers. After being called to attention, those gathered recited the Pledge with hands pressed to heart. Then they went to hammering the decision makers inside. Tom Buffenbarger, president of the International Association of Machinists and Aerospace Workers (IAM), called for a boycott and called Maytag management "the American Taliban." "The fight begins today and we will take the fight every place in America."[2]

Several speakers called Maytag's closing announcement an act of "economic terrorism" and drew parallels between September 11, 2001, and October 11, 2002. Both dates were now infamous markers of a new era, both existential threats to the America they knew. Michael Patrick, now a regional representative for the International, stood behind Buffenbarger. Next to Patrick were Lt. Governor Pat Quinn and Dave Bevard. All three were dressed in dark suits and reading over their notes. "We want the board of directors to look at the other side of their decision, how it affects people," Patrick had said in the town's newspaper the day before, setting the tone ahead of the event. "We won't sit on our hands and let them just say this is a business decision. Our intent is peaceful."[3]

Iowa Senator Tom Harkin, Congressman Lane Evans, and Local 2063's vice president, Doug Dennison, also took turns standing in the bed of the pickup, stirring up the crowd. After the speeches, the crowd escorted the leaders into the Sodexho Marriott Conference Center and cheered them inside.

When Ralph Hake said there would be no more questions, a voice came from the back of the room. "I am the lieutenant governor of the State of Illinois." It created a tense silence. Quinn went on to complain about the Maytag tax breaks and what he saw as the corporation's ethical problems. He questioned if Illinois' Iraq War veterans would find any good jobs when they came home from fighting for their country.

Other voices followed, peppering the normally dull shareholders' meeting with pointed questions and critical commentary. And as more workers squeezed in, there was loud applause for the dissent. Sue Wilson—who three decades earlier had fought for pregnancy and maternity pay for women at Appliance City—stood to question Maytag's market strategy. Is Maytag still a premium company? she asked. Or is it chasing appliance giants Whirlpool and General Electric on cost, surely a losing strategy?

In anticipation of the meeting, the union had collected a tall stack of handwritten letters from its members and sent them to Hake. In his letter, Doug Dennison wrote about his family's weekend. "We used our Hoover (American-made) vacuum before using our (American-made) Hoover steam vac to shampoo the carpets. We did some laundry in our (American-made) Maytag washer/dryer. Made an excellent dinner cooked in our (American-made) Maytag stove. The boys did the dishes which consisted of them loading our (American-made) Maytag dishwasher. They even put the leftovers away in our (American-made) Maytag refrigerator." Like other letter-writers, Dennison promised a personal boycott. All he had left was his power as a consumer.

Dave Bevard also got his chance at the conference room's microphone. Bevard had become Local 2063's president in the unhappy months after the announcement of Maytag's closing. It was then that he began to receive envelopes, with no return addresses, in the mail at the union office. Inside were press clippings and internal memos from Newton. The source had to be a disaffected manager, and he guessed it was someone with a long history in Newton and in Galesburg. In fact, he was pretty sure who it was—an "old school" company loyalist who sat across from him at the negotiating table in April 2002, with his head hung in shame, caught between conflicting loyalties: troubled by Maytag's new direction but always a good "company man." Those envelopes helped Bevard take the public relations fight to Maytag. That morning, Bevard implored Maytag shareholders to think about the wide-ranging impacts of closure. The factory's closing meant school closings and other social consequences.

The questions were charged, but not rude, and Hake did not cut them off. He absorbed the anger and did not reflect it. Perhaps he knew he was in a failing media war and that there was little he could say that day to turn things around. This was why he had avoided requests from U.S. congressmen, Illinois Governor Rod Blagojevich, and others to meet about the decision.

It was a fait accompli. Maytag's 62-acre site in Reynosa had been bulldozed, graded, and a storm-sewer system had been laid. A month earlier the ex-priest Mike Allen had revealed that Maytag had several plants planned, with room enough for 5,000 workers. There was no turning back for Hake, even had he wanted to. It was now time for other Maytag towns—Herrin, Illinois, and Newton—to chew their nails.[4]

Perhaps, though, faced that morning with a verbal onslaught of human troubles, all from people he had to look in the eye, he felt remorseful. "I understand your point of view," Hake had responded to Quinn. The CEO explained that the factory and refrigerator design platform were the problem, not the workers. "The workforce is not the source of the problem," Hake said. "It's not their fault."[5]

Outside, workers marched around the conference center, waving small American flags and carrying signs denouncing corporate greed, Hake, and NAFTA. One read, "There's that sucking sound again!" referencing Ross Perot's famous line from the 1992 presidential campaign about the NAFTA jobs vacuum in Mexico.

The marchers, fists raised, chanted, "U.S.A.! U.S.A.!" Since the closing announcement, the surge in patriotic slogans around town had been note-worthy. It was defensive patriotism, the sort that emerges when people want to hold on to something important. The Midwest's industrial decline had been grinding away for decades, but the Maytag closing seemed like the end of an era, and people were deeply shaken by it. If this admired Midwestern company could leave town, what was left behind? It was a confirmation that America had fundamentally and irrevocably changed. The signs, the T-shirts, the speeches all sought to claim what America meant, and the protest was not just against the company's direction, but the country's. Maytag and America had been synonymous: innovation, workmanship, hard work, togetherness, and a broad conception of corporate responsibility. In the marchers' minds, there was no question whatever of who stood on the moral high ground. This was not idle screaming. They had an important message, one that they were desperate to convey to the rest of the country. "I knew Fred Maytag," an older Newton resident said that day. "He wouldn't go this way. He'd be sicker'n heck about it."[6]

Randy Colwell, a Knox College student whose father worked at the fac-tory, showed up late to the rally. He had missed the ride to Newton and, distraught, called a cab for the 180-mile trip from Galesburg. It had cost him $250. After the march, Local 2063's safety standards representative Aaron Kemp told the demonstrators Colwell's story. They walked to the makeshift stage and dropped $10 and $20 bills in a hat. Colwell stood on stage, blank-faced and speechless. The workers had covered his fare.

TRACY WARNER COULDN'T make the Newton rally. The new point-based attendance policy required her to save points in case her two-year-old boy, Ryan, got sick. She felt awful about missing it. Her father worked the fac-tory for thirty-two years, and she believed in unions. Warner called herself "a loner" but saw worker solidarity as a moral obligation.

After the strike in April 2002 failed, Warner was angry. Three nights in a row, after she put her son to bed, she stayed up, writing a letter to the editor in the back of her little home. A dog barked incessantly in a neighbor's yard, fueling her irritation. In the letter Warner mourned the strike vote and ques-tioned the solidarity of the older members. They were set for life, but what about single mothers or people only halfway to retirement like her? "There is more to being in a union than wearing a union T-shirt," she wrote.

That Monday union leaders made copies of her letter and posted it around the factory and told her they were proud of her. On the factory floor her co-workers were surprised. "We thought you were quiet!" they teased her. Some in her department joked that she had become the "poster child for the union." Ryan's mostly absent father complained that she had called herself a "single mother." "But I am!" she shot back. Sticking your neck out in a place like this provoked reaction, she learned. "I wanted to go on strike, I really did," Warner maintained. "I was ready to make my picket signs, get my lawn chair out of the garage, and call my relatives so I could sign up for picket duty."

Like Annette Dennison, Warner had to look ahead and that meant, as with Dennison, fixing an embarrassing community college transcript and getting her associate's degree as quickly as possible. Trade Adjustment Assistance (TAA) limited recipients to two years of education assistance and one degree. With an associate's in hand *before* her layoff, she could pursue her dream of earning a bachelor's degree in journalism. Her brother was the first in her fam-ily to complete college and was now doing well as a pharmaceutical salesman.

Only a handful of Maytag workers were pursuing bachelor's degrees. In the limited transition time, getting a trade certification, such as for welding or

heavy-equipment operation, or a professional degree, such as for computer networking or nursing, were far more conventional and practical routes. And those
paths were cinches for TAA approval. Pursuing a journalism degree would take
a lot more convincing. And first she would have to prove herself worthy.

Through 2003 and 2004 Warner continued attaching door handles and
tying down liners and water tanks on refrigerators during the day. At nights
and on weekends, she attended classes, studied, and parented Ryan. Her aunt,
Mary Jones—who completed her thirty years and was fully vested in her pension at Maytag three years before its closing—filled the childcare gaps, watching the irrepressible red-headed toddler when Warner was at school.

Right before she was laid off in September 2004, Warner completed her
associate's degree at Sandburg. She carried a C average in high school and
at Sandburg before the announcement. With anxious determination Warner
reshaped her academic record, graduating from Sandburg with all A's. Unlike
many of her counterparts, especially the men, she wanted to make a clean
break from the dull repetitiveness of factory life. She was determined to reinvent herself.

WHEN GEORGE CARNEY rode his Harley around the Sodexho Marriott in
Newton in May 2003, it had been the first time he had taken it out of his
garage in months. He simply hadn't felt like riding. Carney organized twelve
bikers to ride with him that day; only two showed. Carney couldn't blame
them. "Did anybody that went to that rally think that it was going to do any
good? No, it's not going to change a damn thing."

Prior to the 2002 announcement, Carney operated a forklift on the second
shift, alongside Annette Dennison, and logged massive overtime hours. On
long weekends he would sometimes put in fifty-four hours in three calendar
days, eighteen of it overtime. One time he worked thirty days in a row. Carney
also built houses and did odd jobs in the mornings for extra cash.

Carney played as hard as he worked. On weekends he used to take 20-mile
treks on his mountain bike, cruise back roads on his Harley, and gamble on
the riverboats in the Quad Cities with his friends. He loved to go to NASCAR
races, hunt, and play paintball—all with characteristic intensity. All these
things, however, were ultimately just hobbies.

More than anything, Carney needed to work. It made him a good father
and calmed his mind. "I'm just one of those guys that doesn't mind work.

It keeps my mind off things, stops me from thinking about relationships, regrets . . . when I sit down, my mind starts going one hundred miles per hour." Carney had hardly stopped moving since he started at Appliance City in 1984, and he had become fiercely loyal and connected to the place. The factory allowed him to provide his wife, Becky, and his two boys with a good life. At one time they had had it all: a nice home, a swimming pool, and fourteen acres outside the Quad Cities. "I like to think I was a good family man back then. Everything I did was for my boys."

Carney worked too much, though, and it eventually led to a divorce. He'd crash when he got home late at night. Becky would say, "I got the worst part of you," and she was right. The "best part of me," Carney said, was getting up early in the morning, working odd jobs, the Maytag second shift, and every scrap of available overtime. "It's what ruined my marriage, overworking. I mean, it's hard to have a relationship with someone who's not there."

Carney muddled through the end of the 90s after the divorce. He drank, dabbled in cocaine, and tried meth a few times. "I was a real redneck back then," he said, always willing to go after a laugh at his own expense. Carney didn't like meth. He became jittery and his ears itched like mad. The drugs, he said, weren't hard to come by at the factory, but work had always been his drug of choice.

Now, in the summer of 2004, Carney faced an imminent layoff. While Annette Dennison and Tracy Warner were finishing up their associate's degrees, Carney had sunk to a dark place.

The Town Tavern in Avon, Illinois, was his new home. He was a customer; he was also the new owner. Carney threw together all the money he had to buy the bar for $120,000. Without a Maytag wage and pension, the Town Tavern would be his home, his income, and his retirement plan all wrapped up in one.

Avon had less than a thousand people, and the Tavern was one of two bars, located at its main intersection at Washington and Main. Pete's Place, the other bar, was next door. The Tavern had a slow, steady stream of customers coming for beer, karaoke on Wednesdays, and, for a few, the mesmerizing allure of Naked Lady video poker. His motorcycle buddy, "Rooster" Fouts, sometimes played weekend nights with his band, the Texas Barking Spiders. On the eastern wall of the Tavern, above a neon Budweiser sign, Carney had hung the banner that flew behind his motorcycle a year earlier in Newton.

Carney lived cheaply in the bar's upstairs apartment. When he was thirsty, he pressed a drink out of the soda gun or grabbed a beer. When he was hungry, he ate a frozen pizza from the bar's freezer. The rest of the bills, like the groceries, the heat, and the cellphone, were business write-offs as well. His father, who had had nine kids, had been a small businessman and a survivor in thin times. Carney would try to do the same. "The people that go crazy are the ones that can't adapt."

Carney, 45, did not consider retraining or college. "Not everybody is cut out for college," he said. He didn't like school and doubted whether he would get anything out of it even if he did well. His two boys, Eric and Brandon, were in junior college and high school, respectively. Their generation didn't have a choice. "It isn't, 'Well, I can get out of school and start earning a paycheck,' like I did. It's not a matter of an associate's degree either. They're all going to have to have bachelor's degrees. [Employers] are going to take the guy that can sit there and solve a problem in the least amount of time."

Carney maintained that it was too late for him to become a different person. He was a working stiff, and he'd drop his head and plow ahead as he always had. As the night wore on, Carney began to question his adaptability. "I can sit here and say to you, 'Yeah, I'm adaptable.' But does it worry me? Sure. Do I still know that in February I lose my job and that I had nine years left to go and my retirement was set? Oh, heck yeah. It plays on me every day."

His friends had noticed. "He used to be energetic," Mike Smith told me as we sat in his Avon living room. "Now he doesn't want to do anything. He used to care a lot more about Maytag. Now he's like, 'Screw that, screw this.'"

Carney and "Smitty" started on the same day in 1984 in Appliance City, back when it was part of Magic Chef. They'd had a lot of fun and made a lot of friends together through the years. With his shaved head, stern face, tattoos, and long goatee, Carney looked intimidating. But he chatted, mingled, and joked like an overgrown kid, and he made friends easily. In fact, he was as frenzied about socializing as he was about motorcycles and beer-drinking. Smitty, though, was worried about what he'd seen in Carney recently. "We're losing 21 years. And it just seems he's never happy anymore. George has changed a lot, I mean a *bunch*. I'm not going to say much about his drinking habits, but they've escalated. He used to just be the funniest guy in the world, now he doesn't even want to joke anymore."

When Carney left the table to tend bar, Lynn Nelson, his girlfriend and another layoff casualty, took his chair at one of the eight wood veneer tables in the bar. She revealed that Carney had been severely depressed and quick-tempered since the announcement. "His nerves are shot. He's just worried about what the future's going to bring and how he's going to support himself and us, how he's going to take care of his kids. I can see it deteriorating his health because he worries all the time. It's just eating away at him."

Nelson looked at Carney as he poured drinks. People in the bar talked about the St. Louis Cardinals, the weather, and a recent meth bust. "He would much rather just sit around now and not do anything, and he can't spend any money," Nelson said. "And then the more he sits around, the more lethargic he gets. Depression is probably a good word for that."

Carney returned to the table seeming to know what Nelson had said. "At home she ends up taking the brunt of most of it," he admitted. "It's played pretty much havoc with our relationship. It's hard on her. It's putting me to the point where I don't care. It wasn't that way before. But, about our relationship, it doesn't matter anymore." Carney seemed to be disconnecting from not just his job, but from Nelson, his close buddies, his beloved hobbies, and from the social order generally.

Carney's malaise was not universally shared. Tracy Warner and Annette Dennison, in fact, were puzzled, and even oddly frustrated, by how committed they remained to Maytag. They never missed a day of work and never considered even putting a scratch on a newly manufactured appliance. They kept doing their best work despite the urge not to.

But as the final layoffs approached, things started becoming unhinged. Smitty, a mechanic in the warehouse, noted an increase in damaged machinery and dinged and dented refrigerators. An ill and disgruntled retiree made a bomb threat at Butler Manufacturing, the other big Galesburg factory where hundreds of jobs had recently been downsized and health and pension plans gutted. There was even a high-speed police chase after a worker brought a loaded semi-automatic pistol inside the Maytag factory to grind off its serial number.[7] The mood in town turned sour. Conventional wisdom held that spousal abuse, crime, crystal meth trafficking, and alcoholism were sure to increase. Peddling beer and liquor at the Town Tavern was starting to look like a good bet for Carney.

JOE KREJCI, A Galesburg logistics manager who reported directly to Newton, was as miserable as the line workers in the summer of 2004. Krejci and Darla, his wife, loved their home in the comfortable Fair Acres neighborhood. But Krejci saw everything falling apart around him in the two years since the announcement, and knew that he needed an escape plan. "The last few years they've tried to cut their way to prosperity. Every time you turned around, [corporate] cut somebody. It got so miserable that going to work every day was like going to a funeral." Krejci couldn't start his job search in earnest if he wanted to collect his severance; the uncertainty was eating at him and Darla. Krejci started drinking. "It's been extraordinarily stressful," Darla said.[8]

The disorienting effects of the impending closing began to reach well beyond the shop floor. An impact study out of Western Illinois University found that the direct and ripple effects of the Maytag closing would mean job losses not just for assemblers and warehouse workers but also for managers, truckers, bank tellers, hotel workers, accountants, postal carriers, teachers and school administrators, grocery clerks and stockers, dentists and doctors, automobile salesmen, waiters and waitresses, social service workers, home cleaners, hospital workers, and gas station attendants. The study estimated the total drop in area payroll at $111 million, a staggering amount of money for the mostly rural area.[9]

Krejci, a conservative Republican, featured a "W2004" sticker on the minivan in his driveway. But when he talked about Newton, he echoed Local 2063's reaction. "I liked the drivers and people here, but corporate was terrible. They've lost their way. It's really incompetent management. They're in shambles."

The longtime appliance man said it came down to a lack of leadership. It started with Lloyd Ward's "smoke and mirrors" and his obsessive focus on Maytag's stock price. But Hake, Krejci said, was even worse. "I don't think Hake has any vision at all. He's a bean counter. With Hake it's been cost control, cost control, cost control." Hake had cut product development by over half from 2002 to 2004 and had failed to produce any major innovations. Plus, the former CFO was just plain uninspiring, Krejci said. "Hake would give a presentation and it was like, 'Shoot me now!' He'd put you to sleep. You didn't want to go out and say, 'Let's do this!' So it got to the point where you didn't have the aura of 'Maytag' anymore."[10]

Maytag's organizational malaise in Newton was reflected in the Galesburg factory. Managers and line workers alike complained that they did not have the time or human resources to do their jobs properly. Foremen were under pressure to push breakneck speed without sacrificing quality. In some departments, worker–management relationships grew toxic. "It got to the point to where people were screaming at you," Shannon Cummins, a second-shift worker, said. "You were constantly being told, 'OK, look, you've gotta improve our quality!' Then they'd say, 'You're too picky, keep the line moving, you've gotta improve our quantity!' 'Improve, improve, improve! We're going to make your life hell because we need to do better!' "

Joe Krejci was relieved when his layoff finally came in June 2004. But in the transition, as he scrambled to find work to support his family, his drinking increased, and his family life began to unravel. He was unemployed for only six weeks, though, and had a comfortable severance to cushion the transition. In August Krejci headed three hours east to Joliet, Illinois, to become the manager of Toys"R"Us's private fleet, a six-figure job he learned about from a trade group connection. If you were able to move, Krejci said, there were plenty of jobs for people with his business degree, his professional connections, and his skills and experience. He went alone. His wife didn't want to leave Galesburg and was concerned about his drinking. Soon after he moved, Krejci and his wife separated, with a divorce and a bitter custody battle on the horizon. The transition had taken its toll. Still, in 2004, Krejci was more worried about those who were in the midst of much longer transitions and without many viable options. The workers inside the factory had become, he said, "Just another commodity, just another part. I'm not sure what those guys are going to do."

SQUINTING IN BRIGHT sunlight, Lt. Governor Pat Quinn took the Machinists' podium again. It was September 4, 2004, a year and a half after his dramatic interruption at the Maytag shareholders' meeting. It was Labor Day in the midst of a neck-and-neck presidential race between George W. Bush and John Kerry. Quinn stood at home plate of a baseball field, in front of a tall chain-link backstop dressed out in flags and labor banners. A few hundred people were scattered around the infield and outfield. The baseball field sat on a fat finger of land that sloped down into the murky waters of Lake Storey on the north side of Galesburg. Maytag, said Quinn, is going to "yearn for the day when the Machinists' union at Galesburg Maytag made quality products." The company was making a huge mistake, he said. "Fred Maytag, who believed in the American worker and the American consumer, would be most ashamed of the company that bears his name!"[11]

Local 2063 had continued their relentless push against Maytag. If they couldn't save their jobs, maybe their campaign—heard on CNN, in the *New York Times*, and other national media—would make corporate bigwigs think twice before consigning another unionized Rust Belt factory to physical decay and resentful ex-employees. The final shift would be gone in less than two weeks. Most of those gathered that Labor Day were connected to the two biggest industrial unions in town, the Machinists and the Steelworkers. T-shirts read, "Proud to be Union" and "100% Union." On one man's car was a sticker of a devious-looking Calvin, of the Calvin and Hobbes comic strip, urinating on the word, "Maytag."

Following Quinn, IAM president Tom Buffenbarger read a letter from a former refrigerator maker now stationed in Iraq. Buffenbarger contrasted the little guy heroically dodging bullets overseas to Maytag CEO and arch villain Ralph Hake, who ruined a proud company's heritage and betrayed his country. Buffenbarger, with sweat pooling on his bald head, waxed nostalgic about a Galesburg that had once been a place of good jobs, charitable giving, and worker dignity and pride. Then, "the religion of greed found its way to the boss' office in Newton, Iowa." It's a religion that, Buffenbarger said, "knows no borders, has no conscience or spirit, does not value humanity, cares nothing about the future, disavows its promises and obligations, and cares not about the consequences of its actions." Ralph Hake, he said, was now one of the religion's "high priests."

"We need to recognize that corporate greed and Al Qaeda have a lot in common," Buffenbarger continued. "Those may seem like extreme words. But both seek to subjugate people through fear and terror. People can be terrorized by bullets and bombs and people, yes, can be terrorized economically." The mostly white, middle-aged audience applauded enthusiastically. They were happy to see Buffenbarger was not backing down. Maytag had demanded that Buffenbarger, a prominent national labor figure, back off his call for a boycott and from referring to Maytag as "the American Taliban." After the Newton rally in 2003, Maytag executives had sent letters to Machinists leaders at the Amana, Iowa, and Herrin, Illinois, factories, pointedly asking them whether they agreed with Buffenbarger's strident comments. Mark Krivoruchka, Maytag senior vice president for human resources, wrote, "I hope you and your organizations fully understand the seriousness of this situation and the potential results of your actions."[12]

But while the International would fight on, today was the Local's last chance to say their piece.

Doug Dennison took the podium. He was wearing dark sunglasses and his wavy brown hair went down below his neck. He had a sticker with Hake's portrait circled and crossed out on the "MAKE IT IN THE U.S.A." T-shirt that hung long over his slim waist. The crowd was still fired up about Phil Hare's line, "I'd rather have FDR in a wheelchair than Ronald Reagan on a horse!" Hare filled in that day for Lane Evans, the area's longtime U.S. representative and labor champion who now had Parkinson's. Mike Patrick, in cargo shorts, and Dave Bevard, in his favorite black fedora hat, stood behind Dennison. To his left were the next two speakers: State Senator Barack Obama and U.S. Senator Dick Durbin, both with their hands grasped genially behind their back.

It was Dennison's last chance to vent his frustration before Local 2063 dissolved to nothing. Now 43, Dennison, like his union-proud father, had worked in Appliance City nearly his entire adult life. After two decades he had his "dream job" as Local 2063's vice president. By all accounts he had excelled at putting out personnel "fires" on the shop floor. Dennison had a nearly fanatical devotion to fairness that he also practiced in his other passion, coaching boys' basketball.

Dennison had completed nearly three years of college, but, unlike his wife Annette, schooling and retraining had been far from his mind since the announcement. The whole Maytag debacle had really stuck in his craw. In his view, lousy trade policies had put Local 2063 on its heels, forcing it to accept concession after concession. With the concessions came growing antipathy from the membership. People complained about paying their union dues and accused good people of being worthless leaders or in bed with management. From the other side, management said the Galesburg plant was not "competitively viable." From his perspective, they had done everything Newton asked of them to make the plant more efficient. The union even had pictures of Ralph Hake presenting them with safety awards. They had won recognition from *Consumer Reports*, and Newton bragged about their industry-best service call rates for refrigerators. And then there was the "bitter pill" from 2002: the belittling, kick-in-the-teeth, all-takeaways contract. As vice president, he felt obligated to go down fighting.

"This is a problem," Dennison said into the podium's microphones. "This is a real problem. This problem is not a Democratic problem or Republican problem. This is not a union or nonunion problem. This is not a man or woman problem. This is a real American problem. This is an epidemic that touches us all. All of us, everyone. Heck folks, we're still drying off from being tinkled on by Reaganomics. Now we've been defecated on by Bushonomics, with his tax cuts, his policies, and his war." Dennison's voice seethed with anger, making the politely-phrased scatological words oddly discordant. He was usually the quietest guy in the room. His conviction was apparent, though, and the crowd responded. Near the end of his five-minute speech, Dennison sent a message to the politicians standing next to him.

"I want to remind all of you that NAFTA and other trade policies have failed all of us. They have failed Americans miserably. We need your help. *We*

FIGURE 6.1 DOUG DENNISON SPEAKS AT LABOR DAY WEEKEND RALLY
Machinists Local 2063 Vice President Doug Dennison addresses a Labor Day weekend political rally in 2004. To the right of the lectern are Michael Patrick, State Senator Barack Obama, and U.S. Senator Dick Durbin. *CREDIT: Chad Broughton.*

FIGURE 6.2 OBAMA AT LABOR DAY WEEKEND RALLY

Obama follows Dennison at the lectern at a Galesburg political rally in his 2004 run for U.S. Senate. Obama barnstormed union halls throughout Illinois with Dave Bevard and Doug Dennison of Local 2063. Obama had mentioned Galesburg in his star-making keynote address at the Democratic National Convention earlier that summer and was greeted enthusiastically by a crowd of several hundred at the rally. To his right is International Association of Machinists (IAM) President Tom Buffenbarger. *Credit: Chad Broughton.*

are Galesburg, not Maytag, Butler, or Gates. People make this community, not the businesses. The workers of Local 2063 made this Maytag plant what it was, not the CEO, the shareholders, or the Board of Directors. Your responsibility is to serve us." Leaving the podium to enthusiastic applause, Dennison shook Obama's hand.

Obama had become a local hero when he mentioned the Galesburg Maytag workers in his keynote address at the Democratic National Convention a few weeks earlier. In sixteen mesmerizing minutes in Boston, Obama captured the nation's attention and, from that day forward, he would not let go. *New York Times* commentator David Brooks said after the speech, "This is why you go into this business: to watch a speech like that . . . this is like watching Tiger Woods play his first tournament."[13] The people at the rally in Galesburg, dispirited by two endless wars and a muddling economy, felt like they were a special part of that buoyant moment. They had been shouting their message for two years, and now someone had listened and said their story mattered, even if it was just one sentence in the big speech.

After a surprising win in the primary in March, Obama was in the middle of a successful senatorial campaign. Many admitted to coming to the rally just to see Obama, whose star now eclipsed accomplished legislator Dick Durbin. With what local unions saw as a mixed record on trade (Durbin had voted for NAFTA in 1993), Durbin received only a lukewarm welcome when his truck arrived. When Obama arrived, the crowd moved from the baseball diamond to his black Suburban like iron filings to a magnet. When he took the podium, people attended every word.

"When I first started running, not too many people gave me a chance," Obama said. "People said, 'The guy's got no money, he's got no organization, and nobody can pronounce his name.' Everybody called me 'Alabama.' They called me 'Yo Mama.'" The audience, already charmed, laughed along with the "skinny kid with a funny name," as he called himself during his Illinois barnstorming. A muscular woman raised a homemade sign. In neat, black lettering on white posterboard, it read, "KEEP THE AMERICAN DREAM ALIVE."

"Where I learned the most, it was coming to places like Galesburg, Illinois, and meeting with people like Dave, and Doug, and the Machinists." Bevard, Dennison, and a few of their union colleagues had been traveling Illinois speaking with Obama at local union halls. Being among their own made preceding the charismatic speaker a little less intimidating. "The one thing I knew for certain was that the story of Galesburg was going to be in my speech."

"And it was!" a woman yelled.

"And it was because what is happening here is emblematic of what is happening all across the country. And what I also knew was that whatever promises I made on the campaign trail, the one promise that I absolutely could make and keep was to make sure that when I woke up every morning in Washington, facing a day's work at the Capitol, that what I'd be thinking about is how do I make sure that a situation like what's happening here in Galesburg does not happen again." Obama talked about the dignity of work, the "raw deal" ordinary people were getting from Washington insiders, and how Wall Street ruled politics. He drew a sharp contrast between himself and George W. Bush and outlined trade and tax policies that would help places in Illinois like Galesburg, Alton, Carbondale, and the west side of Chicago.

"We're not going to accomplish it just by making fancy speeches. The way we're going to accomplish it is by making sure that all of us believe in the possibility that when we come together, ordinary people can do extraordinary things. That's the essence of America. Just because I'm elected all of these jobs are not going to instantly come back, not all of your problems are going to be solved. Wives and husbands might still argue once and a while. Kids might still talk back when they shouldn't talk back." The crowd appreciated the folksy levity as Obama took a breather before his finale.

"But if I have the honor of representing you I'm going to be standing alongside everyone on this stage. I'm going to be standing shoulder to shoulder next to you because I'm absolutely convinced that if we work hard, if we keep our hopes up, we keep our spirits alive, I have no doubt that John Kerry is going to be elected president, John Edwards is going to be elected vice president, Lane Evans is going to be re-elected to Congress, and all of us together can roll up our sleeves, and remake the kind of America that all of us believe in!" The crowd cheered loudly. "Thank you very much everybody! Thank you!"

Later, as the rallyers began to thin, Bevard offered signs from the protests. "It's our going-out-of-business sale," he said dryly. They were the signs from the previous year's Newton rally: "MAYTAG: MAKE IT IN THE U.S.A. OR THE U.S.A. WON'T MAKE IT." It was likely the last time many in the crowd would go to a political rally. Despite the common refrain of the day—"It starts here!"—"it" was, in reality, an ending—an ending everyone knew in their gut was coming. The pitched battle against Maytag—drawn out over nearly two years, all while the factory was churning out millions of appliances and printing thousands of paychecks—was unwinnable, and yet somehow people came to the parades and rallies. It suggested that something much bigger than Appliance City was at stake. It was an assertion of the right to exist in a world that seemed dead-set on leaving them behind.

The angry resilience on that Labor Day was tinged with an undercurrent of powerlessness. Hake made for a good enemy, but the bigger foes they named—free trade, the "religion of greed," and runaway global capitalism—were faceless, abstract, and hard to mobilize against. In just a couple of weeks, the paychecks would stop coming, and the factory's slow death would be final. The Labor Day rally offered one last moment of defiance and solidarity—and a chance to grieve together. As David Johnson said, "It allows people to know there are other people with them."[14]

Dennison exchanged another handshake and a hug with Obama and thanked him for coming. "I look at Obama as a representative," Dennison said. "I'm just hoping he doesn't become a politician. He's definitely what America needs: someone to work across the aisle and look out for the worker."

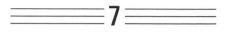

7

"SIN MAÍZ, NO HAY PAÍS"

Reynosa, Tamaulipas, and Agua Dulce, Veracruz

> Veracruz is a beautiful state. Fishing, hunting, natural beauty,
> agriculture, petroleum. We have everything except work.
>
> —Dr. Patricio Mora, Association of Veracruz Workers in Tamaulipas

AFTER THREE YEARS of living in the shadows of the United States, Laura Flora Oliveros returned to Mexico in 2004 to reunite with her daughters and her parents in Tierra Blanca, Veracruz. Erika, her youngest, had just turned five and was now strong enough, Flora hoped, to make the arduous border crossing. If everything worked as planned, Flora's entire family—four generations of them—would be together in central Florida in a couple of weeks.

On her second voyage north, Flora's intuition told her that something was not right. Flora was attuned to the news of rapes and disappearances of hundreds of female migrants and maquila workers at the border, which a United Nations mission had been investigating. Her three daughters dismissed her concerns and begged her to go through with it. Just before the dusk river crossing, and over the girls' protests, Flora abandoned the trip, forfeiting, for the second time in three years, all her savings to a coyote.

"I felt awful about not making the crossing, but I had a foreboding thought. It frustrated all of my plans. My daughters didn't sense the danger. They were happy, saying 'Let's go, Mom! Let's go!'"[1]

Right or not, her decision left Flora, her three girls, and her parents penniless, 1,300 miles from her older children in Florida, José and Deysy, and a new grandchild she had yet to hold. They each had a change of clothing and nothing else, stuck at the border with hundreds of thousands of other migrants, who came mostly from Veracruz. Reynosa had become one of the world's premier meeting places for southern labor and northern capital, the archetypical neoliberal city. And yet nobody outside of the booming city itself seemed to know about it aside from the Veracruzanos who flowed into its slums.

In the decade after the 1994 free trade agreement, rural Mexicans headed north in unprecedented numbers. Much of it was internal to Mexico. The channel from Veracruz to Tamaulipas—Reynosa being the main destination—became the busiest internal pathway in the country.[2] In previous decades Veracruzanos dispersed to other Mexican states, especially the ones around Mexico City. Those states with poor soil and migrant pathways carved out decades ago—such as in Jalisco, Guanajuato, and Michoacán—had traditionally been the launching pads for northward migration. Refugees from those states had fed pre-Depression labor needs in the 1920s, the Bracero Program during World War II and in the postwar years, and, in the 1980s and early 1990s, populated slaughterhouses in Colorado, pumpkin fields in Illinois, and restaurants in Los Angeles. Veracruz, though a poor state, was rich in agricultural wealth and had never been a big exporter of people for that reason. From 1995 to 2000, however, over 425,000 Veracruzanos left their home state, or over 6 percent of its entire population, for Tamaulipas. Another 80,000 made it to the United States.[3]

Flora found that work was plentiful in Reynosa. Through a labor agent she found work at a maquila on her first day there. After two weeks, though, Flora realized that the agent was pocketing her overtime money—the extra money that any maquila worker needs to get by. So Flora left the job and hopped on a bus to search for a new one. In Reynosa, she was beginning to realize, it was just a matter of time before one passed a "help wanted" sign in one of the industrial parks. After a half-hour ride, the bus pulled in front of the newest factory in Reynosa, Planta Maytag III, located on the southeast edge of the city. Hanging from a metal fence surrounding the factory was a big white banner calling for applications from anyone who had finished *primaria* (6th grade) and was older than eighteen. A few days later Flora was making refrigerators for "My-tyg," as locals called it. She had never heard of the company.

When Flora arrived in 2004, it was apparent that Reynosa was struggling to keep up with the migrants pouring into its outskirts. City officials were not keeping their end of the "infrastructure" deal the former mayor had made with MEDC's Mike Allen in 1988. Flora nonetheless managed to find a place to live. Other migrants built their homes wherever they could with whatever they could find. About a mile from the new Maytag factory, one enterprising small businessman capitalized on the new market for ramshackle housing. A handwritten sign behind barbed wire read, "Se Venden Tarimas." On his little plot of former ranch land, amid scattered cactuses, were small mountains— fifteen- to twenty-feet tall—of factory pallets. He sold the pallets for $1 each.

Once settled, Flora began to look back on her time in the United States with José and Deysy like it was a dream. "I think back on the cleanliness, the vegetation. I remember we once went over this beautiful bridge in Florida, with just pure sea below it. I felt like a cartoon character as we passed over it, with long hair, and really pretty." She remembered a chance encounter she had at a Piggly Wiggly—a Southern supermarket chain—where a fair-skinned, muscular man caught her eye. In a grocery aisle, she could not explain in English that her son was not her boyfriend. Embarrassed, they parted ways. It was a bittersweet memory that popped into her mind frequently. In the States, Flora had lived a lonely life, but every week she had sent back money and called her three youngest. Now, at least, she was with them.

Flora didn't second-guess her decision. Staying in Tierra Blanca, she maintained, would have been worse. Like the fading agricultural towns of the Midwestern and Plains states of America, rural Veracruz had little for even the hardiest workers. "If I were still in Tierra Blanca, I'd probably still be working in the marketplace. My mother sold chickens and my grandmother sold *atoles* (a hot, thick drink made from corn *masa*) and tamales. I would have done the same." Despite its perils, Flora thought Reynosa offered the best chance her daughters had on Mexico's side of the border. Schools in Reynosa were congested and troubled, yet more likely to teach the skills young people needed to make it in a rapidly globalizing Mexico. Plus, at the border she and her girls were mere miles from the land of milk and honey— the place with that beautiful bridge. One day, maybe, she and her girls would try again to go there.

As she started assembling stainless steel side-by-sides for gringo homes, though, Flora began to feel alone again—despite being among hundreds of thousands of her fellow Veracruzanos in the dusty border city. "I hope to find someone to drink coffee with in the future. For now, I have to watch over my girls." Like so many others from Mexico's vast hinterlands, Flora suddenly found herself in a new world at the border—a place that, as border scholars David Spener and Kathleen Staudt put it, "offers us a front-row view of history's drama unfolding."[4]

DR. PATRICIO MORA DOMINGUEZ is a native Veracruzano, though you wouldn't know it by looking at him. Of Irish descent, the bespectacled doctor barely stretches to five feet. His hair is a rusty orange, and his skin easily burns. After working as a doctor in Las Vegas for thirteen years, Mora founded the Association of Veracruz Workers in Tamaulipas, which provides information, medical and legal assistance, and other services to Veracruzanos in Reynosa. The energetic, Jesus-inspired man is utterly devoted to his fellow Veracruzanos, especially the destitute and ill-informed just up from the south. Mora's most cherished free service is returning the terminally ill or deceased to their families so they can die or be laid to rest in their homeland.

"If you ask politicians about the migration to the border, they'll say that it's fine, that they have job opportunities," Mora told us. "But the country was not ready for free trade. The *ejido* breakup, with the social land converted to private property, it's killing the country (*matar el país*). Now we're *all* capitalists . . . but without credit." A poster celebrating Papantla and the pyramids in El Tajin, written in the indigenous language of the Totonacs of northern Veracruz, hung on the association's lime-green interior walls next to Mora's framed diplomas and certificates and a rather stunning, lifelike sketch of Jesus. "Why are we so dependent on the United States?" Mora asked. "Because we don't invest in the Mexican countryside."

Mora's teenage assistant sat behind a typewriter and a The Incredibles cup at the front desk of the migrant agency's headquarters. Two older men, sitting on either side of an old mini-refrigerator, listened as Mora spoke over rattling box fans. "For us Veracruzanos," Mora said, "it's very difficult to leave the land behind, because of friends, families, property, food, customs, climate, leaving a natural environment. When we migrate to the North, in pursuit of the famous American Dream, many people die and they find eternal rest. And when they don't achieve the American Dream, they end up stuck in the Tamaulipan Dream."

In order to understand Reynosa, Dr. Mora said, one has to go to Veracruz.

LEANING AGAINST THE Agencia Municipal building was an old bicycle with a holstered machete strapped to its frame. A field laborer had come to see Dr. Javier Gonzalez Rocha, Agua Dulce's mayor. The sky-blue building, situated just off the town's vacant main plaza, housed a mayor's office, a library, and two jail cells—without either doors or inmates. A faded printout of a missing police officer was attached to one of the gated windows, something to do with the ubiquitous border drug violence. The manic intensity of the north felt far away in the slow-moving and tranquil town of rocky roads and scattered homes. The little town sits in the tropical Papantla region of Veracruz, the narrow state that stretches for over 400 miles along the Gulf of Mexico from Tamaulipas to the southernmost state of Chiapas.[5]

Gonzalez's office was already like a sauna. A handsome man in his fifties with a thick mustache and reading glasses hanging from his shirt, he sat behind an enormous and ancient Olympia typewriter. He was in the last year of a three-year term as the town's mayor when we met him in July 2007, but was probably best known locally as a doctor, and as the man who had delivered many of Agua Dulce's younger residents. The population of Agua Dulce, he contended, was 10,000 to 12,000; the government figure, 5,910, was an undercount, a government ruse to loosen the federal obligation to the struggling area.[6] Part of the problem was that half of Agua Dulce was not living in Agua Dulce. Breadwinning fathers, ambitious recent high school graduates, and entire families from Agua Dulce went to Poza Rica to catch the ADO bus heading north toward Reynosa. When they stepped off twelve hours later, they were in an arid, bustling city ready to assemble DeWalt power tools for Black & Decker or radio assemblies for General Motors. A few would undoubtedly work alongside Laura Flora and other Veracruzanos in Planta Maytag III. By 2005, two out of every three Mexicans lived in an area that was depopulating. Among thirty-one states, Veracruz, the state with by far the largest rural population in Mexico, had been hit hardest.[7]

José Luis Cruz Fernandez, the small town's treasurer, tried to explain what was happening. "It hasn't improved here. On the contrary, people's standard of living has declined for both the landowner and the worker."

"The cost of life is up here," Gonzalez said. "And the prices of the agricultural products are down." To illustrate his point, the mayor slowly moved one hand up and the other down.

"And the consequence is that people have begun migrating to other places," Cruz added. "The producer cannot provide a good wage if he doesn't see a good price for his product. So the first to go is the worker." Like Gonzalez, Cruz was a lifelong Agua Dulce resident. With the federal government's rapid withdrawal from rural sector support, he said, seeds, chemicals, gasoline, and other agricultural inputs had increased in price. In addition, remittance income from the United States had induced local inflation, making it more difficult for the majority of impoverished, peso-only families to keep up. At the same time, returning migrants fueled consumptive desires with conspicuous spending and material tokens from the north. These were common problems of economic development and globalization. What had so puzzled locals was how little economic globalization had moved Agua Dulce forward.

The reason behind the mystery, Gonzalez and Cruz said, centered on corn. Mexico, a reluctant partner for decades after its 1910s revolution, began to share a common agricultural market with the United States and Canada in the NAFTA era. Since January 1994, cheap corn from America's heartland had been streaming across the border, essentially unchecked by tariffs and quotas. The agreement had outlined a gradual phase-out of protections in order to avoid a shock to Mexico's rural sector, but Mexico's government, hell-bent on liberalization and pressured by U.S. agribusiness, refused to enforce the protections, foregoing billions in revenues. Instead the shock came hard and fast for unwitting *campesinos* (peasants or farmers). The sudden glut of corn decimated producer prices in Mexico, a kind of free trade–induced austerity that punished millions of Mexico's most vulnerable rural families.[8] Liberalizers reasoned it was necessary medicine for campesinos, who were hopelessly backward and inefficient. The "comparative advantage," as economists term it, lay to the north in the United States, with the industrialized row-crop farms of the biggest corn-producing country on the planet. Lower corn prices would result in cheaper tortillas and other benefits for Mexico, the proponents said.

By 2005 producer prices for corn were down a startling 66 percent, cutting deeply into farmers' incomes while, over the same period, their costs had increased because of the withdrawal of Mexican government support. It was a double hit that amounted to development in reverse for rural Veracruzanos. Before NAFTA, a Mexican corn farmer could buy a liter of gasoline with one kilo of corn. In 2003 it took five kilos. Put in other numbers, in 1980 one ton of corn would purchase about six baskets of basic goods. By 2000, one ton of corn would purchase only about two-and-a-half baskets. As one Mexican farmer said, "There was a time when the federal government, the state government, the agriculture department gave us support with credit, fertilizer, herbicide, and at a very affordable price. Today, well, everything has to come out of our own pockets, out of our hard work."[9]

To make matters worse for rural Mexico, the 1996 U.S. Farm Bill had expanded support for U.S. agribusiness, a power play with a tangible impact on campesinos. From 1997 to 2005, Mexican corn farmers lost $99 per hectare (about two-and-a-half acres) per year as a direct result of the depressing effect that U.S. subsidies had on corn prices in Mexico.[10] To small farmers, typically working a few hectares of rain-fed, hilly land with little access to technology or markets, it was an enormous hit.[11] With the Mexican and U.S. governments against them, and prices plunging, many campesinos and other rural folk headed north.[12]

Others tried to figure out ways to stay. Like the transitioning workers in Galesburg, the first impulse was often to adapt in place. On a drive around Agua Dulce, our guide, a local PAN (Partido Acción Nacional) administrator, Orlinda Garcia Martinez, pointed out denuded hills where farmers had cut down trees to cultivate more land. Others squeezed out higher yields. Still others searched out local wage labor options. Some continued to grow corn and other crops but withdrew from the marketplace in the face of the artificially low prices—a "retreat to subsistence."[13] Oddly, corn output across Mexico increased, especially in Veracruz, in the face of these new realities.[14] This unanticipated response forced economists and technocrats in Mexico City to rethink the basic maxim that lower prices decrease production and to entertain notions such as "non market values" and "shadow prices" to explain what they considered to be economically irrational behavior.[15]

Sticking with corn was hardly irrational in a country where over 18 million directly depended on corn farming for their survival.[16] Smaller growers were reluctant to emigrate or to switch all or most of their production to horticultural crops such as oranges or limes or mangoes, which came with no guarantee of success and could not feed a family. For the Mexican people, these were existential questions. The ancient staple had been a foundation of life for Mesoamerican cultures for thousands of years, intricately interwoven into economy, society, and culture, and having ritual, religious, and healing functions within indigenous communities. Corn farming offered an honorable way to provide for a family and achieve status in rural communities. Traditional seed lines had been cultivated over generations for ease of shelling and processing, color and taste, softness of tortilla dough, and suitability for local dishes and climates. In Oaxaca alone, there are 85,000 unique subvarieties of *criollo* (traditional) corn.[17] "Sin Maíz, No Hay País" (without corn, there is no country).

VIEWED FROM A hilltop, the ejido plots surrounding Agua Dulce make up a patchwork quilt of spectacular shades of green. Here amid the undulating semitropics of northern Veracruz, the land produces corn—and much more—year round, and life revolves around agricultural seasons.

Standing in the bed of Mayor Gonzalez's Dodge pickup, we passed through some of the 250 plots of the area's collectively owned ejido. On a couple of desolate gravel roads, we passed four hectares (about the size of five soccer fields) of orange trees, four of corn, and then four of limes baking in the all-pervasive Veracruz midday sun. In Zona Totonaca, farmers grow corn, citrus, tropical fruits, vanilla, coffee, sugarcane, *chayote* (a squash), sesame, beans and wild lentils, pimientos and chiles, and tomatoes. Locals, including indigenous Totonacos, also foraged the lush landscape for wild potatoes and *quelites* (wild greens).[18]

As we got out of the truck and began to walk Gonzalez's eight hectares, it was easy to see why Veracruzanos in Reynosa waxed nostalgic about the fat, sweet fruits that literally fell from the trees here. Gonzalez had recently become an *ejidatario*, a voting and land-holding member of the area's ejido, having earned the status from his father. He farmed chemical-free, aside from an occasional herbicidal spraying at the base of some trees. The area's land, however, had been cultivated intensively, and few armadillos, iguanas, and snakes remained. "Humans seem to create ecological disasters wherever they go," Gonzalez said. The ubiquitous, loud birds, however, seemed happy as they squawked in the food-filled trees.

Stopping under a banana tree, we met Gonzalez's fieldworker, an older man with a machete who was eating fruit and in no particular hurry. "At the very least, you won't die of hunger here," Gonzalez said. "He doesn't bring a lunch. We just walk down the rows of bananas, papayas, mangoes, and avocados, grabbing fruit to eat."

The colorful bounty was everywhere in Zona Totonaca. People loaded down with fruits and vegetables packed the buses that moved in and out of traffic-snarled Papantla, the municipal seat just ten miles north of Agua Dulce. Each day in the hilly city of 150,000, a small army of women hawked corn, chiles, tomatoes, and oranges at well-trodden spots. Between Poza Rica and Papantla, roadside fruit stands overflowed with ejido-grown banana bunches and glass containers of vanilla and honey. At one stand, a 44-year-old ejidatario in a sleeveless white undershirt and belted dress shorts had hundreds of mangoes for sale in neat stacks of hard plastic crates. It was hard to imagine how such a fertile region, with such hard-working people and vigorous local trade, could be so poor. "Here in Agua Dulce, we have too much space and overproduction," Mayor Gonzalez said. Agua Dulce needed decent prices and access to buyers.

El Tratado de Libre Comercio de América del Norte (or TLC, a common shorthand for NAFTA in Mexico) was supposed to open new markets for Mexican farmers. Mexico had a comparative advantage in the labor- and land-intensive cultivation of horticultural crops. The World Bank, the United States Department of Agriculture (USDA), and the other pied pipers of liberalization counseled Mexican smallholders to transition out of corn to higher-value crops (or out of agriculture entirely). The phase-out of tariffs against Mexican (and Canadian) fruits and vegetables sold in the United States would open lucrative markets to the north and assist export-oriented farming in places like Zona Totonaca.[19]

Gonzalez had already diversified into fruits and vegetables on his eight hectares.[20] Back in the 1960s, his father planted corn on his entire *ejidal* parcel and rented another forty hectares to grow more corn. "Corn filled the truck and it filled the house where we lived. It was overflowing. We filled up the storehouse and our living areas. There was only a tiny area where we slept." The Gonzalez family switched some of their land from corn to oranges in the 1980s, when Florida experienced several freezes and orange prices went up. At the outset of NAFTA, sunshine-soaked Veracruz was far and away the biggest citrus-producing state in Mexico, with half of the country's orange and three-quarters of the country's grapefruit production.[21] With 300 million potential citrus consumers north of the border, Agua Dulce seemed like just the kind of place where economic integration—and the transition from corn—could work.

ORANGE FARMERS FOCUS on costs, yield, and price. A typical *Veracruzano* orange farmer might harvest twelve metric tons (a metric ton = 1,000 kilograms) of oranges per hectare across eight hectares. At 0.75 pesos per kilo, that farmer would earn 72,000 pesos from the 96 metric tons. Fertilizers, herbicides, farm hands, and other inputs cost about 50,000 pesos. In this case 22,000 pesos, roughly $2,000 in the mid-2000s, is left over for the *ejidatario*'s living expenses, savings, or improvements to the land. The most resourceful orange farmers, Gonzalez said, might produce 200 metric tons and earn about $10,000 after expenses.[22]

Orange prices stagnated after NAFTA.[23] Some nasty annual price dips knocked many Veracruzano farmers out of orange production entirely. Several reports from the Foreign Agricultural Service of the USDA noted widespread abandonment of orange groves in Veracruz.[24] The low producer prices hurt ejidatario and landless fieldworkers alike. Field hands in Zona Totonaca see a burst of work at orange harvest time. Like other jobs in Agua Dulce, a harvest worker earned about 70 to 90 pesos, $6.25 to $8, a day, only a little less than what a worker in a border maquiladora earned.[25] If prices were good at harvest time, piece-rate workers filling 20- or 30-kilogram boxes could earn much more, said Treasurer Cruz.[26] But with depressed prices, small-scale farmers sometime didn't even bother to harvest their crop because they wouldn't earn back their labor costs. When this happened, fieldworkers were the first to emigrate. Some ejidatarios might give up, rent their land, and head north as well.

Orange farmers who stayed in the Agua Dulce ejido continued to grow cheap oranges for other Mexicans in the NAFTA era. Orange exports to the United States in the mid-2000s remained less than one percent of the total produced. Unlike the transformative changes NAFTA instigated for corn and other staple crops, it was a "non event" for oranges and most other fresh produce. In fact, almost all of the variation in export levels since NAFTA could be explained by the peso–dollar exchange rate.[27]

Mexican orange production was in part stymied by powerful Florida citrus growers. Florida growers kept their costs low, somewhat ironically, by recruiting undocumented migrant laborers, including Laura Flora in the early 2000s, to work their orchards. The $1.6 billion industry in Florida used its influence to get special protections in the so-called free trade deal.[28] The new game was rigged against the little guys in northern Veracruz like Gonzalez. There were plenty of oranges being produced across North America; the question was who got what market.

Florida growers could ship their orange juice around the world, whereas isolated and scattered Veracruz farmers had to rely on intermediaries. Even if lucrative export markets did develop for ejidatarios in Agua Dulce, there were simply too many barriers to switching out of corn. Many ejidatarios had only two, three, or four hectares. Many had little money to invest in ejidal improvements, and state financing had been eliminated. A hectare of citrus trees, for instance, requires a 50,000 peso ($4,500) investment. Further, lime trees need five to six years to bear fruit, much too long for a campesino to forego income.[29] The same was generally true across Mexico no matter the fruit or vegetable. Campesinos stuck it out with corn, migrated, or creatively combined the two instead of making the switch, again baffling the technocrats. "We understood that the transition from corn to strawberries would not be smooth," agricultural economist Philip Martin said. "But we did not think there would be almost no transition."[30]

Campesinos reported many reasons for not switching to "higher value crops": lack of financing (62 percent), tradition or custom (55 percent), easier to market current crops (43 percent), soil not suitable for other crops (39 percent), didn't find any alternatives (35 percent), better income from current crop (34 percent), didn't know how to produce other crops (28 percent), didn't have the infrastructure (27 percent).[31] To uphold traditions in the global era, Mexican farmers needed credit, an improved transportation and communication infrastructure, and assistance with machinery and technology.[32] Without their government's support, Agua Dulce's ejidatarios dug in as the world left them behind. As J. Bradford DeLong, a Treasury official in the Clinton administration said, "We underestimated Mexico's deficits in physical and human infrastructure."[33]

The truth was that economists in Mexico City knew campesinos and rural economics stood only to lose in North America's new common marketplace. Efficient medium- and large-scale farmers had a shot, maybe, but not the impoverished small farmer. Everardo Elizondo, a leading Mexican economist of the NAFTA era and a former deputy governor of the Bank of Mexico spoke about the government's shift away from agricultural support in a 2013 interview. "Why subsidize campesinos to produce something with no economic value? To keep them poor? It makes no sense! One might think he is in Veracruz where he only need extend his hand and pick up a mango. That's nonsense. That's foolish shit!" He grinned pleasantly to make sure we were disabused of any romantic notions of rural life in Mexico. It had always been hard, before NAFTA, after NAFTA. Elizondo supports safety-net policies to help campesinos transition out of agriculture—not unlike the transitional assistance workers received in Galesburg.

The fact that Mexico still has much of its workforce in agriculture is a sign of underdevelopment, he continued. The border cities, and all those striving migrants, represent progress, development, and Mexico's future. "The real thing is that they live better in Reynosa. They live better in Ciudad Juárez. They live better in Tijuana."[34]

Ejidatarios like Gonzalez, however, felt their government had abandoned them. The ejido had become "more like a savings account" than a place to earn a living, Mayor Gonzalez said amongst the dark green of his fruit trees, some of which went unharvested when prices were low. "You hope to make back what you put in." Many of the wage-earning fieldworkers had traveled on, but the ejidatarios had land. He had seen other farmers rent their land and emigrate, but few sold the ejidal land that was, for many, their last shred of security in a difficult time. "The old people from around here say, 'I'll never sell my land because the land never runs out, but money does.'"

BACK IN TOWN, and again in the bed of Mayor Gonzalez's pickup, we saw the well-tended, colorful homes of Agua Dulce. Interspersed amongst the modest dwellings were a couple of five-table, hole-in-the-wall restaurants and a few *mini supers* (convenience stores) selling eggs, *refrescos* (soft drinks), and toiletries. Modest, neatly landscaped homes, painted in vibrant shades of pink, orange, blue, and green, faced the road. Roaming roosters and hens, hanging laundry, and smoldering piles of trash were in the yards. The nicest homes belonged to absentee migrants and those who had several hectares in the ejido that surrounded the little town. A few homes had a car or truck parked nearby featuring border state plates from Tamaulipas and Texas. There were also modest shacks near the plastic bottle-littered *fútbol* and baseball fields. Most of the shacks belonged to *vecinos* (neighbors)—the landless wage workers from the state of Puebla, as they were called in town—with only loose ties to the area. It was hard to tell to which homes the chickens and dogs, sauntering through midday heat, belonged.

Gonzalez braked in front of a roofless, unfinished home hidden among chin-high weeds. After a family had bought this plot and started building the cinder block home, the husband left to work in the United States. Later the parents divorced; two of their daughters went to Reynosa, and one went to Mexico City. The family was shattered, and there was a fight over the little plot of land. Ruling on property disputes like this was his main duty as mayor. "I see cases like that almost on a daily basis," he said, looking at the half-built building.

A comparatively large, dark-green ranch-style house sat a few lots down on the same street. The house appeared well built, but was as empty as the weed-filled home. It stood behind a tall metal gate, far from the road and at the end of a concrete driveway. This was a "remittance palace," Gonzalez said, one of those built by a successful migrant worker.

"This way of building a house comes from the United States. Here the traditional style is with the house—the windows and the doors, everything—against the street. Here, though, is a house with a gate and a fence and yard in front of the home. They are just little outposts. They are well made, but they don't have life to them. They're white elephants." Gonzalez and Cruz were both skeptical of the idea that remittances had helped their rural town. Most of the money sent back from the United States and the border cities went to private homes, not to improve the local standard of living, pave the streets, or to create jobs.

As Veracruzanos streamed north, remittances to Veracruz alone had grown to $1.4 billion by the mid-2000s. Remittances had become a lynchpin of Mexico's development strategy. At well over $20 billion each year since 2003, it was a top source of foreign exchange for Mexico, alongside oil exports and the maquiladoras.[35] In 2001 the federal government created the *Tres Por Uno* program that matched migrants' remittances sent to hometown associations (HTAs) with municipal, state, and federal funds in order to fund, for instance, church repairs or the building of a local health clinic. By so doing, the government had actively promoted out-migration under Vicente Fox and Felipe Calderón in the 2000s.[36]

Mayor Gonzalez was a traditionalist, though. Like the loyalists of the small towns of western Illinois, he planned to stick it out in Agua Dulce, for better or for worse. He desperately wanted paved roads, decent employment options, and maybe even a maquiladora. Agua Dulce's older residents were deeply troubled by the loss of the labor, vitality, and brainpower of their young people. The absence of youth was conspicuous. It seemed as if the entire town was on vacation. Gonzalez himself sent his children to school in Papantla to avoid the televised teaching of *telesecundaria* and *teleprepa*.

Just as troubling was emigration's social impact on the town. The population of Agua Dulce, now older and more female, was more vulnerable. Gonzalez perceived a decline in civility, one that he pinned on younger migrants. They drop out of school early for their adventure up north and become detached from life back home. They return with a degraded sense of civic responsibility.

"Young people have lost their manners. They don't take off their hats when walking into a house. They don't greet people. Some don't give up their seat for an old lady or a mother with a child riding a bus. Here people don't do that anymore. They bring these customs and manners back from the other side." Orlinda Garcia, our guide earlier that day in Agua Dulce, made a similar point. She said that the single most troubling social problem—ahead of poverty, high unemployment, alcoholism, and domestic violence—was the abandonment of the elderly by their working-age children.

Values about what constituted a "good life" had changed. "The kids just want more and more," Mayor Gonzalez said. "And since their parents cannot give it to them they quit *prepa* (high school). You ask them, 'Aren't you going to study?' And they say, 'No, no, I'm going to the other side.'" That kind of thinking prevailed across the country. By 2002 one of every seven people born in Mexican villages lived in the United States. Most had come after NAFTA.[37]

María Ester Cruz Alvarado decided to stay, for now. When we met her in 2007, she was twenty-three years old and sitting in Agua Dulce's small public library working on a lesson plan for a summer program for local kids. Five years earlier, after graduation, two of her friends had left for Reynosa. One of them kept inviting her up. "She told me that whenever I want to go, I could go. People tell me that it's a little bit ugly there, a little bit dangerous, but I don't know. I don't think that I'd like to go." Cruz was still supported by her family. Her fathers and brothers worked two hectares of banana and two of lime, which earned a modest, but steady income. "That's it," she said. "That's what has provided for us."

Unlike the *vecinos*, families with ejido land like Cruz's were much less likely to leave. For poorer ejidatarios in Agua Dulce, the land provided shots of liquidity at harvest time, a critical part of an eclectic survival strategy.[38] An ejidatario might work another farmer's orange harvest for a few weeks for a daily wage, sort corn husks for tamales with his or her family at a piece rate, and work on a northern farm, at a tourist area, or in the United States for a month, season, or year. Enterprising householders might also use earnings from migrations to buy more land or invest in the productivity of their existing plots. Economists continued to complain about the inefficiency of the ejido. The social property was a drag on the economy. But to a farmer, the ejido plot was often their only asset, a hedge against displacement from their home, especially for the elderly and indigenous. It was everything: a place to grow corn and feed one's family, an insurance policy, a mark of social standing and familial lineage, a source of certainty and stability in a rapidly changing world, and a connection to place.

Young women from farming families such as María Cruz faced a dilemma. Cruz's options were limited in Agua Dulce. Her brothers worked the farm whereas, as a woman, she could only find intermittent work. Her family was landed but poor. She could only afford one university class, which she took on Saturdays in a nearby city.

Her main option was *El Norte*, but this was scary to Cruz. One of her brothers had been detained in the United States for a couple of months, and she wasn't sure if he would make it back. There were stories of lost souls, drug abuse, and criminality that spread like fear through the little town. Mayor Gonzalez said criminals in Veracruz sometimes escaped to the border to hide there until the statute of limitations on their crime expired. At least locals in Agua Dulce could still look out for one another. They were connected to the place through their families, their land, their traditions. That's why Cruz and a lot of people like her stayed, difficult as it was. There was still their corn.

8

"THE END IS HERE"

Galesburg, Illinois

ON THE LAST day there would be a potluck and a drawing for some free appliances and $100 in cash. It was clear, though, that those still around in September 2004 could hardly wait for this drawn-out shuttering finally to be over. Crews were taking down the lighting, removing tables and cabinets, and gathering screws and air gun bits to toss in the garbage. "I don't know if they are going to start with fresh tools down there in Reynosa or what the deal is," Tracy Warner said. The crews also asked workers to remove photographs and newspaper clippings from their workstations. "They are dismantling it all around us, like they can't wait for us to get out of there." The lawn outside, usually covered in pop cans, plastic wrappers, and cigarette butts, was cleaned up and sprayed green by Chem Lawn. Management was trying to sell the old place.

Warner's imminent layoff was part of a sea-change in Illinois in the first years of the new millennium. The pace of the hollowing out of manufacturing in the fourth-largest manufacturing state in the country had been unprecedented. From June 2000 to November 2003, Illinois lost more than 100 manufacturing jobs a day, or one out of every six. Gone were over 150,000 jobs in a state of 12,500,000. In Rockford, the machine-tool industry wilted, and unemployment spiked at over 11 percent. In Harvard, located near the Wisconsin border, Motorola closed its cellphone plant. Developers wanted to turn the site into the world's largest indoor water park. In Peoria, Decatur, and Kankakee, laid-off workers applied for jobs at Walmarts and Home Depots that would pay them maybe half their former wage.

In suburban Chicago, Winzeler Gear went from making 2 million gears a month with fifty-five workers to making 16 million a month with thirty-five employees. A robot the size of a minivan increased the factory's output while also eliminating human labor. Even with the productivity boost, the owner doubted the company would be able to stay competitive. Chicago remained at the top of the United States in manufacturing output, but the jobs were disappearing. People in all corners of the state crammed unemployment offices. The 2000s would be the first recorded decade of zero net job creation. No decade since the 1940s had seen job growth of less than 20 percent.[1]

For Warner, who had been buoyed by the sunny Labor Day rally, the gloomy conditions steeled her determination to reinvent herself as a professional. The single mother had just earned her associate's degree while working full-time and raising her son, Ryan. Just before her September layoff, Warner applied to *The Register-Mail*. She sent in what she would later realize was a sloppy cover letter. She didn't even know to send a resume. She had worked at one place since 1989, a place where she performed such functions as shaving plastic lips off water dispensers so that they would seal snugly on a refrigerator door and never leak. It wasn't relevant experience and may even work to her disadvantage. She was 39, had never learned to write a resume, and was computer illiterate. The newspaper never called.

Warner knew that there were no shortcuts. She needed more schooling to have a chance. But for someone who disliked risks, getting a degree in journalism was a radical idea. Being a single mother in debt made the gamble seem all the more perilous. But on the assembly line, Warner had felt like a robot; she daydreamed about finishing college and becoming a local reporter. If she didn't take the leap now, when would she? Plus, her previous dabbling in newspaper writing had been promising.

Galesburg Works, the Workforce Investment Office in town, had other ideas for her. The office administered retraining monies under the Trade Adjustment Assistance (TAA) program and had to approve displaced workers' degree plans. Her counselor told Warner that they could not approve funding for a journalism degree. The degree, they said, would not train her for a "high growth field." This irked her, though she knew it was probably true.

THE LAST TOP-MOUNT refrigerator went down the assembly line on September 14, 2004. Workers grabbed what they had salvaged from their worksite and the factory's auction, and went home. At 9:30 a.m. on September 16, the last side-by-side refrigerator arrived at the end of the line. Like the last top-mount, it was perfectly functional but would never be used. It was a memento, auto-graphed by all of the workers on that last shift with a thick black Sharpie. Those two refrigerators would join a third Appliance City souvenir—the last wide-by-side (the Galesburg-designed "Z door," in which the upper por-tion has a wide refrigerator and a narrow freezer), which had been sitting in the Labor Temple since that line shut down in September 2003. Covering every square inch of the refrigerators were names and notes: "Stacey Steele," "Kay Emerick," "Bless the hands that touch this," "¡Adiós!" "Dorothy Meyer," "Travis Stoneking," "Sandy Rath, U.S.A." "Renée Hamilton," "Tonia Waugh 9-24-03," and "I will miss Maytag, Joe B."

That was it. A Coca-Cola truck arrived and reclaimed some vending machines from the break room. Three women went out front to take pictures in front of the big Maytag sign. In the pictures the women can be seen mak-ing hand gestures at the big blue letters and smiling. It had taken decades of hard work and slow progress to make the jobs at Appliance City decent and even desirable. The improvements came on the shop floor by means of the small but incremental innovations of workers and the adjustments of local engineers. They had come by means of contract negotiations and grievance hearings. But there was no getting around the fact that the work remained arduous. People left that September day, as they had earlier days, with swollen feet, aching backs, and battered hands.

They would not miss the work as much as they would miss the place and the people. For Tracy Warner, the factory was her social life. "These are peo-ple that you share birthdays with. They can hardly wait to see pictures from big events, like the birth of a child. We have baby showers at work. We have cake and coffee together. I don't know, that is like your second family." There were bonfires and wiener roasts, Christmas parties and gift exchanges, and bake sales and charity auctions for workers who had hit a rough patch. It was "a world within a world," said Deb Pendergast. "There were things that stayed there [that] we never took home."[2]

Perhaps most of all, Maytag workers said they would miss the profound sense of security a factory job once offered. They knew they were headed into an increasingly inhospitable world for those without college degrees. Michael Laun, a worker with fifteen years, like Warner, said that day, "You don't want to be afraid, but you are." Two women politely waved off a reporter as they left the factory for the last time. "Sorry, we've got to get on with the rest of our lives."[3]

That night Dave Bevard, Doug Dennison, and a few others literally turned off the lights at the place once known as Appliance City. In 1905, a century earlier, 19-year-old Roy Ingersoll and his father had built a modest two-story brick building where a darkened, sprawling jumble of buildings now stood, and forty or fifty men had banged out earth-cutting steel plow blades for the Galesburg Coulter Disc Company. In 1936 Midwest Manufacturing made its first refrigerator cabinets on the small industrial site, which had been abandoned in the Great Depression.[4] The signed refrigerators marked the end of sixty-eight years of nearly continuous appliance-making in that spot on the southwestern edge of Galesburg.[5] The factory, which just a few years before had still been a vibrant, miniature city of 2,500, was emptied and put up for sale. People did not expect a suitor to come along.

Now unemployed, Warner continued to plead her case for a journalism bachelor's degree. Her counselor relented and told her to write an essay about the types of jobs for which the degree would prepare her and why she was a good candidate. Her application went to an administrative office in Springfield and eventually came back with an approval. TAA would fund her two years at Western Illinois. She was thrilled. She would start in January 2005. If it all went without a hitch, she would graduate with a bachelor's degree in December 2006, on the very same day that she would receive her last unemployment check.

Like Warner, Annette Dennison had been jumping through hoops for her education. While her husband Doug fought Maytag to the bitter end, Annette drifted away from the rallies, the union activism, and her friends at the factory. She locked herself in her bedroom to study for "Biomedical Ethics," "Family and Marriage," and other classes she had been taking when she wasn't driving a forklift. She spent less time with her two boys. She had been an obsessive, even pestering student since she started two years earlier. "It was hard to go back to school, really hard. But I didn't accept anything less than an 'A' from my professors. I guess I surprised myself."

Dennison had signed the last refrigerator. The next month she applied for one of the eighteen slots for the next radiology cohort. She knew that other laid-off workers would stampede into the retraining programs at Sandburg, but she was optimistic. Where there were once F's on her transcript, she had earned straight A's in science, math, and social studies—the prerequisites for the competitive program.

Unlike journalism, the radiology program qualified as training in a "growth field." Getting accepted would be a big win for the Dennisons, because it would qualify Annette for a second year of unemployment compensation under TAA. Plus, TAA covered all educational expenses—from the miles traveled to school right down to pens and pencils. Doug and Annette worried that they would not be able to keep the home they had bought a few years earlier. They needed a new plan to fund Dylan's and Dalton's college savings, as well as their own retirement. They stopped taking vacations and looked for ways to trim spending. Doug beat himself up for spending too much while he worked at Maytag, and for not being ready for this predicament. A small fraction of the displaced workers would land jobs that paid a wage comparable to the $15.14 average at Maytag—and usually only after considerable retraining and some luck. And those that did would likely have to commute to Peoria or the Quad Cities, both about fifty miles from Galesburg. In February 2005 Annette would learn whether she had gotten into the intensive two-year, X-ray technician program—and whether the hard work and sacrifice had been worth it.

WHEN TRACY WARNER started at Western Illinois in January 2005, she was utterly disoriented. As a "nontraditional student" she stood out somewhat awkwardly, or at least that was how it felt to her. Warner was twice the age of her classmates, and she commuted instead of living in the dorms. The students all seemed young, energetic, and carefree. And the teachers were more demanding than at Sandburg. Some were intimidating because they were "more worldly," as Warner put it. One professor flew jet fighters. Warner expected it would be tough, but WIU quickly cast a harsh light on her academic weaknesses. In her classes—"Persuasive Campaigns," "Beat Reporting," and "Research and Design"—her teachers ripped into her writing. "They tore it to shreds," she admitted. "It was scary. And I'm an older student; I don't take criticism very well." Warner began to question her decision to pursue journalism. She felt like an imposter. Maybe the employment office would fund a trade certification if she dropped out right away.

One afternoon in 1967, when Warner was 18 months old, her mother dropped her off at her grandparents' home in Aledo, a little town twenty-five miles north of Monmouth, and then committed herself to a community mental health facility for a month or two before disappearing to Greece. Warner's father's parents raised her until she started kindergarten. Her grandfather, a retired road commissioner, worked as a custodian at Aledo High School to help pay for Warner's upbringing, while her grandmother took on a second tour of mothering.

When Warner was a senior at Monmouth High School, she heard that her mother was staying in the LeMoine Hotel in Macomb. She wrote a note that the front desk attendant took to her mom's room. Warner's mom came to the lobby and without further ado proceeded to blame Warner's father for everything. With her mother was Warner's four-year-old half-brother, whom Warner had never met. Her mother was in town trying to get her son, who carried a Greek name, U.S. citizenship. Warner had plenty of step- and half-siblings from her father's three marriages, and she may have had a biological brother or sister. Her mother had apparently put a baby up for adoption a year or so before she had Warner.

When Todd, Ryan's father, who had been adopted himself, insisted she put their son up for adoption in 2001, she had been furious. After surviving thyroid cancer in 2000, Warner, a divorcee who thought she would remain single the rest of her life, had met Todd and fallen in love. The relationship foundered, but it had produced Ryan, her miracle. She was 36, cancer-free, and had a baby boy. A year later, the closing announcement came when Ryan was one, throwing her life into disarray again. "I don't have anything real, except for my son," Warner said.

Now, in 2005, laid off and struggling through college, Warner felt an acute financial pinch. Her unemployment income was $794 every two weeks, and it was a lifesaver. All her tuition, books, and mileage were paid for by TAA—the mileage, in particular, added up. She had also secured a court order to get $82 every two weeks from Todd, who worked as a security guard. But some expenses had increased, TAA did not fully cover Ryan's preschool, and she still had debts to pay. She could not afford the $312 a month to maintain her Maytag health insurance through COBRA. She'd have to go without coverage indefinitely.

Before Ryan came along and with fat Maytag paychecks, Warner "never hurt for money." She ordered out on Fridays with her co-workers, went to bars when she felt like it, and spent as many weekends as she could going to concerts. She would camp out for tickets for her and her friends and spend $35 on T-shirts. She saw Eric Clapton, Metallica, Ted Nugent, Kiss, Jimmy Page and Robert Plant, the Rolling Stones, Pink Floyd, and others. Looking back, it was an indulgent time. She probably drank more than she should have and weighed more than she liked. Now, however, she "knew the value of a dollar" and was constantly asking herself whether enrolling in WIU's journalism program had been the right career move and financial strategy for her and her son.

By mid-semester, however, she had realized that there was no going back. This *was* her transition, for better or for worse. There would not be another chance. Eventually, with some support from kindly professors and some younger women working at the school newspaper, Warner began to feel like she belonged at Western. She arrived to class early every day, dressed professionally, and wore makeup. She became consumed with her coursework and her grades.

"I worked harder than anyone else because I was scared to death," Warner said.

BY FEBRUARY 2005, the factory had been silent for five months, and all that remained inside the warehouse across the street were cardboard boxes, litter, and a handful of high-seniority workers. Whether out of logistical necessity or sheer spite, the company made a clean break from the feisty union town, choosing to close its Regional Distribution Center as well. Maytag listed the enormous warehouse for sale for $8 million but then promptly protested Galesburg's tax assessment for that amount, claiming that its market value was in fact only $2.1 million. Maytag did the same with the factory, which had been assessed at $8.56 million. Maytag claimed its value at precisely $3.771 million. The company had gutted the factory so, naturally, as they argued, it was worth less. The devaluation meant higher taxes on homeowners and lower revenues for local government, especially cash-strapped Galesburg School District 205.[6]

Maytag was no longer the revered company from across the Mississippi. Once upon a time, layoffs literally had brought tears to the eyes of F. L. Maytag, who would bring workers back for a few weeks before Christmas even if they were not needed so they could earn a holiday paycheck.[7] The influx of "corporate gypsies," as Dave Bevard called them, had turned Newton into a different place. Maytag's 20,000 workers had become statistics, expenses to be trimmed to boost their bottom line. "It used to be that if you laid people off, it was a badge of shame," Bevard said. "Now it's cheered on Wall Street." Workers and residents alike vowed never to buy another Maytag product.

Local 2063's last meeting was Tuesday, February 8, 2005. Dave Bevard, his wife Pat, Doug Dennison, Sam Bigger, Mike Patrick, Don LeFebvre, Esta Brown, Butch Mundy, Kevin "Fuzzy" Robinson, and Leroy Hutchins convened over pizza for twenty minutes. "The warehouse is all but empty of product today," Doug Dennison wrote in ornate script in the union minutes. "The end is HERE." The leadership discussed a few final grievances and the "Afternoon with Santa" event they hosted in December. Bevard closed the meeting saying, "Local Lodge 2063 has a long and honorable history. It's been an honor and privilege to have worked with so many good people over the years. I wish to thank all past officers and members who sacrificed for what we have now. Everyone in LL2063 has a right to hold their heads high and be proud of our heritage and the jobs we did."

Beginning in the 1950s, Local 2063 had recorded their minutes in tall black ledgers with elegant, thick burgundy bindings. These books documented five decades of office nominations and vote tallies; political support for other area unions; flowers sent to families of deceased members; and the particulars of health insurance, pension plans, and sick-day policies. The last recorded words were: "DBR Mike Patrick adds, 'LL 2063 shall always be together in spirit.' Respectfully submitted, Doug Dennison, VP LL2063, IAM&AW."[8] Dennison also had some good news to share. Annette was one of eighteen students admitted into the radiology program at Sandburg in a competitive year. She would start in May.

Local 2063 was reduced to eighty members that week. They worked the warehouse as the final appliances shipped to Amana, Iowa. Forty finished work on that Friday, while the other half spent two weeks cleaning. The day before the warehouse closed, February 10, the U.S. Department of Commerce reported a record U.S. trade deficit of $617.7 billion for 2004. There was also a story from Quebec about the first union certification at a North America Walmart in a decade. Walmart closed the store.[9]

In April 2005 Maytag, the third largest appliance company in the United States, would miss profit targets and have its debt downgraded to junk status. Its stock price hit a fourteen-year low at $9.12, down 87 percent in six years. Ralph Hake had been hailed two years earlier as "Maytag's repairman" in the business press for his tough surgery on costs, including the Galesburg decision. Now the same press was taking him to task. "You can't manage a turnaround just by managing costs," CNN Money opined. Under Hake's cost-cutting regime, customers began to complain about quality problems and lackluster products. The once-successful Neptune, a premium washer, had become the "Stinkomatic" and a joke on the Internet. Claes Fornell, creator of the American Customer Satisfaction Index, said three constituencies were dropping Maytag: "consumers, retailers, and investors." "But it started with consumers," Fornell said. "Maytag used to be the leader in customer satisfaction. Now it's at all-time lows."[10]

Shareholders had lost over $1.6 billion. A lawsuit brought by a New York investment advisor charged that Hake had made "statements that were knowingly or recklessly false and misleading" because "Maytag's internal forecasts were lower than the public forecasts." The lawsuit claimed that Hake, who owned 789,438 shares at the time, attempted to "manipulate the stock price for purposes of a corporate merger or buy-out." *Fast Company* nominated Hake as its "candidate for spring cleaning," noting his outrageous pay and the near halving of Maytag's share price in his four years at the helm.[11]

None of this was sweet vindication for Bevard, Dennison, or the others who had stuck out the fight. Dennison still felt betrayed. "Ralph Hake, excuse my language, is a piece of shit," he said a few years after the decision. "And I'd tell him that to his face if I get the opportunity. He came into Maytag from Whirlpool and absolutely ruined it in a three-year period. He ruined so many lives."

In June 2005, Haier, a rapidly growing Chinese appliance maker, bid on the weakened Maytag. The Chinese company partnered with two American private equity firms—Bain Capital, founded by Mitt Romney, and Blackstone Group.[12] Haier had recently opened a refrigerator factory in the rural town of Camden, South Carolina, where it had been guaranteed a low-cost, non-unionized workforce, tax abatements, and very low land prices. The 200 jobs in the new Chinese-owned refrigerator factory hardly offset the 30,000 jobs in textiles or the 68,000 manufacturing jobs that had been lost in South Carolina since 1997.[13]

Through the rest of 2005, the three former principals of Local 2063—Bevard, Dennison, and Aaron Kemp—continued to meet in the nondescript back rooms of the Galesburg Labor Temple where they worked for the AFL-CIO Peer Outreach Program. The graffiti-covered side-by-side stood beside them, pushed up against one of the wood veneer-paneled walls (see Figure 8.1). They would later haul the last Galesburg refrigerator to the Galesburg Antiques Mall, where it still stands. Local 2063 existed mainly as a stack of filing boxes next to an extensive CD collection in Bevard's home by mid-2005. There were piles of hardbound meeting ledgers, scratchy audiocassettes of contract meetings, yellowed news clippings, and multicolored contract booklets dating to the 1950s. Local 2063's membership surpassed 4,000 when Rockwell purchased the plant in 1973. Nationwide, the powerful Machinists surpassed one million members in the 1970s.[14] Now Local 2063 existed purely as memories and archives and the International's membership had declined by 40 percent.

Former Local 2063 workers were not alone, of course. The two other big industrial unions—the autoworkers and the steelworkers—had experienced even steeper declines.[15] In 1973, nearly two in five manufacturing workers in

FIGURE 8.1 DAVE BEVARD WITH THE LAST REFRIGERATOR

Local 2063 president Dave Bevard stands next to the last side-by-side refrigerator made at the Galesburg factory. The refrigerator, autographed by its makers, now stands in the Galesburg Antiques Mall. *Credit: Chad Broughton.*

the private sector were union members. In 2005, only one in eight were. In Illinois, union membership dropped by more than half between 1973 and 2005. The same was true for Ohio and Michigan; for Indiana and Pennsylvania, the losses were closer to two-thirds. All these losses came despite rapid growth in public-sector unions across the same time-span.[16] In 2013, union membership was about 35 percent among public-sector workers and only 6.7 percent among private-sector workers.[17]

These numbers, though, do not convey what was lost. People at Appliance City spoke of their "second family" so often that it was a cliché about local factory life. The formal bonds of union membership added another relational layer to these informal bonds of friendship. Being a member of Local 2063 involved an education in the elaborate contract rules meant to ensure fairness and due process for handling grievances and misconduct, as well as those rules regulating voting on representatives and labor agreements. For leaders it required politicking, making your case for union office, and being responsive to members. Union democracy was fraught with disagreement and conflict—but it brought people together to manage and debate their livelihoods, their health-care issues, their plans for old age, and their day-to-day working conditions. Now those communities were gone. The factory closing had cut people adrift, and ex-Maytag workers could feel the difference. "It's become cutthroat, competitive," Town Tavern owner George Carney said. "People will use a ladder to step right over you. It's every man for himself now."

The gutting of the unions paralleled a general erosion of social connectedness. From the early 1970s, Americans did less together—less bowling in leagues, less engagement in political work, less church attendance, less entertaining, less drinking together in bars, and less eating together in diners. Spectator sports, fast food, and in-home entertainment increased to fill some of the void. In *Bowling Alone*, published in 2000, Robert Putnam argued that the changes in how Americans spent their time had led to a profound and qualitative shift in how Americans related to one another. This loss of social capital, he wrote, had led to greater social distrust and the widespread perception that others were less moral, less honest, and less trustworthy.[18]

So it seemed in Galesburg after Maytag had closed. Tim Welch, for one, was hardly nostalgic about Local 2063's departure. "The union is just another racket to get your money." After his 2003 layoff from Maytag, Welch had no health insurance and no life insurance. He dropped his monthly donation to the Knights of Columbus. He parked his boat and put it up for sale.

Many workers felt that their supposed allies had let them down. Union leaders offered tough talk at rallies and in the media, but talk was cheap. They blamed their union for the lousy final contract, for not sticking up for them, and for the layoffs. George Carney said Local 2063 would "sugarcoat" contracts and push them through for the company. He couldn't prove it, but he thought they were probably "on the take." "I like working for a union," Carney said. "If a foreman decides he don't like you, and you might be the hardest worker there, he can't get rid of you for no reason. Unions stop that. But the other part is the guy who does nothing all day, beats his wife, sells drugs, whatever else. The union has to stand up for that man. That's what tears unions down, makes them look bad. I thought our union was a joke."

To Local 2063's leaders, though, that last day in the Labor Temple was no joke. Being a unionist was a way of life. They could no more give up their union label than they could disown their family. And for Bevard, Dennison, Kemp, and the others who stuck with Local 2063, all that was right with the labor movement locally could be traced back to Mike Patrick and leaders like him. Bevard, always an anti-establishment type, remembered taking the oath of office, administered by Patrick in the early 1980s. He was startled by just how seriously Patrick, Chuck Unger, Don LeFebvre, and others in the old guard had taken the leadership vows. "I remember taking the oath of office, and feeling like, oh my God, what am I actually saying here? It meant something to me because it meant something to them."

Not everyone in the union leadership over the years "got it," but to Bevard those guys did, and it had been enough to keep Appliance City humming. "There were no games, no hidden agenda, nothing. While you may disagree with what the proposal is, it's not going to be detrimental to the facility. It's going to benefit our people and we're not trying to damage the business. I'd never cease to be amazed that they could look at something and say here's this language, now to extrapolate from that, what are all of the ramifications as this moves out? Five minutes later they would come back with answers. They were incredibly talented." And they felt the full weight of their obligations. Bevard remembered times when the team did not get something they felt retirees or lower-tier workers needed during a marathon contract negotiation. "It was the worst thing in the world," Bevard said. "We'd feel sick, like we'd failed."

When the Local brought home a good three-year contract, it was big news for the entire region: a relief to countless families, school administrators, local suppliers and business owners, and the company. Bevard had had the miserable job of serving as president for the two-year shuttering under a humiliating contract. Instead of passing the torch to Dennison and the others, he would have to blow it out. It was a no-win situation, even though they had routed Hake and Maytag in the public relations war. Nationwide, despite their membership declines, labor unions maintained reasonably strong public support. Public opinion tracking polls showed that at the time of Local 2063's end in 2005, Americans approved of labor unions as strongly as they did in the 1970s, by a margin of about two to one.[19]

In 2005, even with its economic anchor gone, Galesburg still fit that idyllic portrait of "Rockwell's America" in many ways. People still bowled together. They still drove slowly through town, greeted each other on the sidewalks, and talked to their neighbors. The marquee at the First Christian Church, at the corner of North and Broad Streets, still offered folksy aphorisms. "Have Your Tools Ready, God Will Provide the Work," read one. "Come in! This Church Is Prayer Conditioned!" read another. Middle-aged and connected to family and community, ex-Maytag workers wanted to stay where they were, whether they lived in Galesburg, Monmouth, or off some county road.

But people were scrambling. Up at Carl Sandburg College, Annette Dennison and hundreds of laid-off workers streamed into training programs. Tracy Warner kept at her journalism program at Western Illinois. George Carney, who still flipped off the factory whenever he drove by, tapped kegs at Town Tavern and plowed snow part-time for the Village of Avon. For Doug Dennison, the fiery speeches were over, and it was time to find something else. He had to step into the next stage of what seemed like, as it did for most ex-Maytag workers, a transition without end.

Galesburg, once a place where people earned comparable wages, was now a place with people spinning off in different directions.

Galesburg was now a place where more people would choose the "wrong track" answer in the polling question about the direction of the country.[20] Even with its outward show of resistance and resilience, it was a place marked by distrust and cynicism. Their beef was not with the guy down the street, however, but with distant corporations and big government.

Galesburg was now a place that used to make things.

"America needs to start producing again," said former Maytag worker and history buff Mark Good. "We're the Roman Empire right now. Rome swallowed and consumed everything and produced nothing. We're consuming everything and producing nothing too. Except war."

9

THE MIKE ALLEN QUESTION

Reynosa, Tamaulipas

Trabajar por la patria es forjar nuestro destino.
("To work for the motherland is to forge our destiny.")

—Motto on the Reynosa city seal

FROM THE MOMENT she started at Planta Maytag III in December 2004, Laura Flora's financial circumstances turned bleak. She had earned much more during her peripatetic travels through tobacco fields and orange groves in the United States. In fact, Veracruzanos could sometimes earn an even better wage harvesting limes or picking chiles back in their rural villages than they did at the border. Flora felt demeaned by the low wages Maytag paid and found the work tedious and the factory culture oppressive and demoralizing. Yet she stayed.

As a single mother, Flora lived on the razor's edge of survival, but she had something her friends back in Tierra Blanca did not: steady work. Back in Veracruz, work ebbed and flowed with the weather, the seasons, and the rhythms of rural life. At the border, work was unrelenting, driven by the demands of global competition, time-discipline, and the ravenous consumer market to the north. It was the sheer volume of available jobs for unskilled workers—and the promise of overtime—that lured people like Flora to Reynosa. Based on income figures in 2004, about 50 million people in her country, 47 percent of the population, lived in poverty. With overtime Flora could cross the poverty threshold to move into the nonpoor half.[1]

The border was also where Flora, who turned 41 the week she began at Maytag, thought she could be a better parent. She had failed to sneak her three young girls into the United States in September, and now they were stuck in a place where they knew no one. But at least they would be together, unlike when Flora was in the United States with her two older children. And here in modernizing Reynosa, her daughters—if not herself—had a much better chance at getting ahead than they had had in Veracruz. "The education is better here, a lot better," Flora reflected over a glass of sweet lemonade on a hot July afternoon in 2007. Her boyfriend, Arturo Mireles Guzman, agreed. The girls needed a technical profession, in his view. "So they don't kill them like they kill us. Education, so *they* can be the bosses." Mireles, a native of Reynosa, also worked long hours at Planta III.

Laura Flora's oldest daughter in Reynosa, Laura Suarez, listened quietly in the shade of their peach-colored house. Suarez, a beautiful, dark-haired, and round-cheeked girl, was 14. When asked how she imagined her future, she replied, "To study a career in industrial design or . . ." and, unsure, hesitated. "An engineering degree!" her mother chimed in with excitement. "'That's what I want her to study." When, a month earlier, Laura Suarez finished *secundaria* (sixth through ninth grade), she had told her mother that she wanted to quit school. "I don't know if I can keep going," she had said. "I want to start working." Suarez, protective of her two younger sisters, wanted to help her mother feed their struggling family. Flora spent over half of her Maytag paycheck on food. Still, their mother said that the girls often felt like they had "a hole in their stomach."

"Don't give up your dream of studying," Flora had told Suarez. "I don't know how we're going to do it, but we're going to do it. Look, I don't have an inheritance for you. The only inheritance that I can give you is your education. That's your great treasure. If you don't remember to value education, you're just going to end up the way I did." That fall Suarez would begin grade ten, the last grade her mother had finished in Tierra Blanca.

"I don't want you waking up at dawn by yourself, leaving your daughters alone sleeping," Flora said to all three girls, who were milling around their rocky yard. She looked at us with somber eyes. "My youngest daughter wakes up with me at five in the morning and asks, 'Do you have to go?' and I have to say 'Yes, get up and help yourself to bread or something.' I want them to have time for their families." Flora needed her young teenager to stick with school. It was the thing that kept her returning to Planta III early every morning. It kept her sane. It was why she tolerated this crazed border boomtown.

Flora's gamble was about more than education. Coming north meant escaping crushing gender limitations in all aspects of life in Veracruz. She insisted Suarez be a *licenciada* (degreed professional) before she helped Flora with the bills or started her own family. A single mother most of her life, Flora spoke from experience and regret. "In the long run if there is a problem in their marriages, they'll have their education, and that's worth more than any man."

These were the crucial years. Flora could not let Suarez get derailed. If she dropped out now, Suarez would likely experience the border as Flora had— as relentless toil and loneliness. If the young teen could push through the next several years, though, Reynosa could offer something else entirely. Despite the ceaseless and horrific headlines about drug-related violence, much of it directed at young women, there was a sense of freedom and possibility at the border. There were concrete freedoms, too—access to more occupational fields, contraception, women's health care, and divorce.

The loudest and most articulate critic of the maquiladoras in Reynosa, Arturo Solís, conceded that the border boom had loosened patriarchy's grip. "She has ceased to be dependent on a man," the human rights leader said of women generally. "It has allowed her to be in charge of the family and to decide about her life, her family, her partner, and kids. Here in Mexico, women were confined to housework and had to conform to what her husband said. This has changed. And that is very good."

Younger Veracruzanos often partied on the weekends. Flora went out once with her co-workers, but didn't drink. Her daughters told her to go out and have fun, to break the monotony. "No, I'd rather watch a movie, and sleep with you," Flora said to them. "You don't see me drunk, going out. Learning how to cook, how to make rice, this will serve you when you're older." The two older girls wanted a Caribbean cooler (a bottle of alcoholic punch) so over the holidays Flora had bought them one. "I was right here on top of them, watching them," Flora said. "I pay attention to who their friends are. I watch over them."

The maquiladora was conceived to sop up the unemployed men returning to Mexico at the end of the Bracero Program in 1964. Yet since its inception, women have filled the maquila's lowest ranks. In Reynosa, Zenith Electronics, which spearheaded the first Rust Belt exodus, dominated the early industrial landscape and employed mostly women. In

1977, before Zenith came, Reynosa had a mere eight factories, employing 1,258 workers, fewer than half the number that worked at Appliance City in Galesburg that year. By 1992 Zenith alone had six factories, employing more than 8,000 in Reynosa. In the lowest-ranking *obrero* (assembler) category, women made up 61 percent of the maquila workforce in January 1990 and still constituted the majority at 55 percent in 2007, when we first met Laura Flora.[2]

In the 1990s and 2000s, Mexican women were shattering little glass ceilings in maquilas across the city. Gloria D. Altamirano, bilingual and well educated, shattered one on the former Zenith campus in Reynosa, acquired by the South Korean giant, LG Electronics, in 1995. Korean companies were notoriously misogynistic, but Altamirano worked her way up to human resources manager. She confirmed what we had heard from many in Reynosa. American companies were the best to work for, she said, because they are "culturally closer." The Europeans and the Japanese were next, and then there were the Koreans. She said Korean companies had a "really different philosophy," one that was as ruthless as it was relentless in its pursuit of production quotas and the bottom line.

Altamirano showed us around the spruced-up LG factory, which was located near Flora's home. A sign in enormous raspberry-red-on-white lettering read, in English, "Great Company, Great People" and "The People Company." Former yellow school buses and *micros*—even today several routes are called "Zenith routes"—shuttled workers to and from the expansive campus as they belched black smoke. Semis crawled in and out of the loading zones on its wide streets. A man pedaling a three-wheel bicycle and selling cold treats looked out of place in one of the few open places in a facility designed for maximum density. The televisions from this LG factory were as close as one could get to an American-made television set. Whereas in 1960 there were twenty-seven U.S.-based television manufacturers, including Siragusa's Galesburg-connected Admiral, four decades later there were none.[3] LG closed the Zenith shops in Juárez and Matamoros as well. LG's Reynosa campus was its cheapest and most efficient facility. And Reynosa—from the company's perspective—had the "friendliest" labor climate at the border.

Inside, the scene was not much different than it had been ten or twenty years earlier. Women in colored-coded aprons pieced together the televisions in lines, thirty-two to forty-five to a row. It was more modern and automated than in decades past, certainly, and the company had further pressed "just-in-time" processes to minimize inventory and maximize efficiency. By the mid-2000s, this remarkable symphony of frenetic but utterly rationalized activity, this superorganism of production, pumped out 6,500 televisions every day. The factory's output—anything from its dirt-cheap 14" tube television to some of the first HD plasma screens, which at the time sold for $5,000—could be found in the living rooms of both the rich and the poor, from Canada to Peru.

Altamirano quit the job as human resources manager at LG. It was too stressful, and she had realized that she had made it as far as she was going to go. "It's still a man's world at forty and above, after you reach a certain level. As a woman, you know that you will never be able to report directly to corporate. In a generation, it will be different. Opportunities for women really evolved a lot in our community professionally, politically, sociologically." Altamirano would leave the door open for talented, hopeful young girls like Laura Suarez.

This was the essential fact of Reynosa for parents like Flora. Without a legitimate hope that education and time would bring a better life for their children, the daily grind, the frayed and strained family, and the ubiquitous dangers of the city would not have been worth it, not even close.

LAURA FLORA HAD no idea that she lived in a world created by a charismatic power broker from Texas.

Presidents Bill Clinton and Carlos Salinas, along with a succession of other elite pushers of free trade in Washington, D.C., and Mexico City, had set the stage for the border's transformation. Locally, the cacique union bosses, the city's developers and government officials, and the maquiladoras had all played important parts. And the organized power of local and national maquiladora associations, such as the influential Reynosa Maquiladora Association, made up of mostly gringos, coordinated lobbying efforts at the local, state, and federal levels in Mexico. More than anybody, though, Mike Allen was the main actor in the explosive binational boom taking place in the Magic Valley in the mid-2000s when Planta III and Laura Flora both arrived.[4]

Maquiladora employment in Mexico had surged to 1.3 million in 2001—tripling since 1990—but then dropped (see Figure 9.1).[5] While other border cities suffered, losing tens of thousands of jobs, and while the Rust Belt faced its most severe crisis yet, Reynosa continued to boom.[6] From 1990 to

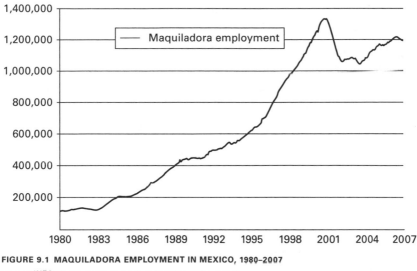

FIGURE 9.1 MAQUILADORA EMPLOYMENT IN MEXICO, 1980–2007
Source: INEGI (Instituto Nacional de Estadística y Geografía).

2006, Reynosa outpaced by a large margin its competitors up and down the nearly 2,000-mile border in employment growth and value-added.[7] From just a handful of factories in the 1970s and 1980s, Reynosa had some 150 factories in the mid-2000s—General Motors, General Electric, Whirlpool, Nokia, Black & Decker, Halliburton, Panasonic, InSinkErator, Kohler, and LG among them—that employed 75,000 people. Reynosa had become NAFTA's darling. Its phenomenal growth in the second phase of border industrialization catapulted this obscure city into third place among the border industrial engines powering U.S. consumption. Reynosa was still behind longtime giants Juárez and Tijuana, but well past Matamoros, Mexicali, and Ciudad Acuña.[8]

Mike Allen and his partner Keith Patridge had little patience for Reverend Ed Krueger and the naysayers. Allen was, after all, bringing jobs to his former parishioners. He resented those, however well meaning, who were as ignorant as Allen said that he himself had once been. "Ed Krueger is one of those, God bless him. He's got a big heart. But he's totally unknowledgeable about the forces that create a good living for the people he wants to help." Allen saw himself as doing God's work in South Texas and Reynosa. Krueger and the others were obstacles.

Some Catholic oblates had recently visited the **border** to scrutinize working conditions and wages among the maquilas when **we first** met Mike Allen in 2003. Angered by the negative media attention that came of it, Allen called a meeting with the bishop of Matamoros. "Bishop," Allen recounted saying, "OK, straight up or down: Would you prefer not to have these maquilas here, to shut them all down and tell 75,000 people to go work somewhere else? You're letting a bunch of gringo priests come here and run the church in Mexico. What is that all about? You talk about the ugly American. Well, you have the ugly priest, too!" Allen maintained that his lobbying sortie to Matamoros had been a success. "No," he said the bishop had told him, "keep doing what you're doing."

This was what one might call the "Mike Allen question": a yes-or-no, "forced choice" question with no room for equivocating and no gray areas to explore. It was another example of Allen's persuasive powers. Even critics on long-winded diatribes would be stopped cold, forced into a stammer, when asked this question. They were forced to admit the obvious; ultimately, in a global, cutthroat contest between job-starved places, it was better to have the factories than not to have them.

Many in the Rio Grande Valley lined up with Allen. John Sargent, an economist at the University of Texas-Pan American, was one. "I know this is kind of a hard thing for people in your neck of the woods to accept, but when companies such as Maytag come down to the border, they really are making life better for people in these communities." "Money is not raining down on them," Sargent said, but it was better than the alternative in Veracruz. There was consistent work, better schools, full access to health care, and "significant opportunity for people who start out at very low levels to work into the lower middle class through working in the maquilas."

That was what Flora was counting on for her daughters. In Reynosa there were plenty of role models for Laura Suarez, Adrianita, and Erika. Those role models were not, perhaps, in Flora's rundown neighborhood, but when Flora saw the well-dressed women working in factory offices, commuting in nice cars, or walking downtown, she saw her daughters' futures.

Erika Barbosa Muñoz was one of these women. Her father, a poor agricultural worker for most of his early life, had raised her in Reynosa. Barbosa felt obligated to repay her father's struggles and to take advantage of the freedoms she found amid the chaos of the border. She focused obsessively on schooling and work. In 1995, at 19, Barbosa started putting buttons on car radios in General Motors' Delnosa plant. She did tedious finger work and, four months later, worked from 7:00 a.m. to 4:30 p.m. doing low-paid data entry. From 5 p.m. to 10 p.m., Barbosa attended the local technical college. At 27, the ambitious and energetic *norteña* (native northerner) was a quality-control supervisor working in Delnosa's offices, off the shop floor, and interacting with clients from Ford, Toyota, Nissan, and General Motors. "We have the capability to do things just like men, not to just stay at home taking care of kids. My co-workers and I, we have this mentality. If I get married, I get married, but I want to develop myself, my profession." Barbosa made the standard wage for her first few years at the global auto parts giant, but she had quadrupled her income in eight years, adjusted for inflation. She saw other women in higher positions and dreamed of joining them, but they all spoke much better English. That's what she needed to do next, she had determined. After that, maybe she would start a family.

Edna Avila, Barbosa's friend from the technical school, said it was a different world for women at the border. "In states without maquilas, women are still very repressed. My husband has a profession and he understands my aspirations," Avila told us. "He has his and I have mine. I'm not just going to conform to what he wants to achieve." Avila said that she and her friends were picky about men. "I try to tell my neighbor lady [who, according to Avila, spoiled her son], 'You are hurting your son! It will be difficult for him to find a woman who will do all that [cooking and cleaning] for him!'"

The border was especially open to those already with solid footing in the middle class, such as Gris Cruz, another lively and sociable norteña. While Flora worked 50- or 60-hour weeks, Cruz and her husband, Arqueles Garcia, devoured what the burgeoning cosmopolitan city offered. When we first met them in 2003, both were talented artists in their early thirties, bilingual, and well educated. Garcia, a photographer, music fanatic, and Apple devotee, zipped us around town in his tiny black Chevy, showing us sites. Their little home, with a prolific lime tree out back, was just off Miguel Hidalgo, a teeming river of cars and trucks that cuts a broad gash south and west out of Reynosa toward Monterrey.

By 2007 the busy thoroughfare was much faster and more developed than it had been four years earlier thanks to big public works projects. Just off the road there was a massive new federally funded Infonavit development where homes were packed together as tight as Lego blocks. There were car dealerships and new SUVs everywhere. Nearby there was an Applebee's, a Sirloin

Stockade, and a Sam's Club. There was also a renovated stadium that could hold 10,000 fans of the Broncos de Reynosa of the Mexican Baseball League. After dark, seen from the top of the thoroughfare's towering bridge above the stadium, the city's far western edge—virtually all of it new—lit the landscape for miles.

Further south on Hidalgo was a big shopping mall and a big theater that would have looked at home in just about any American suburb. The mall sat across the highway from Empresora Donneco Internacional. That's where R. R. Donnelley, a Chicago-based, Fortune 500 company, printed and bound books in the 890-acre Parque Industrial del Norte. Just outside the book maquila, interspersed among a couple of bland, boxy buildings, is the company's brownish soccer field.

We had first met Cruz and Garcia in 2003 at CEFPRODHAC, the Reynosa human rights organization directed by Arturo Solís. They had recently assisted on an interview and photojournalism study critical of the maquiladoras. Four years later, Cruz was working for Delphi, the automotive components company founded by General Motors. Conversant and comfortable with both Mexican line workers and American managers, Cruz found a niche in "communications" at the factory. Her job was "to encourage loyalty" in order to stem chronic turnover among line workers. The job offered some professional development, but Cruz did not feel like her work there was respected.

One Saturday night Cruz and Garcia took us to Plaza Principal to offer us a glimpse of what Reynosa looked like to them. That night the downtown plaza throbbed with the hip-hop sounds of a popular Mexican musical group, Semilla de Mostaza. Packed tightly, adoring young fans waved their arms back and forth, chanting lyrics in an uncanny unison. Dressed in sleek, body-hugging black clothing, the polished ensemble featured a female lead with a deep, soulful voice. An edgy, frenetic younger man named Fermin IV, with a shaved head and a goatee, skipped across the stage as he ripped out rhymes that, somewhat incongruously to us but not to our evangelical friends, praised Jesus. The middle-aged keyboardist, Heriberto Hermosillo, Garcia told us, was a famous Monterrey musician known for his past indulgences with drugs and alcohol. With the joyful smile of a saved man, Pastor Hermosillo held down the rhythm section, sweating in the hot evening air. It was hard not to be swept up in the buoyancy of the crowd and the slick musicality of these postmodern missionaries. I knew then that Cruz and

Garcia would give Mike Allen a couple more "yeses." The new Reynosa, at least the parts they loved, after all, would not have existed if not for Mike Allen and the maquiladoras.[9]

THERE WAS JUST one restaurant near Planta Maytag III. La Palapa, as efficient as the factories around it, bustled with middle-class managers at lunchtime. In 2004, a tasty quesadilla, guacamole, and Coke lunch for two cost 75 pesos (about $6.75), roughly what Laura Flora and the other refrigerator makers down the street made in a day without overtime. There probably had not been an assembler in the restaurant all year. Flora ate all her daily meals, aside from her morning toast, at the factory. When a kitchen worker at Maytag gave her a plate of food, Flora would joke, "This is nasty! What a bunch of *cochinada* (hog slop). But put more on! I'm hungry!" Veracruzanos like Flora were notoriously frugal, and she bargained for every extra taco or burrito morsel she could get. Flora squirreled away packets of dried milk from the factory's cafeteria. The meals came out of her paycheck, but they were cheap, about 45 pesos ($4) for a week of lunches.[10]

Newspapers routinely reported that maquila workers earned an average of $2.60 an hour in the mid-2000s, often taking the McAllen Economic Development Corporation's numbers at face value.[11] Locals knew this was nonsense. Even María Prieto, Reynosa's director of industrial development, said the average in the maquilas was 70 pesos, about $6.25, per day, or roughly 78 cents an hour, without overtime. Speaking for the Mexicans that worked at Planta III, Maytag's vice president of manufacturing, Steve Ingham, maintained that Maytag's wages were about in the middle compared to other maquilas. What was important, what Americans needed to understand, Ingham said, was that the border factories offered a leg up for Mexican workers. "When they come from Veracruz they've automatically arrived in the middle class in Mexico. From their perspective, their culture, in their country, this is a huge step that makes them very proud."[12]

Pablo Lara Sanchez was, like Laura Flora, an early hire at Planta Maytag III, where he hung doors and did other line work for fifty to sixty hours each week. His home was on an unpaved road in the southern reaches of Reynosa's outer slums in Colonia La Joya. On weekends Lara had built his large family's sturdy home by himself, enclosing it with a chain-link fence held up by thick tree-branch posts. His address, "601," was spray-painted in black on the makeshift gate to his home. After years of work, the Lara home was nicer than most, with smooth concrete floors and good rain protection. Coffee mugs and skillets hung from nails in the tidy kitchen (see Figure 9.2). A blue Smurf dangled from a wall hook in the bedroom, and children's books were lined up neatly in a tall bookshelf.[13]

Lara showed us his Maytag ID when we first interviewed him in December 2004, just as Maytag revved up production in its first year in Reynosa. Lara's daughters, Genesis and Noemi, rushed out with a backless, flowered cushion chair and a homemade wooden stool for us. His teenage son, Jesús, looked on as we talked. Lara and his wife, Carmen, are both from Alamo, a little town in northern Veracruz. Lara dropped out of school when he was 13 to work for his father, a hard-working but abusive alcoholic. The young teen started each morning at 6 a.m., when he delivered 125-pound sacks of corn *masa* on a hauling tricycle to a mill. That work for his father's small corn-processing business brought their household about $140 a week, which was roughly

FIGURE 9.2 PABLO LARA SANCHEZ'S FAMILY

Lara's wife, Carmen, and their children in their kitchen in Colonia La Joya on the outskirts of Reynosa. *Credit: Chad Broughton.*

twice as much as he made now, but it was harder work than the line work at Maytag, the kind of constant physical toil that wore one down. "You had to work unbearably hard to maintain yourself or get ahead a little bit," Lara said of his little hometown.

By 2004 Lara had worked for Zenith, Converse, Seagate, Motores (GE), and other maquilas in his ten years in Reynosa. The state-of-the-art Planta III was more comfortable, cleaner, and more safety oriented than the others. Lara still felt like a commodity at Maytag, just as he had at the other maquilas. On his first day, the company put him through a battery of tests: for dexterity, a psychological test, a medical exam and urine test, and even an examination for tattoos. Soon after he started, the indignities of unpaid breaks, uncompromising attendance policies, and poor pay piled up fast. When he described having to skip morning meals, his eyes welled with tears. "There are Americans at the factory who have seen that we don't even make enough to eat a real meal in the morning and it seems like they don't care. That's really painful for me. They've bought off our union and intimidated people with the threat of being fired."

Lara was magnetized by the evangelical writings of James Dobson, founder of the conservative Christian organization, Focus on the Family. It was a way to handle the damage wrought by his father's physical and emotional abuse and his untenable economic situation. A social conservative himself, Lara still clung proudly to the sole breadwinner ideal, working overtime to keep his wife at home with their children. "This job doesn't pay nearly enough to raise a family. My family's economic situation would never allow me to buy one of the refrigerators I make. I don't have enough to buy fruits and vegetables."

Lara worked 54.57 hours at Planta III in the third week of November 2004. At the end of the week, he cashed a check for $60 (669 pesos), or about $1.10 per hour in take-home pay. The top line read "Tiempo Normal" (regular time), $35.75. This meant that during the first 48 hours of the six-day week, Lara had earned 74 cents an hour. Itemized below were "Septimo Dia" (seventh day), the legally required payment for Sunday ($6); overtime for 6.57 hours ($9.75); an early arrival and attendance bonus ($6.50); a transportation allowance ($6.50); a company contribution to savings (also in deductions) ($2.50); and a government cash payment ($4.25). Deducted were IMSS, a social security and health care tax, ($1.00); cafeteria charges ($4.00); union dues ($0.75); and a savings account deduction ($2.50). Lara also received 105

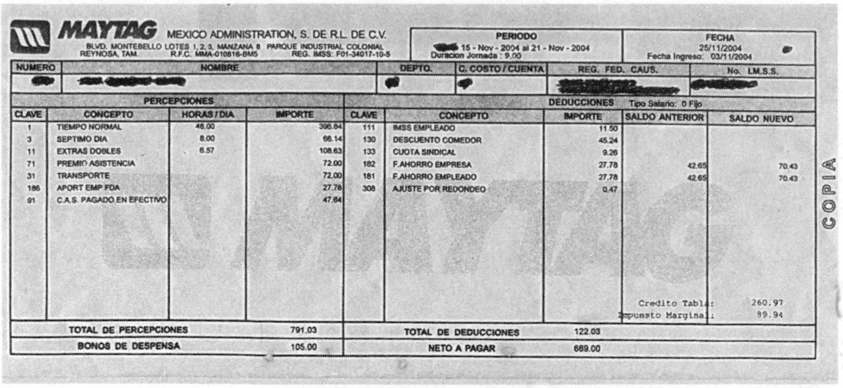

FIGURE 9.3 MAQUILA PAYSTUB

Pablo Lara Sanchez's paystub from November 2004 showing $1.10 per hour take-home pay. Laura Flora Oliveros' paystubs from Maytag and other maquilas from 2004 to 2013 reflect take-home pay averaging closer to $1.35. Maquila wages, adjusted for inflation, were about the same in 2012 as they were in the early 1980s.[14]

pesos ($9.50) in "Bonos de Despensa," an untaxed grocery voucher similar to food stamps (see Figure 9.3). If Lara worked fifty weeks in a year, averaging 6.5 hours of overtime a week, he would earn about $3,000. The Lara family, through Pablo's sheer volume of work, lived above the official poverty line for urban dwellers.[15]

In early 2005 Maytag's public relations claimed that the Reynosa factory was blowing away expectations. According to Maytag vice president Ingham, safety, quality, delivery, and cost had all dramatically improved since the relocation, and, as a result, "our competitive position has improved significantly." It was a win-win for the company and its new workers, according to Jeri Penn, the director of cost improvement at Planta III. "There are opportunities for anyone to broaden their education, gain technical skills, and progress through the ranks, even from the operator level," she said.[16]

Lara disagreed. Perhaps there were brighter possibilities for someone with no children, some English proficiency, and a solid educational footing, but not for him. His parents did not enroll him in *secundaria*; at age 28, he was still trying to finish high school. The only way Lara made material improvements in his family's life was when he was fired for agitating in the maquilas. As he gave us a tour of his home, he pointed out the parts of his home he had added with the influxes of cash he had received with each of his severance payments. Lara had vague dreams about becoming a lawyer, but the fact was that he was an *obrero* and that meant he and his family would likely remain mired in poverty for another generation.

Most maquiladora workers seemed stuck, unable to make it into the lower middle class. One maquila worker, Nivorio Suarez, said in a focus group that he came to Reynosa for youthful adventure as a 16-year-old in 1986. In his thirties, he still worked the line. "The resources aren't there. The economics always stop you regardless of what you want to do. If I went after a career it would have been a dream in vain. That's why I don't get ahead. You get used to it."

The 1994 peso crisis and devaluation had made Mexican workers cheaper for foreign corporations—and expanded the wage gap between Mexican workers and minimum-wage workers on the American side. Reynosa's boom during the NAFTA era had not lifted the average worker's wage. In fact, a maquila worker like Pablo Lara or Nivorio Suarez in 2006 made about the same wage, adjusted for inflation, as a maquila worker in 1990, even as productivity increased (see Figure 9.4).[17]

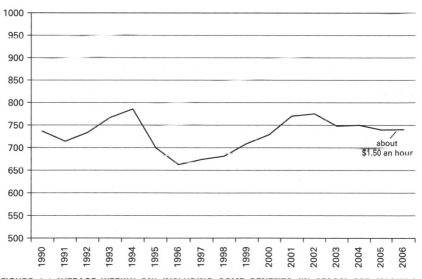

FIGURE 9.4 AVERAGE WEEKLY PAY INCLUDING SOME BENEFITS (IN PESOS) FOR MAQUILA WORKERS IN TAMAULIPAS, 1990–2006 (IN 2002 PESOS)

Source: INEGI (Instituto Nacional de Estadística y Geografía). INEGI wage data includes cash, in-kind payments such as food stamps and transportation stipends, and some benefits. The take-home wage rate was lower.[18]

That's why Laura Flora, Pablo Lara, and Nivorio Suarez would have been quite surprised to learn they were "automatically" members of the middle class when they arrived in Reynosa. Maybe a single worker could get by on $60 a week, but none of their families had enough food to eat. The cost of food in border grocery and corner stores was higher than the marketplaces of the south. The border was "dollarized," which was perhaps the most jarring adjustment Veracruzanos faced in Reynosa.

The Comité Fronterizo de Obreras (Border Committee of Women Workers) determined a basic food cost at about 900 pesos ($81) a week for a family of four in Reynosa in a report. María Elena García, a single mother who worked with the CFO said, "I dream of having a budget like that! [The maquila] pays me 400 pesos [$36] per week in the maquila. That is half of what I need to give my kids a balanced diet. And from that comes the poor education of kids, because if they have a poor diet, they can't learn well. So it is difficult." The cost of the official "market basket" of food, housing, and essential services rose 247 percent in the first six years of NAFTA, according to the CFO.[19]

Laura Flora and Pablo Lara could not afford to buy the wide array of consumer goods now available across the city. Kids' shoes were $5 to $25 around the plaza. Children's books were $5 to $13. Enfamil was $6.50 for 400 grams. A two-liter of Coke was $1.35. An air-conditioning unit was $260. CDs were $10. Low-end jeans around the plaza ran from $8 to $16. Ham was $2 a pound. Some things were cheap, including dental work and pharmaceuticals, especially antibiotics. No prescription was needed for antidepressants, but Prozac was pricy: $52 for 28 capsules.

There were flea markets everywhere in the city, and some had good deals if you knew where to look. However, buying the signifiers of the middle class—a stereo, air conditioner, even a weekly six-pack of microbrews—was simply not plausible. The Nike Shop on Plaza Principal was as expensive as an American store. Many shoes sold for $135 or more. Telephone and Internet service, gasoline, car rentals, hotels, and taxis were likewise as expensive as in the United States.

A 2003 study comparing prices of basic food items in nearby Nuevo Laredo, Mexico, to Minneapolis, Minnesota, found that prices were comparable. Milk, rice, beans, chicken, cooking oil, and tomatoes were cheaper in Nuevo Laredo, whereas bread, eggs, potatoes, beef, toilet paper, and corn flakes were cheaper in Minneapolis.[20] In 2007, Laura Flora estimated the food cost for Erika, her youngest, alone was a few dollars a day for milk, bread, and a dinner. For the four of them, her weekly $55 to $70 paycheck and $9 in food stamps simply did not add up. "Every week I buy 500 pesos [$45] of food. My daughters are at an age where they are growing. It's not enough."[21]

When asked whether a Maytag wage could support a family, Maytag's Ingham said in January 2005, "From the discussions I've had with individuals down there, there's not been any specific concerns communicated to me." In November 2004, second-shifters at Planta III (Pablo Lara worked the first shift and Flora would be hired in the subsequent month) had staged a work stoppage over wages owed to them. Fifteen to twenty of those workers were fired the next month. Workers were cycling in and out of Maytag because of low wages, leading Maytag to offer a bonus for workers that recommended a new hire. "In other words," the Comité Fronterizo de Obreras noted in an article, "Maytag is begging for people."[22]

Lara left Maytag in early 2005, after the holidays, to continue his hitherto fruitless search for a living wage. He had two messages. "I want to ask workers in the U.S. to support us as we fight for a dignified wage. I don't want to be seen with pity, but with dignity. And I'm sending another message to any businessperson in the U.S. that has businesses here in Mexico. It's good that you come, but you must see your workers as human beings. We're not animals. We're human beings and we have the same blood flowing through our veins." The stony-faced Veracruzano then turned to us. "They forget that we all have a Creator and that there is a God above and that, one way or another, there will be justice."

DURING OUR TRIPS in the mid-2000s we continued to ask the Mike Allen question around Reynosa: "OK, straight up or down: Would you prefer not to have these maquilas here, to shut them all down and tell 75,000 people to go work somewhere else?" Despite his earlier concession as to progress for women, Arturo Solís answered in the negative. "The only thing maquilas have done here is occupy the workforce," he said. "The maquilas don't resolve the problems that they generate. There is overpopulation, a lack of social services, a lack of schools and health care. There is no water, drainage systems, adequate housing for families. All of this, *all of it*, is what the maquiladora has brought."

Solís led CEFPRODHAC from its Spartan second floor offices just off Plaza Principal. On the wall were pictures of Solís with Kofi Annan and then-Mexican president Vicente Fox. Reynosa, he said, had been a sleepy agricultural and petroleum town of 70,000 in the 1950s. When the maquilas came, Reynosa's population, and its problems, exploded. In the nearly two decades since Mike Allen's fateful handshake deal with the mayor in 1988, Reynosa had added about 45 people every day.[23]

From 1990 to 2005, the city grew from 282,667 to 526,888, according to INEGI, Mexico's census bureau. Herber Ramírez, the city's secretary of economic development in the early 2000s, said the official numbers were a massive underestimate of Reynosa's true size. He contended that the federal government intentionally undercounted border cities to lower its spending obligations. The real population of Reynosa, extrapolating from local social security numbers, "could easily justify 1.2 million." Locals on both sides of the Rio Grande, including rivals Solís and Allen—men who agreed on little else—backed Ramírez's population claim.[24]

"The city is growing a block per week," Ramírez told us in his municipal government office in 2003.

"It's a block per day!" one of his staff members interjected.

The secretary smiled. "The truth is somewhere in between. The city doesn't have the monies to equip all the new colonias with infrastructure, electrification, water, sewer systems. That's something we have to live with." A former manager at Zenith, where he had worked for a number of years, Ramírez noted that, contrary to popular belief, the maquilas do pay a fair amount of taxes. Almost all of the money, though, goes to Mexico City. In the United States, Canada, and other industrialized countries, localities generally keep 30 percent of total tax collections. In Mexico, the figure is closer to 5 percent.[25] The social and infrastructural challenges facing Ramírez dwarfed the tools he and the city government had to address them. María Prieto, then the city's director of industrial development, told us, "Those guys in Mexico City, they don't know how it is in these colonias in Reynosa."[26]

Jorge Cantú Resendez, a developer of federally supported Infonavit housing, told us that the federal government financed 4,000 to 5,000 units a year in Reynosa. Even by INEGI's conservative population growth estimates for 2000 to 2005, the city was growing at over four to five times the rate of these low-income housing starts.[27] Although McAllen-Reynosa, NAFTA's best example, was still growing jobs in the recession of the early 2000s, migration was far outpacing job growth. Jobs streamed in, but people were streaming in faster.[28] Young people were crammed four, five, or more into apartments to save money. Families squatted and pieced together shanties in corn fields at the city's edges. As economist John Sargent put it, people were "voting with their feet" when they trekked to the border, and that lent support to Allen's view. But finding housing and basic services was another matter.

In response to the Mike Allen question, Solís pulled no punches. " 'No' for Mexico," Solís said. " 'Yes' for Mike Allen. Ask him why they don't use all that infrastructure that they are building in Mission [Sharyland Plantation and other Texas-side infrastructure]. Why not here?" When we asked Allen about the infrastructure and social responsibilities of the maquilas, he responded, exasperated, "That's not what they're there for! They're there to provide jobs for people!"

For the bean-counters —as many saw them—who had taken over Maytag under Lloyd Ward and Ralph Hake in the early 2000s, this was an appealing point of view on the nature of responsibility. Decades before Ward and Hake, there had been the $15,000 pipe organ and the $250,000 public swimming pool that F. L. Maytag had donated to Newton. And there had been the time when his grandson, Fred Maytag, insisted on building a new factory within Newton's city limits, so that the company could be taxed to support its hometown. More recently, in Galesburg, there had been Maytag's 8,000-person, all-you-could-eat buffet out at Lake Storey with Schwann's ice cream trucks, fountain drinks, and big giveaways. Workers put their timecards in a big barrel for a shot at TVs, washers and dryers, cash, and prizes at the enormous, union-organized family picnic.[29]

With economic globalization, companies like Maytag had found a way to slough off not only union wages, pension obligations, taxes, and regulations, but also any sense of obligation to the place where they made their money. In Reynosa, Maytag could be practically anonymous in a sea of factories that did nothing to address the urban anarchy their presence had spawned. Solís was well aware of the bygone social contract that bound together American corporations and American localities. "That you don't see in Reynosa."

By the mid-2000s, Reynosa was dotted with hip disco bars, coffee and natural fruit juice cafes, air conditioning-blasted superstores, and American hotel chains. The city seemed simultaneously exhausted and overwhelmed by it explosive growth. Streets were filled with potholes, and uncollected trash littered the streets. In the void of basic services, *carretoneros* (cart drivers) collected much of the city's trash. For 30 or 40 pesos ($3), they pulled their horse- or mule-led wagons—sometimes with their entire families in tow—through neighborhoods to collect trash and then burn it or dump it out of sight. The carretoneros, rumored to be associated with organized crime, lived in dismal conditions on the banks of the city's irrigation river.[30] Their ubiquity on the main roads was a daily reminder that Reynosa was as much a city of slums and desperation as it was a global economic hub. Solís' answer to the Mike Allen question was to tell us to look around. Allen, Solís said, was "the man who causes all of Reynosa's problems, the maquila's main man."

Mexico's cities are filled with pockets of severe poverty and seemingly hopeless disorder. However, Solís was talking about something else—a crisis of near social collapse in a city that could not control its own destiny—and the evidence was everywhere. Like some post-apocalypse film, horses, mules, and chickens grazed in vacant, trash-strewn lots. Children played parentless amongst the rubble. Traffic seemed to clog the city at all hours. The rules of the road were nothing more than loose guidelines. Cars nudged into and through intersections in quick rounds of "chicken." Traffic moved like life here—spontaneous, frantic, and improvised. The same went for Reynosa's street-smart stray dogs, who hustled through the less-crowded streets, sometimes alone and sometimes in packs.

Armando Zertuche, twice Reynosa's director of economic development in the 2000s, offered us a tour of the city in his big SUV in 2003 during his first term. When he was in office, the sharply dressed and dynamic Zertuche began all kinds of projects in tourism, hosting regional meetings and expos, and working with the maquilas. Zertuche recounted Allen saying to him, "Stop, let us help you." When Zertuche declined Allen's "help," he ran into problems. "They go over your head!" Zertuche said. If he protested, Zertuche found himself being attacked in the local media for being "against the maquila industry, against the development of our city."

We asked Zertuche the Mike Allen question. "Yes," he answered. "But be careful with that yes or no question! Was it good that they came, yes. Good that they keep coming, no." Zertuche, a psychologist who consulted for some maquilas, was fascinated by Allen. "Mike Allen is going to be considered one of the greatest men of the last two centuries here in the Valley. He is brilliant, his team is extraordinary. He does his job very, very well and we are doing our job very, very badly. There is no balance."

In short, by the mid-2000s, Mike Allen was winning. His question was no longer even a question. He had people on both sides of the Rio Grande thinking on his terms. Bringing Maytag and the other maquilas to Reynosa was a simple up-down proposition, like a choice between capitalism and socialism. It was black and white. There was an obvious answer. No need to explore the innumerable ways that the market, the state, and civil society interact. No need to over-think, add nuance, or explore a "third way." The question itself was a way to judge his success exclusively in the language of business and economics, in discrete numbers: jobs, the number of factories, and economic growth figures. It was also a way to avoid responsibility for what was happening in Reynosa.

Allen was not the only one evading responsibility. Indeed, all of this was the point of Reynosa's existence. In this paradise of raw global capitalism, after all, the market was the arbiter of resources. The maquilas were simply there to make a buck and provide jobs. The local government evaded responsibility by blaming the federal government for its stinginess. The federal government claimed it could not tax the maquilas more because market forces would push them to China. The unions said they could not push back on the multinationals for the same reason. So everyone saw the mess for which nobody was responsible. Although Adam Smith likely would have been appalled by the lack of public spending, the powerful in McAllen and Reynosa could shrug their shoulders and say that the magic of the invisible hand was at work.

OVERTIME WAS HOW Laura Flora made ends meet each week, and how she racked up points toward an Infonavit home, which would be a huge step up for her family. But all the hours came at a high cost. One cool, early summer morning in 2007, Flora saw a strange man a few houses down. He had a black duffle bag at his feet and was changing his shirt and shoes. Fetid water from a recent rain pooled in the muddy backstreet that ran past her home, leaving only a thin walkway. Flora ignored him as she walked passed him toward her bus stop.

When her *micro* arrived a few minutes later, Flora let it pass and circled back. The man was still sitting there, clearly intoxicated. Drugs, she thought. She went inside and told Laura Suarez, Adrianita, and Erika about the man and warned that they must not open the door for anyone. The front door was weak, though, and vulnerable to a modest kick or shoulder bash. She told them that she had to leave and would not be back until late that evening. With a round of kisses, she said she would call to check on them if she could.

Flora arrived tardy to Planta III that morning. Over her two-and-a-half years there, though, Flora had accumulated some good faith. Her supervisor, who knew she was a single mother, covered for her until she arrived. When Flora explained what had happened that morning, he offered to work her spot on the line until she checked in with her daughters with a phone call.

When Flora returned, the supervisor asked, "Is everything OK?"

"Blessed be to God, it was OK," she responded. Flora then settled in for her 13-hour shift testing for leaks on Maytag's side-by-side refrigerators.

That was just the quandary she was in. Flora had almost no time to watch over her young girls. Sometimes she doubted whether she could get them through school unscathed in this chaotic and anomic city. And these were not idle worries. Predators seemed to lurk everywhere, concealed by the social disorder of her neighborhood.

A month earlier a young man had made an explicit sexual advance to 14-year-old Suarez, who then ran into their home in a panic. Flora raced outside and confronted the man aggressively, as if to make up for the times when she had not been there. "There are so many fucking women in this world," she recalled yelling. "And you come to fuck around with a young girl? You're going to remember me, buddy!" Flora said her husband was a police officer, and the young man left.

"I was terrified because the girls are vulnerable here. But I was enraged as a mother. My daughter is unprotected, she's just a girl. She doesn't really know what a man can do to her. She has to make it to her wedding with her virginity intact. I want them to have a good marriage, a good home. Like little doves, they'll go off and make their own nest."

Flora then looked at Erika, who was leaning against a fence made of discarded factory pallets. Her youngest had been listening with her eyes lowered on the white-faced baby doll in her hands. Erika's sky blue shirt was decorated with butterflies and flowers.

"What would you say if a man came over, and you were alone?" Flora asked her.

" 'No!' Mama," she replied with enthusiasm.

Flora had returned from the United States for the girls—so she could watch over them like a "mother hen" ought to, she said. But now she found herself unable even to do that. Not only was Flora being tugged mercilessly between work and mothering, but so were Laura Suarez and Adrianita. The young teens both cleaned houses in the afternoon and on weekends, leaving Erika to fend for herself. Flora told Erika to yell for the neighbors if there was a problem. The neighbors, she said, are good. They were the only people she trusted.

Flora also felt pulled back to Florida. She had not seen her two older children in years, and she had yet to meet her three American grandchildren. José, her oldest child and only son, was a construction worker near Orlando. "You care more about my younger sisters," he had told her over the phone recently.

"You're full grown," Flora said that she had replied. "If there was a flood, you and your sister [Deysy] could grab on to the branches of a tree and save yourselves, but the three younger ones would be swept away in the current. As a mother I'm always going to take care of the most vulnerable. You and your sister are going to find a way to float, but they would drown." Gone from 6 a.m. to 9 p.m. six days a week some weeks, that was, however, precisely her worry. She was sure she had made the right decision to leave her home in Veracruz—as long as she could keep her three girls from being swept away in a place that had said "yes" to Mike Allen.

10

CHILES, *COYOTES*, AND VANILLA

Volador, Veracruz

Among us there is no single time: all of our times are alive,
all of our pasts are present.

—Mexican novelist Carlos Fuentes[1]

ON THE ROAD to Volador were tree-lined, rocky hills, as well as a fútbol field where a few kids kicked around a ball. A boy on a wobbly-wheeled bicycle navigated the dirt path next to the road, spinning his legs as fast as he could to keep up with our truck.

Just outside of town, a group of ten women and girls were picking *chile piquín* on a steep slope above the road. As Josh and I spoke in English to prepare our questions, the women chattered in rapid-fire Spanish to one another, clearly welcoming the work interruption. They had stopped plucking the tiny red and orange chiles, which they collected in two-liter Coke bottles with the tops cut off. Before we could introduce ourselves, an older woman said in Spanish, "It sounds nice, like what we've heard on soap operas." They said they had seen gringos from time to time in Papantla, the municipal seat, and at the pyramids of nearby El Tajin, the spectacular pre-Colombian archeological site. But they claimed during our trip in 2007 that we were the first gringos to visit tiny Volador.[2]

The rugged but fertile land around Volador was planted with corn, beans, papaya, chiles, bananas, oranges, mangoes, and other crops. It was more difficult land to farm than that of Agua Dulce. Volador was also more isolated, and it had fewer people. The main difference, though, was that Don Beto Cruz, an absentee landlord from Papantla, owned nearly all of the land surrounding the village. There was no ejido here. Locals traded their labor with Cruz for little plots of land to farm. Wage work in the fields earned about $8 a day, but it was irregular, maybe one or two days a week.

Several of the fieldworkers were high school–aged girls earning summer money. Despite the blazing heat, they dressed in jeans or sweatpants and had layers on top to protect against the scratchy fieldwork and the sun. One of the girls wore a white-and-blue shirt that read, "Telesecundaria Mariano Matamoros." The shirt featured a television with a smiley face inside.

A short, older woman of 37 named Lucia said Volador's plight was "unjust" and was fatalistic about the area's prospects. "There's nothing here," she said. "Here everything is hard. It's always the same thing. It's never going to change." Lucia's skin was a deep, sun-drenched brown. She wore a Seattle Mariners cap to shield her eyes. "We always sell low, and they always sell high to us," she said. "They should pay us a good price because we're the ones who are poor! But, no, they just want us to give it away to them."[3]

Lucia had worked in the fields of this semifeudal world since she was ten. She and the others picking chile piquín had not heard of El Tratado de Libre Comercio de América del Norte or TLC. Despite tectonic shifts in Mexican agriculture and vast improvements in technology and efficiency, they remained in practical serfdom, continuing to plant, grow, and harvest chiles on land they rented with their labor-time and fetch the same low prices they always had. When they did wage work, their daily earnings were about the same as they had always been, they said.

Even if Lucia had been given a crash course on the implications of NAFTA for Volador, it wouldn't have changed her fortunes. She had neither the business skills nor the capital to invest in and grow a smallholding. Volador's principal deficit may not have been government support or human or economic capital, but rather social capital of a particular kind. The conventional view, articulated by Robert Putnam in *Bowling Alone*, involves horizontal linkages, in which church groups, block clubs, and close neighborly and reciprocal social relations are indicative of social capital. This kind of social connectedness is empowering and economically beneficial. "Inequality and social solidarity," Putnam argues, "are deeply incompatible."[4] Volador, population 2,343, had the hallmarks of a tightly knit, hard-working village with abundant social capital.[5] Old and young alike, along with a few stray dogs, gathered in the tree-shaded public square to mingle on the hot day. They traded homemade mole for tamales and looked after each other's children. Every

August there was a big festival when migrants would return from afar to celebrate their hometown and reconnect with their families and friends.

Although people in Volador had strong horizontal linkages, their social connections did not extend vertically far beyond the village. If local connections between people were all that mattered, political scientist Jonathan Fox writes, ". . . then many of Mexico's poorest regions would be considered to have large stocks of social capital." Rather, in isolated places like Volador, "dense concentrations of social capital may well be highly segmented . . . and lack the clout to offset concentrated elite power."[6] This was Lucia's and Volador's problem.

Christy Getz, an expert at the University of California, Berkeley, in community development, argues that the smallholders of rural Mexico could not shift to changing market signals because they did not have market information or the extralocal market connections. The vast majority, Getz writes, have "neither the resources nor experience to diversify on their own, much less connect to global markets." According to a report about Veracruz, the state government has invested some in crop diversification and in programs to facilitate contract production of crops, but "most farmers in the state remain outside export channels." The result, then, is that large landowners and savvy *coyotes* (meaning, in this context, market middlemen) grab the new opportunities.[7]

Mayor Gonzalez had said the same thing about Agua Dulce, which had the advantage of being closer to the two cities of the region, Papantla and Poza Rica. "Whatever the farmers do, the intermediaries eat them up," Gonzalez said. "Farmers have to pay the coyote's price." Some ejidos and farmer groups across Veracruz developed cooperatives to increase bargaining power, but they still faced disadvantages in the global marketplace. Gonzalez gave the example of *chile seco*, which sold in Monterrey for ten times what it did in Agua Dulce. The coyotes, the link of both Agua Dulce and Volador to regional and global markets, pocketed the difference.

LUCIA TOLD US that her older son, with no hope for ejidal land and seeing no future in Volador, had migrated to Reynosa that January. He worked in a maquila there, though Lucia wasn't sure which one. They talk once a week. Her younger son attended the *telesecundaria*. Despite her pessimism, Lucia's spunkiness suggested she would have been up for a good fight if she had a chance. As we left, she joked, "You could be our coyotes [here referring to a migrant smuggler]!" A second later she added with a laugh, "Eh, *la migra* would just kill us." Lucia added she would never go to Reynosa. Her husband was dead set against it. Despite endemic poverty, some simply wanted to stay, especially those in their middle and later years. Volador is nestled among verdant green hills and tropical trees. Locals were friendly, close-knit, and crime wasn't a concern. The pace of life was calm and peaceful.

It was getting harder to stay, though. In town we met Aaron Barrera, the plump and amiable PRD (the leftist Partido de la Revolución Democrática) mayor of Volador. He sat behind a bulky typewriter at an empty steel desk in the otherwise vacant administration building. "Oranges and papayas sell for 50 centavos [$.05] a kilo," he said. "Imagine that! A few years ago orange prices were so low that farmers didn't even bother to harvest them." At that price, fieldworkers in the area were making less than a U.S. penny per pound during the labor-intensive harvest. "The coyotes are the ones screwing it up around here," he said, echoing his colleague in Agua Dulce. "They're scavengers." With low prices for their only local exports, fruits and vegetables, how was it that people made ends meet in Volador, we asked. "They leave," the mayor said without hesitation.

A month earlier, in June 2007, after spring graduation, over a hundred young people had left. It turned out Volador's most valuable export was its young people. "These are the best-educated young people we have," said the mayor, sadly. "Those are the ones that go." Emigration of *prepa* graduates had become a yearly rite of passage. Barrera said some went to Mexico City, Monterrey, or New York City. But most had been going to Reynosa. "In Reynosa younger people can find work more easily compared to Mexico City. Legal work." Some went to work in the factories, some went to study, and some went to Reynosa to earn money for the second leg of their trip into the United States. He said brothers, sisters, aunts, and high school friends helped newcomers navigate the disorienting entrance into border life. Sociologists call this targeted and self-perpetuating social process "chain migration." And what a stunning adaption it was. In the absence of land, regular work, and equitable connections to outside markets, Volador's youth managed to make their own connections to families, friends, and jobs all across North America.

Barrera led us up a steep hill on one of Volador's rocky streets. We passed a small store selling bottled *refrescos*, water, and bagged snacks. Inside a fan buzzed, and music played. A family opened the tiny store, Barrera told us, with remittance money from their son. At the top of the rocky road, there was a pair of donkeys under a tree, standing motionlessly beside a sleeping dog. Across the street, perched above everything, was the town's largest building, a sky blue church.

Barrera took us out of the blazing sun and inside a health clinic near the church. A physician's examination chair sat in the middle of the room next to an open window. On the concrete floor were spots of blood. The mayor introduced us to Elba Cortez Rosas, 38, who worked part-time at the clinic. Cortez's husband had been estranged from the family since he left for Mexico City to find work in 1994. She lived with her husband's parents and made large batches of bread, mole, and tamales to sell in town. Her husband, whom she saw every few years, had promised that he would one day take her to Mexico City. Both of Cortez's sons worked in Reynosa.

"Three weeks ago my youngest left," Cortez said. "I said to him, 'You're my youngest, you're my baby. I don't want you to go.' He said, 'Mom, I'm a man now. I want to meet my responsibilities myself.'" The afternoon heat inundated the little clinic. Cortez, though, gesticulated energetically in a bright turquoise dress as she spoke.

Cortez, who had never left Volador, said that she did not plan to visit her sons up north. She had never heard of Maytag or TLC, but was pleased her sons were there. Reynosa migrants were more likely than others to return for the annual festival, and they were more likely to conform to community norms than those returning from Mexico City or the United States. Mayor Barrera confirmed her assessment. "Those who return from Reynosa are more educated and disciplined because Reynosa is a very rigorous place, but it's better than Mexico City. There are a lot of lost youth from both places, but especially from Mexico City because of drugs." They said Reynosa was the most popular destination for young migrants because of its reputation for abundant low-skill jobs and a lot of overtime. Cortez said her youngest, Lázaro, worked in the maquila from 7 a.m. to 4 p.m. and then took classes and studied from 5 p.m. to 11 p.m. "I always told him that in order to get ahead, high school is not enough," Cortez said. Still, she worried. Border newcomers were sometimes preyed upon by unscrupulous coyotes, labor agents, and maquila operators.[8] Maquila subcontractors, said Mayor Barrera, sometimes even sent empty buses to towns like Volador to recruit young workers directly. Preying upon the hope for a better life, they offered transportation to Reynosa, vague housing promises, and sketchy employment contracts.

As Cortez reflected on her life and her fragmented family, she underscored the problem of land. "It's not like it once was. Nobody has their own land here anymore. That's why my husband left."

A CENTURY AND a half ago, this area of northern Veracruz was sparsely settled with independent Totonac farmers. Subsistence farmers tended communally owned *milpas* (fields) of maize, beans, chiles, and vanilla and gathered beeswax, rubber, fruits, nuts, roots, fibers, and flowers from the rainforest to eat, use, and trade.[9] Papantla's earliest chronicler, Juan de Carrión, wrote in 1581 that in the lush, tropical area, "Foods grow in such abundance that there are not enough people to enjoy and eat them, and so the birds eat them." Without mines or geography conducive to agricultural or livestock *haciendas* (large estates), the area had remained largely untouched by Spanish colonizers.[10]

Trade in vanilla, begun modestly in the 1700s, exploded in the last quarter of the 1800s as the first wave of economic globalization hit Papantla, ushered in by advances in transportation and communications. After the American Civil War, steamships connected the city of Veracruz—a major port along the southwesternmost shores of the Gulf of Mexico—to New York with biweekly voyages. Farther north, the port of Tuxpan, a full day's ride from Papantla by mule train, connected directly to the United States as well. A local telegraph line linked Papantla to Tuxpan, Veracruz, Mexico City, and even New York, ending the area's historic isolation, at least for merchants and leaders in town. The international vanilla trade blossomed, and the Papantla region shifted away from low-volume exports to France's gourmet culinary market. Papantla increasingly fed mass production in the budding ice cream and confectionary industries in the United States.[11]

Decades earlier, in 1826, just after Mexican independence, the Veracruz state congress had mandated the elimination of collective landholdings. The legislation, along with Article 27 in the Constitution of 1857, was inspired by the republican idea that individual private property was the foundation of citizenship, liberty, and social progress. Liberals of the time rejected the idea of communal property relations as part of Mexico's inherited "Indian problem." However, it was not until the international vanilla boom of the late 19th century that the notion of private property came to Papantla, according to Emilio Kourí, a preeminent historian of Mexico and of the area.[12]

The booming export economy created a handful of propertied Euro-Mexican merchants and Totonac elites in town, Totonac *rancheros* (local leaders and prosperous farmers), small-scale, but propertied Totonac farmers, and a bulging stratum of the propertyless. About half of the resident Totonacs were displaced from their land, forced to rent land or work as *jornaleros* (day laborers), ranch hands, or tenant farmers—sometimes on the same land they once owned. A rebellion simmered and erupted in the 1890s, leading Mexico's long-time authoritarian president, General Porfirio Díaz, to send federal troops, heavy artillery, and warships to Papantla. After much bloodshed, public executions, and reports of torture and piles of skulls scattered across the countryside, the rebellion was crushed.

Papantla had had its revolution. Now the whole of Mexico was on the verge of its unraveling. During the *Porfiriato* of 1877–1910, Porfirio Díaz had for over thirty years pushed export-led economic growth, foreign investment and trade, industrialization, the consolidation of land into haciendas, and Mexico's first era of assertive integration with the United States. According to historian John Mason Hart, Díaz came to power in 1877 supported by "Texas landholders, New York bankers, railroad tycoons, the state and national print media, U.S. congressmen and senators, officers of the Texas state government, and U.S. Army officers." U.S. interests supported Díaz with money, weapons, and even armed fighters, as Díaz aggressively pushed U.S. land purchases and railroad building in the north and increased trade and investment.[13]

During Díaz's 33-year rule, the U.S. and Mexican economies became intertwined. Trade between the United States and Mexico grew from $15 million in 1880 to $166 million at the dawn of the revolution in 1910. That year Americans bought 76 percent of Mexico's exports and 57 percent of Mexico's imports were from the United States.[14] Foreign interests, mostly American, controlled nine out of ten of the largest businesses in Mexico. Large U.S. companies and wealthy individuals owned over 100 million acres in Mexico. American investment in agriculture in Mexico exceeded $200 million.[15]

At the end of the Porfiriato, the staggering inequities had reached a breaking point. Indigenous communities had lost 90 percent of their land, and 57 percent of Mexico was controlled by fewer than 11,000 haciendas. Still an overwhelmingly rural country, four of five Mexicans depended on the land for survival, but only four in 100 owned land. Emiliano Zapata rallied the disenfranchised for "tierra y libertad" (land and liberty) in the south; in northern

Mexico, Pancho Villa confiscated land from *hacendados* (owners of haciendas) during a bloody decade of revolutionary strife. U.S.-owned haciendas
were initially spared by the revolutionaries, who relied on American support
and were mindful of how they were represented in the U.S. press. After 1915,
however, Villa clashed with U.S. forces, and relations soured, almost leading
to war. Subsequently, although American land in Mexico was not confiscated,
it went unprotected and highly taxed. It was the end of prosperity for U.S.
landowners in Mexico.[16]

The Mexican Revolution ended the hacienda. Agrarian reform sought a
return to the indigenous Mexican ideal of land as social property, the ejido.
Land reform, especially in the 1930s under Lázaro Cárdenas—called Mexico's
FDR by some—allowed many indigenous and dispossessed campesinos to
reclaim their traditional rights to the land.[17] Ejidos eventually covered 52 percent of Mexican territory, and 70 percent of forested area.[18] For most of the
20th century, Mexico turned inward, emphasizing rapid modernization, protection of domestic industries, and resistance to integration with the United
States. From the 1940s through the 1960s, the "Mexican Miracle" produced
rapid growth and the development of a middle class under an import-sub-
stitution model. The Partido Revolucionario Institucional (PRI) monopo-
lized power and ruled through clientelist relations with business, labor, and
campesino groups. In the 1970s, however, the Mexican economy ran into a
serious crisis due to fiscal imprudence and the 1973 oil shock, setting the stage
for the neoliberal policy regime that reopened Mexico to the United States
and the world.

President Miguel de la Madrid ushered in sweeping economic reforms in
the 1980s. Like Carlos Salinas de Gotari and Ernesto Zedillo who followed
him, de la Madrid, who had a master's in public administration from Harvard,
was a new sort of PRI leader, a budget-minded technocrat. From the 1980s
on, Mexico turned toward privatization, deregulation, lowered social spending and supports, and unrestricted trade. These shifts were heavily influenced
by the International Monetary Fund (IMF), the World Bank, and the U.S.
Treasury—the Washington Consensus—which steered de la Madrid toward
far-reaching reforms. The de la Madrid administration joined the General
Agreement on Tariffs and Trade (replaced by the World Trade Organization
in 1995) in 1986, sold off state-owned or partially state-owned enterprises, and
reduced tariffs and protections.[19]

With Mexicans divided over laissez-faire capitalism, Mexico's next president, Carlos Salinas de Gotari, with a Ph.D. in economics from Harvard, pushed further shock tactics to restructure Mexican agriculture as he vigorously pursued NAFTA.[20] In Salinas' eyes, NAFTA was the key to unleashing a modern, global Mexico. But to enter the trade agreement, Salinas, still facing pressure from the United States and the World Bank like his predecessor, needed to reverse the agrarian reform of the revolution and move again toward privatization of land. In the 1992 land reforms, Article 27 in the Mexican Constitution was changed again to allow for selling and renting of ejidal land. Technocrats pushing the reform predicted that the titling of land to individuals would provide access to private credit and create a dynamic land market. A dynamic land market would also lead to increased agricultural productivity as inefficient farmers sold to large, more efficient ones.[21] Discarding the revolutionary framework, wherein "land was a social right and not a commodity," land redistribution was off the national agenda. Reflecting a new market-oriented understanding of *tierra y libertad*, the new land regime "redefined liberty as the freedom to compete in land and commodity markets with less government regulation."[22]

The free market ruled in Volador, as it had in the Papantla region a century and a half earlier in Mexico's first embrace of laissez-faire. One man had gobbled up most of the property worth owning, and the coyotes controlled the distribution channels and local prices. Urban technocrats had tilted policy in favor of large farms over small ones, food trade over food sovereignty, and commodity crops over investments in diverse crops and subsistence farming. A century after the radical liberalism of the Porfiriato, the prognosis was again bright for large-scale corporate farms, land speculators, agricultural market makers, and absentee landowners. Indeed Lucia and the *chile piquín* harvesters in 2007 were not altogether different from the *jornaleros* and land-renters working the fields in the 1890s, aside from the Mariners cap and the two-liter Coke bottles.

"There are a lot of people here losing their property," Mayor Barrera said. Ejido-based communities like Agua Dulce have more bargaining power and market reach for their crops, he explained. It was difficult in Agua Dulce, too, but land-owning families were more rooted, more attached to their hometowns in fertile northern Veracruz. "We rent from Don Beto Cruz," the Volador mayor continued. "He requires you to work two days a week in his fields. If you don't, he will confiscate your crops and not let you back on the land you've rented. We wish things were ejido around here. If it were, things would be different."

ON THE RIDE out of Volador we picked up a woman and her ten-year-old daughter. She was in the middle of a hot, hour-long walk to meet her husband, a bricklayer, for lunch. "I have a daughter studying computers in Poza Rica, and she is about to graduate," the woman said. She spoke quietly as we bounced down a hill in the bed of a small pickup. She and her husband were landless like Lucia and the Cortez family. "I'd like her to find something close, because moving away is an investment as well, and there are risks. I don't want to send her [to Reynosa], but that is, more or less, where they use computers. The truth is, they're also girls. And as parents it seems very far away, and you feel for your children when they are far. And there have been a lot of examples of girls who have gone and messed up. Young women can make mistakes in Reynosa. There are vices there."

11

FROGS, MULES, AND LIFE AFTER MAYTAG

Galesburg, Illinois

> Justice . . . does not allow that the sacrifices imposed on a few are outweighed
> by the larger sum of advantages enjoyed by many . . . in a just society
> the liberties of equal citizenship are taken as settled.
>
> —John Rawls, *A Theory of Justice*, 1971

IT WAS A cold evening in early December 2006, and Tracy Warner had just returned home from Willits Primary School. Ryan had just sung in the "Winter Wonderland" musical there. Christmas lights dotted F Street, adding some warmth to her modest block in the heart of Monmouth, Illinois.

She looked like a new woman, and, judging by her smile, she knew it. The jeans and T-shirt—the uniform of the anxious, soon-to-be-unemployed line worker and picketer of a couple years earlier—had been replaced by a red V-neck sweater, silk blouse, and an aura of confidence. She was wrapping up four fall semester classes and a journalism internship at the school's newspaper, the *Western Courier*. She had done this while raising Ryan and frantically looking for a job. She was set to graduate on the following Saturday from Western Illinois University. The dream Warner had dreamt a thousand times while piecing together refrigerator doors on the Maytag line for over fifteen years was coming true.

"Look at this," she said, handing me an essay. "It's a paper on Rawls' theory of justice. He said that we have to stand behind a veil of ignorance to make fair decisions."

Her reference fit the moment. John Rawls' 1971 *Theory of Justice* poses a hypothetical world in which all societal roles are shuffled behind a metaphorical "veil of ignorance." Behind this veil, one does not know to what role he or she will be assigned in the new social order. It is only from there, Rawls argues, can one truly judge the fairness of various social roles and relations. The CEO, for instance, would have to experience the lives of workers he put out of work.

Warner still saw Ralph Hake as a great villain—and it was not just because of the factory closing and the gutting of her working life as well as the working lives of her friends and co-workers. Warner had embraced the changes as best she could, and she and Ryan would find a way to survive. What still stung, like fiberglass wedged under a fingernail, was the injustice of it all.

Earlier that year—Friday, March 31, 2006, to be specific—Whirlpool had acquired Maytag, with the blessings of anti-trust regulators. On the following Monday, Hake resigned, triggering a change-of-employment clause in his contract that netted him a golden parachute worth between $10 and $20 million plus millions more in Whirlpool stock. (Two months earlier—before the severance payout—an executive compensation expert had called Hake the "poster child for what's wrong with CEO pay.") The fact that Hake's former employer had bought Maytag at a favorable price raised eyebrows—and some full-blown conspiracy theories—in Newton and Galesburg. With Maytag in its pocket, Whirlpool became the biggest appliance company in the world, with, in recent years, revenues approaching $20 billion and nearly 70,000 employees. In his resignation statement, Hake sounded as if he was heading to the next item on his bucket list. "I have many things I still want to pursue and accomplish in life," it read.[1]

The bad news kept coming for workers. On May 10, 2006, Whirlpool announced that it would shut down Newton—both Maytag headquarters and the laundry plants that had been the foundation of the company for most of its remarkable 113-year run. Whirlpool also announced the closing of the washer and dryer plants in Herrin, Illinois, and Searcy, Arkansas, eliminating a total of 3,000 jobs, most of them union. In July, the investment manager's lawsuit against Hake for misleading investors in 2005, and which sought class-action status, was dismissed.[2] Maytag, as anyone cared to remember it, was gone, another nearly meaningless brand name in Whirlpool's extensive list. There was no way for customers, shareholders, or workers to hold Hake, or anyone else, to account.

In fact, after the unrelenting ineptitude that led to Maytag's death—for that's how people like Tracy Warner viewed it—the end proved bitterly ironic. As difficult as the appliance business had been for Maytag, one man was to blame for Maytag's unraveling, and, in the end, that one man was the person who benefited the most.[3] Maytag had become an example not only of how income inequality continued to grow, but also—and this is what enraged Warner and other workers the most—of how a system of performance and workplace reward had lost any semblance of fairness.

This still angered Warner, but at least she had Rawls and this class, "Ethics and Journalism," to put it in perspective. Her classes not only gave her a place to reflect on what had happened, but also a window into a new life. Beyond the excitement of graduating with a BA in a few days, Warner felt like a new woman. She saw the world and her place in it differently, more clearly. She was alive with hope about what lay ahead and was excited to tell me.

After an awkward start at Western, Warner became the go-to person in her classes in her second year. "It was fun to have cute twenty-year-old guys texting me for help. I sort of shocked myself in college. I couldn't cut, copy, and paste when I came to school, but now I'm running T-tests in SPSS [statistical software] in my research class and writing ten- and twenty-page research papers."

In college, Warner could assert control on her life circumstances and that was deeply reassuring. Success was measured with the definitive clarity of grades. She knew that even an outstanding GPA would not give her an upper hand in the rural labor market, but she obsessed over grades nonetheless. They assessed more than academic performance. To Warner, each grade was a judgment as to whether she was smart enough, persistent enough, and nimble enough to make it in this new economy, one that demanded her mind and not her hands.

She thought she could do better than the C averages from her high school and community college days. That legacy and the passing of time, though, had left big doubts in her mind—doubts that had driven her compulsively through each semester.

Warner recounted stories from the past two years. During a recent group project, one student in her trio left early to visit her family for the Thanksgiving holiday. The other, a young veteran of the Iraq war, went on a hunting trip. The assignment was to examine research on the relationship between violence in the media and violent crimes. She did the entire assignment by herself and got an A for the group.

In the end, Warner pulled a 3.6 grade point average. In an awards ceremony earlier that week, Warner had been presented with the $500 Wayne

Thompson Undergraduate Scholarship Award. A journalism professor of hers approached her at the ceremony. "When I first met you, you had a long haul," Warner recalled him as saying. "But you made it."

If only real life were as straightforward as college, Warner thought: work hard and get rewarded. These younger kids at Western did not see what was in store for them. They would see soon enough that in the real world the link between hard work and reward had come undone.

Focused on school, Warner had drifted away from some of her friends in Monmouth. They were not interested in talking about computer programs, survey design, or the "worldly professors" in Macomb, Illinois. She felt she had to hold her tongue not to convey an air of superiority. Her sister had only an associate's degree in child care that now compared unfavorably against her two siblings' bachelor's degrees. Warner said that this weighed on her sister. Her Maytag friendships waning, Warner began spending more time on MySpace and Facebook.

The following week Warner would join her former co-workers, many of whom were still bouncing around like lottery balls in this thing that was called "the transition," waiting anxiously to be vacuumed into a slot. Like the others, Warner wanted to work again, to be useful, needed, and secure. Her degree, she hoped, was her ladder back up into the middle class. Despite Warner's newfound glow, the impending reality of her post-college life was all too real. In the preceding month, Warner had scattered a resume, which read "Bachelor of Arts, expected December 2006," all around Galesburg and Monmouth. She was not choosy, applying at the local copying place, a Sherwin Williams paint store, a car dealership, Hibbett Sports at the mall, Pizza Hut, ShopKo, Sears, J. C. Penny, and *The Register-Mail*.

In fact, earlier that wintery day Warner had interviewed with *The Register-Mail*'s editors. Being a local journalist had always been her deepest aspiration, and the memory of sending a clunky cover letter to the newspaper without a resume embarrassed her. This time, she nearly had her degree in communications with a minor in journalism in hand, and with honors. She hoped for some good news soon.

Warner would receive her last biweekly $794 unemployment check on graduation day and then have to take the first job she was offered to make ends meet, at least for the time being. At Maytag, Warner had grossed about $1,380 every two weeks, earning about $15 an hour. After federal, state, and payroll taxes, union dues, a savings deduction that went to her local credit union, and a small outlay for the Christmas Club, she used to bring home a $1,000 two-week paycheck, about $26,000 per year. Like most former Maytag assemblers, Warner's income two-plus years out was about 50 percent to 80 percent of her former Maytag income. And for those two-plus years, knock on wood, she had managed to get by without health insurance.

It was a tight squeeze for Warner; there was simply no way she could have pursued her dream without help. At Western, Trade Adjustment Assistance covered all of her educational expenses: tuition, books, school supplies, and mileage. Five days a week Warner made the 64-mile round trip to Macomb in her 2001 Chevy Malibu, at a cost of about 48 cents a mile. Along with the additional year of unemployment benefits, TAA covered $7 of her $18 daily child-care bill. The reimbursements for travel and child care sometimes took time to obtain and often came late, but she was grateful. She had paid into the system for more than fifteen years at Maytag, yet she nonetheless felt ambivalent, and sometimes downright guilty, about the aid. The bottom line, though, was that the safety net had been indispensable for Warner. It had helped one determined factory worker reinvent herself as a budding professional.

Warner's brother, a pharmaceutical salesman who was doing well, had been the first in their family to graduate college, and Warner would be the second. Warner was among just a handful from the factory who would complete a bachelor's degree in the transition. With her unemployment running out that Saturday, with as yet no clear job leads and without health insurance, Warner was still beaming. She had done her part. Now it was time to see if her liberal arts gamble would pay off.

A FEW DAYS later Annette Dennison, on the other side of Monmouth, was wrapping up her second-to-last semester in the Sandburg radiology program. She had started a year and a half earlier, in May 2005, after finishing her associate's degree while still working at Maytag. Like many displaced workers, she had played the odds, rushing headlong into health care, which everyone declared the profession of the future. But now she was concerned that the field had become too saturated. "People need to retire!" she said. She would hit the job market in six months.

With their income halved and credit card balances growing, the Dennisons were taking the long view. But it was risky, and it was not at all clear that they would keep their Monmouth home through the transition. Following Doug's layoff in 2005, a patchwork of federal and state programs had helped to sustain them, just as they had for Warner.

The Dennisons kept their Maytag health insurance for four months after Doug left Maytag. After that, though, the COBRA payment would have been $800 or $900 per month and few displaced workers extended their health insurance this way; it was simply too expensive. Instead they were forced to roll the dice. Fortunately, because Annette's second year of unemployment benefits did not count as income, the Dennisons were eligible for KidCare, an Illinois program developed in conjunction with the State Child Health Insurance Program. At least for the moment, Doug, Annette, Dylan, and Dalton all had a Medicaid card, part of a dramatic trend locally for the public health assistance program. As private-employer insurance waned, Medicaid enrollment rates in Knox County—rates that had sat unchanged in the 1980s and 1990s—nearly doubled from 11 percent to 20 percent in 2009, the year of the explosive Obamacare debates.[4]

Like Warner, the Dennisons appreciated the federal and state benefits, but it all seemed to treat the symptom rather than the cause of the problems for ex-Maytag workers. "Sure, they've earned these benefits," Doug said. "They've busted their tails at these jobs. Had we not had the free trade agreements and all that crap, though, none of this would have been necessary."

Annette was taking everything offered to her though. She was reaching for one of the few ladders up in the area; radiology, she believed, was not the kind of profession that could be shipped overseas. Health care was expanding to meet the needs of aging Baby Boomers and a population that was living longer and longer. She had thrown herself into her reinvention and was not about to look back.

The program had been both exhausting and exhilarating. She had pushed through physics, anatomy, and lab classes for two long days each week. Three or four of the other days, she did eight-hour clinical rotations—without pay—at area hospitals in Galesburg, Monmouth, Geneseo, Canton, and Aledo. On weekends she worked at the Methodist Medical Center of Illinois in Peoria, a 50-minute drive away. As she had in her last two years at Maytag, Annette worked virtually every day and hit the books for two to three hours after she and Doug fed their two boys and sent them to bed. "I study whenever I can kick everyone out," she said.

Although reluctant to complain, Annette was taxed by her schedule and uneasy about her age and her competitiveness when the retraining ended. "It's exhausting. I'm getting old, and my body is falling apart. It's still physical like the factory with moving patients and all, but it's mental and emotional, too. Most people want to hire younger people. So we'll see how it goes." Annette was 39-years-old.

Even though Annette had always wanted out of the factory, life outside seemed like a relentless strain. When she added the weekend job at Methodist in Peoria, though, she brought her income near her old Maytag wage. With TAA's extra year of unemployment benefits, her weekend hospital pay, and TAA's reimbursements for mileage and school supplies, Annette had pieced together a workable transition wage. "They even pay for my work scrubs."

But with the credit cards, the mortgage, the boys' college in a few years, and a lost pension, she felt the need to earn more. "I was half-way to my retirement," she said. This was a thought that a number of former Appliance City workers found themselves revisiting, despite its futility.

The Dennisons had cut back on expenses. Annette's car had 157,000 miles on it. They almost never went on vacations. They held off on remodeling a bathroom. Doug quit smoking, though that strategy apparently did little to help their budget. "What he's saved on cigarettes, he's eaten instead," Annette said, ribbing her smiling husband about the extra pounds he started to carry since leaving the factory.

Finally they realized they did not need to cut back on expenses as much as they thought. Doug was working, too, administering a five-year federal education grant at Westmer Junior and Senior High School, about a 40-minute drive north of Monmouth. The job was time-limited, but he was earning about $15 an hour, just less than what he earned at Maytag.

"We're the fortunate ones, very much. But it hasn't come easy," Doug said. "She's worked her tail off at it, and I'm proud of her. She's a grouch sometimes, but she deserves to be. There isn't anything that this gal can't do. If you tell her she can't do it, she's going to prove you wrong."

Annette laughed. "I'm lucky to get four or five hours of sleep. Before I went back to school I was getting seven or eight. I'm exhausted. I can't wait to have a couple of weeks off. It's just draining. School, clinicals, working, kids."

"In the past when you would have driven up in December, the outside of the house would have been lit up," Doug said. "The inside of the house would have been lit up. The Christmas tree would be out."

"Yeah, the tree isn't up," Annette said. "I don't have anything out yet. I don't have time."

Despite less time for her boys, sleep, and her Christmas rituals, Annette brightened when she talked about her new line of work. "I feel like in my work now, I'm helping people. At Maytag I wasn't helping people. Now I see people daily that need help: newborn babies, people dying of cancer. It's awesome to help those people."

WHILE TRACY WARNER and Annette Dennison pushed relentlessly toward getting their degrees, others took a different route. George Carney wanted nothing to do with school. He fretted over his two 20-something boys, Eric and Brandon, getting enough education to make it in a new economy, but was utterly uninterested in his own. He was part of the 70 percent of workers at the plant who could only claim a high school diploma on their resume.[5] Many had not done well in school. At 35, 45, or 55, laid-off workers like Carney felt that more schooling would be either impractical—too late in life to do much good—or simply not for them.

"Not everybody is cut out for college. Not everybody's going to be cut out for higher learning. I never liked school when I was in it." On his Facebook page, Carney listed his college as "Drove past one once" University, Class of 2000.

Carney knew that if he did not choose retraining within a year of his layoff, his window for TAA funding would close for good—and so would his chance at a second year of unemployment benefits. It was, realistically, his last chance to further his education. But was it worth it? One year of community college yielded a 4 percent to 8 percent income boost for older men, studies showed.[6]

Carney did not need studies to tell him that the gains of further education were modest and uneven. And approaching 50, he doubted all the talk of "reinvention." Frankly, he said, he did not want to change. He was a blue-collar worker and not ashamed of it. And the thought of sitting in a classroom, 25 years after his mediocre stint at Winola High School in Viola, Illinois, was entirely unappealing. There was pride in his rejection of more education, but there was also a complicated mix of fear and doubt—both about his ability to make it in the new economy and about the value of retraining. Whatever its source, it kept Carney from seriously considering a return.

Besides which, he liked his bar. Here was his chance at trying to make it as an independent small businessman. That was what he loved about America: the chance to make it on your own. "I like my freedom, not being told what I have to do. That's what America is all about," Carney said, "Trying to do things for yourself, trying to better yourself." He did not want to be told what classes to take or what new fields to pursue. He did not need to have his anger defused or his expectations lowered. This "housebreaking," as it was called by some in the retraining business, was, after all, the first order of business in any retraining regimen.[7] For Carney, then, it was also a principled, even defiant choice to cut his own path through the thicket ahead.

In 2006 and 2007 Carney continued to get by financially at the Town Tavern in Avon. Despite his somewhat menacing appearance, Carney turned out to be an engaging host at the bar, known for his charmingly irreverent intensity. It drew in plenty of people. The Town Tavern brought in $12,000 in a good month. Monthly revenues paid for the mortgage, insurance, utilities, sales tax, staff wages, and lots of beer and liquor. Carney still did not take a paycheck and continued to sleep in the apartment upstairs. He paid most of his expenses through the bar. "I have my own little economy," he explained with a laugh.

Without a 60- or 70-hour workweek at Maytag to occupy his mind and hands, though, Carney "got lazy," as he confessed, and felt a profound loss of structure to his daily life. He would stay up late drinking and then sleep until noon. He became preoccupied with the finances, staffing, and inventory of the bar, even while on vacation, which drove his girlfriend, Lynn, crazy. For extra money, but mostly so Lynn could get him out of the bar, Carney cleared snow and read meters for the City of Avon for $7.80 an hour. He never cleared enough to afford health insurance. As time passed, this concerned him more and more. The lower back pain that had started at Maytag had not gone away. He was still unable to carry kegs up the basement stairs without throwing his back out. Carney started to question whether being a proprietor-customer at the Town Tavern had been the best choice for the long run after all.

IN THIS CARNEY was not alone. Nearly half of the former refrigerator makers chose not to retrain after the layoffs. Men opted out at a much higher rate.[8] According to the 2010 Maytag Employees in Transition survey, which was undertaken by journalism professor Marilyn Webb and other researchers at Knox College, 58 percent of women retrained, compared with 45 percent of men.[9] Of 902 laid-off line workers, men enrolled at Carl Sandburg College—the closest and most likely choice for retraining—at only half the rate of women.[10] When laid-off men did retrain, more often than women they aimed elsewhere for a specific skill with an immediate payoff, such as certification programs for a Commercial Driver's License (CDL), HVAC maintenance, or welding. On average, men seemed less interested in "inventing" their futures, the survey suggested, than women like Annette Dennison and Tracy Warner.[11] There were exceptions, of course, but men typically sought the shortest path to a decent job, and the shorter the better.

Some men, and women, did well with this strategy. One of them was Mark Semande. In June 2006, before Dennison and Warner had even finished school, Semande had already completed the two years necessary at the BNSF Railway Company to bump up to full pay, about $20 an hour. Semande was a grinder operator for BNSF. He teamed with a welder to repair "frogs"—those slender but crucial little triangles of magnesium steel that guide a train onto another track. He did this work all across the expansive BNSF rail network throughout western Illinois. The railroad giant was expanding both at its massive Galesburg hub, the second largest in their system, and nationally, partly because of increased trade with China.

"I'm not a real religious man," said Semande, "but maybe the Lord gave me this job." Divinely influenced or not, Semande's timing and planning were impeccable in a pinch. With two young daughters at home and a wife, Christy, in graduate school for library science, he did not consider retraining for even a moment. "I would just work at McDonald's or Kmart or Walmart. I mean, I'm *going* to have a job."

Because he lived 25 miles south of Galesburg, Semande did not consider John Deere in Moline or Caterpillar in Peoria, two of the largest employers in the area. Instead he regularly scanned the railroad's hiring announcements like a prairie hawk. Because they were unsure whether he would keep his Maytag job, though, Mark and his family bought full family health insurance through Christy's work during open enrollment. Combined with Maytag's health insurance premium increase, their family health insurance costs jumped from $120 to $730 per month. That was a big chunk of what Semande had grossed at Maytag, about $2,500 a month. The Semandes cut their expenses to the bone.

In January 2004 BNSF posted an announcement and Semande pounced.
He applied online, got the job, and started work on June 1. After a weeklong
video crash course on railroads—featuring "hazmat" (hazardous material)
handling, explanations of how frogs worked, rail composition and mechanics,
use of a spike maul and other railroad-specific tools—he got his real training
under the sun, mending and hammering rail ties and earning a dollar or so
more than his Maytag wage.

That summer, on four days a week, Semande worked with a railroad-tie
gang on ten-hour shifts a few hours to the north in Wisconsin. The other
three days Semande worked at Maytag, crating refrigerators in the back of
the factory. To join the railroad union, Semande needed sixty days at the
railroad. Accounting for missed days and the vacation days he had stored at
Maytag—which he took on the days he skipped work to be in Wisconsin—
he knew he would be fired on August 3 under the new attendance policy. But
that would get him to sixty-four days, just enough to have a union job with
the railroad. His Maytag co-workers thought he was crazy. Leaving Maytag
early meant a lost severance, which Local 2063 had negotiated to one week
of pay for every year of service—about $6,500 for Semande, an eleven-year
veteran of the plant.

It was a grueling summer for both Mark and his wife, but their plan
worked. In August, Semande was fired from Maytag, six weeks short of his
layoff date. He lost a good-sized severance check, but gained one of the best
jobs around. In 2006 and 2007, the Semandes still lived in their modest but
comfortable country home outside London Mills, Illinois. And with Christy
now the district librarian for five schools in nearby Canton, they could afford
to turn their cable back on and take yearly trips with the kids to places like the
Grand Canyon and Disney World.

Semande thinks that he might have been the first Maytag casualty hired
by BNSF. Other men—and it was mostly men—followed. Aaron Kemp, the
former safety standards representative for Local 2063, was hired in April 2006
at $16 an hour to work in either tie gangs or steel gangs—forty-member crews
who mend and lay rail all over the country. Kemp endured a four-month layoff
in his first year and had to travel far and wide to make the money. In his first
six years at BNSF, Kemp estimated that he logged 400,000 miles as he traveled almost every week between his Illinois home and Texas, New Mexico,
Louisiana, and California. To pass all those hours in the car, Kemp talked to

his friends, drank coffee, and, when he needed a shot of irritation to jolt him awake on a dark highway, he would tune into Sean Hannity. In Kemp's new life, he was either working the rails, at home with his wife and five children, or on the road between the two.

"It changes your idea of what home is. I can't lie, there's a lot of times when there's something going on at home that you really wish you were home for and you're 900 miles away in a hotel room, and you just got through working in the freezing rain all day, or something like that. You start to have a little bit of a pity party for yourself, and get pretty down. But it seems like things just kinda work out just at the right moment to pull you out of it. My wife is unbelievably strong. I don't know how she does it."

On several occasions, when he was working relatively close to home in Rochelle, Illinois—only a few hours' drive—and got off early, Kemp would drive to his son's baseball game in Galesburg, watch it and maybe coach a little, hug and kiss the family, and then drive back to the hotel. Kemp preferred the railroad work to Maytag assembly work, and they were now better off financially, but if he could have gone back to Maytag, he would have because of his family. "It's really hard to be away from them when they're growing up."

After Maytag's closing, BNSF became Knox County's largest employer, and it would grow to 1,115 employees, including 200 to 250 who had lost their jobs at Maytag and Butler.[12] Galesburg, and this entire patch of the western Illinois prairie, was grateful. A BNSF vice president acknowledged that increased rail traffic had had an adverse impact on the quality of life in the otherwise quiet little city. In twelve years in his job, though, he said he "had never once received a complaint from a citizen of Galesburg" about the railroad company.[13] The increasingly frequent sound of the 100-plus car trains rumbling through the center of town, the long and shrill nighttime whistles, and the clanging of the rail yard were all welcome sounds in Galesburg.

Mike Smith, one of Carney's Harley-riding buddies from the Newton rally back in 2003, had also improved on his Maytag wage. Like Semande, "Smitty" started early. His anxiety about the transition drove him. "Fuck yeah, I have tons of worries," he had told me in the summer of 2004. "It doesn't do me any good to worry about it, but I worry every day." Smitty was an imposing guy. He could bench press 565 pounds and sported more tattoos than clear skin on his body—including an incredibly painful dark blue tattoo capping his shaved skull that had been featured in a magazine. But with the impending layoffs that year he had lost his appetite and 35 pounds and had stopped lifting weights. He would soon lose twenty-one years of seniority and health insurance. And instead of vesting a solid thirty-year pension in 2014 at 52, he would have to start over at zero.

Smitty had sold his half of the Town Tavern to Carney. The two of them figured that its modest profits would not be enough for them both to live on. Smitty was not as sociable as Carney, and he did not drink. He was more of a tinkerer; he collected guns and swords, and worked on his motorcycle for fun. Plus Smitty had a leg up in the job market on Carney. He had made $18.90 an hour at Maytag because he was a skilled mechanic. He had worked on mules (forklifts) and fixed machines in the factory.

Smitty heard from a maintenance friend at Deere that they needed welders. Demand for welders in the region had been slack; rumor had it that it was picking up. So in the summer of 2004, he enrolled in a seven-week program at the American Welding Institute in Rushville to learn the skill before his layoff. At the end of the class, he found only one job nearby, fixing mules at $8.90 an hour—a $10-an-hour pay cut. He wasn't picky, but that was too low. "If there's a 'one' in front of it, call me," he told them and other local employers.

Smitty eventually learned that his friend had been right about John Deere, headquartered in Moline, Illinois, one of the Quad Cities, 50 miles north on I-74. Three years after his layoff, Smitty started earning $20 an hour at Deere fixing mules and spot-welding, and began slowly building back his seniority and pension. Harvester Works, the name of Deere's 2,000-employee East Moline factory on the east bank of the Mississippi, manufactures massive combines and other heavy harvesting equipment for Big Corn and other industrialized row-crop farmers. As a central player in North American agribusiness, Deere—along with its new welder—emerged as a winner of the global era. Deere & Company is now the world's biggest agricultural machine maker and employs over 65,000 around the globe.[14]

MARK SEMANDE, AARON Kemp, and Mike Smith were exceptions. Among those who responded to the Maytag survey in 2010, only 29 percent said they were making a higher wage six years after the layoffs.[15] Had Maytag stayed, of course, they would have been earning a higher wage after six years anyway, making an apples-to-apples comparison difficult. Henry S. Farber, a researcher who has tracked the national Displaced Worker Survey for decades, found that full-time workers who reported losing their jobs in 2004 and 2006 saw, respectively, a 20 percent and 14 percent drop in their real weekly earnings—*if*, that is, they were able to find a replacement job in the first place.[16]

It was even tougher than that in a rural labor market. Galesburg Works was the temporary Workforce Investment Act agency created to respond to the departure of Maytag and other companies. It aimed for an 80 percent replacement wage, a goal stipulated in some of the agency's federal and state monies. David Lindstrom, an employment counselor at the agency at the time, said, "For the people that make it through a program and they get a new job, I'd say they make close to 80 percent, or at least have the potential to do that if they stick with the job for a few years." To make 80 percent, observed Lindstrom, was the "ideal result." This revealed in no uncertain terms the degree to which downward mobility had become the norm in western Illinois.

Locals, Lindstrom noted, seemed both weary of and accustomed to less security and lower wages in the 2000s, and he sympathized. "I have a great deal of respect for all these folks, these marvelously talented people who went into the factory because they knew they could get a job. But then the world turned." Compared to the massive layoffs in the 1980s in Galesburg, there was now "a little more mobility, a greater willingness to commute maybe, and a little more open-mindedness about trying something different." Lindstrom said he had met people who had gone through three separate layoffs. "Boom, boom, boom! They're getting bruises all over themselves."

Jackie and Shannon Cummins listened to what all the counselors had told them about the importance of being adaptable, of pursuing retraining. Given their young family, there had been no choice. A month before the Maytag closing announcement in 2002, the Cummins had adopted Shannon's brother's two children, Rain and Jordon, from foster care. Her brother was in jail for meth distribution in Idaho. After Jackie and Shannon were laid off in September 2003, they both dutifully enrolled in a program in a "growth field." It didn't work out for either of them.

By 2006, Jackie and Shannon found themselves working the hardest job they had ever worked, though one which didn't require any schooling or training, other than, perhaps, some weightlifting classes. For a seemingly endless 12-hour shift, Jackie and Shannon chucked 60-pound boxes of laundry detergent and 20-pound bags of dog and cat food onto a conveyor belt at the gigantic Walmart distribution center in Mt. Pleasant, Iowa. Seen from Google Maps from miles above, the several hundred semi-trailers that surround the building look like the stubble of tiny gray whiskers on a square-jawed face. The warehouse takes in Chinese-made and other products and by means of just-in-time distribution methods, sorts them to its retail stores across the Midwest, including an enormous Walmart Supercenter in Galesburg. A BNSF line, connecting Burlington to Galesburg and to Chicago, runs just a half-mile south of the distribution center, right through the heart of Mt. Pleasant. The steady growth of BNSF and Walmart were so intertwined that BNSF has won Walmart's annual Carrier of the Year award several times.

Jackie and Shannon, both then in their late thirties, were commuting 80 miles in each direction, leaving at 4 a.m. on Fridays, Saturdays, and Sundays to get in 36 hours a week. Gas prices had just risen; they were spending $400 a month on gas and leaning heavily on Jackie's mom and niece to care for their adoptive children. All this was for $14.40 an hour, a dollar less than their Maytag wage, at a nonunionized job that was four times as hard, according to Shannon, as the worst job at Maytag.

"I wake up on Monday feeling drunk," Shannon told me a few days before Christmas in 2006. "We get the kids to school, and we crash. It's overboard. I thought Maytag expected a lot. Not even close! We didn't know how good we had it. I swear we didn't know. If they would just slow down. The boxes are coming too fast, and they're expecting me to do 5,000 boxes in my shift. My body is killing me. I'm too old for this!"

Jackie's and Shannon's retraining hopes had not panned out. Jackie had doubted the benefits of retraining from the beginning. "There were people working at Maytag with associate degrees who couldn't get jobs." At the time, she had thought, "We could still be jobless with these degrees." As with so many others, Jackie's reluctance to retrain was mainly rooted in a troubled past in schools. Her father, a strict Pentecostal minister, moved her family nearly every year when they were young. Jackie responded by rebelling against his authority, and the school's. She drank alcohol, smoked pot, and spent more time with her friends than with her parents. And, one day, arguments about Jackie's sexuality reached the breaking point.

"I just left home, was like, 'Whatever, I don't need this!' And I never went back home," she said. "I was 17."

Jackie Cummins eventually finished high school at 20 in Abingdon, a small satellite of Galesburg in Knox County. Jackie and Shannon, her partner since 1993, still live in the 3,000-person town. After high school, she dabbled in community college courses, but she needed to earn money so she set out to work. "Our parents and families told us we couldn't turn down $15 an hour to go to school. They looked down on us for wanting an education."

So when her Maytag layoff came in 2003, it was Jackie's one chance. She decided to try a marketing program at Carl Sandburg College and to learn Spanish. The decision was something of a blind guess. It sounded interesting and "marketing" was a government-approved growth field. But when Jackie tried to imagine a career for herself, her mind would go fuzzy.

"I've never looked outside of a low, entry-level position. You know, I can't imagine what the future's going to be with an education. I just can't even make a guess. It's so far from the persons we've been that I. . . . People keep asking me, 'What are you going to do when you're done?' I just don't have a clue."

While she was in the marketing program, Jackie applied and got accepted for a job at BSNF. She was thrilled and ready to leave school. A few weeks later, though, she was medically disqualified because of an old shoulder injury from the refrigerator factory. "Maytag lost me that job, too."

The marketing program didn't work out. Sandburg had been overwhelmed by a surge of incoming students and having a hard time finding qualified people for the low-paying teaching jobs at the community college. Better-established and more selective programs, like Annette Dennison's, which only permitted eighteen students per radiology cohort, tended to have better-trained and more experienced teachers.

"I was so excited to take marketing fundamentals and marketing sales, but those teachers were very inadequate," Jackie said. "No skills, or enthusiasm. They're not suited to teach this stuff. I could just read the book. My mom could teach this better." On top of that, her program in Spanish hadn't been approved. She left after a year and, before going to Walmart, went to work at the Iowa Army Ammunition Plant, located just west of Burlington, Iowa, where she assembled a small part that went into missiles.

Shannon finished her degree in computer networking at the end of 2005. She did well in her classes, but could find nothing. She felt as if the two years away in school had hurt their chances. "I couldn't even get a crappy job in Galesburg. I sent out tons of resumes, I was doing them left and right. It was just crazy. Once we moved out of the area, I was getting offers but again never anything in my field. I had no experience. They wanted someone with experience. It seemed like around Galesburg employers were saying, 'We're the only game in town so we can be picky.'" That was how they ended up as "extreme commuters" to the Walmart distribution center in Iowa.

"The programs and the two-year degrees just don't match up with what's available," Jackie agreed. "The programs offered were not tailored for what we can do locally. But, then again, there's not much around to do locally anyway."

"I guess you have to adapt," said Shannon. "You swallow some pride. You learn to accept things that you didn't think you would. You realize you have no choice. I didn't believe that I'd be almost 40 and be in the same spot. I had hoped that we'd be better off. Maytag's closed, well, 'Cool, here's my chance!' I got my degree, but now I feel like I wasted my time. I should have been smart like the rest of them and gone to John Deere. I have a piece of paper that does me no good."

According to the Maytag Project survey, of 133 laid-off Maytag employees sampled, about half retrained. Of that half, 57 percent were happy with their retraining, and 53 percent got jobs in the field in which they had trained.[17] It was a fairly small sample of the 1,600 production workers who lost their jobs, but in my interviews and fieldwork I found a similar split—about half were happy with their training, and about half worked in the field in which they had trained. Darin Shull, for instance, got a degree at Sandburg in computer-assisted design and—despite having teachers who literally sat at the front of the classroom and did no teaching at all—got a job in town making $12 an hour at Midstate Manufacturing. For him the TAA benefits were indispensable, a real lifesaver. Some, like Deb Pendergast, were still eking their way through a nursing program in 2006 and 2007, without clear prospects. For her, TAA put her on a seemingly endless road that would inevitably end in a tough job, with tough hours, and a lower wage than Maytag's. She was undecided. Others completed their certificates only to find, like Jackie and Shannon Cummins, that they had wasted their time. "Retraining does not help if there is not satisfactory employment available," said Wilden McKown, then 61. McKown had attended classes for a CDL but found there weren't driving jobs once he graduated.[18]

For some, TAA had opened their lives up to new possibilities. To others, it was a waste of taxpayer money and a waste of their time; some viewed it simply as a cynical way to quell the discontent in the area. It was like displaced workers from the factory had been shot out of a spinning cannon, flying off in wildly different trajectories and with distinct experiences and comprehensions of what had happened. The homogenizing equality of life in Appliance City, with its fixed schedule and factory wage, had been replaced by a profound variability in life circumstances and stark inequality in post-layoff wages. Three and four years after the Maytag closing, many were still up in the air, unsure where they would ultimately land.

= 12 =

"ESA ES MI VISIÓN"

Reynosa, Tamaulipas

It's not about winning, it's about being faithful.[1]

—Ann Cass, Proyecto Azteca

LAURA FLORA OLIVEROS woke at 5 a.m. and used water in a plastic tub to wash off. She then ate toast and drank watery coffee before leaving around 6 a.m. to make her 7 a.m. shift. On the *micro,* maquila workers, most of them in their 20s and 30s, usually kept to themselves as they headed to the factories. Sometimes Flora sold *manualidades* (handicrafts), like the vibrant carrot-orange crocheted dress she had recently finished, on the bus to work. She made them on her day off, Sunday, and had been teaching Laura Suarez how to embroider a tortilla warmer. She also sold lotions and perfumes for JAFRA—a multilevel marketing company along the lines of Amway—to other women on the assembly line. By 2007 a three-year veteran of Planta Maytag III, Flora continued to believe that her girls had a better chance in Reynosa than in Tierra Blanca. In any case, there was no looking back.

Production had recently intensified at the refrigerator factory. They were working on a big order to ship across the Rio Grande to Home Depot. The feeling in the plant was one of utter exhaustion, Flora said. They had been producing mountains of scrap as a result. By this point Flora despised Maytag, but she hated scrap more. It was demoralizing, a sign of a collective failure. The Mexican refrigerator makers felt the same weird devotion to production that Galesburg workers displayed even in the final days of production there. At the end of good days, days when the lines ran continuously and little scrap was produced, they'd congratulate one another and go home a little happier.

For weeks Flora had often been on her feet until 7:45 p.m. in steel-toed shoes, performing the same tasks over and over again. She had learned thirteen jobs at Planta III, all of them tedious, some of them hard. Overtime bonuses, her paystubs revealed, inflated her average hourly take-home pay to as high as $1.80 an hour, though it was more typical for her to earn around $1.35 in 2007. Flora embraced the extra work because of the money and housing points she had been earning. Working 60 hours a week was her choice, she reasoned, if feeding your children is a choice. The formal sector work—so difficult to find back in Tierra Blanca—also provided health insurance, vacation bonuses, and even $45 toward glasses a few paychecks back.

When Flora began at the border factory in 2004, she had been timid and mild-mannered, she said. Now, she was a loud, irreverent voice on the factory floor. "I can be crude, a real bitch. I get frustrated with work, my hands and joints getting sore, the boredom. So I joke that I'm going to blow up a machine so I can stop. My co-workers say, 'Fine, go ahead and break it!'"

After Flora left the factory at 7:45 p.m., she collapsed on the *micro*. "You put your head down and don't look back. You don't have the will to look back at the plant. The work environment inside is just so miserable." "We're all tired," she said of the Home Depot–order intensification. "My fingers have been rubbed rough and raw, like the hands of a man. And I have varicose veins in my legs from standing all day."

When Flora got home at 9 p.m., Laura Suarez had already cooked the girls' dinner, cleaned up, and readied the youngest, eight-year-old Erika, for bed. Laura Suarez and Adrianita shared one small bed, while Flora and Erika shared the other. Two boxy dressers separated the beds and opened a walking lane in the 250-square-foot, one-room home. Stacks of magazines and books and a small propane stove sat on the floor next to the dressers. The girls' artwork hung on the house's wooden endoskeleton that held up the plywood exterior. Outside were a latrine, a faucet, and a clothesline for drying laundry on Sundays.

After two years in the slums, Flora had moved to this peach-colored home as part of a union program for single mothers. It was an improvement, except that water pooled inside when it rained. Flora was sure the dampness was behind Erika's chronic cough and sore throat. She was desperate to get out, and so she needed Planta III to hold out for a little longer. Each paycheck she earned points toward a federally subsidized Infonavit house, and she was just a few points away.[2] If she left Maytag, she would lose all of the points she had earned. "You feel imprisoned. Like you're tied up with a cord."

The glossy Infonavit brochure listed two options, both tiny "pigeon holes," as they were sometimes called, but new and dry (see Figure 12.1).[3] One was 470 square feet and went for $16,200; the other was 550 square feet and went for $20,600. There was a smaller option at the new Puerto del Sol development that listed for $13,500. The mortgage would double her monthly housing expense, but the government kept a ceiling on the payments. The cinderblock homes had electricity, a proper sewage line, and an indoor water line. Her father suggested hiring a contractor to pour a concrete floor over the "rustic" one. "You can tint the concrete floor," she said. "It looks nice."

Flora had seen Infonavit developments—including some that extended for miles and would house tens of thousands—being carved out by bulldozers, heavy machinery, and armies of construction workers on the city's ranch and farmland frontier, and adjacent to the industrial parks.

FIGURE 12.1 INFONAVIT BROCHURE

A 2007 brochure lists two options in San Valentín, an Infonavit housing development on Reynosa's southern perimeter. One option offers 470 square feet and is listed for $16,200. The other option is 550 square feet and is listed for $20,600. Maquila workers earn points to qualify for the federally financed Infonavit mortgages.

Across the road from Planta III when it first opened was one such half-built row of miniature-looking Infonavit homes. Gray and identical, it was as if they had been churned out in one of the nearby factories. When we visited four years later, the block had become a vibrant palette of homemade paint jobs and idiosyncratic front lawns. Despite Reynosa's arid climate, the new residents had added flowers, small trees, and vegetable plants to their front yards. A pink Big Wheel tricycle and a small grill sat in front of one earth-colored home. A few homes down, someone was stacking cinderblocks on his roof to add a second floor to his little blue "pigeon hole."

Jaime Martinez Gonzalez, a 40-something Veracruzano, had transformed the front of his Infonavit house into a neighborhood store with bagged snacks and candy, oatmeal, toilet paper, baby formula, bottled water, and other items. Two men sat in the shade of the store's big blue awning, which read, "Mi Tiendita" (my little store). Martinez purchased the house with money he had earned in Atlanta as a house-painter but said almost everyone else on the block was a maquila worker. There was graffiti, overgrown grass, a gutted car, metal gates on windows, and electricity lines hanging almost down to the sidewalks. However, like so many of these drab developments that sprung up during this historic building boom, it had become a lively neighborhood filled with busy migrant strivers. Mexico's federal government financed an astonishing 4.6 million mortgages between 1995 and 2010. The boom would allow 15 million poor and working-class Mexicans to make a modest step up.[4]

Laura Flora hoped that she would become one of the millions to get that little toehold into Mexico's lower middle class. It was something to daydream about during the six-workday weeks. What she most looked forward to, though, was the chance to lie in bed at the end of the day. Erika, her *dependiente* (her little one), rubbed her aching back at night. "You'll look after me when I'm older," Flora told her. "Yes, you'll take me around when I walk with my little cane."

ANGEL "TITO" RODRIGUEZ was the boss of the union to which Flora and the several hundred other refrigerator makers at Planta Maytag III belonged. Rodriguez was one of the three old labor caciques affiliated with the CTM (Confederation of Mexican Workers), the national union that dominated Reynosa's labor politics and represented all but a handful of its 75,000 maquila workers.[5] A Veracruzano like Flora, he was a middle-aged man with crooked

FIGURE 12.2 REYNOSA'S SOUTHEASTERN EDGE IN 2003

FIGURE 12.3 REYNOSA'S SOUTHEASTERN EDGE IN 2013

FIGURE 12.4 CLOSE-UP OF REYNOSA'S SOUTHEASTERN EDGE IN 2013

Mexico's federal government financed an astonishing 4.6 million Infonavit mortgages between 1995 and 2010, many of them in Mexican border cities. The building boom assisted 15 million poor and working-class Mexicans, including Laura Suarez Flora and her family. Suarez's young family lives among tens of thousands in the new and densely packed southeastern edge of Reynosa, shown here. Reynosa's outlying areas have been transformed from ranchlands and sorghum and corn fields into fourteen massive maquiladora campuses and busy migrant neighborhoods filled with row upon row of tiny Infonavit homes. Credit: Google Earth Pro.

teeth, bushy eyebrows, and a common touch. When we entered his office, unhurried CTM staff members socialized and drank coffee on the first floor. We were led up the stairs to his spacious, well-appointed office on the second floor.

"We have just one purpose," Rodriguez said with careful deliberation. "It is to represent the workers in a dignified way and with respect for human rights." He said his union was constructing soccer fields and volleyball pitches next to the Maytag campus, but his main job was to respond to the problems and concerns that workers brought to him, like news of a cruel supervisor or an ill mother back in Veracruz. Rodriguez said that in the first situation he would tell the supervisor that "to discipline is to teach, not to harm"; in the second, he would provide money for the worker's ailing mother. After she had put in two years at Planta III, Rodriguez had helped Flora get her little peach-colored home.

Rodriguez was an old-school, government-appointed *charro* boss of the PRI. His role was to maintain "labor tranquility," he said, among the 10,000 workers he represented.[6] He worked with Mike Allen to sign secret labor agreements with companies, including Maytag. Workers were unaware of the contract and did not receive a contract when hired, according to the Comité Fronterizo de Obreras (CFO), an organization defending women working in border areas.[7]

"We make an agreement for one purpose," Rodriguez told us. "That the companies are happy so there is growth in Reynosa." Rodriguez did not go beyond that. Reynosa's growth, after all, was determined to a large extent on the U.S. side. "We don't put an ad in the *New York Times* or the *Tribune* saying 'Come to Mexico,'" he said. He may have been the labor boss, but Tito Rodriguez acknowledged that Allen was the real power in town. He knew his role and made little attempt to sugarcoat his perspective. "The Mexican border is attractive because the cost of the workforce is cheaper here. If you get a company here, you try to protect it. How can you protect it? With a workforce that is more accessible, not as expensive. Those businessmen have to look out for their capital."

Some critics—including those at the CFO—argued Rodriguez had been utterly co-opted by multinationals and the status-quo–oriented PRI government that still held sway in the state of Tamaulipas. Until recently, Reverend Ed Krueger said, "Almost all of the workers, if you asked them who was it that was oppressing their lives, instead of naming the company, they would name the union leader." It was the *lucha doble* (the double struggle). Reforms at the CTM had been as slow and deliberate as Rodriguez's manner of speech, with some modest improvements, in part because of Krueger, the CFO, and others agitating for union action. It was not only activists that criticized the unions. María Prieto, Reynosa's director of industrial development, told us that the unions "don't want trouble, just their percentage." She added the unions were not a problem for companies. "They have money, it is very corrupting."[8]

The problem was not simply one of co-optation or corruption. It was one of balance. In a balanced system, unions, the government, civil society, and corporations keep each other in check. However, in Mexico, unions do not act as what John Kenneth Galbraith called a "countervailing power."[9] Rather, they serve American and other global corporations, assisting with labor discipline, regularity, and control. "It's a marvelous amount of power these maquilas have," Armando Zertuche, Reynosa's two-time director of economic development, said. "A maquila comes to Reynosa to establish itself, and they decide where, who, when, why, with what union, and so on."

This was the simple political reality, one that the "Mike Allen question" pushed to the side. Like the farmworker struggle of the 1960s, all of the institutions of any consequence in the McAllen-Reynosa area were lined up on one side of the capital–labor fight. Unions did little or nothing to drive progress in the maquilas. In fact, when there was a wildcat strike or a protest, the union would be invoked to get workers back onto the assembly lines. Meanwhile, the McAllen Economic Development Corporation, the Reynosa Maquiladora Association, and CANACINTRA Reynosa, the local branch of the powerful industry association in Mexico, promoted the maquila agenda.[10]

To Rodriguez, his duty was to keep the gears of industry greased and turning in Reynosa. In fact, the compliant position of Reynosa's unions was precisely what had made it exceptional in recent years, and the powerful magnet for international capital that it was.[11] It was the key difference between busting Matamoros and booming Reynosa. Management-friendly unions were something the MEDC trumpeted. "The labor union climate in Reynosa," its website read, "is very favorable to industry."[12] Locally the euphemistic assertion was not at all controversial.

Rodriguez seemed proud that "an important corporation like Maytag" would come to his border town. It was his job to make sure the budding relationship succeeded. A big part of this job involved teaching discipline to fellow Veracruzanos and Veracruzanas, fresh from the rural countryside and the natural rhythms of the fields. They were inexperienced with the rigors of border life, to the modern world of work in Reynosa's maquilas. "Many times one thinks that working continually is bad," he said. "But it is an obligation to fulfill your schedule. That isn't violating any human rights just to work your schedule. They eventually become accustomed to industry and have their discipline."

THAT THE FIGHT was lopsided did not mean people were not engaged in it.

A short walk from Planta Maytag III, Teresa Chávez convened a meeting at her dining room table. Each of four women assembled there had a legal pad and a planner in front of them. One had a baby in her lap. In the center of the table sat a blue stapler, Elmer's glue, Wite-Out, and a half-emptied baby bottle. In front of Chávez, the leader of Derechos Obreros y Democracia Sindical (DODS) (Workers Rights and Union Democracy) sat their one weapon: a thick copy of *Ley Federal del Trabajo*. Mexican labor law was the most advanced in the world when it was codified after the Revolution nearly a century earlier. It recognized workers' rights to organize unions, to bargain collectively, and to strike; it also limited the workday and the workweek, while outlawing child labor and gender discrimination. It was still potent law, but largely unknown to those emerging from the Veracruz countryside.

Chávez knew firsthand about workers' ignorance. Already a mother of five at age 20, she ventured north in 1988. Like Flora, she had only a change of clothes and no place to go when she found herself stuck in Reynosa. By 1997 Chávez, a compulsive worker who started informal street work when she was just eight-years-old, had risen to a fourth-level position at Delphi, the automotive parts company, doing data entry on computers.

That year an assembly-floor protest changed Chávez's life.

Hearing a commotion, she got permission to leave her office to see what was happening.

"*Tere, Tere,* help us!" she recalled the line workers yelling when they saw her. Knowing that she had access to the other floors, the workers implored Chávez to get their union delegate, who was hiding out in the office.

"We need to get fucking rid of the union delegate!" they yelled, "He's not doing anything to help us!"

She did as they asked, but the delegate wouldn't get involved, probably scared he would lose his job. A few moments later—it happened that fast—Chávez found herself with a megaphone in her hand, leading an impromptu strike at the big factory. The workers shut down assembly, blocked all outgoing shipments, and called the local newspapers and television and radio stations. Chávez said that several workers were beaten by security guards.[13]

She might not have been so brazen had she known she was up against Mexico's largest private employer at the time (soon to be surpassed by Walmart, today's largest). General Motors had fifty parts factories in Mexico under its subsidiary Delphi Automotive Services, which employed 72,000

Mexican workers, most of them along the border. The labor-intensive jobs—assembling car stereos, steering wheels, and instrument panels—had been exported from Kokomo, Indiana; Flint and Saginaw, Michigan; and elsewhere in the Midwest.[14] Starting in the late 1970s, with television makers such as Zenith, General Motors led the Rust Belt exodus across the border.

After a week-long work stoppage, workers got some concessions. Chávez, though, was fired and blacklisted. That was when she joined the struggle and became, in her own words, "an enemy of the company." Panasonic would not hire her. General Electric would not hire her. The word was out.

Chávez showed us scars from her carpal tunnel surgery. Her disproportionate arms and damaged spine were harder to see, but, she said, even more painful. A decade of near-continuous work had taken its toll. "Mexicans are very hard workers. We can end up disabled with tendonitis, carpal tunnel syndrome, strokes, cancer, and sterility because of the chemicals. My job is to make the companies conscientious and realize they are treating us worse than animals. *Esa es mi visión.*"

The four women sitting around Chávez's table had come to the struggle through tragedy. Aneth Delgadillo, a law student and longtime maquila worker, had recently lost her younger sister to uterine cancer and brain tumors. Delgadillo was sure it was from the strong solvents, including one called toluene, which has the sweet smell of a paint thinner. Her sister cleaned car dashes and electrical components starting when she was 16 when it was General Motors. There were no gloves and no masks, but assurances from both management and the union that it was safe. By 21 she had severe acne, dermatitis, and an aching midsection. Two years later, in January 2003, she was dead.

Delphi, Delgadillo said, disavowed that her sister was a Delphi worker and had her removed from Mexico's public health insurance system. This flung Delgadillo's father and brother, a successful engineer, deep into debt for cancer treatments, the hysterectomy, and other surgeries. "This is what we get for all our labor?" Delgadillo was still grieving and furious. "My sister worked from Monday to Thursday from 4 p.m. to 7 a.m. Sometimes she worked more than forty hours of overtime on the weekends and that is how they rewarded her: cancer, two brain tumors, sterility at 23 years of age. You asked me what my goal was. This is my goal. To get my sister's case out into the public light." Delphi, she said, did not even give Delgadillo's sister her last paycheck.

What rankled Chávez and the others about Delphi was its unabashed deceptiveness. Floor supervisors would make workers wear safety gear and provide work chairs when outsiders came to tour the factory. Once gone, they said, the managers put the safety gear away and took the heavy-duty chemicals out of hiding. They cut corners, skimped on overtime, and made employees buy the protective footwear required by federal law. "Just notice the discrepancy in how the largest companies deal with the most humble of people," said Delgadillo, who was an aspiring labor lawyer. "They don't look at you like a worker. They call us their robots. We are disposable."

You don't have to be a wide-eyed socialist to wonder what F. L. Maytag would have thought about this. The Maytag patriarchs were conservative Republicans and as business-minded as they came, but it became family tradition to start one's career on the production lines, to lunch with the workers, and to take an expansive bottom-line position that included responsibility not just to the shareholders and consumers, but also to employees and the hometown. In Reynosa, F. L.'s famous question for workers, "Is everybody happy?" seemed like cruel nostalgia.

Not all employers were as despised as Delphi, according to Delgadillo. A small Australian dialysis equipment maker had recently done right by its employees. Assemblers there, including Delgadillo's other sister, had been bleeding and fainting when working with a certain adhesive. The company switched glues. The new glues didn't work well, though, and were more expensive to produce. The company returned to using the original glue, but had their engineers design special gloves and masks and instituted penalties for not wearing the equipment.

As the four women reviewed cases, preschool-aged kids in bright colors scurried around the car tires and broken cinderblocks outside. A gray cat watched them calmly from the middle of the empty street as the sun set. Teresa's daughter, Marina Ferror Chávez, held her baby and reported some intelligence she had gathered from a nearby maquila. Chávez and her daughter had posed as job applicants to learn about wage rates and working conditions.

Ferror had only half-listened to her mother in the past. She remembered the maquila workers who came to Chávez with mangled fingers or with stories about sexual harassment or cancer diagnoses. But when Ferror's sister had died from cancer at 21, Ferror joined the fight with her mom. She had worked in the maquilas since age 15 when she was propositioned by a supervisor. At the time of our visit, Ferror was out of work because she had had so many doctors' appointments related to a high-risk pregnancy and problems in one of her breasts.

María de la Luz Potero, the fourth woman at Chávez's table, was devoted to DODS. "I'm participating in the group so that not one more person has to go through what I have suffered for my own ignorance," she said. "If I had known my rights, everything that happened to me wouldn't have happened."

Like Laura Flora's daughters, Potero started cleaning the homes of Reynosa's middle class when she was eight. At 15, she altered her birth certificate to work at General Motors. After thirteen years, at 28, she started to miss work. The terrible headaches, dizziness, and fatigue weren't unusual in a place where, as she put it "the smoke in the plant smelled of plastic," or where they used toluene to clean circuit boards, or where women whispered about vaginal bleeding and *abortos* (miscarriages). Until 2000 there were no warnings from GM or the union or even any gloves.

"No protection whatsoever," she said, even when she was working as a solderer. It took an oncologist to tell her that she had to wash her hands with soap and water every time she handled toluene, which has been recognized as a toxin with serious health effects (but not as a carcinogen by the authorities in either Mexico or the United States). By then, though, she had been dipping a little cloth in the colorless, high octane paint thinner and degreaser for over a decade and breathing in its vapors.

"I know you're not sick," she recalled the *licenciada* (plant official) saying to her. "You're just tired because you've been working here so many years. If you miss one more time you'll be fired."

She knew that when the licenciada talked to her that day she was giving her the legally required warning before a dismissal. As she suspected, she was escorted out of the factory the next time she came to work. The very next week, Potero had a lump removed from her breast and learned she had cancer.

"I just about went crazy. I got really scared. I was in bad shape." She went through chemotherapy and radiation while her children—ages 8, 4, and 3— watched her grow skinny and bald. Fired from the Delnosa GM plant, she became responsible for all the medical bills. Ed Krueger connected her with Susan Mika, an American Benedictine nun, who got her treatment with a private doctor.

Despite all that happened to her, Potero nonetheless still felt blessed to be in Reynosa. When her family back in San Luis Potosí asked her whether she wanted to come home, she would tell them she was happy where she was.

"Although the work pays poorly, at least there is something for the kids and we battle." Her dream was that her children would "study a career, and not be treated like an animal."

After the DODS meeting adjourned, Potero told us that, despite everything, she wanted to work again in the maquilas once she got her strength back. The maquila, she said, offered something secure and certain, and she missed that. That tiny Christmas bonus and the couple dollars that she and the company put away in savings each week gave her something beyond the money itself, something intangible. Working in the maquila again would mean Potero wouldn't have to say to her kids, as she had the previous Christmas, "Well, sometimes Santa Claus makes a mistake." It made her a better mother, and it gave her hope that her life was moving in the right direction.

"WE HAVE A joke about Veracruzanos," Herber Ramírez told us in his office overlooking Reynosa's Plaza Principal. I noted that his staff in the Secretariat of Economic Development smiled, apparently knowing what was coming. "There were four Mexicans on a plane. The guy from Veracruz had a big sack of seafood. The guy from Jalisco, a sack full of cactus leaves. The guy from San Luis Potosí, a sack full of *tunas* [cactus pears], and the guy from Reynosa had *chile piquín*. The plane had problems so the guy from Veracruz threw out his sack of seafood. The guy from Jalisco threw out the sack of cactus leaves, and the guy from San Luis Potosí threw out his *tunas*. The guy from Reynosa looks at his bag of chiles and then throws out the guy from Veracruz. 'I'll keep the chiles,' he says, 'there's a lot more Veracruzanos in Reynosa.'"

Jokes about Veracruzanos were inescapable. When we visited a technical college, one of the instructors quipped, "Why should you never kill a Veracruzano?" "Because their family would come for the funeral and stay."

Many, including those instructors from the local technical college, blamed the impoverished newcomers for the border region's increasing violence and exchanged stories of people being chopped into tamales and worse. "People from the north just don't do that! It's a whole different ball of wax." Also thanks to the rash of outsiders, basic utilities were intermittent. The list of complaints was long. Native *Reynosenses* had become a minority, and some felt encroached upon and defensive.

"If there's a robbery, a Veracruzano did it," Arturo Solís told us, to illustrate kneejerk thinking among some locals. "People don't want to realize that the problem is here, with people from Reynosa, even very prominent figures who've gotten rich off of crime." Veracruzanos were scapegoated, and even called *Veracruchangos* (Veracruz monkeys). "Veracruzano" had become something parents used for a misbehaving child. "You'd think he was a Veracruzano. . .," people said of some miscreant.[15] For some, the migrants were an uncomfortable reminder that Mexico still had one foot firmly fixed in the Third World, no matter how many microbreweries and Sirloin Stockades opened along the border.

At Solís' organization, two human rights workers, middle-class norteñas, described Veracruzanas (women from Veracruz) as darker skinned, with almond eyes and wider jaws. You could always identify them. They dressed more provocatively, were louder, and drank, danced, and partied more than the norteñas. Veracruzanos crowded family members into small homes, worked hard, and kept to their own kind, the two human rights workers said.

This perception so troubled Dr. Patricio Mora that he started an association to support workers from Veracruz (the Association of Veracruz Workers in Tamaulipas), despite local resistance to the idea. The border economy had been built on the backs of these desperate migrants. Yet the Mexican government had forsaken them, Mora contended, focusing instead on protecting investors and maquilas as it "enslaved" the migrant workforce. Mora saved his sharpest criticism for union boss Tito Rodriguez.

"Tito is crazy because he considers himself a real Veracruzano. He has a million-dollar house on the other side of the border. He has lost his identity and sold his people out."

Veracruzanos formed a ring around old Reynosa, like an army laying siege. They often lived in colonias named—officially or unofficially—after their hometowns, such as Volador, Sombrerete, Agua Dulce, and Papantla. The roads were usually unpaved and difficult to walk after heavy rains, much less drive in anything other than a truck with high ground clearance. Each home was a distinct mix of cinderblocks, wood pallet scraps, corrugated tin, wood, and other refuse. Brightly painted Coke trucks bounced into the neighborhoods, bringing refreshments to the *mini supers* and the hole-in-the-wall stores opened by entrepreneurs. Maquila worker and Veracruz native Nivorio Suarez said that, even after twenty-five years in the outer slums, he still felt like an outsider in Reynosa. "I'm living in Veracruz of the North."

In Reynosa the southern migrants found a working world like nothing they had ever experienced. Everything was different: its massive scale, its unrelenting rhythms, the demanding exactitude of its time-management, and its utter disregard for anything unrelated to efficient production—a child who was sick, a complicated pregnancy, or family and religious traditions.

The clash of cultures resulted in skyrocketing turnover in the factories, especially among the most recent migrants. Whereas three generations of a family might have crafted refrigerators in Galesburg, workers in Reynosa cycled in and out of jobs that were so deskilled that anyone could be trained to do them within a matter of hours. LG's Gloria Altamirano said she had seen this culture shock hit newcomers every week when she was a human resources manager. Being thrown into the workings of these vast mechanized systems was deeply disorienting. E. P. Thompson once characterized the transition from the "task-orientation" of peasant society, where "work" and "life" are largely integrated, to an industrial system of disciplined time-measurement as one of the most disruptive possible. This new time-sense of the industrial world required a "radical restructuring of man's social nature and working habits."[16] It sometimes took several hirings for a worker to adapt, Altamirano said, which is why the three-month probationary rule was strictly enforced by most companies.

"Punctuality is a problem across the board. Views of time are just different," said Dave Bullon, a former production manager at Black & Decker in Reynosa. "Likewise, in Mexico you don't really get things done because it's your responsibility, but because of your relationship with someone."

Bullon said American managers become frustrated with the lack of responsiveness among Mexican workers, who sometimes disregard emails or phone calls because the communications were not face-to-face. "It's really hard to drive change and progress when people don't fully buy into what you're doing." From the Mexican side, Bullon acknowledged, there was the "feeling that Americans were too micro-managing or slave-driving."

Armando Zertuche, a maquila critic discussed previously, thought the new work culture was the biggest boon the maquilas brought to the area. People learned to be more responsible, to be on time, to know quality, and to develop professional competition. "We have high-quality people from the hands all the way up to the brains of the operation now, people with two or three languages, master's degrees, specialists, even doctorates. That was something not in Reynosa twenty years ago." Despite the rapid accretion of human capital in the 2000s, there was a palpable sense of discontent across the city, Zertuche maintained, because low wages and salaries did not match the growth in skills.

Others saw the changes not in terms of what was gained, but of what was lost during the border's boom era. Journalist Carlos Peña described a "degeneration" of rural migrant culture under the pressure of constant work and cramped slum living. "The maquila depersonalizes people. Yes, it brings immediate benefits, but people's customs are altered, American customs are celebrated. It's transculturalization, but it's forced. I might be fatalist, but to me this is a permanent crisis."

Ed Krueger and migrant advocate Dr. Patricio Mora did not dissuade people from leaving Veracruz, but they wanted them to make informed decisions. They wanted them to know that, although their wage might be higher and the work more plentiful, the costs of living were also higher and the dangers greater as well. In Veracruz people lived in reasonably sized houses, perhaps with shade trees around, and maybe chickens, a cow, and other animals, and ways to get good, inexpensive food, they said. They are lured away when they hear about the maquila wage and the long workweeks, tempted by the prospect of earning 500 or 600 pesos a week. At the border they are often far from family, friends, and community, and "totally uprooted," Krueger said. Veracruzanos complain about the processed food, the Reynosa weather, which is hot and dry, and the unforgiving pace of life. They miss Veracruz, where the meat and cheese are fresh and the fruit is "falling from the trees," as a Reynosa woman, originally from Naranjos told us.

It was that *everything* was different in Reynosa for the Veracruzano—the food and drink, the nature of the work, the way people interacted with their neighbors, the daily routines and rhythms, the loss of stillness and security. The symbolic illustration Dr. Mora and others used to explain the shift was the substitution of Halloween, the consumption-based holiday imported from the north, for *Día de los Muertos*, a commemoration of dead ancestors that has been practiced for thousands of years in Mexico. Although the changes wrought were hard to encapsulate, the primary cause was not difficult to pinpoint for Mora. It was time. "The maquila worker only has time to wake up, go to work, work overtime to earn enough to survive, and then go home to sleep. People don't say they want to give up traditions, but rather they simply don't have time to maintain them."

CHÁVEZ WAS ATTEMPTING to register Derechos Obreros y Democracia Sindical with the state of Tamaulipas as an *asociación civil,* a recognized citizens' group. She hoped that this would open funding streams for the strapped organization. She also thought it would confer legitimacy to DODS when meeting with maquila managers, union delegates, and grass-roots groups.

The women knew that their main job as labor rights *promotoras* (grass-roots educators), though, would always be hitting the sidewalks and knocking on doors. And that was tough. The issue, again, was time. Nearly all the adults in maquila neighborhoods worked six days a week. In the evenings families were busy feeding their children and hanging out laundry. Chávez and the others ran into widespread skepticism. Some pretended not to be home or said they were too busy to talk. If the DODS women managed a short conversation and pressed a workers' rights pamphlet in someone's hand, a visit was deemed successful. "There are lots of really small steps and lots of closed doors," Chávez said. They did their best work on Sundays in the small, makeshift neighborhood churches. With the blessings of a church leader, people listened and maybe even told their workplace story. "Even if the unions are on the maquila's side, they'll see that we are on the workers' side."

Consciousness-raising was a struggle. Young Veracruzanos, ignorant of their rights and eager to please, were hesitant to make trouble. Chávez was, by comparison, too knowledgeable, too feisty—and too old. When she was fired from Delphi and blacklisted, the maquila manager told her that she was "no longer productive," Chávez recalled. "They used cruel words." The girls with cleavage and miniskirts get hired, her daughter added. They like them young, pretty, nimble, and ignorant.

A vast well of worker passivity was, of course, one of Reynosa's great attractions—along with low wages, compliant unions, and its charismatic development czar across the border in McAllen. Laborers in places like Newton, Iowa, and Galesburg, Illinois, had been organized for generations. They were therefore steeped in the rights and obligations of their contracts and work roles. Michael Patrick admitted that Local 2063 in Galesburg had been, in a way, a victim of its own success. Over the decades they had learned to shape their destiny and advocate for how work was compensated, organized, timed, and managed. After Maytag-lifer Len Hadley vacated the CEO's chair, experienced, participatory workers suddenly went from being assets to liabilities. Under CEOs Lloyd Ward and Ralph Hake, Maytag joined other multinationals as it searched out a workforce that was more pliant and controllable. That's what they found in Reynosa. In Reynosa, Chávez said, "we have two enemies: ignorance and the maquila."

Progress for DODS was slow, and the odds were long. But these women's ferocity and emotional commitment seemed a competitive match. For them, raising their kids, tending to their homes, and fighting the struggle were one and the same. To raise a family they had risked their health to work in the maquila, and then they had risked their jobs to take up the struggle. Tito Rodriguez may have genuinely cared for the 10,000 workers he represented, but from a detached place. For these women, the struggle was visceral and personal. It was the same for Reverend Krueger, the man who brought them together. He had been walking Reynosa's slums for decades, spreading information, connecting people, and cultivating social capital one conversation at a time.

Nonetheless, the movement seemed stuck at the grassroots. CEFPRODHAC (Arturo Solís' human rights organization), DODS, and the Comité Fronterizo de Obreras were at odds with each other. There were personality conflicts and strategic disagreements. Part of the problem was that some of the goals of the movement—such as reducing apathy and fatalism—were difficult to measure in order to demonstrate success to potential funders. It also didn't help that the activists' side lacked the resources to pay the army of promotoras needed for an enormous boots-on-the-ground effort among the tens of thousands of Reynosa maquila workers. Further, funding an epidemiological study on GM/Delphi workers, to take one example, was well beyond any of the grassroots organizations' financial capacities— not to mention the problem of addressing the complicated scientific and methodological questions, such as those involved in studying cancer clusters. Without government or union support, the resources simply were not there. In 2003, as Planta III was being erected, the income of Krueger's Comité de Apoyo (Support Committee), for example, had been $13,726.98.[17]

That same year Delphi, as the largest automotive parts maker in the world, took in $28 billion. In the mid-2000s, the company was also engaged in alleged accounting irregularities, shuttering a number of U.S. factories, an executive pay scandal, and trying to discard pension liabilities to workers.[18] Given this, the multinational was hardly worried about complaints about safety gloves or even cancer clusters in Reynosa—if, indeed, any higher-ups even knew about these problems. Unlike small activist groups, Delphi and Maytag were part of an organized, powerful, bicultural, and bilingual network in Reynosa. At the hub, facilitating the global recruiting, cross-border interactions, and national and local public relations, was Mike Allen's MEDC. In a twenty-page advertising supplement in the Rio Grande Valley's newspaper, *The Monitor*, the MEDC authored an advertisement meant to look like a newspaper article. "As the region celebrates the success of NAFTA and the maquiladoras," the article read, "plant managers seem to understand that the real treasure are the people."[19]

While Allen worked the globe, DODS and Krueger remained intensely local in orientation. Krueger relished the minutiae of real, if piecemeal, change. He advised the fledging activists to focus their comments on one tangible change, such as protective eyewear, in each meeting with a union delegate. He ran role-playing exercises, demonstrating how to compliment union leaders and enlist their support. By this point well into his 70s, Krueger cultivated leaders like Chávez and Delgadillo with what seemed like infinite patience. Nothing made him happier. Like the farmworkers' struggle in the Magic Valley decades earlier, this was where Krueger lived and breathed—at the grassroots. The work was slow and daunting, and with sad, early deaths and intractable sexism, it often seemed that it was a losing fight. But as Ann Cass—a colleague of Krueger's who had also put Catholic social teachings into practice for decades—said about work in the Valley, "It's not about winning, it's about being faithful."[20]

LAURA FLORA SENSED Planta Maytag III was in its death throes by 2007. She had noted production breakdowns, small factory fires, and major material thefts. So it came as no surprise when Whirlpool, which had purchased Maytag in 2006, shuttered Planta III early in 2008, leaving the newly built factory and putting it up for sale less than four years after it had opened. Flora and 750 other refrigerator makers lost their jobs.[21] Flora was ready, though, having secured enough points for Infonavit financing. Soon, with Laura Suarez, Adrianita, and Erika, she would move to a new home.

Before the closing, the trash-strewn and congested city had still been an oddly inviting place. Aside from a few teens yelling "gringos!" when they saw us, the people were hospitable and welcoming. The street vendors, government officials, waiters, maquila workers, 7–Eleven and Oxxo cashiers, and taxi cab drivers were uniformly warm, open, and helpful. Children playing amongst pallet fences and building scraps on muddy roads in the colonias acted like they had the best playground in the world.

By the time of Planta III's closing in 2008, though, you could see and feel the difference. The disorder had grown darker as Mexico's drug war spun out of control as cartels battled each other and the *federales* (federal police). Reynosa, Juárez, and other increasingly lawless border cities turned out to be perfect hosts for the deadly war, waged with virtual impunity, as Reynosa continued to serve as a freewheeling gateway to the north for flat-screen televisions and tropical fruits; landscapers and nannies; and cocaine, meth, and pot. Labor kingpin Tito Rodriguez died of a heart attack in September 2008; his replacement, José Piña Ortega, was murdered execution-style three months later, apparently for upsetting the labor status quo that Rodriquez had so effectively maintained.[22]

The term "development" seemed suddenly to ring hollow in the borderlands, where multinationals had reaped nearly all of the rewards. Juárez boasted an extraordinary 165,000 export-oriented manufacturing jobs, but wages had been stagnant for years—decades even—and the grisly femicides and disappearances—many of the victims being maquiladora workers—escalated again and went largely unsolved and unexplained.[23] The border cities were losing the struggle to police their streets, electrify new settlements, pave muddy roads, and clear the trash. A newspaper account said Reynosa remained mired in the "dark ages" on these counts. Even in 2008, two decades after Mike Allen sparked the area's boom with a simple handshake, Krueger told of a woman who could make more in two days working the local dump than in a week in a maquiladora.[24] Was this development? Many wondered.

María de la Luz Potero went back to the maquilas around the time Whirlpool shuttered its plant in Parque Industrial Colonial. Adjusted for inflation, she made about what she had in 1988, when she began as a precocious 15-year-old girl. In those twenty years, the years of Mike Allen's reign, the gap in purchasing power between Mexican and U.S. workers had grown steadily, spurring more Mexican migration to and across the border.[25] One editorial page that had supported NAFTA for its promise of higher wages in Mexico and, thus, less illegal migration, conceded its error. "Clearly," its editorial read in 2007, "the opposite has happened."[26]

In the midst of growing disorder in Reynosa, Whirlpool moved side-by-side refrigerator production to Ramos Arizpe, a small industrial powerhouse nestled in the mountains south of Monterrey.

13

LOOKING NORTH FROM BARRA DE CAZONES

Barra de Cazones, Gulf Coast, Veracruz

Poor Mexico, so far from God and so close to the U.S.

—Popular saying in Mexico

IN BARRA DE Cazones, Veracruz, we ordered Modelos at an empty beach-front restaurant, La Palapa de Kime, on a muggy July afternoon. A handful of vacationers were scattered on the expansive, pebbled, brown sand beach. This was not the tropical paradise of Cabo San Lucas brochures—with expensive hotels and fine white sands—but the scarcity of tourists in this beautiful and serene Gulf Coast village was puzzling at first glance. The roads into town are good—pleasant, twisting runs through a remote and picturesque rainforest, in fact—and a couple of medium-sized cities and an airport are within an hours' drive.[1]

We later learned that the electricity in town was sporadic and that the hotel accommodations were expensive but shoddy. And along the downtown strip, half-constructed buildings seemed frozen in their incompleteness, as if they were as ambivalent about the future as the inhabitants were. Roofless, these cinderblock buildings stood mute and abandoned alongside the central beachfront road, rusting rebar jutting out of the tops of their gray walls. In front of them, stacks of bricks lay idly on the sidewalk.

This quiet fishing and farming village of a few thousand would like to reinvent itself as a tourist destination. Government efforts to create fishing cooperatives and plants for processing and freezing fish expanded Mexico's annual catch in the 1970s and 1980s, but today Mexico's coasts are dominated by U.S., Canadian, and Japanese boats, which catch ten times what Mexican boats do.² Small-scale fishermen in places like Barra de Cazones fetch low prices for their fish, and high fuel prices take a sizable chunk of their meager earnings. With fishermen struggling, little investment in infrastructure, high interest rates, and few jobs, this lonely town's main business, like that of the nearby villages of Volador and Agua Dulce, is out-migration.

Archimedes, a proud and boisterous local entrepreneur, was frying several freshly caught fish in a wide skillet and extolling their virtues in a theatrical baritone. "This one is flaky and delicious. You must try it," he crooned, pushing toward us one of the larger fish, one with particularly bulbous eyes.³ Our local companions in Barra de Cazones, Emilio and Ismael Fuentes, approved "Kime's"—as Archimedes prefers to be called—suggestion, and we returned to our Modelos and some deep-fried and pleasantly greasy Gulf appetizers. Emilio, an unemployed father of two, had been giving us the royal treatment since we arrived in town an hour earlier, insisting that he was our tour guide. Ismael, his younger brother, just back from several months of farm work in the United States, looked at us curiously from across the long plastic lunch table. Emilio's son, Lenny, also joined us under Kime's thatched roof where we sat, protected from the sun but exposed to the thick air from the Gulf.

After passing orders to his cooks, Kime quickly returned, ready to talk. "When a gringo comes, it's as if a comet crossed the sky," he announced. "We have a tourism plan. We have a beautiful spot here, but we haven't been able to take advantage of it. You see that I'm flying the American flag next to the Mexican flag. I fly it so people from America will feel comfortable. The U.S. has a lot of respect in the world, and they run everything."

Ismael then pointed to the Mexican flag, hanging lifelessly below the American flag. "The American flag flies tall," Ismael observed. Everyone laughed at the obvious metaphor.

Kime laughed along, but the sight set him off. A self-professed conservative, Kime turned to us with a serious look. "You came to find out how we really live? We live on fucking leftovers! We don't live well. Thankfully, I'm a businessperson, I have enough to eat. But there are people who have to slave all day just to eat." Kime proceeded to rant with wild gesticulations about Barra de Cazones, blaming lazy Mexicans, the drug trade, the high cost of credit, patronage and corruption in the Mexican government, and greedy coyotes for the area's ills.

Kime saved his harshest criticism, though, for migrants. "People come back from the border, from the U.S. with AIDS, addicted to drugs. Those bastards are really screwed up. They get themselves a car and they don't even know how to drive, and they crash because they're drugged up. They show up here with dollars and they're drunk." After pausing for effect, Kime pressed ahead. "But the biggest problem is the disintegration of the family. Men and women leave their children behind. So if kids are drunk or pregnant, doing drugs, who is going to tell them anything?"

AFTER LUNCH, AND after a few more Modelos at Kime's, the Fuentes brothers gradually worked their way into a vociferous debate in Spanish, which lasted most of the afternoon. We later learned that it was not the first time the two brothers had fought over issues involving migration, family, and lifestyle. Ismael, a native of Barra de Cazones, had been migrating to the United States for nine years, first illegally and later with an H-2A work visa. He was 38 when we met him in 2007, and had attained some success from his travels. He lived in a bright lime-green, two-story home with running water, a television, air conditioning, and a stereo. Emilio and his family lived just blocks away, without running water, a stove, or much else in their tiny, but neatly painted and orderly home. Somewhat resentful, Emilio insisted that his younger brother's material success had come at a high cost to his character. Ismael took offense.

"People do not emigrate because they're stupid, Emilio. What is this concern about people emigrating, Emilio? That's where the future is! People who leave Mexico, who leave Veracruz, they make progress in their lives. They're better off."

In a lawyerly fashion, Emilio, 40, looked at us. "Look, there are two different ambitions. My highest ambition is my family. His highest ambition is money. But with the money he makes, he cannot have the family he wants. If I went to the States and came back once a year, my children could become drug addicts, or delinquents."

Emilio then pointed to Lenny, a well-groomed 18-year-old who had been sitting attentively, saying nothing over the course of several hours. "He wouldn't be talking about going to the university right now if I weren't here. Sure, you can see my house is more humble than Ismael's, but I have family security and he doesn't. There are two different kinds of ambition. Mine is real and his is a fantasy, because the United States is not his country." Emilio concluded his oral argument with a paternal look at Ismael. "I want to tell you something. The United States is never going to be your country."

"Well, of course not, I love Mexico," Ismael replied, annoyed.

"But what are you doing for Mexico?"

"I'm not doing it for Mexico; I'm doing it for me. You have to look out for yourself. What did Mexico do for me? What did the local mayor do for me? Nothing! I'm the one who built my home."

"What you're trying to do is a fantasy. You're trying to conquer the unconquerable." Exasperated, Emilio looked at us. "He wants to conquer the United States, to make the United States his own."

"For God's sakes, Emilio, if you don't go to the richest country in the world, you won't do anything in your life. Don't talk about the people who have failed, talk about the people who have triumphed! I mean Hollywood is in California—how come they didn't put it in Guatemala?" Ismael looked at us sheepishly, as if to say he would have nailed his final point if he had one or two fewer Modelos.

"Ask him who he lives with." Responding to his own question, Emilio said, "He lives alone."

Ismael looked away, shaking his head in denial. Pressed further, he conceded. "Fine, the truth is I like being alone. I've been living alone for ten years, and I like it. Gringos and gringas live alone. I like that what's mine is mine; it's my television, my stereo, and my house. Emilio, you'll never try something new."

"Nor do I want to," Emilio replied. "For me it's just the unknown, an adventure. It's a huge land to want to conquer, a land more difficult than your own. With my family, I have more needs than he does, but I have a plan for my life that I created a long time ago and I like it. Him? He is not from the U.S., and he's not from here. If I fall, at least I know where I've fallen."

The brothers eventually wore themselves out after the hot afternoon of drinking and debating. Despite their hardline stances, each seemed to long for what the other had. Emilio and his immediate family were tight-knit, proudly law-abiding, and deeply rooted in their impoverished but neat neighborhood. Ismael, on the other hand, was alone for most of the year. He had girlfriends and even children scattered around Texas and Mexico whom he rarely saw, Emilio told us. Emilio, methodical and careful with his speech, though, conveyed a quiet sense of despair. In the following days we would come to know a tearful man who was torn up by the fact that he could not provide more for his family. Despite his persuasive case against it, he had for some time considered migrating north. Out of fear and moral reservation, he had always decided to stay.

REFLECTING ON HIS brother after the debate, Ismael told us, "My brother is a good person, he is honest, he leads a good life. But that just doesn't work here."

Earlier that afternoon at Kime's, Ismael, an illiterate, middle-school drop-out, tried to teach his well-read, older brother about making it up north. "Why are you stuck thinking the way you think, Emilio?" Ismael had said. "You think about the 'zero' when you should be thinking about the 'one,' and then the 'two,' because that's how you get ahead. At first, I didn't have any-thing, but then I got to 'one'—say, a cellphone. And then to 'two'—say, the little pickup truck that I own. And then to my home, which is 'three.'" Ismael continued his lecture on upward mobility as Emilio listened with a disap-proving look on his face. "But if I just get stuck on 'zero,' I'd get depressed. I might start using drugs. Emilio, even if you don't have a trampoline, you still have to jump."

Marking his life through material consumption may not have brought Ismael happiness, but it earned him standing in Barra de Cazones—and per-haps brought structure to the chaotic and self-destructive life he had led dur-ing his younger years. Ismael seemed genuinely concerned for Emilio, as if he wanted to help him to see through the small-minded parochialism that paralyzed him. Though less refined than his older brother, Ismael possessed a worldliness born of his travels.

Since the number plateaued in 2005, some six million Mexicans have been estimated to live in the United States illegally. Then, as now, they have worked in California's vegetable fields, pumpkin canneries in Illinois, hog slaughter-houses across the Midwest and Great Plains, and fast food as well as gour-met restaurants nearly everywhere.[4] Immigration had boomed so much in NAFTA's first decade that nearly one-fifth of working-age Mexican men lived in the United States by 2005.[5]

Like other migrants, Ismael simply found the math too compelling, par-ticularly after hearing stories from friends and relatives who had made it to the United States. "The truth is everything is based on the dollar, and you earn dollars in the U.S.," he said. "So you think at $5 an hour, well that's $50 a day when I make only 70 pesos [$6.25] a day here. And that's *if* there's work. So then your uncle might say, 'Oh, no, I work construction and earn $11 or $13 an hour,' and you say, '*Chinga su madre!* I'm going to go!' "[6]

Under the work contract, Ismael started in the tobacco fields of the Carolinas and then moved through just about every agricultural state, running an exhausting gauntlet across the American countryside that included sweet potatoes, cucumbers, squash, sweet peppers, cabbage, and finally the melon harvest. The work typically extended to the beginning of November, when the contract ended and immigration law required the migrants to return to Mexico. Ismael often overstayed his visa and visited one of his "wives" in Dallas, did some informal work painting and in construction, and eventually made it back to Barra de Cazones for a few months of sunny relaxation. Emilio complained that his brother drank and philandered away his off-contract time.

An admitted failure as a student and a delinquent as a teenager, Ismael tried to persuade his brother that he had matured through his nine years abroad. When asked about Kime's "lazy Mexicans," Ismael responded, "I agree with none of that. Workers should be well protected. We should have social services. The lifestyle and prosperity of the United States is supported by agricultural workers. We hold up the whole country." Mexican workers worked hard and never spoke back to employers because they feared retaliation—even when they had papers, he said. That is why American employers like us, Ismael concluded, and that is why the union work he did was important.

Ismael said he could make about $9,000 on a contract for a season's worth of agricultural work, which was better than the $8 an hour average for seasonal workers in 2007.[7] "It is absolutely backbreaking work," he admitted, "but I don't care because I don't want to deal with the sadness here, this humiliation. Here in Mexico I have to work that hard for much less money."

Even with papers, Ismael endured abuse. He was beaten in a sweet-potato field for not harvesting fast enough. He still remembered the grower's name. He was defrauded of his dues by a phony union before a legitimate union, the Farm Labor Organizing Committee (FLOC), began their aggressive, grassroots organizing campaign with H-2A visa holders. He said that he also had his hours undercounted and was forced to work days on end with serious illnesses.

While in the States, Ismael stayed in cramped dormitories, often employer-owned, with no television or music, frequently sleeping on tile floors with just a blanket and a pillow. For months at a time, it was just work and sleep, work and sleep in the rural pockets of the United States, hidden away from American grocery shoppers. Ismael would return, exhausted, to Barra de Cazones, with cuts and bruises, lots of stories—some good and some ghastly—and wads of pesos and dollars. A marginal laborer in the United States, Ismael arrived home to be part of a local elite in this little Gulf Coast village.

Despite his brother's trials, Emilio was right to call Ismael one of the lucky ones. Ismael's H-2A work visa is so valuable in rural Mexico that swindlers come to places like Barra de Cazones to round up locals for elaborate visa cons. In 2007 Ismael was one of only 76,814 agricultural workers certified to work in the United States on H-2A visas—a puny number in comparison to the nation's estimated 1.1 million unauthorized field and livestock workers (nearly all of them are Mexican).[8] The Fuentes brothers told of some men who had recently driven around town in an official-looking car with a loud-speaker, making announcements about work visas. The con men took their marks—desperate visa-seekers—to the U.S. consulate in Monterrey and tricked them out of $300, then left them stranded hundreds of miles from home. As with coyotes, there seem to be just enough legitimate visa agents for the illegitimate ones to exploit the inexperienced.

On top of having the H2-A visa, Ismael's union membership is unheard of among temporary workers from Mexico. In 2004 FLOC signed a union contract with the North Carolina Growers Association, ending a five-year boycott against the Mount Olive Pickle Company, the second-largest pickle company in the United States and which purchases cucumbers from the growers.[9] Ismael happened to have been there and joined FLOC after a visit in the field from one of its leaders. The contract was a first for Mexican guest workers, and a small victory in a long struggle that has been fought for decades by braceros in the 1940s and 1950s and labor organizers led by Cesar Chavez and Dolores Huerta in the 1960s and 1970s—including Ed Krueger and the "scab melon"-picketers of the Magic Valley.

At Kime's, Ismael flashed his FLOC photo identification with somber pride. He claimed that FLOC's representation had checked any previous mis-treatment. In a recent, painful stint with gout, the union demanded, against the grower's protests, that Ismael be able to go to the hospital for treatment for the acute arthritis that accompanies the disease. Historically, illegal immigrants and their employers have preferred avoiding doctors and emergency rooms out of fear of being caught by immigration agents. Because of this—contrary to popular belief in the United States—illegal immigrants draw far fewer public resources than their population-size would suggest.[10] The California Hospital Association estimated that only 10 percent of the state's uncompensated care was for illegal immigrants in 2007.[11] Only about one in ten farmworkers—whether citizens, visa holders, or the undocumented—have employer-provided health insurance, and only 15 percent are enrolled in Medicaid.[12] The Affordable Care Act, "Obamacare," requires that farm labor contractors provide health insurance for field workers by 2015.[13] But before pushing for health insurance and public services, Ismael's union was starting with the basics: availability of drinking water in the fields, rain and protective work gear, and means of processing workers' compensation claims for workers injured on the job.[14]

"As long as I'm there under a legal contract," Ismael proclaimed, "I have all of the rights that you have, all of the labor rights of an American citizen." Under the visa program, Ismael received a book put out by the U.S. Department of Labor as he crossed the border bridge, listing numbers to call if he had problems with his employer. "Apparently, slavery has ended."

It had taken Ismael nearly a decade and some plain good luck—being in the right place at the right time—to learn to navigate the complex pathways of seasonal, cross-border migration. To newer farm migrants, the disadvantages of the language barrier, lack of education, and physical and social isolation result in what is essentially indentured servitude to savvy and organized American growers. Though H-2A work visas provide fairly expansive legal protections, those protections exist in practice only if and when the U.S. Department of Labor enforces them, attorneys protest their violation, or workers assert their rights, either individually or through unions.

Since migrant workers are typically unable to switch employers or to lodge their own labor complaints, employer control is nearly absolute. And while FLOC, improbably, unionized 7,000 guest-workers in North Carolina, including Ismael, another million-plus unauthorized farmworkers are routinely subject to blacklisting, being shortchanged for their work, and punishing work quotas, and are sometimes the victims of sexual harassment and rape.[15] This massive army hoes, thins, transplants, **harvests**, packs, sorts and grades, prunes, irrigates, and operates farm equipment almost entirely in the shadows of the American economy. For decades, Mexican and Mexican American farmworkers have quietly put food in American grocery stores, fruit and vegetable stands, and restaurant kitchens. And for decades, they have been despised for coming.

EMILIO AND ISMAEL Fuentes were born into a family of fourteen children. Their father fished at night in the local river that flows into the Gulf of Mexico, and in the Gulf itself, on a small boat. After school, they and their siblings worked the fields and collected firewood for cooking. Fishing put food on the table, though not much more. Emilio and Ismael have family scattered in Reynosa, Mexico City, and nearby Poza Rica, a city of 200,000 about twenty-five miles away, as well as in the United States.

Emilio admitted that he was unsure whether he would be able to resist the border's pull. The 470 miles that separated Barra de Cazones from Reynosa—a nine-hour drive—seemed vast. "There is a lot of cultural distance that separates us, the North and the South. Globalization hasn't arrived in Cazones. It's just at the border, and in Monterrey, in *El Norte.*"

There was one way in which globalization had arrived in Barra de Cazones, though. It was in the form of the U.S. dollar. When Ismael returned to the little Gulf town with a season's earnings of $9,000, his and other migrants' ability to spend the money distorted the local economy, driving up prices and pressuring more holdouts, such as Emilio, to leave. The dollarization of Barra de Cazones created stark divisions between those who "vivir con el peso" (live with the peso, as Emilio phrased it), and those who return with American earnings or receive them as remittances. Robert Courtney Smith, a sociologist and author of *Mexican New York*, calls the latter group the "remittance bourgeoisie." Smith terms those who cannot or will not migrate the "transnational underclass."[16] Every household in places like Barra de Cazones that moves toward the dollar makes surviving on the peso in that community more difficult. "I respect what he does, and I respect what I'm doing," Emilio said. "Everyone has his own way. He lives with the dollar. For me, I can live with the peso."

Emilio's plot of land was, unsurprisingly, well tended. Nothing was out of place. The lines of the Fuentes' property were neatly marked on three sides with a cactus hedge. The grassy backyard appeared to extend for a mile down a treeless hill to the river, which widened and slowed as it mixed with the Gulf of Mexico.

Toward the back of the property was an outhouse—a box made of corrugated metal with an opening covered for privacy by a squash-yellow blanket. Chickens strutted in the shade of the palm fronds and fruit trees around their home.

The Fuentes family practically lived outdoors. The corrugated metal roof protected them from the rain, but their brick, cinderblock, and wood home did nothing to keep out pests or hot or cold air. Inside, on a floor of uneven concrete, the three bedrooms were large enough for a bed, a dresser, and little else. Two of the interior brick walls were painted with cheerful colors, hot pink and bright turquoise. On a small altar sat various images of the Virgin of Guadalupe and two lit candles in little glass cups. In the rear of the house, which was about 500 square feet, was an open-air cooking area where Fuentes' wife heated water for coffee over a log fire. They drew water from the neighborhood well and washed dishes in a tin basin and rinsed in a plastic one. A blue-and-white Coleman cooler served as their makeshift refrigerator for milk and *queso fresco* (a homemade, soft white cheese).

When we arrived at Emilio's for breakfast, he showed us his administrative law book. He said he enjoyed reading about the law, and the bookmarks, sunk deep throughout the thick tome, suggested that he did. His penchant for law, order, and family seemed to trump his desire to "vivir con el dólar" like his brother. Ismael's travels, while appealing, had raised concerns for Emilio, both moral and practical, about leaving his family.

"Migrants become impressed with the kind of life that people have there. They start comparing their lives to the lifestyles of the people there, and they start making mistakes. My brother, Ismael, he's changed a lot. He's estranged from his family. His wife in Texas is illegal. His children are illegal. They've changed, but not for the better. Yes, they've earned some dollars, but they've lost their origins, their values, their identity, and each other." Ismael had admitted as much at Kime's. "Once you leave, you're not thinking about money just to survive and to eat," he had said. "You're thinking about building a house, a car, jewelry. You start to think a different way."

Emilio knew he would change, too, and that the gamble of leaving, should he ever do so, would be unlikely to pay off in the short term. And, though he did not say it, he clearly feared the unknown. "The government, the money, the language, the culture—everything is different," he said. "For me, everything belongs to its own place. Things from the U.S. belong to the U.S., and things here belong to here."

A few years earlier Emilio had started working as a volunteer with Dr. Patricio Mora, of the Association of Veracruz Workers in Tamaulipas. As Mora's liaison in Barra de Cazones, Emilio advised new migrants on the realities of life in Reynosa. Mora brought Emilio to the border twice to show him those realities: people living far from their work and stuck in the underdeveloped margins of the sprawling city, being paid low wages, and too often victims of violent crime. "It's not our job to say to go or not, but migrants need to know that the rent is expensive, that you need a month saved up before going, and to be aware of what life is like there. I give them Dr. Mora's address if they decide to go." At times, Emilio wasn't sure how to advise himself on the question.

During breakfast, Emilio showed us Lenny's flawless report card. He glowed with pride, and even mentioned Harvard as a possibility for his talented and mature boy—despite the fact that he thought Harvard was located in Los Angeles. Soon Lenny would leave for more schooling and, Emilio hoped, eventually a good job. Lenny resembled his father. He loved the natural beauty and slower pace of Barra de Cazones. On clear nights in the right season, Lenny and his friend would gather food and supplies and, after a short boat ride, hike forty-five minutes up a nearby beach to a sea turtle nesting area. He and his friend, who had recently taken a university entrance exam to become a marine biologist, would stay until 3 a.m. prowling the nesting grounds and marking nest sites for a local research project.

Emilio had years before placed a bet on Lenny—namely, that a solid, two-parent upbringing would pay off down the road for his family. Emilio now had to decide how to support his son and his family through the next few years while Lenny was in school. As he considered heading north, Emilio thought about Ismael and the striking contradictions he embodied. He was worldly but illiterate, an advocate for the weak but a *machista* womanizer, and a hard worker who squandered his money. Flawed as he was, Ismael had embraced the rough opportunities that economic integration between Mexico and the United States had fostered. What it all meant on balance was ultimately hard to say for Emilio, who simply wanted to stay.

"In the end, migrants acquire some things, but lose others," he said. "They get dollars, but later they've lost everything they've had, everything that they wanted to come back to. I see the life of immigrants as very insecure, more difficult than the life that we have here. I'd say, 'Fine, take me with you,' if I knew I would have guarantees there, but there are none."

14

GETTING BACK TO WORK IN THE 'BURG

Galesburg, Illinois

TRACY WARNER BEGAN to worry after she got a rejection letter from Pizza Hut a few weeks after graduating from Western. She hadn't heard on some manager-level jobs at the Carl Sandburg Mall, but she expected at least some positive responses from the entry-level ones. "We wish you luck in finding a job worthy of your skills," read the Pizza Hut letter.

"What's that?" Warner said, exasperated. "Either my skills suck, or I have too many skills. Which is it? 'Cause I'm kind of curious! It's flattering to be overqualified but it doesn't pay the bills."

Warner hadn't expected a dream job to suddenly appear, but she had hoped for more than a quiet phone and a growing pile of rejection letters. She just needed something, anything, to get by. Several months into 2007, the newly minted and distinguished WIU graduate was still unemployed and uninsured. Although sworn off factory life, a desperate Warner applied to Farmland Foods.

When Maytag shuttered in 2004, Farmland, a massive, loud, hog disassembly operation, became the largest employer in this part of western Illinois. With about 1,200 to 1,400 cutters and slicers and a $60 million payroll, the slaughterhouse employed a couple hundred more than BNSF, the largest employer in Galesburg. Like Mike Smith, Warner was just looking for a wage, any wage, with a "1" in front of it, and Farmland, on Monmouth's northern edge, was close. It was so close, in fact, that on some days Warner could smell the tangy mix of rendered hog, hydrogen sulfide, methane, and whatever else made up that vile smell in her house, a mile to the south.

Farmland was a last resort for former Maytag workers. The jobs there, involving tearing apart pig carcasses with razor-sharp knives and powerful pneumatic tools were, frankly, tougher than appliance work. Perhaps worst was the "sticker," which slit the throats of about 1,000 shrieking animals each hour for about $12 an hour. That was one pig every four seconds, at about a penny per kill. It repulsed her to the core, but Warner admitted to herself that the regularity of factory life was calling to her again. It was regular work, and she needed the money.

Warner never received a call. She suspected Farmland management was suspicious of former Maytag assemblers. Local 2063's activism was well known in the area, and Farmland was headed in the opposite direction, having actively recruited a workforce that was mostly Mexican. In the previous decade, Farmland had gone from a majority white workforce to an almost exclusively Hispanic one, with an unknown number of unauthorized migrants. Patrick Anderson, the safety supervisor at the plant, said that of twenty new employees invited to a training session, eighteen might be Hispanic.[1] The world's largest hog producer and pork processor, Smithfield Foods, had purchased Farmland in 2003.

Farmland was famous for its anti-union stance and brushed off half-hearted union organizing efforts in Monmouth just about every summer. At the time Warner applied, anti-union signs were taped up and down the hallway inside the entrance. It's all she had seen in the first thirty seconds walking into the plant. The posters claimed that workers at Farmland in Monmouth made more than workers in their unionized Nebraska plant and didn't have to pay union dues.

Former union workers disliked Farmland as much as Farmland disliked them. Tim Welch, a hardworking Appliance City veteran, had lasted only ninety days at the Smithfield plant. "They use you up," he told me. "What, just to whack that meat up and get it out, get it done. And they're assholes, man. There's no union there so you either kiss their butt and get along with them or take the other path." What had emerged in the Monmouth labor market in the mid-2000s was an odd segmentation; the highest-paying entry-level jobs were nonunion, and those jobs typically went to locals in the growing Hispanic population.

With no phone call from Farmland, Warner began to despair. Her biggest disappointment came a few weeks later with, oddly, a long-awaited offer from *The Register-Mail*. The editors asked if she would be the Monmouth bureau reporter. She was thrilled, initially. The job required coming up with several story ideas each week, taking a newspaper writing class, and covering the police department and courthouse. Most evenings she would also have to attend school board and city council meetings in Monmouth and its surrounding towns.

It was an entry-level job and therefore paid poorly, but Warner knew that's where she would have to start if she wanted a career in journalism. She spoke to Carol Clark, the previous Monmouth bureau reporter. Clark told Warner that the job required sixty hours a week and that the newspaper "didn't like to pay overtime." Beyond the low pay and long hours, Warner would need childcare in the evenings. As much as she rolled it around in her mind, she couldn't make it work. A few days later Warner called *The Register-Mail* to turn down the job. She hoped that she was only postponing a move into journalism.

Weeks turned into months, and Warner found herself at the local welfare office in March 2007. She hadn't wanted to go. She had always thought public aid was for other people. She justified it to herself, as she had with the TAA benefits, by noting that she had paid into the system for years and that she needed the help. She had no income other than the court-ordered $82 in child support from Todd every two weeks. Now back in Ryan's life, Todd added his son to his health insurance plan and took him for a night or two each week.

The tiny welfare office for Warren and Henderson counties sat between a cornfield and a farm equipment dealership on the town's southern edge. The exterior was dismal, as though designed to keep people away. The Illinois Department of Human Services (IDHS) sign and the decorative wood shingles behind it were weathered and ragged. Inside, the spare lobby was covered with information about people's rights to food stamps, medical benefits, and assistance with translation into Spanish, Polish, and several other languages. One brochure targeted seasonal farmworkers. Warner noticed posters about fraud. She felt uneasy, defensive even, as she waited for her caseworker to call her name. The pride and excitement she felt that past December as she displayed her term paper on Rawls had vanished.

The meeting with her caseworker did not go well. Ryan, then 6, was bouncing around the office the entire time. Her caseworker, older and no-nonsense, insisted that she control him. Warner stayed long enough, though, to complete the interview and fill out a pile of paperwork. She applied for food stamps and Medicaid, but left the office crying after the tense interaction turned into a full-blown argument. "They treated me like a criminal. They don't know me! They don't know my situation! They shouldn't judge me, at least not to my face."

To her surprise, Warner received a Medicaid card and a LINK card that was credited each month with $284 in food stamps. Finally, she had health insurance again. Even though her only income was child support, she received no cash benefit. Since welfare reform in the late 1990s, cash benefits—usually a few hundred dollars a month—had been tough to get. IDHS had used "diversionary" strategies to keep women off the rolls—a "help-and-hassle" orientation, with an emphasis on the latter.[2] Illinois had cut the number of cash recipients by an astonishing 91 percent in the decade before Warner walked into the Monmouth office in 2007. By 2010, in the clutches of the Great Recession, Illinois ranked first in the states' race to gut the cash welfare system.[3] If you were able-bodied, you would find something, the policy screamed, and you didn't have a choice anyway.

Warner finally found a job cashiering weekends and nights at Farm King, a retail farm supply store, in late March. The Farm King job paid $6.50 an hour, then the Illinois minimum, but the hours were predictable and limited enough so she could manage her home life. Starting at Farm King was like a "kick in the teeth," Warner said. The wage was low, the technology was slow, the people were rude, and the store was poorly run. "Standing at that register, I kept thinking to myself that I shouldn't have to work here; I shouldn't have to put up with this. I know that I shouldn't have thought that, but I did."

In May, Warner took on a 20-hour per week janitorial job at Warren Achievement, a not-for-profit for people with developmental disabilities. The cleaning job, also at minimum wage, was a good fit. She could do it on her own time, after the "consumers" had left for their group homes or to be with their families for the evening. And she could bring Ryan, who liked to wonder around the quiet and empty building.

In her next visit to IDHS, Warner told her caseworker that she was working two jobs. The schoolmarmish caseworker snarled, according to Warner, informing her that she had to report income as soon as she earned it. Now the caseworker would have to report Warner's income retroactively to a special unit in Springfield dealing with food stamps fraud and overpayments. Earning $1,100 a month still kept Warner under the official 2007 poverty line of $14,291 for a single mother with one child.[4] Despite being officially "poor," Warner qualified for only $10 in food stamps. As a result, the state had overpaid Warner $274 each month since she got the jobs. In August, the Springfield unit ordered her to repay $1,096. Warner was shocked. Hat in hand, she worked out a deal to pay IDHS $20 a month for several years to make good on her debt to the State of Illinois. Warner could not help but think about the $10- or $20-million golden parachute that Ralph Hake got after he downsized her job and ran Maytag into the ground.[5] It was absurd.

Although the safety net had served her well in the transition out of the factory, Warner knew that she had sunk lower. At least retraining was approved of by people around her. Settling in the safety net's lowest layer, Warner felt the judgment of her caseworker and others around her. "They were trying to teach me a lesson, trying to show me that I'm a bad egg, a burden to the system. [My caseworker] asked me, 'Why would I use food stamps as a crutch even if I qualified for them? Why would I want to make life for me and my son harder than it has to be?' "

Warner's caseworker, an IDHS worker for decades, insisted she had never said that and didn't pass judgment. "Of course people take advantage of the system, that's human nature. If you can, you will. And there is more to the job than number-crunching, but my job is not to be a judge."[6] At the end of 2007, in a state of nearly 13 million, fewer than 9,000 adults, all of them parents or guardians, were deemed worthy of TANF (Temporary Assistance to Needy Families) cash benefits. (About 50,000 children received TANF benefits; the total Illinois caseload was 58,882.)[7] TANF cash support for adults had basically ceased to exist in Illinois.

Warner kept applying for a better job, and at the end of summer 2007 she found one at Galesburg High School. Five years earlier she had cast a vote to strike against Maytag in the school's auditorium. That fall she would start as a teacher's aide in the school's extensive special education department. Finally, she thought, she would use her degree.

It was a taxing job. She assisted in classrooms filled with adolescents carrying a variety of unfortunate diagnoses—autism, developmentally delayed, behavior disorder, learning disability, bipolar disorder. But she could work during Ryan's school hours, the job paid $8.55 an hour, and it came with health and retirement benefits. Warner kept her job cleaning for Warren Achievement in the evenings and weekends and happily left Farm King behind. The job at Galesburg High School fit the skills she had developed in college a little better and engaged her mind. Warner would be working two jobs, more hours, driving more, and yet still earning about half her Maytag income, but she finally felt like she was climbing out of the hole she had found herself in since graduation.

DOUG DENNISON WAS not particularly fond of changing directions. However, when the funds for the AFL-CIO peer counseling program dried up in the summer of 2006, he had to find something else. He lucked into work managing a grant at Westmer Junior and Senior High School in Joy, Illinois, a tiny town of 417 just east of the Mississippi.[8] The school faced falling test scores, declining enrollment, and impending consolidation. The Illinois State Board of Education's Regional Office of Education had been awarded a five-year 21st Century Community Learning Centers grant from the U.S. Department of Education to turn things around. It funded before-school, lunchtime, and afterschool programming—and Dennison's position.

Dennison was excited about his new job. He started with fifteen kids who, after grabbing lunch in the school cafeteria, came to spend their meal with Dennison. "They eat with one hand and read with the other. I try to instill some self-respect, positive behaviors, study skills. I'm a college dropout, but I tell them that I'm a graduate of the school of hard knocks." Dennison also started coaching the varsity basketball team at Westmer. He felt strangely comfortable in this job, different as it was from Maytag production-line work.

"I like helping people. I like to root for the underdog. I like to stand up for the underdog. And in a way that's what I'm doing in my new job. I'm earning a couple dollars less, and I'm not sure what happens when the grant runs out but I can't complain. I guess we're not quite as set in stone now as we were when we were working at Maytag. We've had to become a little more flexible, to go with the flow a little more."

By this point, it had been over two years since his fiery Labor Day speech before the 2004 election. Things had changed plenty. "I actually like my current work more. But if I could go back in with my 21 years, I'd give up my current job and go back. I would have been content to retire at Maytag." He had been just nine years away from a fully vested pension, and he missed his work with Local 2063. But this new job was simply more rewarding, and there was no sense being nostalgic or considering a return to factory life.

"I'd rather not go back to a factory setting. I'd rather do something like I'm doing now, working with kids. The unions aren't the same anymore anyway. Dad was a union man. Each night you sat with the family, ate dinner, and we talked union. Now you think less of the 'team.' It's more, 'What can I do for myself?'"

What had motivated Dennison in the three years after the closing announcement was the fight: a fight for fairness that he had learned sitting at his parents' dining room table, on the Maytag shop floor, and in Labor Temple meetings. But, he now saw, the fight had cost him. Planning the rallies, going on the speaking tour with Bevard and Obama, making classroom visits, and talking to the media had taken him away from Annette and the boys. He had missed Annette's aunt's funeral to speak at the Labor Day rally, which had really irked Annette. She was looking out for the family's future; he seemed stuck in the past.

"Give it up, Doug," Annette had said to him many times. "It's a losing battle. Move past it! Corporate America, you can't fight them." Annette supported Doug's union work but wondered when he would face reality. "The union is going to save our jobs, blah, blah, blah," Annette said. "I didn't buy it."

"I thought we were going to save the world," Dennison added. "I was going to go down with the ship and be a hero. I even thought we could keep the plant from closing. Silly me. The plant still closed. People still suffered. Maybe I took the easy way out. Annette was more in touch; she reinvented herself."

In May 2007 Annette graduated at the top of her radiology cohort of sixteen, down from the eighteen that started two years earlier. Mounted on her bedroom wall was a plaque for the Nancy Gilman Outstanding Student award, an award voted on by the program's clinical instructors. She was proud, and rightfully so. Her program was among the most selective at Sandburg, with some of the best teachers, and the best prospects, and she was at the top. At the end of over four years of prerequisites, science classes, clinical rotations, and part-time work at Methodist, Annette, a few months shy of age 40, could really say she had reinvented herself.

Methodist Medical Center in Peoria scooped up Annette right away as a full-time, emergency room X-ray tech at $20 an hour, a good 30 percent higher than her Maytag wage. Annette would leave for work at 9:45 p.m. to start her shift at 11 p.m. She and her friends at work took "lunch," as they called it, at 2 a.m. She worked the ICU at 4 a.m. and then went to the cardiac unit after that. Annette was out the door at 7:30 a.m. Once home, she wound down with chores or errands and then slept from 10 a.m. to 3 p.m., provided her mother—who did not fully get the idea of "third shift" for the first year or so—did not call.

"Every day is different. Peoria, it's kinda of city, it's right downtown. We get all the crazy stuff, the drunks, the shootings, the stabbings. It's fun!" She laughed a wry laugh. "No, but it does make it interesting."

Annette kept at it through 2008 and 2009 but began to think about squeezing in a semester for MRI certification or a year and a half for ultrasound. Her schedule was tight but it was appealing: more day shift jobs, jobs closer to home, more money.

"Someday I'll have a normal shift and spend more time with the kids. Right now there's just nothing out there." She was starting all over with her retirement savings—her Maytag pension would have vested in 2019. She still had a distinct advantage over older women and men who started the reinvention process in their forties and fifties. She had more time. Looking back at the past few years, Doug and Annette felt much different than they had in 2004. They were more settled, more content with the changes.

"We're pretty lucky," Doug said. "She worked hard at it. I just sort of fell into something."

"It was a tough transition, I guess," Annette said. "We got through it, just figuring out what we wanted to do and then doing it, setting a goal."

"I still don't know what *I* want to do!" Doug said, only half in jest.

"Yeah, Doug still doesn't know what he wants to do when he grows up!"

"I'm going to fake it until I make it," Doug said with his characteristic self-effacing humor and boyish charm.

Annette had become the primary breadwinner, not to mention the handyman in the family. Doug cooked more. Because of Annette's upside-down work schedule, the balance of parenting Dalton and Dylan had shifted his way as well.

"I'm the man, he's the woman," Annette joked.

I asked if it produced any friction in their relationship. "We always have conflict," Annette replied with a smile.

"Not really," Doug corrected. "I wear the pants in this house! I set them out, and she presses them!" Slouched in the couch, Doug laughed. He was about to head out to a yearly fantasy football draft with his buddies.

"Yeah, OK," Annette said, humoring him with a playful scowl.

THE WALMART COMMUTE and the Walmart job were too much for the Cummins family. In 2007, Jackie left the distribution warehouse gig and got a job at Farmland Foods ripping out the spinal cords of eviscerated hogs. The money was good enough to keep her there for a year, but she found it grueling and humiliating. "I've been reduced to this!" she remembered thinking to herself. "It was disgusting." However, the slaughterhouse job had a wage "with a '1' in front of it": $13 an hour. And she didn't have a long commute.

Shannon found a local job, too. While at Walmart, she had been substitute teaching in a couple of elementary schools. In the fall of 2007, she was offered a job working in an Abingdon school as a student aid. It required her new associate's degree but paid only $8 an hour, just over the Illinois minimum wage of $7.50 an hour. Nonetheless, she liked it. "The kids are fun. You go with them to the specials like gym and music. Gym is hilarious. They just do whatever they want. They don't listen to the rules." Shannon, a warm, maternal presence, worked closely with autistic children and kids with behavioral problems.

Shannon and Jackie stubbornly stayed on in an area where the good jobs had already been carved out, and in a tiny town that might not welcome a lesbian couple with children. Jackie said she had faced discrimination a couple of times at the Maytag factory, but nothing she couldn't handle. Once an older lady who had rushed to Jackie's aid when she got a cut later demanded a blood test after she was reminded that Jackie was a lesbian. It was an ignorant thing to do, but atypical, Jackie maintained. In fact, in the five years they were at Maytag, the couple made all kinds of friends. Jackie's department threw them a shower when they learned they were adopting Rain and Jordon.

"It would be nice to live in a place where we were more accepted, with more gays and lesbians, but it wouldn't feel like home," Jackie said. "So many people in larger areas are different from us. It is sometimes hard to fit in. I think we're just little old farm girls at heart. We love apple pie, baseball games. We're just kinda cheesy Midwesterners."

Jackie preferred that "political types" focus on bread-and-butter issues rather than on gay rights. "My life doesn't have to be the focal point of America. How I live as a gay person doesn't have to be the issue that is first and foremost, because it's not. Education, jobs for all Americans is ten times more important. The prime example is this school here in Abingdon never once said anything to us about being gay parents. But they *have* talked about budget cuts. I mean the focal point right now for us is not gay rights; it is money."

"We aren't advocates," Shannon added.

Jackie and Shannon had worried about their adoption being stalled by local prejudice. But they found a lawyer in Galesburg—a "great man"—who helped them through the process without a hitch. Despite the downward jolt in their economic lives, things were good in their family and in their community. Jackie had reconciled with her father, and both Shannon's and Jackie's families adored the kids and were nearby to help. They had a community.

In 2003, a month after they were laid off from Maytag, and on the very day they had left to pick up Rain and Jordon from Idaho, a gas explosion in the house next door caved in their house and rocked it off its foundation. It was ruined. For weeks, people they knew and people they didn't know brought by furniture and food. More recently, Jackie said, a man had walked by their car and shut the door to turn off their lights. That's what made Abingdon their home. They had been around a while, and they felt accepted and didn't want to start over with that. "It may be behind our backs, but they're doing a good job of hiding it," Shannon said of the seeming absence of prejudice. They didn't want to leave.

Further, moving to St. Louis or Chicago just didn't make sense. They had lived in cities and suburbs before but, as Shannon put it, hadn't cared for the "hustle and bustle" and living so close to so many people. It wasn't for them. "I don't feel like competing," Jackie said. "Clearly it's a competition there, to get a house in an OK neighborhood, a better parking spot. Well, I have those things. If someone has a bachelor's degree or master's degree, I think they can do much better in the city. But I think someone with a small, two-year degree, well, you're looking at being below poverty level incomes. What's the point? You're really going to be at the bottom."

David Lindstrom, the counselor from Galesburg Works, said that the Cummins' sentiments were widely held. He estimated that only 5 to 7 percent of the workforce had left, and if they did leave, they likely didn't wander far. Displaced Maytag workers routinely chose the familiar, the secure, and the people they knew—and, consequently, lower incomes—over the unknown. As Adam Smith wrote about the initial churning of the industrial revolution in *The Wealth of Nations*, workers generally resist moving if they can. "After all that has been said of the levity and inconstancy of human nature, it appears evidently from experience that a man is of all sorts of luggage the most difficult to be transported."[9] Plus, Lindstrom said, "You can sell your house here, and you can buy a brick in Chicago." He was about right. The Cummins' two-story, three-bedroom home was worth around $45,000 in 2007.

Jackie left the hog slaughterhouse and settled into a job as a dental assistant for Dr. Kandy Sayrs in Galesburg during the summer of 2008. The work was fairly steady and paid $10.15 an hour. Together, she and Shannon would make $27,000 in the year that followed, less than half of the $60,000 they had earned at Maytag—a cash-rich time when they didn't have Rain and Jordon. When they had worked at Maytag, Jackie would buy a new pair of shoes every month and sometimes crank up the heat to 80 degrees in the winter and wear shorts. Now it was an everyday struggle to cut costs. They planned every meal, shopped in bulk at Aldi, and delayed even essential purchases until they had the money. They still lived above the poverty line, which for their family was $21,834 in 2008.[10] The Cummins family, though, had fallen to about 125 percent of the poverty threshold, arguably a better indicator of severe material hardship. One in five Americans fell under this threshold in 2010.[11]

Between 2000 and 2008, manufacturing in Knox County nearly evaporated entirely, making it a poignant reflection of the precipitous and historic nationwide loss of 5.8 million (about one in three) manufacturing jobs in the 2000s (see Figure 14.1). The labor-friendly county lost 4,139 manufacturing jobs, or 78.7 percent of its total. About the same number of people trickled out of the county from 2000 to 2009, as if a Smithian self-correcting mechanism had been set in motion. The population dropped steadily over the decade from 55,836 to 51,648, or 7.5 percent. Education and health care added the most jobs, 428, but these jobs—most of them tied in one way or another to public funding—made only a small dent in the loss.[12]

Many commuted to Peoria, the Quad Cities, or elsewhere for work, but Jackie and Shannon had chased that chimerical full-replacement wage long enough. It took time, but they had learned to expect less. "Are we ever going to have that again in life, in America?" Jackie asked. "The American Dream is not a cute little house with a white picket fence anymore. It's just an OK job that pays the bills, that's close by you, and fits your time schedule. And maybe even *that* is just a dream. I still haven't found that niche like I had at Maytag."

"You just accept it," Shannon said. "You realize there's no other alternative, that you have no choice but to deal with it and move on. Well, this is what it's

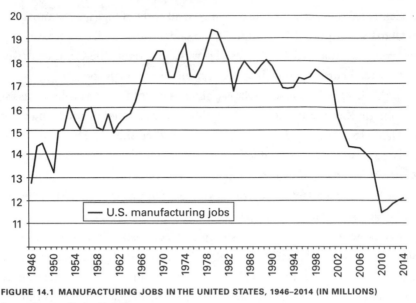

FIGURE 14.1 MANUFACTURING JOBS IN THE UNITED STATES, 1946–2014 (IN MILLIONS)
Source: Bureau of Labor Statistics.

going to be. It's never going to reopen. Everybody's not going to get their jobs back. You get to that point. You can't hang on to what used to be. You can't be constantly mad at Maytag. Yeah, I still go by every now and then and think about it, cuss it out." She laughed. "But really you just accept it. You have to, there's no going back. You just have to become different people."

Jackie and Shannon had seen many friends and former colleagues follow their own circuitous paths to this rather plain realization. One friend, they said, worked really hard in school but didn't make it. She became resigned, started using meth, and, soon after, lost custody of her children. By 2008, however, she had become clean, reunited with her children, and was working a low-wage job. She finally had settled. Looking across the post–Appliance City landscape several years out, it was clear these Midwesterners—and probably people everywhere—were simply not hard-wired for downward mobility. People knew they had to settle. Doing so, however, was another matter entirely.

Jackie learned that she couldn't fix it, and that trying was tantamount to beating your head against the wall. But she was equally frustrated that nobody else seemed to be trying to fix it either. She had been an avid supporter of the union, but looking back she had a more cynical view. When I asked her if it mattered that her job at Farmland was nonunion she said, "Not anymore. There's not a difference anymore. It used to matter."

"This is hard for me to say," Jackie went on. "But I think unions are losing steam and power. I think it's being stripped away. Corporate people don't want it anymore." Jackie was quite fond of Dave Bevard, Aaron Kemp, and others in the union, but as a whole, it had failed in her eyes. "Maytag steamrolled them. They didn't stand up for us." The local, with AFL-CIO funding, had hired Jackie as a peer counselor, a job she felt was just meant to pacify laid-off workers by telling them about things that they already knew about, such as the Workforce Investment Act and food stamps.

Jackie and Shannon knew they could rely on their family and their neighbors, yet felt isolated otherwise. Even at the climax of the Obama and Clinton primary contest in June 2008, they didn't bother to vote. Shannon appreciated the first serious female candidate being in the race, but Bill Clinton's signing of NAFTA still upset her.

Jackie enjoyed her work at Dr. Sayrs' office more than she had the Maytag job. Plus, she had beautiful white teeth as a result of the dental work and her mild obsession with Crest Whitestrips (and despite having been to the dentist maybe twice in her life). And Jackie quickly learned not to "scream her co-workers a new one" at her new workplace (as people had done back in the factory). Her new job in the service sector helped people directly and even changed people's lives if they had an embarrassing or painful dental problem. But like so many others, Jackie would have left this or any of her post-Maytag jobs in a heartbeat to return to Appliance City. She missed the pay, the benefits, the friends, and the regularity. They were basically "trained monkeys," she said, but it had simply been a good job.

Shannon didn't miss Maytag at all. She loved the work with kids and wouldn't have traded back despite the much lower wage. "It's goofy but I like being called 'Ms. Cummins.' It's cute. You come in the door and they're like, 'Hi, Ms. Cummins!' It makes me feel more worthwhile, I guess, like it's more of a career. Maytag really just felt like a job."

ON JANUARY 1, 2008, after the Smoke-Free Illinois Act went into effect, George Carney's Town Tavern suffered. Fewer people came, and when they did, they didn't stay as long and drank less. Carney estimated that his revenues at the little bar dropped by a third in 2008. In the midst of the Great

Recession, he thought he would be in one of the few businesses that would remain steady in Avon, population 799. Like Galesburg, Monmouth, and the smaller towns scattered in Knox, Warren, and Fulton counties, Avon was slowly shrinking. One in every eight Avon residents left in the 2000s.[13]

Carney sold the bar in April 2009 for a loss and left Avon, too. The property's value had declined as a result of the new law and, on top of that, Carney learned it had an old lien he had to settle. He was left penniless. The confident workingman with a family, a big house with a swimming pool, a beautiful Harley, paintball and NASCAR buddies, and plenty of overtime cash, found himself living alone in a small room in his son's apartment in Matherville, Illinois. "I walked away with nothing. Lost everything. Started with basically the clothes on my back and the stuff I had in my apartment, and that's it, that was all my belongings."

His son's room was just big enough for a bed, a television, and the twenty cases of hard liquor Carney had salvaged from the Town Tavern. Jobless and depressed, he seldom came out of his room, choosing instead to watch crime dramas from morning to night, week after week. When he needed gas money to drive around looking for work, he would go to a bar and sell a bottle of Captain Morgan or Jägermeister for cash. The worst part was that Carney was alone; he and Lynn had parted ways. "I wouldn't say I took it out on her, but I was more reserved to myself," Carney admitted.

Occasionally, whenever he was feeling masochistic, Carney would calculate how close he would have been to retirement at Maytag. That year it was just five years until 2014, which would have been the year. Now, if he could even find a job in the midst of the Great Recession, he would probably have to work for as long as his body would hold up.

GALESBURG

1. MAIN STREET, GALESBURG, ILLINOIS
CREDIT: DAVID SAMUEL STERN.

2. THE SIGN COMES DOWN, NOVEMBER 15, 2004
CREDIT: KENT KRIEGSHAUSER/*THE REGISTER-MAIL*.

3. RUSTING LINE INSIDE SHUTTERED APPLIANCE CITY, 2008

CREDIT: DAVID SAMUEL STERN.

4. DOUG DENNISON AT WESTMER JUNIOR HIGH, 2010
CREDIT: CHAD BROUGHTON.

5. TRACY WARNER IN HER MONMOUTH BACKYARD, 2010
CREDIT: CHAD BROUGHTON.

6. GEORGE CARNEY AT WELCOME INN IN MILAN, 2013
CREDIT: CHAD BROUGHTON.

7. CUMMINS FAMILY AT THEIR NEW HOME IN ABINGDON, 2013
CREDIT: CHAD BROUGHTON.

8. MICHAEL PATRICK AT CLOSED FACTORY, 2013
CREDIT: CHAD BROUGHTON.

REYNOSA

9. COKE TRUCK RUMBLES THROUGH REYNOSA COLONIA, 2007
CREDIT: DAVID SAMUEL STERN.

10. FACTORY PALLET FENCE AND PAINTED PLYWOOD HOUSE, 2007
CREDIT: DAVID SAMUEL STERN.

11. PLANTA MAYTAG III IN PARQUE INDUSTRIAL COLONIAL, 2007
CREDIT: DAVID SAMUEL STERN.

12. LAURA FLORA OLIVEROS AND DAUGHTER ERIKA, 2007
CREDIT: DAVID SAMUEL STERN.

13. LAURA SUAREZ FLORA, 2007
CREDIT: DAVID SAMUEL STERN.

14. CONSTRUCTION OF A ROW OF INFONAVIT HOMES, 2007
CREDIT: DAVID SAMUEL STERN.

15. NEW INFONAVIT HOUSING NEAR PLANTA MAYTAG III, 2003
CREDIT: CHAD BROUGHTON.

16. SAME ROW OF INFONAVIT HOMES, FULLY LIVED IN, 2013
CREDIT: CHAD BROUGHTON.

17. ERIKA SUAREZ SHOWS ED KRUEGER VIDEO OF BANA BOX MAQUILA FIRE, 2013
CREDIT: CHAD BROUGHTON.

18. DODS LEADER TERESA CHÁVEZ (RIGHT) AND DAUGHTER MARINA FERROR, 2013
CREDIT: CHAD BROUGHTON.

19. MAYOR JAVIER GONZALEZ OF AGUA DULCE IN OFFICE, 2007
CREDIT: DAVID SAMUEL STERN.

20. ABANDONED, HALF-BUILT HOME OF FORMER AGUA DULCE FAMILY, 2007
CREDIT: DAVID SAMUEL STERN.

21. EJIDATARIO PRODUCE STAND OUTSIDE OF PAPANTLA, 2007
CREDIT: DAVID SAMUEL STERN.

22. WOMEN HARVESTING CHILE PEQUIN OUTSIDE VOLADOR, 2007
CREDIT: DAVID SAMUEL STERN.

23. MAYOR AARON BARRERA OF VOLADOR, 2007
CREDIT: DAVID SAMUEL STERN.

24. EMILIO FUENTES (RIGHT) LISTENS AO BROTHER, ISMAEL, DEBATES, 2007
CREDIT: DAVID SAMUEL STERN.

25. EMILIO FUENTES'S HOME IN BARRA DE CAZONES, 2007
CREDIT: DAVID SAMUEL STERN.

26. MARISOL OVERSEES CORNHUSK EXPORT OPERATION
IN AGUA DULCE, 2007
CREDIT: DAVID SAMUEL STERN.

15

HOJAS, BLACKBERRIES, AND
THE TORTILLA KING

Agua Dulce, Veracruz

ON A BLISTERING morning in July 2007, four middle-aged men, already quite drunk, stood shaded under the eaves of a long, white stucco building. The building, which was derelict, sat in the middle of Agua Dulce in semitropical northern Veracruz. Our guide, Orlinda Garcia, asked the four men where we could find an *hoja* (husk) processing plant. Mayor Javier Gonzalez and Treasurer José Cruz stood with us as well. Gonzalez's sky-blue municipal office was just a few hundred feet away, on the other side of the vacant town plaza. The adjacent plaza was littered with rusty rides and empty prize booths from a traveling summer carnival that had recently ended.[1]

"This is it!" a man in a Pittsburgh Pirates cap shouted. He pointed to a concealed entrance.

Part of the wavy clay tile roof was missing and had been replaced with corrugated metal sheets. Plastic bags and bottles specked the ground outside. A slick, red PRI campaign banner hung on an electric pole next to the building with a candidate's portrait. "Fiel a ti" (Loyal to you), the banner read. The plain building stretched alongside a wide, bumpy road—deserted except for a few chickens. It did not look like the site of a profitable foreign-trade operation.

A young *encargada* (supervisor) named Marisol greeted us from behind a black metal gate. We asked her if we could see inside the facility. "The *patron* is not here," she said. "I cannot let you in." She was apologetic but firm. In a pink blouse, capri pants, and faux gem-studded flip-flops, she appeared to be dressed more for a Saturday of shopping in Monterrey than managing an export business in this half-ghost town in far-flung Veracruz. "The boss is very particular, and he doesn't allow people from the outside to see the operation."

Another neatly dressed young woman looked at us while she embroidered some clothing in a chair behind Marisol. She sat next to a pile of plastic bags swollen with corn husks (called hojas or *totomoxtle*). In the darkness further inside, there were several young women busily stuffing husks while keeping their eyes on us. Marisol said they worked six days a week. The four *borrachos* were attracted to this building for more than the shade.

We pressed Marisol for a quick tour, but she was unimpressed by the fact that Garcia was a PAN representative from Papantla, the municipality's seat. Mayor Gonzalez tried his luck, but Marisol remained unimpressed. It was clear that she would not let us in, but she agreed to talk from behind the gate.

Competition among cornhusk exporters, we learned, was fierce. Husk exporting had become big business in the past couple of decades as Mexicans living in the United States sought out tamale husks for their kitchens and restaurants. Not just any husk would do. They demanded sturdy, traditional white *criollo* maize husks to make tamales, the Mexican comfort and festival food filled with meats, cheese, or sweet ingredients that is steamed in the husk.

"In the past, farmers just discarded the husk," Marisol said. "The grain was worth more. Campesinos are now planting for the husk, not the ear." In a twist of the post-NAFTA world, the exportable tamale cornhusk was now more valuable than the actual grain in Agua Dulce. On the side of nearby country roads and around town corn ears lay discarded in browning pyramids, left to rot or be used as firewood.

Some Agua Dulce farmers, pinched by sagging prices and rising costs, contracted with norteños from Monterrey, Sonora, and elsewhere to grow corn for the husk. For many, the mini-export boom had reshaped daily work life. Young men sawed or "disked" off the base of the harvested corn with a carpenter's saw so the hojas were light for export. Fumigators then gassed the hojas in sealed rooms with sulfur gas to whiten them and remove impurities, fungus, and bugs—leaving an eggy smell lingering in certain parts of town. From there, entire households, including grandmothers and children, sorted the husks by quality grades in their living rooms, not unlike the putting-out system of preindustrial England that turned rural cottages into little family workshops for spinning thread, sewing, and making shoes.

Once sorted, the husks came to Marisol and her packing crew or one of the other local exporters. Marisol said big trucks came periodically to pick up the boxes, but she didn't know where they went. Although the hojas connected Agua Dulce to the dynamic global marketplace, the work relations seemed feudal. There were no benefits or opportunities for advancement, and everything was subject to the whims of owners, the weather, and the seasons. The work was paid in cash by the day or by the piece.

We left Marisol and walked a couple of blocks through town. We found a door that was apparently propped open for ventilation, for inside the heat was nearly stifling. Women in colorful tank tops stood on a concrete floor layering sorted, papery husks on tables. With a few fluorescent lights dangling from above, this miniature packing factory looked more like an unfinished garage than the engine of another hoja export operation.

The women stuffed stacks of the papery husks into thick plastic "Azteca"-branded bags. The bags, which were heaped in a waist-high pyramid in the center of the room, were then put into Azteca cardboard boxes and readied for pickup. "The workers are from here, but the owners are from elsewhere," Treasurer Cruz said. "They have capital, they know the market over there in the U.S., and they have connections. Even if you had economic resources here for starting a business, if you don't have contacts, it doesn't matter."

Gonzalez expressed mixed feelings about the local husk exporters. "Here the husk work almost never ends. We think it's because we have cheap labor here."

"The majority of people shoot to make 80 to 100 pesos a day [$7.25 to $9.00 a day]," said Cruz. "They'll do that and then they'll feel like they're done for the day."

Although global markets had entered Agua Dulce, Agua Dulce as a whole had not moved forward. What the capitalists from Monterrey and elsewhere had managed to create were protected islands of private moneymaking. The outsiders came in to buy local husks, made cheap by the glut of corn, as well as the surplus labor: for soil plowing and harrowing; sowing and weeding; fertilizing and spraying; harvesting and sawing; and fumigating, sorting, and packing. For all this labor, local workers earned pennies from each box of husks bound for the United States. The norteño husk exporters did not make the federally required social security or savings account payments to their workers. Unlike those doing formal work in the maquilas, husk farmers and workers did not accumulate housing credits or receive food vouchers or over-time bonuses.

Gonzalez echoed the complaint of city officials up north in Reynosa; he was powerless to shape these islands of transnational trade to local interests. As with the border maquiladoras and Maytag after Hadley, the owners of the hoja enterprises had only a commercial connection to the place where they made their money. It was development without progress.

However, in jobs-starved Agua Dulce, it was better to have the hoja work than not. One farmer in Zona Totonaca asked worriedly whether the Chinese exported maize husks. He said he had read an article online about it. Many still had little idea what El Tratado de Libre Comercio de América del Norte was, but people in Agua Dulce sensed outside forces at work in their corn fields, orange groves, and husk workshops.[2] The hoja story is just one story from a revolutionized North American food system. The repercussions have been felt from the ejidos of semitropical Agua Dulce to Mexico's new export-oriented blackberry and hog farms, from the hole-in-the-wall tortilla makers of Mexico City to new tortilla factories north of the border and in China, and from the expansive corn landscapes and tractor factories of Illinois and Iowa to supermarkets and chain superstores across the continent.

CAÑEROS—THE 155,000 SMALL-SCALE sugarcane growers in Mexico— also faced a new economic landscape. Sugar, cultivated since the time of the *conquistadores* and culturally significant, supports over two million Mexicans.

In the mid-1990s, high-fructose corn syrup (HFCS) from the United States began to spill into the Mexican soft drink market as the continent moved toward free trade in all sweetners. A trade war—that continues to this day—commenced. Mexican sugar growers complained that HFCS, like all American corn products, was unfairly subsidized and demanded access to the U.S. market, where sugar prices were higher. The U.S. sugar industry, in turn, lobbied for import controls to avoid a deluge of cheap Mexico sugar. Sugar prices in Mexico dropped and the industry was thrust into crisis. Several big mills closed or were expropriated by the government because of debt, and cañeros everywhere found themselves at a crossroads.[3]

One of the shuttered sugar mills, San Sebastián, was located just outside of Los Reyes, Michoacán, about 440 miles directly west of Agua Dulce. Like the corn farmers of Veracruz, cañeros were supposed to switch their ejidal lands to "higher value" crops—those in which Mexico had a "comparative advantage"—to survive in the global era. Enter blackberries, a luxury fruit virtually unknown in rural Mexico until 1994.

Although the sandy soil and temperate highland climate of Los Reyes are perfect for blackberries, few cañeros could reinvent their ejidal sugarcane plots on their own. In Michoacán, blackberry production costs ten to twenty times more per hectare than sugarcane. It requires costly irrigation systems, washing facilities, and packing and chemical sheds. And, for good yields, growers have to follow a highly scientific process, involving mowing, burning, irrigation and fertilization, hedging and chemical defoliation, growth promotion, and pruning of the "Tupy" cultivar, a blackberry variety.[4] The cañeros didn't get the help they needed.

Instead, the Mexican state welcomed in transnationals and supported larger-scale, higher-tech growers who could generate economies of scale and be more competitive in the globalizing fruit market. In the mid-1990s, Driscoll's and SunnyRidge from the United States, Sun Belle from Chile, and others descended on Los Reyes to grow the labor-intensive luxury export. They found the perfect place for a global enterprise. First, cheap land. Renting ejidal land, in fact, was preferable to buying, which entailed tax liabilities.[5] They were also attracted to Mexico's lax environmental standards, which permitted pesticides that were banned in the United States. And, like maquila owners in the north, they found a ready pool of workers. With the closing of the sugar mill, which was unionized and government supported, campesinos of the Los Reyes region were desperate. Finally, from central Mexico the global giants could put freshly hand-picked berries into U.S. supermarkets in merely three days. It was the perfect arrangement, and just the sort of market-oriented shift that President Carlos Salinas de Gotari had imagined for rural Mexico with the 1992 changes to Article 27 of Mexico's constitution concerning the ejido. The "black gold rush" was on.

Like Papantla's export-led vanilla boom a century earlier, the blackberry boom reshaped the region. It brought investment, grew wealth, and drove economic growth and exports. There were jobs for construction workers, irrigation mechanics, truck drivers, agronomists, and engineers. Women, often indigenous Tarascans who were desired for their "natural" ability to pick the small berries, had wage work opportunities. Fourteen years after the transnationals entered Michoacán in 1994, Mexico's exports of fresh blackberries had grown by a staggering 101,615 percent by volume and by 224,997 percent in value.[6] Today, nearly all of Mexico's blackberries are grown in Michoacán, and SunnyRidge has added blueberries and raspberries. In 2014, Chinese and Mexican authorities met in Los Reyes to lay the groundwork for berry exports to China.

According to Donna Chollett, an anthropologist at the University of Minnesota-Morris, the black gold rush in Los Reyes undermined local traditions related to land stewardship, family, and community. It also exacerbated inequality, imposed foreign control, and etched new class strata and gender relations in sharp relief. In her longitudinal study, Chollett found that most of the former cane lands had been converted to blackberry production by the late 2000s. Although the hacienda of prerevolutionary Mexico had not been recreated, larger blackberry growers (some of the better-off, former sugar growers) and big transnationals have cobbled together de facto fruit plantations on rented ejidal lands. Today, the berry companies rent to grow their own crops, but also contract with larger local growers. With contract farming, corporate buyers can demand the cheapest and best produce, impose production rules, and reject crops entirely at their discretion—and face none of the risks of a bad crop, sick workers, or pest problems. Like American chicken farmers in the South who contract with Tyson or North Carolina tobacco growers who contract with Philip Morris and Reynolds American, the risk is pushed to the agriculturalists, in this case, to the local blackberry growers.[7]

Chollett also found that an increasing number of divorced and abandoned women headed households in Los Reyes. The men who used to grow sugarcane (and couldn't make the switch) had been pushed into unemployment, wage work, or the rural exodus. The social property was still there, but fewer ejidatarios farmed it, reflecting a nationwide trend. In 1999, 1.8 million ejido landowners were classified as farmers, according to the U.S. Department of Agriculture (USDA). Just four years later the number was 1.3 million. Many women took title to ejidal lands during the upheavals. In 2006 the Secretariat of Agrarian Reform announced a "feminization" of the ejido.[8]

The women fieldworkers of Los Reyes, who worked with hazardous pesticides, formed the base of the agro-industrial food chain. In 2008 women could earn, if they picked proficiently, about what a maquila worker did in a day. Each container of Los Reyes blackberries the women filled for Trader Joe's or some other American supermarket, where they sold for about $4, made them 9 cents.[9] The work fluctuated seasonally, but as with packing cornhusks under a dangling light bulb in Agua Dulce or soldering plasma screen television components in Reynosa, picking berries—as labor intensive and tedious as maquila work—was how economic globalization looked to poor women across the Los Reyes countryside. Chollett's conclusion, in fact, could have been written about the maquilas. "More women have jobs, but fewer men do ... Women's wages fall at the bottom of a chain of profit that transfers millions of dollars outside the region."[10]

Studies of rural Mexico have found that, as in the border region, women have faced both greater risks and greater opportunities in Mexico's opening. In the middle of the rural squeeze, households had been forced to maximize income-generating opportunities, meaning, most notably, out-migration and women's wage work. One study of rural households found that the percentage of women in charge of the farm, generating income, managing households, and remittance income had shot up. Another study found that in households in which the woman's earnings had increased, male alcoholism and violence declined. Another study found that women developed more intra-household bargaining power in the post-NAFTA era. Another study found that rural households were more likely to have televisions, nondirt floors, and more meat and dairy in their diets, though these changes would likely have arrived without liberalization as well.[11]

Michoacán blackberries turned Mexico into the third-largest blackberry producer in the world by 2007. American consumers, hungrier than ever for fresh produce, luxury fruits, and antioxidants, were delighted to have sweet, off-season berries on their supermarket shelves.[12] The USDA, in fact, argued that the availability of off-season produce from Mexico helped drive the shift in U.S. consumption patterns toward fresh produce over processed fruits and vegetables.[13] And with more avocados, limes, and people from south of the border, the agency proclaimed, Americans were integrating not just economically but also culturally with their southern neighbors.

Yet despite a boom in fruits and vegetables, most of Mexico's agricultural exports were losing export share in the United States. Asparagus, mangoes, melons, cauliflower and broccoli, eggplants, and cucumbers, to name but a few, had increased in absolute value but lost market share. Bananas, coffee, and live cattle declined as well. In fact it was a rare case, such as blackberries, avocados (up 33,397 percent in volume over fourteen years), and beer—particularly Grupo Modelo's Corona—(up 801 percent), where Mexico capitalized decisively.[14] The new exports were not enough to replace what had been lost as traditional crops like corn and sugar became less viable. Fruits and vegetables accounted for a small fraction of cultivated land, and much of Mexico was unsuitable for fruits and vegetables because of soil, climate, and topography reasons.[15]

Former president Salinas' promise to "export goods, not people" ultimately relied on free trade's ability to create jobs in export-oriented agriculture and manufacturing.[16] Over a decade and a half into the experiment, however, the math did not add up in the countryside. Agricultural employment in Mexico dropped from over 8 million in the late 1990s to less than 6 million in 2010. And the nature of the farm work had changed; seasonal work such as blackberry-picking surged by 3 million, while work in the family farm sector plunged by 5 million.[17] To some, this was progress toward a more modern, urbanized Mexico. The pain of rural displacement was unfortunate, but necessary from this point of view. The market needed to have its say. Open competition would ultimately lead to better uses of land and labor, more productive farms, and lower prices for everyone.

AT VERACRUZ'S MOUNTAINOUS western edge is Perote Valley. The rugged, semi-arid valley sits at 8,000 feet above sea level, a steep, forty-minute climb from Veracruz's capital, Xalapa. It is a strategic location for Mexico's biggest hog farm, Granjas Carroll de Mexico (GCM). Mexico City and its 20 million residents are a mere three-hour drive to the west and the busy port of Veracruz, Mexico's largest, is just two hours to the east. For millions of Mexicans, this is the birthplace of their favorite pork dishes, from shredded pork tacos to *cochinita pibil*, a traditional pork dish of the Yucatán that is slow roasted in banana leaves. GCM is massive; it sent over a million hogs to slaughter in 2013. Two decades earlier, this highland valley had no pig farms at all.[18]

Pork-eaters in Mexico City and other urban areas have seen lower pork prices since the 1990s but may not know why. Livestock farmers in Tierra Blanca, where Laura Flora Oliveros grew up, certainly did, though. With the swiftness of a stroke of the pen, small- and medium-sized hog farmers in Mexico found themselves in the mid-1990s competing on their own turf against pork giant Smithfield. As it did for Michoacán's cañeros, economic integration with the United States for hog farmers meant inviting in foreign competition, dialing back government protections, and scaling up production.[19]

In 1994 Smithfield went into business with Granjas Carroll and later purchased the massive production and feeding operation in Perote to gain a foothold in the enormous Mexican pork market. Smithfield, led by Joseph W. Luter III, emphasized fully industrialized hog farming and "total vertical integration," wherein the company controls each stage of a pig's six-month existence, from birth to bacon. No need for fields or feedlots here; the concentrated animal feeding operations (CAFOs) of western Veracruz provide unprecedented economies of scale and cheaper meat. In rows of wall-to-wall pens, sows live in tiny "gestation crates" where they are unable to turn around. There, without sunlight, straw, or fresh air, they are artificially inseminated to become efficient piglet factories. In CAFOs, and with the benefit of hormones, antibiotics, insecticides, and pharmaceuticals, the birth-to-slaughter term was shortened, and the young pigs were fattened up by 20 percent. GCM became the most productive hog farm in Mexico.[20]

Smithfield imported the cutthroat lessons of the U.S. consolidation experience in which the number of hog farms in the United States declined by 90 percent from 1975 to 2008—while "total hog inventory" grew by 16 million.[21] The Smithfield empire grew in the tail-end of the consolidation era—1,000 percent from 1990 to 2005—as it mastered the mind-boggling logistics of killing tens of millions of pigs and handling tens of millions of tons of pig excrement each year across its growing empire. By 2006 Smithfield was slaughtering 27 million hogs (which included its Farmland slaughterhouse in Monmouth, Illinois, where Jackie Cummins and other former Maytag assemblers were working) and wielding enormous political clout in both the United States and Mexico.[22] The American pork industry—to take one example of how it sought to translate political power into competitive advantage—pushed for labeling and safety-testing requirements in the newly integrated marketplace that were onerous to small- and medium-sized Mexican hog farmers.[23]

Smithfield was a main beneficiary of U.S. farm policy. With billions in American taxpayers' subsidies for U.S. row crops, Smithfield saved hundreds of millions *each year* from 1997 to 2005 by buying corn and soybeans—by far the company's largest expense—at prices well below the actual production cost.[24] Smithfield could import this subsidized animal feed directly from the United States through the nearby port of Veracruz to their CAFOs in Perote Valley. Smithfield was a "winner" of free trade.[25]

On top of producing cheaper hogs in Mexico, Smithfield and other American companies flooded the Mexican market with U.S.-slaughtered pork. From the early 1990s to 2006, pork exports to Mexico increased by 700 percent.[26] In a few short years, Smithfield had become the giant competitor down the road for small- and medium-sized farmers—and also the foreign multinational dumping cheap pork in local markets. As a result, producer prices for hogs dropped, and Mexican hog farmers struggled. Even successful medium-sized, middle-class farmers with a handful of employees were put out of business. Eugenio Guerrero, unable to compete with the U.S. corporations that controlled 40 percent of the Mexican pork market by 2002, had to auction off his 2,000 hogs. His costs had gone up, credit was unavailable, and cheap pork was drowning his family business. He let his workers go and opened a small paint shop. "Mexico will not be a country of producers; it is going to become a country of salesmen," he complained. "We are becoming a country that depends on foreigners for food." Like folks in western Illinois, Guerrero was clinging desperately to his spot in the middle class in an era of mounting inequality.[27]

Pork imports cost 120,000 Mexican farm jobs from 1994 to 2012, according to Alejandro Ramírez, the general director of the Confederation of Mexican Pork Producers.[28] Some former hog farmers became wage laborers at Smithfield's Mexico operations, the place that had put them out of business.[29] Like the displaced Totonacs of Papantla a century earlier and the cañeros of Los Reyes, former pork farmers and their families sold or rented their land, worked as *jornaleros* (day laborers or ranch hands), or emigrated north to Reynosa or beyond.

It wasn't what the politicians had promised. Inviting in investments from the likes of Smithfield was supposed to mean jobs, and more jobs would mean less migration. President Clinton had echoed Salinas' promise to "export goods, not people" as he tried to sell the controversial trade legislation to a wary American public. "As the benefits of economic growth are spread in Mexico to working people," Clinton said at a NAFTA signing in 1993, "they'll have more disposable income to buy more American products and there will be less illegal immigration because more Mexicans will be able to support their children by staying home."[30]

Many Veracruzano hog farmers decided they couldn't stay and North Carolina became their destination. They worked outside the little town of Tar Heel at Smithfield's world's largest hog slaughterhouse. Like displaced tobacco farmers from Veracruz working for wages in North Carolina's tobacco fields, former hog farmers were doing what they knew best, slaughtering hogs. Although the company denies it, Smithfield actively recruited Veracruzanos to come to North Carolina.[31] By 2010 undocumented workers made up at least a quarter of the "animal slaughter" workforce, and there's ample evidence that Smithfield used undocumented workers to undercut wages and unionization efforts at its plants.[32] In the case of Tar Heel, though, the anti-unionization effort ultimately failed. Smithfield deployed riot police, a factory "jail" for agitators, and Immigration and Customs Enforcement to intimidate and dissuade, all the while racking up labor and human rights violations. After the bitter decade-plus fight at the Tar Heel plant, the mostly Mexican slaughterhouse workforce voted in a union in 2006.[33] The social landscape of rural North Carolina and rural southern Veracruz alike had been transformed.

The literal landscape had been radically altered as well. The parched terrain of Perote Valley was dotted with 80 hog-feeding complexes, each with as many as 20,000 hogs. The complexes consisted of neatly ordered pens with automated food-preparation and feeding systems. Next to the pens were perfectly rectangular black lagoons for excrement and urine, which baked in the sun. The three linchpins in this new era of industrial meat were an efficient use of space, a high hog-to-worker ratio, and ultra-low wages.

Smithfield employed 1,200 in the depressed valley. David Torres, an eight-year worker at the farm, worked eleven-hour days and earned $180 a month. CAFO workers, according to investigative reporter David Bacon, suffer from myriad health problems, including acute bronchitis, asthma, heart palpitations, headaches, diarrhea, nosebleeds and eye irritation, and brain damage. The town of Perote, Galesburg's twin in size, has protested these public health problems, a declining water table from the water-intensive pig operations, and water and air pollution.[34]

In May 2009, Perote Valley earned an international spotlight when the swine flu (H1N1) outbreak, the first pandemic in forty years, was traced to a five-year-old boy living in the small town of La Gloria in the valley. The outbreak prompted renewed debates over the rapid growth of CAFOs. Smithfield deflected the blame coming their way and were helped along by Mexican health officials. The H1N1 origin story proved "operatic and knotty," according to one science writer. The new virus was a triple genetic reassortment of swine, bird, and human viruses that then reassorted again with Eurasian swine flu genetic material. According to the Centers for Disease Control and Prevention, pigs are "a mixing vessel" for different species to swap genes and then spread them. *Science* suggested a lack of regulation in developing countries was part of the problem when it condemned "a lack of surveillance in swine populations that may harbor influenza viruses with pandemic potential." The CDC said that "the mixing of live pigs from Eurasia and North America through international trade" was likely the source. That left plenty of room for debate over the new virus' precise genesis. Local farmer Fausto Limon said that no one in Perote, where 60 percent of the population eventually got sick, believed Smithfield.[35]

By the end of the 2000s, the takeover was nearly complete. Half of the pork eaten in Mexico—and Mexicans were eating a lot more pork—came from the United States. More than a third of the domestic Mexican pork industry was controlled by transnational industrial operations.[36] Perote Valley had become everything that both NAFTA's proponents and its critics said it would be. It was a magnificently productive, efficient, ultramodern operation that provided formal sector jobs for the area and cheap pork for the nation. It also wiped out pork farmers and their ranch hands; offered vile, degrading jobs; and poisoned the valley's air with volatile chemicals and its water with toxins, blood and afterbirth, and microbial pathogens.[37]

School-age kids in Perote Valley said it best, though. Taking the bus to school, they complained, was like riding in a toilet.[38]

THE NEW, STATE-OF-THE-ART shredded pork was folded into a new tortilla.

Traditional tortillas are made from large kernels of white corn mixed with calcium from slaked lime, simmered in water, and then ground into *masa* (corn dough) and cooked. This age-old process, researchers have found, releases antioxidants and niacin. The traditional corn-dough tortilla is sturdy but pliable and has a toasty, sweet corn taste. It is a nutritious food, a utensil for scooping beans, and a sturdy plate to hold braised meat and vegetables. The average Mexican consumes ten tortillas per day and it is the main source of calories, protein, and fiber among the poor. There are anywhere from 65,000 to 200,000 tortilla makers in Mexico.[39]

The avalanche of cheap American corn was supposed to mean lower tortilla prices. Mexicans did indeed get cheaper, factory-farmed pork and lower prices on eggs, rice, fish, and other meats. Lower food prices were a big deal for Mexico, where households spend 35 percent of their income on food (compared to 11 to 12 percent in Canada and the United States). Food price inflation, though, exceeded overall inflation. And, oddly, the price of tortillas, the very basis of the food system—like pasta to Italians or potatoes to Peruvians—tripled from 1994 to 2000 even as Mexico was awash with cheap corn. As corn farmers earned less, tortilla consumers paid more. It made no sense.

This was the era of the self-proclaimed "King of Tortillas," businessman Roberto Gonzalez Barrera. A lifelong friend of President Salinas, Gonzalez and his company, Gruma, received government support for his Maseca corn-flour tortillas. Mexican consumers initially rejected the dehydrated, less nutritious corn-flour tortilla. "They say it tastes like dirt," explained one tortilla shop owner in Mexico City.[40] But Salinas and his brother, Raúl, tipped the scales in favor of corn flour over *masa*.[41] Gruma enticed small tortilla makers to convert to flour by offering new machines and greater supplies to those that made the transition. The Salinas government subsidized the shift and punished tortilla makers who didn't convert by giving them low-quality and reduced amounts of corn. The Salinas Commerce Department even signed a decree that declared that all growth in the market be filled by corn flour.[42]

While pushing the virtues of modernity and free markets, Salinas' crony capitalism helped transform Mexico from a country of public to private monopolies. The billionaire King of Tortillas was the first to buy a formerly nationalized bank, Banorte, to add to his private fortune. Salinas helped make his friend, Carlos Slim Helú, one of the world's richest men by granting him a monopoly with Telmex. Salinas had updated traditional Mexican corruption for the neoliberal era. He enriched himself, his brother, and a new breed of Mexican plutocrats by selling off state-owned properties and banks and rigging the rules of the game in favor of big business. "The art of back scratching between politicians and businesses," one reporter noted, "seems to have become a science under Carlos Salinas."[43] A study in the *Journal of Economic Issues* found that the concentration of economic power in Mexico expanded dramatically during this period as the direct result of trade liberalization.[44]

Gruma came to dominate the tortilla sector with control of 80 percent of the flour tortilla market in Mexico. In the United States, on the outskirts of Los Angeles, Gruma opened the largest tortilla factory in the world in 1995. Soon Barrera controlled 50 percent of supermarket sales of tortillas in the United States, which had become big business, constituting nearly a third of the bread market. In the United States, salsa began to outcompete ketchup, and tortillas would eventually overtake white bread. Gruma, the largest tortilla maker in the world—with brands Maseca, Mission, Guerrero, Buena Comida, El Ranchito, Calidad, Super One, and others—dominated supermarket shelves on both sides of the border.[45]

In 2003 Gruma was alleged to be paying hefty fees to retailers for shelf space and to eliminate competitors in the United States. "They have attempted to monopolize markets and restrain trade," plaintiffs in a lawsuit told the *Los Angeles Times.* Major retailers like Food 4 Less were excluding smaller American tortilla makers because of Gruma's anti-competitive tactics. Its American subsidiary had cornered 90 percent of the corn and flour tortilla market in southern California and became the major supplier to Taco Bell. Soon the company's tortillas were sold up and down Latin America, and in 2007 Gruma opened a factory in Shanghai to make tens of millions of tortillas for KFC's chicken wraps in its restaurants in China.[46]

In Mexico, corn mills shifted to increased amounts of U.S. corn. American export agencies helped U.S. corn sellers to bull their way into the Mexican market with favorable loans for big corn buyers if they bought U.S. grain. Gruma bought cheap American corn in part because ADM (Archer Daniels Midland), which stores, transports, processes, and trades corn and other grains, had a 27 percent stake in Gruma. Soon one out of three tortillas was made with flour from U.S. corn.[47]

This was what economic integration in North America had become: a lucrative symbiosis between government-supported grain giants on either side of the Rio Grande. Three binational grain cartels—ADM-Gruma, Cargill-Continental, and Minsa-Arancia-Corn Products International—all but controlled the cross-border grain market. The food cartels were linked to other corporations in agrochemicals, animal health care, genetically engineered seeds, and biotechnology that stood to benefit from the new industrialized food market. These big grain companies, along with livestock transnationals, sat on the Mexican import committee that made critical decisions that impacted trade quotas and commodity prices.[48]

American agribusiness had found what it desperately needed: new markets and new uses for its chronic, government-subsidized overproduction. In addition to dumping yellow corn into Mexico, the U.S. food industry had creatively inserted corn and its invented byproducts—corn oil, dextrose, cornstarch, maltodextrin, xanthan gum, livestock and salmon feed, and more—throughout the North American food system. High-fructose corn syrup was particularly useful in absorbing corn overproduction, becoming nearly ubiquitous in processed foods, such as soft drinks, commercial breads, salad dressings, candies, and Twinkies. Soon, it seemed, every fast-food and grocery product in North America—not to mention batteries, charcoal, diapers, and Motrin—would contain cheap yellow corn from the efficient corn producers of America's Heartland—including those around Galesburg and Newton driving satellite-guided John Deere tractors and combines made, in part, by displaced Maytag workers such as Mike Smith.

The mega-merger era led to the five largest grain companies controlling three-quarters of the world's grain market. Consolidation in cattle processing, hog processing, chicken production and processing, seeds, biotech, and retail food sales proceeded with little interference from the Clinton and Bush Justice Departments.[49] As Gruma grew by moving into the United States, big American companies got bigger by moving into Mexico. Green Giant, for example, started to manufacture frozen foods in Mexico. Cargill bought a beef and chicken processing plant in Saltillo, Coahuila. American food companies bought low-wage, low-regulation plants across Mexico to make vegetable oil, process soybeans, and crush oilseeds. Profits for Cargill, ADM, and other agribusinesses surged.[50]

Outraged Mexican farmers complained that Mexico's public monies that once were used to support poor rural producers went overwhelmingly to big farm operations—and even to Cargill's Mexican subsidiary, Cargill de Mexico.[51] Campesinos protested by blocking bridges and border crossings and by shutting down electricity and gas installations. In 2003 hundreds of thousands converged on Mexico City's *Zócalo*, snarling traffic for weeks with theatrical demonstrations, featuring tractors, horses, and straw-hatted farmers carrying colorful signs. There were loud nationalist demands for food sovereignty and big banners reading, among other slogans, "Sin Maíz, No Hay País." Protesters even rode into the Mexican Congress on horseback to demand a renegotiation of the free trade agreement.[52] "El campo no aguanta mas" (the countryside can't bear more) was the name of the campaign. Working-class urbanites joined the farmers to protest high tortilla prices. Alejandro Nadal, a leading analyst of the Mexican corn industry, wrote, "The monopolistic behavior of cartels that control the tortilla industry have prevented the 50 percent cut in corn prices being passed onto consumers of corn products."[53]

By 2007 Mexico found itself in the grips of a full-fledged food crisis as tortilla prices continued upward.[54] There were food riots and reports of poor urbanites switching to instant noodles and other cheap, low-nutrition, high-sodium foods. The conventional explanation was that high oil prices had driven up demand for ethanol and, as a result, the international price for corn as well. That, in turn, had forced up tortilla prices. Farming groups, tortilla makers, and members of Mexico's Congress continued to point to Gruma and Cargill, to alleged collusion and price-fixing. Critics argued the grain companies hoarded the 2006 and 2007 corn harvests to make false claims of scarcity and then pushed up prices through commodity speculation.[55]

While a new class of economic elites shot into the financial stratosphere, the median income in Mexico stagnated, and income inequality increased. As in the Porfiriato of a century earlier—when oligarchs ruled alongside the iron fist of Porfirio Díaz—Mexico had relinquished much of its labor and food sovereignty. Mexico's import dependence in corn had grown from 7 percent in the years before NAFTA to 34 percent in 2012.[56] Kristin Appendini, a Mexico expert writing in the *UN Chronicle*, warned policymakers to attend to "the contradictions of depending on external markets for food, while rural people were marginalized into informal, low-paid, non-agricultural jobs, migration and even illegal activities that lead to social and cultural fragmentation."[57]

THE SPIKING INTERNATIONAL corn prices didn't matter in isolated Agua Dulce, where discarded ears of corn, left behind in favor of their exportable husks, lay scattered across town. Back in the sky-blue Agencia Municipal building, Treasurer Cruz said corn prices had been low and stagnant in the area for decades. When the coyotes representing Maseca—a brand of Gruma—came to town, he said, the buyer could offer less than the grain's value. Sometimes they would say it was low quality, but generally they didn't need to give a reason. With the government buyer CONASUPO, the National Company for Popular Subsistence, eliminated, agribusiness had assumed effective control over the prices that campesinos saw. And, with tortilla subsidies and price controls (which had kept tortillas affordable) also eliminated to make trade "free," "market forces," which to a large extent meant transnationals, shaped the consumption end as well—in supermarkets, restaurants, and *tortillerías*.

In Eric Schlosser's *Fast Food Nation*, rural sociologist William Heffernan describes America's agricultural economy with an hourglass metaphor. At the top, he says, are millions of farmers, ranchers, and fieldworkers. At the bottom are hundreds of millions of customers. In the narrow passage in the middle are a dozen or so multinational corporations profiting from each transaction.[58]

In Agua Dulce, the perceptive small-town treasurer described something similar, suggesting the hourglass model itself had been imported throughout much of Mexico. "No, the price of corn hasn't changed much," Cruz said in the midst of the tortilla crisis in 2007. "But this is a question for business people, those in business dealings. It's not the person at the beginning of the supply chain, or at the end, who makes the money. It's not the producer or the vendor that makes the cash."

$$=== 16 ===$$

TREADING WATER IN THE
GREAT RECESSION

Galesburg, Illinois

Happiness is like a butterfly; the more you chase it, the more it will
elude you, but if you turn your attention to other things, it will come
and sit softly on your shoulder.
—Henry David Thoreau, posted on Tracy Warner's Facebook wall,
November 2012

IN APRIL 2010 George Carney found himself stacking and banding wooden
boards to be made into roof and barn trusses. His new workplace was Roberts
and Dybdahl, a lumberyard in Milan, Illinois. Carney was paired with a partner, an automated cutting machine with five enormous shark-toothed saw
blades that bit loudly into lumber and dropped boards onto the tray below.
Now 51, Carney was using his body to earn a living again, even if the job paid
only $9 an hour, a shade above the Illinois minimum. The first week he put in
60 hours. "It was a hard job. It was perfect for me."

On April 29, his ninth day on the job, Carney's life changed forever,
again. Two days after an unremarkable Occupational Safety and Health
Administration inspection, a two-by-six shot out of the saws like "a ball out of
pitching machine." Its long side smacked right into Carney's skull, and in an
instant his world went dark.

In the previous year Carney had been bartending while he lived in his son's
extra bedroom in Matherville, Illinois. He served "fancy, high falutin" drinks
at the Oak View Country Club starting in late May 2009, after being unemployed for a couple of months. Members liked Carney because he would
remember their names and favorite drink. The "whisky-beer man" learned to

make cosmopolitans, martinis, manhattans, and other country club mixes. "I always told myself I was shy, but everyone tells me I'm not. I feel uncomfortable with it, but I seem to be fairly sociable." In August he added a day job at Milan Lanes, a bowling alley and bar, and was working almost every day. Still, it was a "pretty low point" to be a working-age man living in his son's extra room. It was a role-reversal that neither of them relished. "You don't feel like you got anything," Carney said of the year after leaving the Town Tavern.

Then Carney's father succumbed to cancer in March 2010. With his Town Tavern earnings, Carney had been able to contribute to a few years of treatment, but ultimately the cancer won. After his death, Carney's mother moved to Texas to live with Richard, Carney's older brother. Carney then moved into his mom's home in Rock Island, Illinois, one of the Quad Cities. Nearby, Roberts and Dybdahl was hiring. Carney took the gig and dropped the country club job. He had his own place, a good job, and, most importantly, a job that, after the probationary period, carried health insurance. "I thought, I'm makin' it up in the world!" he said with a laugh.

Carney was clothes-lined by the rocketing board, which slammed his head onto the cement floor. His face and skull were broken in four places and his spine was badly bruised. The next couple of days were fuzzy, as Carney went in and out of consciousness. "I woke up to people holding me down so I didn't move. Next thing they were cutting my shirt off. Next time I open my eyes they're putting leads on me, and I'm in the emergency room. Next thing, it's the next day. Every time I closed my eyes, I was waking up with a different thing going on."

During his two weeks in the hospital, Carney's boss from Roberts and Dybdahl came every day at lunch to visit. And Carney's mother moved back from Texas to help with his recovery at home. In a few weeks Carney could limp along and was thinking he would return to work soon. That's when he started feeling a pain in his hand like he'd "smashed it in a car door." Soon after his whole right side felt half numb. It then moved to his chest. "It felt like someone put a ten pound bag on my chest, like I was wearing a wetsuit." Carney complained that he wasn't getting the care he needed, but got the runaround from Liberty Mutual, the company handling his workers' compensation claim. Carney hadn't worked at the lumberyard long enough to qualify for its health insurance. As such he would only get care if it was related to the work accident. He had to hire a lawyer.

Getting worse each day, Carney despaired. He was in constant pain, had trouble breathing, his eyesight blurred at times, and his hand began to claw to avoid the pain of straight fingers. Some days he wouldn't get out of bed, drowning in his thoughts and inactivity, feeling worthless and watching an endless stream of crime dramas. "I didn't care about anything. I figured I was better off dead. I wished that board had been turned around." Doctors said that if that had happened, it would have killed him. Carney even asked his brother where he kept his gun. Richard told him it was still in Texas and tried to lift his spirits, but it was little use. And then on July 28, 2010, Carney says he did something he'd never considered doing before: he prayed. Like George Bailey in *It's a Wonderful Life*, he told God he wanted to live.

The next day, while sitting in his recliner, Carney had a seizure and stopped breathing. Richard was nearby and managed to wrestle Carney to the floor and onto his back to perform CPR. He started breathing again. An ambulance sped him to the hospital for another stay. Carney was able to get a laundry list of prescription medications for nerve pain, swelling, sleep, and seizures. He saw doctor after doctor for surgical evaluations as Liberty Mutual, he thought, attempted to get some doctor to say the seizure was the result of a preexisting condition from which Carney suffered, spinal stenosis. He kept getting the same advice. As one doctor put it, "Your option is surgery or an autopsy. You need to have this done."

Early, in the predawn quiet of September 7, Carney couldn't sleep. He shuffled out to his Rock Island porch and slowly lowered into his recliner just after 4 a.m. He prayed silently for things to get better. Feeling selfish, he made prayers for other people he knew. As he sat in a black Harley T-shirt and a foam neck brace, he tried to clear his head of swirling thoughts, but his mood often turned dark.

That afternoon when we spoke, he told me, "I don't blame anyone but myself. I used to blame Maytag for a lot of things, but now I don't think I do. Life is what you make of it." It was sincere. He wanted to be positive. He wanted to turn around this seemingly endless decline in his physical, emotional, and financial standing since he had been laid off six years earlier. But he just couldn't seem to shake his animosity.

"If Maytag had been there, then this would not have happened to me," he said later in the day.

Carney was candid to a fault. He wasn't proud of his resentment, but he also wasn't going to pretend that it didn't exist. Carney's self-deprecating sincerity and his fury somehow coexisted. "I'd be three years from retirement and I wouldn't be hurt like this. I wouldn't have been lookin' for a job. I might still be with my girlfriend. Maytag cost me a lot. If I drove by it today, I'd probably still flip it off." He laughed.

Carney needed surgery on his spine, and it took a lot of doctor's appointments to get it approved. He received $1,000 every two weeks from workers' compensation, which helped. But other than that, the safety net he once had was gone. He had no assurance he could go back to his job. He had no guarantee that the biweekly checks would continue. He had no health insurance. He had no retirement health care to look forward to and only a tiny pension lined up. He had no life insurance. He had no union. His decline and his frayed emotions had cost him his patient and warm girlfriend. All he had was his family and his morning prayers. He was hanging by a thread.

BY THE FALL of 2010 Tracy Warner was feeling competent in her job at the high school. From 7:40 a.m. to 2:40 p.m., she worked one on one with autistic children, supervised students who were thought to be a threat to themselves, tutored, made copies, ran errands, filled out paperwork, and read tests to learning disabled children. It was grueling at times, and a certain cynicism and gallows humor emerged from the work. "You can't fix crazy," the teachers would say in the break room over lunch as they exchanged war stories about their mornings. Warner usually kept to herself during the lunch break, checking her email and feeding her Facebook, Tagged, and MySpace interests.

Warner's main task was helping to maintain some semblance of classroom order with students who were constantly challenging authority. When she was in charge of the classroom one afternoon, a student refused to stop talking while she was supposed to be working on a project.

"You need to be quiet, or you're going to the yellow room," Warner recalled telling her, referring to the school's disciplinary purgatory.[1]

"Oh, hell no, my mom and daddy don't even talk to me like that," the student responded. "So you're not going to talk to me like that!" Warner walked over and picked up the student's purse and put it into her arms. "Did you all see that? She's trying to get in my business!" the student said.

"I don't want any drama," Warner said. "Just get your stuff and let's go wait outside for the teacher to get back."

"I ain't going nowhere!"

Warner then pushed the table aside and moved her chair, clearing a path for the student. "Let's go, now!"

"You're not going to get me out of this chair," the student said.

After more back and forth, the teacher returned and demanded that the student go to the yellow room.

"I'm not going to the yellow room," the student yelled, as she moved aggressively toward Warner. The teacher hustled Warner into the adjoining classroom for her protection. The student followed and began banging on the door with her hands, yelling at Warner.

"Come on out of there, I'm going to whoop your ass!"

The teacher pushed a button, and Joe Luna, the Galesburg police officer stationed at the high school, came down the hall and took the student away. The student dropped out of school a couple weeks later, a few months before her graduation.

Galesburg schools struggled as the area slowly got poorer. By 2013 over two-thirds (68 percent) of the school children in the Galesburg district were "low-income," up from 43 percent in 2002, the year of the Maytag closing announcement. It was among the sharpest increases in Illinois. With total employment and population declining over the decade, schools in the region had closed and consolidated as well. Despite that, "educational services, health care, and social assistance" had become the largest occupational category in Galesburg.[2]

Each semester Warner had a different schedule. In 2010, her fourth year at the school, Warner was sitting through three 84-minute blocks of English, two in the morning and one in the afternoon. That September the special education teacher was reading *I Know What You Did Last Summer* to the students. It's a suspenseful book, Warner said, but it was not enough to hold the attention of the students. Warner's job was to "redirect."

"They listen to their headphones on full blast, stand on tables, and I sometimes find them researching Glock pistols and pit bulls online or drawing disturbing pictures." Warner's factory toughness served her well in the classroom. She told herself time and time again to let the teacher be the authority figure, but she found herself constantly being pulled into classroom conflagrations.

Once a student needled her about her "ugly sandals" and eventually provoked a reaction from Warner. "What about you? You've worn the same Southpole shirt for three days in a row."

"Treated!" some of the gathering kids shouted gleefully. "Miss Warner treated you!"

"It ain't none of your business what I wear to school."

"Well, when you wear it three days in a row it is," Warner said. "It's the same shirt. I'm sure you're not washing it."

"Ah, that's what you get!" another onlooker said.

"Well, I got news for you. You're a humpback," the boy said to Warner. "You need to get back surgery!"

"Is that the best you got?" Warner asked, trying now to rein in her reaction. It was the sort of fight that she and her Maytag co-workers would engage in playfully. But here it was different. The spat died down, and the student was sent to the yellow room to await discipline; the incident was more or less forgotten.

Warner had her misgivings, but she was happy that the job had started to feel more permanent after a few years. She had avoided being "riffed" ("reduction in force," a bureaucratic euphemism for a layoff) three summers in a row despite colossal fiscal problems in the state. She was earning $9.79 over 32.5 hours and two years away from a year-round paycheck (same pay spread over twelve months). Adjusted for inflation, her Maytag wage would have been $17.25 in 2010.

Over the summers, and for extra money during the year, Warner kept the cleaning job at Warren Achievement (WAC) for ten to twenty hours on evenings and weekends. Outside the neatly landscaped brick building where she cleaned, a yellow marquee, in crooked numbers, read, "THE STATE OF ILLINOIS OWES WAC $1,542,430.82." Warren Achievement cut back on caseworkers and some other full-time workers but kept inexpensive part-timers like Warner. (The executives refused a pay cut.) That summer Warner power-washed the lime off the accessibility decks and ramps at the group homes, taped and painted, mowed grass, checked and replaced light bulbs, and did deep cleaning behind refrigerators and inside vents.

Warner and Ryan squeezed by in the summer on the WAC paycheck of about $925 a month. The bumps to the state's minimum wage helped, and she was doing better than when she had first graduated from Western Illinois.

Now she only dipped below the poverty line in the summertime. Because her total yearly income in 2010 of $18,675 surpassed the official poverty threshold of $15,030, she and Ryan were no longer officially "poor."[3] Warner now knew to report her income frequently to her businesslike caseworker, and to her surprise Warner received $234 each month in food stamps over the summer when her income dropped—even as she continued to pay her food stamps debt each month. Ryan's father was still paying $82 a month in child support, and his family was chipping in for expenses like school supplies and clothing. Nonetheless Warner and her son were living between 100 and 150 percent of the poverty line. The single mother earned about half her 2004 Maytag income in 2010.

At the end of the 2000s, inequality was being discussed at dining room tables across the country. The Aughts had been the first recorded decade of zero net job growth and falling median income.[4] Everyone had heard the statistics about the gains accruing to the top one percent, which had seen a 154 percent increase in real income from 1980 to 2010 and had taken nearly 60 percent of the gains of growth over roughly the same period.[5] The problem, though, was systemic, and spread across the income distribution. From 1950 to 1980 incomes had more or less doubled across each fifth of the income distribution—with the fastest growth, in fact, among the bottommost quintile. Growth had "lifted all boats" in the postwar years. Income growth between 1980 and 2010, however, was strikingly uneven (see Figures 16.1 and 16.2). The tight link between productivity growth and wages in the American economy had been severed in the 1970s; since that time productivity had continued upward while the hourly compensation of workers flatlined.[6]

For former Appliance City workers like Carney, Warner, the Cummins, and the Dennisons, the most troubling aspect of increasing inequality was what it might mean for their children. As the Pew Economic Mobility Project put it, "the up-escalator that has historically ensured that each generation would do better than the last may not be working very well."[7]

ON A CRISP autumnal afternoon, I found Doug Dennison burrowed comfortably in a former technology cubbyhole in Mercer County Junior High School. In his makeshift office, he sat in the same chair he had sat in at the Labor Temple and plied the same file cabinets. A framed poster of Rosie the Riveter saying, "We Can Do It!" hung over his desk. Wedged in the bottom

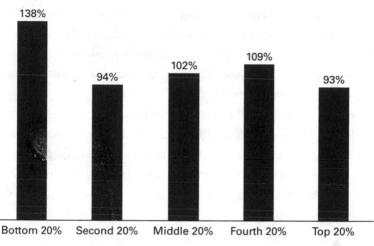

FIGURE 16.1 FROM LIFTING ALL BOATS

Average family income growth by Income group, 1950–1900 (adjusted for inflation)

Source: Author's calculations based on data from Lawrence Mishel, Josh Bivens, Elise Gould, and Heidi Shierholz, *The State of Working America*. 12th ed. Ithaca, NY: Cornell University Press, 2012.

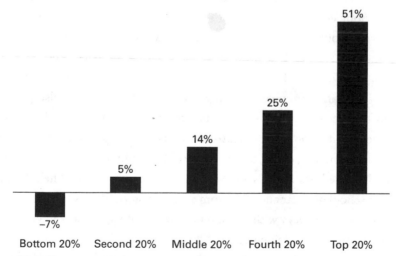

FIGURE 16.2 TO SINK OR SWIM

Average family income growth by income group, 1980–2010 (adjusted for inflation)

Source: Author's calculations based on data from Lawrence Mishel, Josh Bivens, Elise Gould, and Heidi Shierholz, *The State of Working America*. 12th ed. Ithaca, NY: Cornell University Press, 2012.

of the poster's metal frame were wallet-sized pictures of Dennison's middle school-aged boys in their basketball uniforms. The 2010 school year had just started in Joy, Illinois. The school's 21st Century grant would expire at the end of the year. It was Dennison's fifth and final year as a self-made education specialist at the struggling school.

Dennison and the federal Department of Education monies he helped to steward for the Regional Office of Education had made a mark. He showed me a gorgeous, wall-sized mosaic made from thousands of recycled crayons. The vibrant mosaic mapped western Illinois in a rainbow of colors. There was an oversized yellow corncob, a grim bust of Lincoln, a dark-blue Mississippi River with a giant jumping bass, and a colorful array of fields, barns, and churches and buildings. The junior high, consolidated in the preceding year, had been sculpted into the giant artwork with black and yellow crayons with a waving American flag on top. Young teens at the school had designed and pieced the mosaic together in one of Dennison's programs, an art enrichment program funded by the grant. The grant funded teachers to work in after-school and summer programs in art, fitness and health, and career preparation. It also funded homework help and tutoring, test-taking and study skills classes, transportation for the afterschoolers, and snacks.

When school let out, Dennison met with four boys and one girl in a second-floor classroom. Dennison had neatly outfitted the classroom and halls with motivational posters that read "Excellence," "Success," "Focus," "Goals," and "Aspire." One poster showed a setting sun over a rocky beach. It read, "When all is said and done, the only thing you have left is your character," a quotation from country singer Vince Gill. There were also posters of Einstein, the digestive system, and metric prefixes. On a bookshelf was a thick book, *Adventures in Food Nutrition!* Outside the opened windows, over the drone of a noisy box fan, the afterschool kids could see and hear fifty boys, nearly half the boys in the school, doing drills on the football field below. The old school drew far and wide from across western Illinois to fill its shiny, squeaky-clean hallways with 217 seventh and eighth graders, known, since consolidation, as the Golden Eagles.

Dennison started the session with a game. He asked his students to unscramble "values" words like "character," "choices," and "goals" while they ate federal government-funded cinnamon Teddy Grahams and sipped fruit juice. The main focus that afternoon, just as it was every afternoon, was getting homework done. Dennison, who had himself steered clear of school for some time, was amiably prodding the kids to "show your work" and explaining the difference between simple and compound sentences.

Four years earlier, when Dennison first arrived, teachers' grade books had been littered with zeros. That year the adults at the school, including Dennison, began an effort to turn around lousy homework habits. Some kids refused, didn't care, or thought it was uncool to do the work. Other kids didn't have the support they needed at home from parents with limited educations. Some did their work but weren't organized enough to turn it in on time or keep it from getting buried in their locker. It was a nearly all-white student body, 41 percent of which was low-income.[8]

Like so many schools across the country, Mercer was pushing for a shift in school culture and beginning to track homework and tests electronically. Dennison said it had been working, too, though some students still lagged behind. It was the second year of the "Zeros Aren't Permitted" (ZAP) program. Kids that had been "zapped" for missing a homework assignment were sent to the ZAP room to catch up on their homework during lunch. If they didn't catch up, they might get an afternoon detention.

Caleb and Adam, two of Dennison's students, walked in late that afternoon.

"Did you come from detention because of ZAPs?" Dennison asked. They nodded, and Dennison moaned loudly with frustration. Shifting to upbeat, he asked, "We got everything all done?"

"Yeah," said Adam.

"You're sure?"

"I think," replied Caleb.

"You think? Are you using your planner to write everything in it?"

"Somewhat," Caleb responded, still sheepish.

"Now, we've talked and talked and talked about this."

"I got some stuff written in it. Not all of it."

"How's that working?"

"Not really well," replied Adam.

"Okay," Dennison said with a gentle laugh. "I'll make you a promise. If you would use that planner and write everything in it that you're supposed to, and cross it off, you wouldn't forget to do an assignment."

"I do, and I do," Adam said. Dennison looked at them in silence. After a pause, the boys, resigned, offered to look through their lockers for their planners.

"Good idea," Dennison said. "Good idea." Dennison was a natural with these boys.

That Wednesday there were 83 homework assignments that got "zapped," a sign that the homework problem, for some kids, was close to intractable. Caleb alone had been "zapped" three times that day. Despite a general upward trend, that year the school didn't make "Adequate Yearly Progress" (AYP) under No Child Left Behind. Only 20 percent of Illinois schools did.[9] There were plenty of bright kids there, but some kids were still being left behind despite the school's efforts and the federal money.[10]

Dennison was concerned about kids like Caleb. In five or six years he would move into a rural labor market with no Maytag, no Butler, and a down-sized Gates Rubber Company. Dennison brought in guest speakers—union representatives he knew, people in various trades, college counselors—to talk about careers. And he had learned federal grant reporting and the Byzantine intricacies and formulas of No Child Left Behind. He had done what he could in the five years he had with the grant. But he had to wonder: Did these kids stand a chance in the new economy? Where would the jobs be for the farm boys and girls in and around Joy and Aledo? And what about the "river kids" from around Muscatine?

That there's an education gap between wealthy and poor children is well known. What's shocking, though, is how rapidly the gap has grown alongside the decades-long widening of income inequality. Sean Reardon, a Stanford sociologist, compared the math and reading test scores of children in families with incomes in the 90th percentile (about $160,000 in 2008) with the children of families with incomes in the 10th percentile (about $17,500 in 2008). He found that since the mid-1970s the income achievement gap had jumped by an astonishing 40 percent, moving well ahead of the black–white achievement gap, which had narrowed over the same period. Family income was now nearly as predictive as parental education in forecasting a child's school achievement, a momentous sociological shift for the country.

One of the main drivers of the divergence has been a big jump in the spending of higher-income and college-educated parents in the cultivation of their children in the preschool years.[11] Schools like Dennison's struggled to close a gap that is opened in early childhood and has been shown to persist steadily through high school. Two studies recently found that the gap in college completion between rich and poor youth has also grown rapidly since the 1980s.[12] All this doesn't bode well for the kids in Joy or Galesburg wanting their shot at the American Dream.

As the afternoon wore on, the sole girl was focused and attentive while a special-needs boy high-stepped around the room and had a hard time staying in his chair. Three other boys, all sporting crew cuts, dark denim jeans, and paunches, did their work slowly. Two of the boys wore the same black T-shirt reading "Annihilation" in ornate blue-and-white graphics. I asked one of them if it was a band's name. He said, shyly, "Oh, nah, I just got it at Kmart. I got some good shirts."

Dennison and the kids read and discussed an article from *Scholastic Choices* magazine about different types of bullying. Dennison asked, "Has anybody in this room been bullied, been called names?" When all five of them half-raised their hands, Dennison asked how it made them feel.

"Sad and mad a little bit," one kid replied. "But I just ignored them."

Dennison liked working with these kids; he found it paralleled his union work. He returned to the underdog metaphor he had used years earlier. "They're kind of the underdogs I guess. And we were kinda the underdogs back then." He had himself resisted education in the transition, yet had reinvented himself as an educator. He had had some successes, but had also seen the limitations of the small program that the federal dollars supported, at least in comparison to the vast advantages that kids in other places had on their way into an increasingly demanding labor market.

"Sometimes it feels like we take two steps forward, and you get to feeling really good. But then the next day you take four steps back."

He thought about his two boys' futures all the time. Dylan, his oldest, had struggled the previous year as a freshman. "We are on them every day about grades. We're always saying that there just aren't those good paying jobs that you can fall into. You've gotta have the education." Dennison said that Dylan was a talented kid and that he wanted to be a video game designer. "If they had an Olympic sport for video games, he'd be the team captain!"

Annette and Doug, like other squeezed middle-class families, had no choice but to believe education can still be the Great Equalizer, even in an era of widespread income stagnation and downward mobility. The opposite seemed to be true. Incomes in places like Joy and Galesburg are eroding just as income has become more predictive of children's academic achievement and cognitive skills, which, in turn, have become more predictive of adults' earnings. Rather than being a Great Equalizer, the decades-long growth in income inequality has created a feedback mechanism that may decrease inter-generational mobility. As Sean Reardon soberly concludes, "As the children of the rich do better in school, and those who do better in school are more likely to become rich, we risk producing an even more unequal and economi-cally polarized society."[13]

From Parents to Children: The Intergenerational Transmission of Advantage is the most thorough examination to date of how the United States stacks up against other advanced economies (Canada, Belgium, Norway, France, Denmark, Sweden, Australia, the United Kingdom, Germany, and Italy) on the question of whether economic inequality in one generation leads to inequality of opportunity in the next. In the United States, inequality has grown faster in the past thirty years than in the other countries. And fam-ily background has become more tightly linked to children's cognitive, socio-emotional, educational, and economic outcomes than in other coun-tries. In the country where social class is nearly a taboo subject, it has the greatest impact on a child's chances. Despite having "the least intergenera-tional mobility and the least equal opportunity for children to advance" of the countries in the study, though, Americans generally remain optimistic about the American Dream for themselves in public opinion polls.[14]

It is common to think that rural places like Joy, Monmouth, and Galesburg have always had a much less educated citizenry. In fact, in the mid-20th cen-tury, college graduates were spread evenly across the country. Urban and rural communities all had their share of educated professionals in business, medicine, law, and education. As higher education opened to a broad range of people, college graduates increasingly located in metropolitan areas, espe-cially global cities, creating, "a new, highly unequal, post-industrial educa-tional geography," according to sociologist Thurston Domina.[15] Although segregation by race remains a dominant organizing principle of U.S. urban housing markets, racial segregation levels plateaued and even declined in recent decades. In the late 20th century, educational segregation was the leading segregation trend. In a remarkable shift, college graduates are now more residentially isolated than African Americans within highly educated counties. Economic polarization, in short, has spawned a new geography of inequality in education—just at a time when education is more essential than ever. Talk of a rural renaissance in the early 1970s—the very time Appliance City hummed with the work activity of upward of 5,000 workers—has been replaced with concern over a "hollowing of the middle," as sociologists Patrick Carr and Maria Kefalas put it. The young "achievers" of these little towns head to places like Chicago and St. Louis, while an aging population stays behind and slowly dwindles.[16]

On my way out of Joy, I scanned the radio as I passed little churches next to mobile homes and antique shops with homemade "Stuff 4 Sale" signs. On a Christian station, a woman was recounting a mesmerizing story about overcoming her drug problem, finding God, and being forgiven by her family. Moving through the radio dial, I heard country music, an advertisement for hunters, the J. Geils Band's "Centerfold," and a livestock report. After the report, which was upbeat, came an advertisement from a local monument business proclaiming the power of scripture on your tomb. Next, I heard an advertisement for the Monmouth Prime Beef Festival featuring carnival rides, a parade, and a demolition derby.

ON A WARM September afternoon, Tracy Warner and I went to pick Ryan up at Lutheran Preschool and Day Care in Monmouth. We then headed to her evening janitorial job at Warren Achievement on the southern edge of town. If not for teal aluminum siding, the Monmouth not-for-profit's wide, gable-roofed building would look more like a livestock barn than a social services center. Inside, the building was cut up into various service areas for its disabled "consumers." There was also a new jungle-themed room that Warner had helped to paint over the summer and an area for tai chi.

That evening Warner swept and mopped the hard tile floor of the common area and cafeteria, which had gathered a lot of food over the course of the day. While she swept, Ryan played a video game on an old computer, watched the weather report on the one-station television, colored, and drank pop. What the nine-year-old looked forward to the most was combing the vending machines in the lonely building for dropped coins. He found a nickel that night.

Even though Warner was making about half her former income working these two jobs, she said her life was better in important ways. "I was more overweight back then. I know how hard a dollar is to come by. And the stress of the job, the drama between the company and the union, us fighting for our rights all the time. It was draining." It had been fun to have the money to spend weekends going to Metallica and Pink Floyd concerts, she said, but, now that she was a mother and college graduate, she spent her time and her money in better ways.

Since her layoff she had felt the support of her family in a way she hadn't before. Her mother, who was also struggling with downward mobility as a nurse, watched Ryan frequently. And her aunt, Hazel Baker, and her cousin, Toby, came to her aid when her basement flooded and, to her horror, she lost all of her college essays and papers—including the one on John Rawls—and her washer and dryer. They helped Warner clean out her basement, build a first-floor laundry room, and repair her garage. Baker was the Chair of Missions for the Good Hope United Methodist Church in Good Hope, Illinois, a town of a few hundred residents south of Monmouth. She brought in help from the church, including the minister, who redid Warner's plumbing.

The widowed Baker lives in a 30-foot Maverick by Georgie Boy RV and is an active member of NOMADS, Nomads On a Mission Active in Divine Service. In the winter Baker does mission work in Donna, Texas, just east of McAllen in the Valley. When it's safe, she also works in the colonias across the border in the Reynosa area. She spends summers parked in Warner's cousin's driveway in Good Hope. Baker said her lifestyle is a way to "share her Christian faith and experience different cultures, lifestyles, and geographic areas."

Like her aunt, Warner defied the stereotype of the parochial rural Midwesterner. She told me about a virtual friendship she had with Hasnain Sabih Nayak, a magazine editor living in Dhaka, Bangladesh. Nayak edits *Toitomboor*, a children's magazine. The name means, she told me, "full to the brim." After Ryan had a story about a Monmouth ice storm published in the magazine, Warner and Nayak began chatting regularly online. And when Nayak won a peace-building fellowship from the SIT Graduate Institute in Vermont, he was able to visit Warner and Ryan in Monmouth. Although her mom and sister adored Nayak, a couple of Warner's co-workers questioned her judgment about bringing a Muslim around her child and struggled to believe that she actually slept on the couch while he slept in her bed. Warner threw up her hands recounting what she considered to be the small-mindedness of her co-workers.

Warner promised Nayak that she and Ryan would visit him and his family in Dhaka since he had made it to Monmouth. At tax-filing time in recent years, Warner had received $2,000 to $3,000 tax refunds because of the Earned Income Tax Credit, a lump-sum wage supplement that was always most welcome. With the dramatic shift away from welfare and toward work support in the past twenty years, the EITC is now arguably the most effective anti-poverty tool that low-income Americans have—and it's designed precisely for low-wage workers such as Warner. She received a $2,739 EITC in 2010, which she used to catch up on bills. In 2011 Warner planned to use it for plane tickets to Dhaka.

HIGHWAYS I-80 AND I-280 encircle the Quad Cities in a broad, concrete loop. The Mississippi River flows right through the center, dividing Bettendorf and Davenport in Iowa from Rock Island and Moline in Illinois. On the southwest curve of the circle highway, just west of the efficient little regional airport, are parcels of trees, soybean and corn fields, and a couple of golf courses. It's a mixed-class exurbia smattered with some roomy homes with expansive lawns and swimming pools alongside small, boxy working-class homes with gravel driveways. Interspersed in this nearly all-white area are also a few mobile home communities.

Early in 2011 George Carney and his brother split the cost of a mobile home in Woodland Mobile Home Park on Coyne Center Road. It cost them about $6,500. Some ran as cheap as $2,000, but in those you had to be careful not to walk through the rotted floors. A couple of nicer trailers listed for $10,000, which was more than Carney and his brother wanted to pay.

After Carney's surgery in October 2010, the stress of four adults crammed into a small home had proved too much. He and his mom fought, and four days later Carney, Richard, and Richard's girlfriend, Beth, moved into the single-wide. They joined the nearly 18 million Americans living in mobile homes.[17] America's 60,000 manufactured-home communities are tucked away in rural pockets in northern Florida, Georgia, Texas, New Mexico, the Carolinas, Appalachia, and southern Illinois.[18] In Rock County, Illinois, there's only a smattering, but across rural America mobile homes make up 16 percent of all housing.[19] Manufactured housing grew rapidly in the 1980s and 1990s, when it made up 15 percent to 25 percent of all new housing starts in the country.[20]

In the summer of 2011, Carney and I spoke above the din of cicadas buzzing next to us in a tall tree. It was a warm, pleasant August morning. Young people walked the streets of the trailer park. Carney and I sat on a concrete patio next to a small gas grill. He wore a green Town Tavern T-shirt and showed me that his arm had improved from the accident at the lumberyard, though he still couldn't lift it above his shoulder, which came out of its socket at times. He tired easily and dragged his left leg after walking for a while. The injuries and his isolation had taken an emotional toll, but he had started driving again.

"This is probably the longest I've been outside in a long time," he said. He lived on one side of the trailer. He had everything he needed: a recliner, a bed, a television, and his cellphone. "Other than going to a doctor's appointment, I don't leave. There's lots of days I don't even leave my room. If I'm hurtin', I'll stay in there all day, come out long enough to get food, go to the bathroom. I stay in probably more so than I'd like to admit. Probably 80 percent of the days are like that." As always, Carney wasn't afraid to talk about his troubles. He was depressed, but that was what it was.

Between his shoulder and his neck, Carney couldn't sleep. "I'm back and forth all night. It looks like there's been a wrestling match in my bed every night, which would be okay if there were a female partner. But by myself it's kinda sad!" Each night he would pop four or five generic "Sleep Aid" pills from the Dollar General but wished he had access to real sleep medication like Ambien. He would typically wake before dawn and turn on the television to avoid "thinking about shit."

"I just sit there and stare at the TV. It distracts me. When I lay down, my mind starts going hundred miles per hour. Even now, sitting here talking, thinking about those damn cicadas, I wish I could get up there and pluck them out of that damn tree and shit. Stupid stuff!" He shook his head and chuckled. "If I was a stock broker that'd be good, probably. I could put it to good use."

The income trends of the past three decades noted previously had been most pronounced for men and the less-educated. When Carney was 35 in 1994, men in their thirties were making only about 5 percent more than their father's generation, adjusted for inflation.[21] But at least in 1994, Carney and his generation hadn't *lost* ground, which was what happened to younger men. In 2004 men in their thirties had 12 percent less personal income than men in their father's generation in 1974. Working-class and poorer men with less than a high school diploma had seen a 28 percent decline in real earnings since 1979, and high school graduates with no college had seen a 15 percent decline.[22] Men, the research showed, were much more sensitive than women to downward mobility and changes in household income. Lower income and job loss led to ill-defined familial roles, problems with intrafamily communication, less emotional concern for and responsiveness to others in the family, increased inability to maintain standards of behavior, and lower overall family functioning.[23]

Carney's thoughts were still tinged with gloominess and sometimes turned to masochistic fantasies of suicide. "I think about that a lot—a lot more than I admit to anyone around here. I got no life, man. I got no companion, no nothing." Carney's self-deprecating humor had vanished. "These guys [Richard and Beth] are great to me, they'd do anything for me. But, yeah, I think about it a lot. If not for him, I know I'd be buried. I know I would. There is no doubt in my mind. I would have found a way already."

Richard was living on disability after several spine surgeries. He had "all kinds of hardware in his back," including two or three vertebrae in cages. Carney and Richard had grown close in the previous couple of years as Richard was taking care of their dying father, their mother when she broke a kneecap, and now Carney.

"You never know about a person. He's proven to be one hell of a person. Yeah, he's a special man." Beth, a certified nurse assistant who worked in a nursing home, also helped the threesome stay afloat.

"We have our differences; that's part of a relationship. But I thank them all the time. All the time. There is no way in hell that I'll be able to repay them for what they've done."

Carney couldn't drink or ride his Harley anymore, and he was embarrassed to stagger around in public on his gimp leg. But what deflated him the most was that he felt useless. On doctor's orders, Carney couldn't kneel, squat, get on a ladder, or take more than eight steps without a handrail. He couldn't work on a platform or lift more than ten pounds. "That's a gallon of milk!" he said. For a workingman, it was a death sentence.

"I don't mind being alone. What I don't like is the way I am," Carney said with tears pooling in his eyes. "I don't want to feel like he has to take care of me."

He had been told that the lumberyard was looking for a job he could do. "It'd have to be a desk job. But I'm not smart enough. I've never done a desk job."

Carney was plenty smart, but that wasn't how he viewed himself. And it was true he had no experience in office work and no desire to do it. This was a man who could get through exhausting 54-hour weekends at the factory but was terrified of office work. "I'd like to go back to the same job I had." He felt he needed to be in a place where other men—and it was mostly men at the lumberyard—were working. It made him feel connected, of use, and alive.

"Work is how I was social. I bullshitted with people all the time. That was my social life. There wasn't a lot of extra things I used to do. I just worked." That year, his son had connected him to Facebook and Carney took to it. It helped fill the void. His phone was almost always connected, waiting for news feeds from friends as he watched his crime dramas in his little cave in the Woodland Mobile Home Park.

Carney knew that in 2014, at 55, he would be able to collect a paltry $200 monthly pension check. Had he continued at Maytag, he would have instead had a generous pension vested at that age (a full pension in 2004 was around $1,600 a month). He would have kept working well beyond 55, but with "peace of mind" in the face of old age and a declining body. Acute or chronic injuries in the fifties and sixties were inevitable at the factory. The Maytag pension and retiree health benefits, along with Social Security and Medicare, wove together an ample safety net. It was not perfect, but that public-private formula provided for America's most productive workers when their bodies were used up or when an accident happened. It kept them in the middle class in old age. As pensions and employer-sponsored health insurance declined across the nation, Medicaid and Medicare had to expand to fill the void (further expansion of the federal role in health care is the nub of the ongoing debate over Obamacare).[24] But much of the everyday burden fell on people like Richard and Beth, people with troubles of their own.

For Carney the loss of a good wage, health insurance, a pension, and "peace of mind" did not capture the full extent of the new American problem of downward mobility. Day and night, alone in his dark room, Carney had to face the fundamental questions. He had lost the way in which he contributed to and participated in society and connected with others. The place where he had demonstrated his ferocious work ethic and earned his dignity was now a hollow shell. Carney felt cast aside and left behind. In a nation that valorizes self-reliance and hard work—and abhors dependence—could he still even claim cultural membership anymore? Those were the thoughts that left him with restless nights and suicidal thoughts. There didn't seem to be a way forward, or even hope of one.

IN LATE DECEMBER 2012, with a heavy blanket of snow on the ground, people in Galesburg and Monmouth nestled in for winter. Annette Dennison continued to commute to Peoria to work nights at Methodist Medical Center. She was now the family's well-trained and steady provider with a career. Doug's temporary job in Mercer County ended when the 21st Century grant expired there. That same year Monmouth-Roseville High School, a few minutes from the Dennisons' home, received the same grant. His boss at the Regional Office of Education was impressed with Dennison's work, and so Doug started as the five-year grant's site coordinator at his beloved alma mater in town. It was only a temporary job but everything seemed to be working out for Dennison, whose post-Maytag life had admittedly been as unplanned as Annette's had been planned. Without the long commute, Dennison shifted his extra time to his avocation, coaching, and a new passion for Facebook. He posted on a near-daily basis with unmitigated enthusiasm about the boys' junior varsity basketball team that he coached at the school. Coaching, after his family, was Dennison's passion. Life was good. That fall Dennison also became a Rising Star Director for Body by Vi, a multilevel marketing weight loss program that supplemented his income and helped him lose thirty pounds.

It had been a long decade since the anxious months surrounding the Maytag contract dispute and closing announcement. There were still occasional stories about former Butler or Maytag workers in the local papers, but for the most part people had put the bad memories out of their minds and weren't particularly eager to discuss them. Locals often referred to the "stages of grief" when discussing their post-Maytag years. Passing through the stages took different amounts of time for different people, of course, but most had made it to some version of begrudging "acceptance" a while back.

The angry talk, dire predictions, and revolutionary fervor of a decade earlier were now more town lore than present sentiment. In 2002 people had reacted angrily and predicted unmitigated devastation for individual workers, their families, and the community as a whole. "I think the entire Galesburg area has been raped by Maytag," pronounced Eric Ekstedt on the day of the announcement. Another Maytag worker, R. J. West, had said that day, "This town is going to die."[25] Former appliance maker Tim Welch talked about an impending revolution and an inevitable increase in crime. "Man, if they can do that to us, what are we going to do to other people? When somebody gets hungry enough, they're going to do whatever they got to do. Prison ain't that bad. Three squares a day and $20,000 a year to take care of you. What the hell? Why not go try to rob that bank? They're taking shit from us. Hell, you can even get an education in prison. Whereas out here, there aren't no guarantees."

In 2002 the mood was dreary, and the forecasts grim. And yet eight years later, when asked to rate their "level of satisfaction" before and after the Maytag layoffs, 133 workers reported on average only a slight decline in the Maytag Employees in Transition survey. On a scale of one to ten, their satisfaction went from a median score of eight while at Maytag down to seven in 2010.[26] Annette Dennison was busier and more stressed, but also more satisfied as an X-ray technician. "It's bettered me. I've gone to school and got a degree, and I like what I do now. I don't know if I'd say I was 'glad' because it turned our world upside down. And all the other people, look at what it's done to them. But it's bettered me. That door closed and a better one opened."

Mark Semande was so pleased with his railroad gig that it had made him think twice about the existence of God. "For my family it was a blessing," the BNSF railroad worker said. He felt like he was "nothing to the billion dollar company" but, nonetheless, that the high-skilled, physical maintenance he did at rail junctions really mattered. "I look at it as if my children were riding on that train. That's how I take my job." Semande was among the 34 percent that reported higher life satisfaction six years after the 2004 layoffs.[27]

So why was there such a discrepancy between the 2002 predictions and 2010 reports of life satisfaction? Psychologist Daniel Gilbert writes that human beings are simply not very good at prospection. Simulating, or "prefeeling" the future is a unique human ability, but it's fundamentally flawed. Concrete feelings about the present get in the way of our forecasts. "We cannot feel good about an imaginary future when we are busy feeling bad about an actual present," Gilbert writes in *Stumbling on Happiness*. "When we try to overlook, ignore, or set aside our current gloomy state and make a forecast about how we will feel tomorrow, we find that it's a lot like trying to imagine the taste of marshmallow while chewing liver."[28]

Gilbert contends that we tend to underestimate our ability to cope with adversity. He tells us that in big traumas our "psychological immune system" kicks in, and we adjust, in part, by cooking the facts so that we can adapt to new realities. He writes that intense psychological states, such as the life-changing shock and distress of a layoff from a good job, may abate more quickly than milder irritations. "Intense hedonic states are especially likely to trigger the psychological processes that attenuate them," Gilbert and his colleagues note. "Because people are unaware of these processes, they mistakenly expect more intense states to last longer than less intense states."[29] We overestimate the impact (intensity and duration) of the unhappiness that will come from a romantic breakup, a disturbing medical diagnosis, or a job loss.[30] This "impact bias" makes us likewise overestimate the intensity and duration of the happiness we will get from buying a new car, getting cosmetic surgery, or being admitted to a good college. As Adam Smith wrote in *The Theory of Moral Sentiments*, "The great source of both the misery and disorders of human life, seems to arise from over-rating the difference between one permanent situation and another."[31]

In the survey, former Maytag workers said the American Dream was lost for manufacturing workers, and everyone in town knew sad stories of friends and former colleagues. For themselves, though, people were less pessimistic about the American Dream and their own satisfaction. On average they were making much less and had fewer benefits, but their resiliency had kicked in. While we mis-predict the future, we are excellent at "motivated sense-making," or adjusting psychologically to unanticipated new circumstances. Under our mental radar, we engage in dissonance reduction, motivated reasoning, self-serving attributions, self-affirmation, and positive illusions. These psychological processes are largely unconscious, and that's what makes them work. Layoff victims adapt cognitively to trauma by searching for meaning, regaining mastery and control over the traumatic event, and through self-enhancement (often through making favorable comparisons against less fortunate others).[32] As a result, on average, many former workers had nearly made it back to their level of life satisfaction prior to the layoffs.

But Gilbert's explanation only went so far here in rural western Illinois. Tracy Warner didn't fill out the survey. Only 31 percent did. If she had, she would have rated her life satisfaction at eight or nine while at Maytag. "I had lots of money coming in and felt very secure in my life. Life was really good when I worked at Maytag. I could pretty much do whatever I wanted to do in life. The sky was the limit." In December 2012, Warner said she would rate her life satisfaction at a five or six. "I have a lot of stress in my life, mostly because I don't make very much money. I'd love to do more things for my son and as an only child he should have more than he does, but the money is just not there. Sure, I feel more accomplished because I went back to college and have a respectable job now, but I'm not really doing what I want to be doing and I'm working two jobs and barely getting by." Warner and Ryan hadn't been able to travel to Bangladesh that year as she had hoped.

George Carney didn't fill out the survey either. He said he had gone from an eight to a three but was "growing out of it." One could almost hear his psychological immune system busily at work as he willed himself toward optimism and acceptance. "Life is what you make out of it. It changes, and we have to adapt to what we are given." It was unlikely, though, that Carney would grow out of the dark place he was in until he earned a regular paycheck again. As psychologists Max Haller and Markus Hadler write on the subject of happiness and life satisfaction, "What counts most is the ability to cope with life, including subjective health and financial satisfaction, close social relations, and the economic perspective for improvement in the future, both at the level of the individual and at that of the society."[33] For former Appliance City workers Warner and Carney, it was difficult to conjure happiness from the realities of downward mobility. The psychological immune system may be adept, but it cannot, as Gilbert argues, make an argument out of nothing.

17

LITTLE DETROIT, *EL CÁRTEL*,
AND *AGUAMIEL*

Ramos Arizpe, Coahuila

There was this belief that the market solves everything.
—Rogelio Montemayor Seguy, economist and governor of
Coahuila, 1993–1999

THE SECOND-SHIFTERS FILED in slowly on a late Thursday afternoon. From the outside, the factory was a long (nearly a third of a mile), nondescript white box, baking silently in the desert sun of the Ramos Arizpe mountain valley. Inside, it was fairly dark and noisy, with long rows of metal-stamping machines, soldering stations, and assembly lines. Neat green pathways edged with yellow lines, stretching as far as the eye could see, marked the safe routes through. Full-sized and colorful cardboard cutouts of a smiling man and woman greeted workers, highlighting appropriate safety gear.

The operators, an even mix of men and women, meandered down the green paths like high school students reluctantly heading to class. There were young men with sagging jeans and others with Def Leppard and Metallica T-shirts. One young man sported a fauxhawk. Another had a pony tail and looked slightly hungover. Many of the women wore tight-fitting jeans, some of them bejeweled. A large number appeared to be in their teens.

The factory in Ramos Arizpe—a desiccated and spacious industrial valley just southwest of Monterrey, Nuevo León, and just north of Saltillo, Coahuila—was on a refrigerator continental divide. The Whirlpool, Maytag, and KitchenAid refrigerators they assembled here—including the side-by-side, which had been perfected and popularized by Galesburg's Admiral plant fifty years earlier—flowed north. The hip and colorful Brastemp side-by-sides shipped south to Brazil.

The enormous Whirlpool factory was only seven years old in 2013, but it paled in comparison to the massive Dodge Ram truck plant we visited on the other side of Saltillo. Planta Ensamble Saltillo had its own valley, rigorous security, and produced 220,000 trucks a year in nearly infinite combinations of engine sizes, body types, and colors. It sat next to a Chrysler engine factory and a DHL logistics center, which handled some of the highly complicated sequencing for the massive operation. From the back of an electric cart, we saw Dodge trucks start off as metal pieces, pressed out and shaped by hundreds of enormous robotic arms, jerking precisely from position to position, sending up sparks behind tall metal cages. Engines, drive trains, cabs, and boxes (beds) were being joined by the all-male assembly force.[1] There were scores of detailed digital displays, quality-control team stations, and neatly organized bulletin boards pinned with spreadsheets, performance measures, and "World Class Manufacturing" goals. Electronic jingles like the theme from *Jeopardy!* played when a particular shop-floor group needed attention. Planta Ensamble Saltillo was a modern marvel.

The Whirlpool plant, by comparison, was human labor-intensive, low-skill, and low-tech. Its 3,200 workers produced about the same number of refrigerators—around 2,500 per day—as had Appliance City in the 1960s. A Galesburg worker could have discerned the layout and workflow of the new factory. Some of the jobs were the same, like hanging doors, but many others had been stripped of any skill requirements and made into the most rudimentary of movements. Whirlpool's HR manager, Javier Chávez, said that turnover was extremely high. This came as no surprise, given that turnover has been the norm in Mexico since it opened itself up to foreign factories in the 1980s. It was reflective of the low-road industrialism of North America: low wages, low skill requirements, and low retention. Neither side had much interest in a long-term relationship.[2]

"You could call it survival," Gustavo Félix, a Saltillo economist, told us. "But it's really difficult. Everyone in the family has to work to get by, and there aren't many opportunities to get ahead. Public education is inadequate, and wages are low. It's that way in the whole country. There is a lot of unemployment, and workers do not have many alternatives." As we walked through the cafeteria at the Whirlpool factory, the looks directed at Chávez felt decidedly unfriendly. Perhaps we inferred too much, but we left the plant feeling like the place was a tinderbox of discontent. "The multinational corporations come to decrease costs," Raul Vera, Saltillo's courageous and outspoken Catholic bishop, had told us over dinner the previous evening. "But the costs are always paid by the workers."

Maquila workers in Ramos Arizpe-Saltillo had it tough, but the area had managed growth better than had Reynosa. It had the luxury of being close to the beating heart of northern Mexican capitalism, Monterrey, and was known as Mexico's "Little Detroit." The Saltillo region had moved through light industrialization starting as far back as the 1840s, when immigrant families, including Irish, set up textile-making in the area. The last of those older textile factories had recently closed, lost to Asian competition, but the area had progressed gradually, rough as it was, through all the stages of industrial development rather than leapfrogging into the global economy. Workers were not, as they were in Reynosa, displaced agricultural migrants thrust abruptly into an industrial revolution, grinding away at full bore. The workforce was generally better educated, and the social infrastructure more robust.[3] Ramos Arizpe-Saltillo was still close enough to the border for American companies to reap the communications, logistical, and cost-savings benefits of "nearshoring," especially for heavy, bulky items like trucks and refrigerators.[4] In February 2014 Ramos Arizpe-Saltillo had 77,200 export-oriented manufacturing jobs. Industrial goliath Ciudad Juárez had 204,300 and Reynosa had 94,300 (see Figure 17.1).[5]

Rogelio Montemayor Seguy, governor of Coahuila during the early NAFTA years, took a far different development approach than the border cities. Montemayor, like Mike Allen and everyone else, set out to woo and persuade multinationals to come to Coahuila. But instead of seeking out all and any foreign direct investment, his administration strategized around geographic clusters of particular higher-value-added industries, meaning those in which the Mexican contribution to the product was more meaningful. He helped ease the burden of red tape but focused on recruiting companies that paid taxes and planned to stay and be part of the community. His administration developed technical schools and apprentice programs based on company needs. "You need this type of industrial policy," the former governor told us in his art-filled but modest Monterrey home. "This will help you accelerate the growth of the linkages between the dynamic modern sector that you already have with small- and medium-level companies."[6]

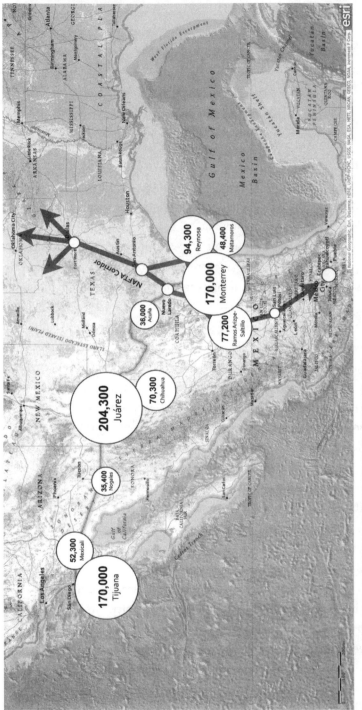

FIGURE 17.1 BORDER STATE PRODUCTION CENTERS AND NAFTA CORRIDOR, 2014

This map shows the ten largest urban production centers in Mexico's border states by IMMEX (export-oriented manufacturing) employment. Total IMMEX employment in 2014 exceeded 2.1 million jobs in over 5,000 factories across Mexico. Juárez, Tijuana, Monterrey, Reynosa, and Ramos Arizpe-Saltillo account for one in three IMMEX jobs. The arrows indicate a central transnational pathway—sometimes referred to as the "NAFTA Corridor"—for legal and illegal trade and migration. Nuevo Laredo-Laredo and Reynosa-McAllen are the critical border nodes of the corridor. In 2013, 3.5 million trucks, 500,000 rail cars, and $180 billion in imports and exports crossed the border at Nuevo Laredo-Laredo alone. *Credit: National Geographic, ESRI.*

Source: INEGI (Instituto Nacional de Estadística y Geografía) data, February 2014; Laredo Development Foundation.

Economic growth came fast for Governor Montemayor and Coahuila. In the mid- to late 1990s, Coahuila had an average of one investment over $30 million per week. He went into the process mindful of "minimizing the collateral damage that growth brings." Montemayor has an economics Ph.D. from the University of Pennsylvania and, like so many of the U.S.-trained Mexican economists who returned to revolutionize Mexico in the 1970s and 1980s, had been taught that the market solves all problems. But Montemayor also had experience in planning in the upper echelons of the Mexican federal government. His administration in Coahuila promoted the development of schools, health clinics, and child-care centers as much as it did industrial growth. Coahuila still has its problems, but Montemayor's tenure as governor is considered a model for smart and strategic integration into global markets and broad-based development.[7]

"It's a lot of work, you have a lot of long-term planning and negotiating to do, but it's doable," Montemayor told us. "But if you don't believe it's necessary, you'll never do it. You have to be convinced that you have to help markets. You're not trying to suppress markets, but there are always inequalities, always the big guys who can just do whatever they want. Well, maybe the small guy can't compete now, but maybe he can tomorrow if you take the trouble to think ahead."

Montemayor did what he could at the state level, but he was swimming against the tide nationally. "The federal government didn't have a policy for linking growth to smaller producers and dealing with growth's collateral damage," he said, "and didn't believe there was a need for it. There was this belief that the market solves everything."

LAURA FLORA OLIVEROS and her girls finally moved after Flora's layoff in 2008. Flora may have put in more hours at Planta Maytag III, where retention was notoriously low, than anyone else. She had kept all her paychecks from Planta III, the dates of which span from December 2004 to April 2008. Another document showed her sizable severance of $2,675.[8] Their new Infonavit home on Reynosa's southwestern side was small, but the new construction was a big step up. Flora was intent on a break from the monotony of the maquilas, so she set up a little store in her home with her severance. Two years later, though, Flora fell behind on her payments, lost the home, and had to return to maquila work.

Flora and her youngest, Erika, then had to move to Colonia Nuevo México, ten miles from Reynosa's downtown. Laura Suarez had gotten married and moved out, and Adrianita had gone to study and live with her aunt down south in Tierra Blanca. The roads to Nuevo México, not much better off than they had been ten years before, made for a long car ride when we visited her in 2013. To get there, we bounced over curbs, spun through mud, and plowed through bumper-high brown pools that had collected after only a moderate rain. It felt like the edge of the world or a frontier outpost in the Old West. And sometimes it sounded that way. In the barren farmland just to the south was a shooting range for *El Cártel* which is how Flora and other locals referred to *El Cártel del Golfo* (the Gulf Cartel), or CDG. The CDG had recently reclaimed Reynosa from *Los Zetas* after a long series of vicious street fights. Near Flora's home, the Jabil maquila stood as a monument to one of the clashes. The front of the factory was pockmarked with spackled-over bullet holes and grenade damage.

After dark, the CDG's pickup trucks would roll through little Colonia Nuevo México. The night, Flora said, belonged to them. In the colonias, the CDG loomed large, and the municipal police and the federales did not. Still, she said, the CDG was far preferable to the ruthless Zetas, who run protection rackets, steal cars, and engage in grotesque violence. Flora said the CDG kept order in Nuevo México, and, in an odd way, she felt she and 14-year-old Erika were protected. El Cártel is most concerned with its exporting business, Flora suggested; you just have to stay out of its way.

In a city owned and run by multinationals, the underground hustlers of the CDG seemed to be the only thriving entrepreneurs. Some of Erika's male teenage friends were involved, seeing cartel life as a place where ambition, hard work, and loyalty earned money and mobility, and made them attractive to women. On our last night in Reynosa, we watched a big soccer match at Sierra Madre Brewing Company. Nearby, a group of CDG men (identified by our driver and security specialist) and their dates—young women in tight-fitting dresses and high heels—made no effort to hide who they were.

El Cártel had become a regular part of everyday life. Nobody denied that fear hung over the city like a proverbial dark cloud. But a few said the media coverage had been sensationalized, and the violence was largely avoidable. If someone stood in its way, though, the CDG was as vicious and skilled a guerrilla force as there was. They hijacked semis or buses to block highways and could essentially shut down the city if one of their own was jailed. They kid-napped with impunity, bribed widely, and killed police if they tried to step in. El Cártel came in armored convoys to assault the federales or the Zetas when their turf was threatened or when they had a score to settle. Like a U.S. street gang, the CDG's violence was targeted and, usually, business-related.

Up and down the U.S.-Mexico border, a bloody war had raged since President Calderón came into office in 2006, promising to crack down on the cartels. The scale of the trauma it has inflicted on Mexican society nearly defies comprehension. Americans might think of the Boston Marathon bombing in 2013, which killed three people, injured 264, shocked a nation, and led to a massive federal, state, and local law enforcement response that shut down a major U.S. city. In Mexico's drug war, people have been burned alive in oil barrels (called "el guiso" [the stew]) and hanged from highway overpasses, penises have been hacked off and found in the mouths of the dead, and hun-dreds of women disappeared without a trace in Juárez. Since 2006, 85,000 people, more than the United States lost in Vietnam, have been slain in the drug war. More than 26,000 are unaccounted for. More than 100,000 have been arrested. And 1.6 million have left their homes because of drug violence.[9]

Martha Ojeda, director of the Coalition for Justice in the Maquiladoras and originally from Nuevo Laredo, said it was all of a piece. "It used to be on the Pacific. The drugs would come through Tijuana. Now it's north through the NAFTA Corridor, so Laredo is the biggest city for import and export for Latin America." Narcotrafficking has grown alongside trade as the rails and highways of the corridor pump manufactured goods, food, people, and drugs north, starting in Chiapas and moving through Mexico City, San Luis Potosí, Saltillo, Ramos Arizpe, Monterrey, Nuevo Laredo, or Reynosa, and then to San Antonio and beyond (see Figure 17.1). Though nobody knows the exact number, authorities estimate that tens of billions a year—probably on par with legal remittances from migrant workers in the U.S.—flows back into Mexico to the drug traffickers, much of it as bulk-smuggled cash.[10]

As key points of entry into the biggest consumer market in the world, the border nodes of the NAFTA Corridor (Nuevo Laredo and Reynosa), along with Juárez, have become flashpoints. South Texas, according to a report from the Justice Department, has been the epicenter of cross-border drug trafficking in recent years.[11] One of Ojeda's organizers had recently disappeared, and her cousin had been killed. "The violence is worse than people think," she told me in 2012. "It's impossible to organize right now. It's a hell."[12] The drugs spilled into Texas, but the violence rarely did. El Paso, Texas, on the other side of the trickle-thin Rio Grande from Juárez, was ranked the safest city in America for the fourth straight year in 2014.[13]

Arqueles Garcia and Gris Cruz stuck it out in Reynosa. The married couple had become accustomed to the military and cartel convoys on the streets and keeping their eyes averted from the quiet CDG safe house next door. The afternoon in 2009 when their cul-de-sac erupted into a massive gun battle, however, they knew it was time to leave. Garcia saw a CDG leader, a man with a gold-plated AK-47, and others boasting about their kills while washing blood off their trucks like it was just another day. That same year federal police raided a CDG safe house in Reynosa and found 500,000 rounds of ammunition, 165 hand grenades, dynamite and tear gas launchers, handguns, and 540 assault rifles. The federal government claimed it was the largest seized weapon cache in Mexico's history. Most of the military-grade hardware, it turned out, came from licensed dealers in Texas.[14]

Garcia and Cruz moved to the other side of town. When there was a flare-up of violence, they relied on Twitter and Facebook updates to figure out what routes were safe to drive and when. Bloggers and YouTube users also attempted to reconstruct events in the absence of reporting and reliable government alerts. Locals made deft use of Internet social networking to share practical advice—and to commiserate. During one gun battle, a mother tweeted, "#ReynosaFollow Q feo los niños preguntando Q paza ii uno pss nada mijitoo. . . Q impotenzia vdd!!! ("How horrible. The children are asking what's going on. I tell them nothing. How defenseless we are!!!")[15] One of the few journalists to report from Reynosa, Tracy Wilkinson of the *Los Angeles Times* wrote that Reynosa "may be the single largest city in Mexico under the thumb of the cartels."[16] Even Reynosa's mayor was displaced. He fled to Texas.

"It's pretty intense here," Garcia told us. Cruz told of being held several times on lockdown at PEMEX, her workplace, as the military came to secure the big local oil and natural gas refineries in town. She told of seeing eight-year-old boys with assault rifles in their hands. Garcia and Cruz—talented artists, aspiring young professionals, and kind and loving parents—had embraced evangelical Christianity in the previous few years. "We've seen evil," Cruz said.

"The root of that problem is the maquiladora phenomenon," Governor Montemayor maintained. Border industrialization had been too fast and chaotic. Local governments received little revenue and had been overwhelmed by its costs. When the young women recruited to the factories had children, there was nothing for them. Many were single and child care was hard to find. "They grew up alone, like in the wild," Montemayor said of the next generation. "When you have that going on for many years, you start seeing the kind of person who has no attachment to anything. The pool of people in Mexico without work and without education, looking for anything to do, is huge. They argue about the figures, but the lowest I've seen is 7 million."

The unglued quality of border life seemed to have unraveled the "Mike Allen question"—exposing a yawning hole in the logic of market fundamentalism and its faith in laissez-faire to meet all needs and solve all problems. In the near absence of government authority, effective regulation, grassroots democracy, and law and order, the powerful ruled unchecked. During the day, the multinationals held sway over the formal economy. At night, El Cártel dominated the lucrative informal sectors. After twenty-five turbulent years, Reynosa seemed held together only by greed and desperation. The border boomtown, Montemayor suggested, was no longer governed by government, and lacked balance, a center, and a plan. "The benign 'invisible hand' may have been a favorable inaugural condition for commercial societies," the late historian Tony Judt wrote, "but it cannot reproduce the noncommercial institutions and relations—of cohesion, trust, custom, restraint, obligation, morality, authority—that it inherited and which the pursuit of individual economic self-interest tends to undermine rather than reinforce."[17]

"Maquiladoras-narcos-migration—that's the triangle," said Mexican author Julian Cardona, referring to Juárez. "If you keep these things separate you will never understand what is happening in this city."[18]

ONE MORNING IN Saltillo, our driver, a security specialist, was busy on his cellphone. He was gathering intelligence on a shooting in front of the Coahuila governor's palace; five security officers had just been shot. He suspected it was a message from the Zetas or El Cártel to the governor and Saltillo's mayor. Later reports indicated that the assailant was ex-military and was demanding action in the case of disappeared relatives.[19]

There had also been a recent rash of kidnappings as the cartels clashed. When we asked how many there had been in Saltillo in the last month, the driver replied, "Un chingo de secuestros" (a shitload of kidnappings). Although the chaos of the border had infiltrated south, down the NAFTA Corridor to Monterrey and Saltillo, so, too, had ordinary Mexicans' insistence that life move on. That same night we went to Saltillo's main square—the very same spot where the early-morning shooting had happened—in which 15,000 were gathering for a big cumbia concert.[20] The crowd mingled alongside municipal, state, and federal police armed with shotguns, assault rifles, and body armor. There were police dogs, undercover cars, road blocks, and a police pickup truck hauling a black mobile watchtower dotted with video cameras. The festive, hot night went off without a hitch.

The Zetas held sway in Saltillo, although the Sinaloa cartel and the CDG pinched in from the west and east, respectively. In General Cepeda, a tiny little town just west of Saltillo, Emilio Arizpe had learned, like so many in the area, to coexist with the Zetas. Since 1980, Arizpe, a warm, articulate man with rugged good looks and laid-back charm, has cultivated the land at Villa de Patos, an organic farm dedicated to land conservation and traditional production methods. Arizpe works with ejidatarios to produce maguey sap (or *aguamiel*), a viscous agave sweetener he uses in nutritious drinks for health-conscious and well-off consumers in Monterrey and around the world.

Arizpe sits on the board of ARCA Continental, the second-largest Coca-Cola bottler in Latin America and seller of Bokados bagged snack foods. He grew up playing in his grandfather's bottling plant in Saltillo, which in 1926 was among the first to bring Coke to Mexico after the worst fighting of the Revolution had ended. Northern Mexicans initially didn't take to the strange black liquid that "tasted like medicine," Arizpe said. The Americans from Atlanta advised his grandfather to give it away for free. Today Mexico's per capita consumption of Coca-Cola products far exceeds that of any other country. We asked Arizpe if Mexico's economic liberalization had helped ARCA. "Yes, of course. The main consumer of Coke and chips are working people, and they have more money to spend." In 1992, Mexicans drank 292 Coke drinks per person per year, fewer than the average American at that time. Today Mexicans consume on average 745 Coca-Cola beverages per person per year, hundreds more than second-place Panama.[21]

Arizpe was the rebel of his family, having turned his back on the family business for a time to join student protests in the 1960s and to build schools in remote villages in Oaxaca. Though he prefers his aguamiel drinks to Coke, he has no political objections to the soft drink. "Imagine that campesino working in the heat all day and then tasting a cold, sugary Coke. It's something fantastic. It's *la chispa de la vida* (the spark of life)." Yet for that reason, Arizpe fights an uphill battle in promoting his aguamiel drinks. Coke is still a potent status symbol in Mexico. Even his workers, with free access to the agave drinks, choose Coke. Nonetheless, he views his work at Villa de Patos as a long-term mission—and the dividends from ARCA support it. As Beatriz, the manager of his Monterrey store, said, "The one feeds the other." Even though he seems to be working against history, Arizpe is passionate about sound ecological practices and linking small-scale ejidatarios to profitable export markets around the globe.

A major consequence of NAFTA has been the industrialization, reorganization, and consolidation of the North American food system. After two decades, Mexico's food environment, as "Exporting Obesity," published in the *International Journal of Occupational and Environmental Health* argues, is increasingly obesogenic (obesity-causing). "Mexican diets have shifted away from traditional food staples toward energy-dense, processed foods and animal-source foods—foods that tend to be high in fats and/or sweeteners." Consumption of white bread, sugary drinks, fast food, bagged chips, ice cream, processed meats, and other refined foods and sweets have all increased in the NAFTA era. "There has been nothing short of a 'supermarket revolution,'" according to the article.[22]

Nothing was more apparent in Reynosa in 2013 than the proliferation of low-cost superstores like S-Mart, Soriana, Walmart, and Bodega Aurrera (Walmart's "discount compact hypermarket" in Mexico). The brightly colored stores stood in near-cartoonish contrast to the mangled roads, rows of tiny cinderblock houses, and dreary-looking schools. The big retailers had sopped up and formalized much of Reynosa's low-end consumption, as they had across the country. Since Walmart entered Mexico in 1991, it has become the country's largest private sector employer and now controls half of the retail and 20 percent of the total Mexican food retail sectors. Other U.S. retailers, such as HEB, Safeway (Casa Ley), Costco (Comercial Mexicana), Pricemart, Fleming (Gigante), Kmart, Oxxo, 7-Eleven, and Circle K, also pounced on the newly open and urbanizing markets south of the border. It was the same story with fast food chains.[23]

Across the Rio Grande, McAllen-Edinburg-Mission sits in first place on the list of America's poorest metropolitan areas—and among the areas forecasted to grow fastest through 2020.[24] In 2005, *New York Times Magazine* writer Elizabeth Weil uncovered an obesity epidemic in the colonias of the Magic Valley, still a fecund producer of healthy vegetables, citrus fruits, and melons. In Rio Grande City, where Eugene Nelson, Ed Krueger, and the UFW mapped strategy during the 1967 melon protests, half of the boys and 35 percent of the girls were obese or overweight when they entered elementary school. It had become normal, Weil found, for poor children in oppressively hot South Texas—where you can get "an Extreme Gulp, which is 52 ounces of soda, and a bag of chips for a dollar"—to be overweight and prone to Type 2 diabetes and other health problems. A new food culture had taken hold and public health workers found it difficult to push back. When one Valley school changed to a healthier breakfast and lunch menu, the school kids staged a protest. They hung signs outside some cafeterias reading, "No more diet" and "We want to eat cool stuff—pizza, nachos, burritos, cheese fries."[25]

Reflecting on these changes, the authors of "Exporting Obesity" asked that we reconsider the "unexamined assumption that increasing volumes of low-price (and low-quality) food is good for producers and consumers." This model, they argue, fails to account "for the very real costs to taxpayers and public health agencies" in the United States and Mexico.[26]

So to the "maquiladoras-nacros-migration" triangle, one must add "Big Food" to understand the experience of hypercapitalism in today's borderlands.

WHAT DID THIS all add up to, two decades after NAFTA and three decades after Mexico began to open in the 1980s? In 2014, the Center for Economic and Policy Research issued an assessment of NAFTA on its 20th anniversary. It reported low per capita GDP growth (0.9 percent per year), little to no progress in reducing poverty, and basically flat wages since 1980 (average wages, adjusted for inflation). The authors calculated that if Mexico had continued on the growth path it had been on from 1960 to 1980, it would be a high-income country today, and among European nations in per capita income. Instead, Mexico ranked 18th of twenty Latin American countries in growth from 1994 to 2013.[27]

For millions of Mexicans, the era of integration with the U.S. has been the era of displacement *to* the U.S. Today, the United States has more immigrants from Mexico alone (12 million) than any other country has from all other countries combined.[28] Most, though, have been forced into the shadows because of a contradiction at the heart of the free trade agreement. Although NAFTA had freed the movement of goods, services, and capital, the agreement—unlike the ambitious integration of the European Union—ignored the transnational movement of people, and in fact cracked down in Juárez and Tijuana around NAFTA's implementation. As a result, many northbound migrants found themselves stuck in the swelling border cities, the places in Mexico most changed in the past two decades. Here was a peculiar industrial revolution, shaped profoundly by its northern neighbor, powerful outside interests, and the ravenous demands of U.S. consumers for goods, legal and illegal alike. *Pobre México, tan lejos de Dios y tan cerca de los Estados Unidos.*

Chad Richardson and José A. Pagán, longtime authorities on the border, explained why development has been so uneven in the borderlands. "The benefits of cross-border development flow toward the centers of each nation," they wrote, "while the costs must be absorbed by border residents." There are hundreds of thousands of jobs at the border, but the low wages enter the area as paychecks and then quickly exit through the cash registers of S-Mart or Bodega Aurrera. The limited taxes the maquilas pay, along with federal income and other taxes, exit south, to Mexico City. Further, the linkages to local economic activities that promote self-employment, small suppliers and other businesses, balanced growth, and broad-based industrial development do not exist in low-road, maquiladora-led development, Richardson and Pagán found.[29]

In this brave new border world, it was somehow unsurprising that a cold-blooded and criminal paramilitary operation could make nonchalant and reasoned appeals to the masses, offering a better life for ambitious, hard workers. In one audacious example, the Zetas hung a huge banner from a highway overpass in Reynosa. It read, "The Zetas tactical force wants you if you are military or ex-military. We offer a good salary, food, and care for your family. You will not be mistreated or fed cheap ramen noodle meals. Lazy people, refrain from calling."[30]

And yet Reynosa's industrial machine plowed forward, fueled by Laura Flora and other Veracruzanos desperate for the hours. In 2014, workers in Reynosa's sea of over 150 export-oriented factories logged upwards of 20 million hours each month.[31]

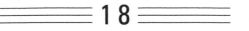

18

RESHORING UP

Galesburg, Illinois

The issue of government has always been whether individual men and women
will have to serve some system of government of economics, or whether a system
of government and economics exists to serve individual men and women.

—Franklin Delano Roosevelt, campaign address at The Commonwealth Club,
San Francisco, September 23, 1932

IT WAS LATE on a sunny, but bitterly cold mid-February afternoon. Michael
Patrick, red-eared from the chill, cast a long shadow across the rough concrete that used to be the Appliance City factory floor. A few months earlier,
two-thirds of the expansive ruin had been razed. It was now an extended chin-
high pile of crumbled bricks, broken cinderblocks, mangled rebar, and corn-
yellow insulation chunks. Patrick, dressed in a corduroy jacket, wool trousers,
and a brown wool fedora, remarked that there was little now to stop the bitter
Arctic winds that swept through the enormous demolition site. One could
see clear through to the Henry C. Hill Correctional Center across the tracks
and farther north on Illinois Route 41. The razed portion of the former factory was big enough to fit twenty football fields, side by side. The newest part
of the factory was still standing, but vacant. The California-based investment
company that owned the property hoped that clearing the "old, antiquated
industrial real estate" would make the remaining property more attractive to
potential buyers.[1]

"When you're here," Patrick said, "you think about the people. It was the
blood, sweat, and tears of the workers that made this place run. It was ours,
you know? We had different owners come and go but *we* made it run." He

pushed his hands deep into his jacket pockets and shrugged. It was early 2013, and Patrick could mark fifty-four years since he and Bob Dennison, Doug's father, started packing insulation at Admiral's Midwest Manufacturing plant on January 26, 1959.

Patrick lived alone in a modest brick house on South Pleasant Avenue, just across the BNSF tracks, less than a mile away. The 72-year-old retiree hibernated in the winter, but managed to make each of his granddaughter's sixth-grade basketball games. When the weather warmed, Patrick took his late model minivan to antique shows, estate sales, and collectors' conventions. He collected license plates and license plate toppers, die-cast cars, and other trinkets.

Earlier that day, over lunch at the Landmark Cafe, we had discussed the wage pressures, retiree obligations, and foreign competition that faced Maytag in the early 2000s.

"Do you think this plant could have made it?" I asked.

Patrick thought for a long moment, as if it weren't a question that had run through his head a thousand times. "I don't know, Chad. I don't know."

Joe Krejci, a longtime appliance industry manager and Maytag's logistics man in Galesburg, had once told me that he thought Maytag could have made it as a niche player, had it focused on innovative design and high-quality, high-end products. In other words, Maytag could have made it by doing what it had done for over a century. Former Local 2063 president Dave Bevard, and other traditionalists, agreed. Maytag should have stuck with what made it great, rather than try to compete on price with Whirlpool and General Electric, the two domestic giants. It had always been about the Maytag name, the design, the workmanship, and the quality. It was about the *product*. The *product* commanded the price premium. The *product* made Maytag distinctive. When that was lost, so was Maytag.

Perhaps Maytag was stuck untenably between the high-volume appliance giants and the luxury producers when foreign competitors like Haier started to roll in. But it had weathered many crises before, most recently in the early 1990s under Leonard Hadley. "Can the company do even better?" *BusinessWeek* asked in 1999.[2]

Maytag's ignominious end in 2006 broke Hadley's heart. "I was very sad and upset," the aging and still widely admired former CEO said from his home in Cedar Rapids, Iowa. "I thought I left them hardwired for success.

I was astounded at how quickly the wheels came off." He had been hesitant to comment on Maytag's collapse. The Maytag lifer—he had started at the company in 1959—had been the epitome of a loyal and tight-lipped company man. With the Maytag name all but destroyed, though, he allowed himself a little latitude.

"Foreign competition wasn't something I had to deal with, and certainly Grandpas Maytag never saw those challenges in their lives. But the board in my view had enough time with Successor Number Two [Ralph Hake] to judge him inadequate and make another change rather than sell the company. They didn't do it." Regarding Hake's focus on costs, Hadley replied, diplomatically, "There's a limit to what you can do with that." Hadley added that when he bought Iowa refrigerator-producer Amana, he did not expect Galesburg to be closed down. "I never saw the cost reports to prove that he was right," Hadley said of Hake.[3]

When I told Patrick what Hadley had said, he seemed to appreciate it. "We had a great relationship with him," Patrick said.

Hake typified the "MBA bean counters" infecting American business, according to iconoclastic automobile executive Bob Lutz. Lutz, a conservative Republican, argues in *Car Guys vs. Bean Counters* that "the drive to reduce cost, skimp a bit on service, ruthlessly pursue quarterly earnings targets no matter what the negative consequences has hurt American business from automobiles to appliances." When "number crunchers" took charge at General Motors, the maker of the Corvette and Cadillac was putting out cars like that hideous focus group creation, the Pontiac Aztek—or as Lutz called it, the "Quasimodo of crossovers." Lutz's conclusion: "Shoemakers should be run by shoe guys, and software firms by software guys."[4]

After Hadley—the hands-on, detail-oriented "appliance guy"—left, Maytag went from being the leader in customer satisfaction to "all-time lows," according to the creator of the American Customer Satisfaction Index.[5] In turn, its market share hit all-time lows, its bonds downgraded to junk status, and its stock price hit a fourteen-year low.[6] "More than anything," a CNN business writer wrote, Maytag failed, "because Hake followed a compass more attuned to Wall Street than to his loyal customers."[7]

Hake, who put in four years as Maytag's CEO, took his $10 to $20 million in severance and headed west in 2006. He bought a McMansion in the gated Anthem Country Club of Las Vegas later that year. The Hakes' back patio and swimming pool overlooked Hole 11 of the club's golf course and, ten miles to the north, the Las Vegas strip. In the 2008 election, the semiretired University of Chicago MBA donated to both the Libertarian Party candidate for president, Bob Barr, and to its vice presidential candidate, Wayne Allyn Root. Root, Hake's nearby neighbor at Anthem, describes himself as a "capitalist evangelist." He is author of *The Ultimate Obama Survival Guide*, which promises strategies for building wealth and securing freedom during the socialist "Obamageddon." Back in Iowa, Hake was sued by a couple that had bought his Newton home. The couple claimed that the $641,000 house, less than a decade old, suffered from poor-quality materials and framing, leaks and roofing problems, and generally shoddy workmanship.[8]

Blaming Hake and his predecessor, Lloyd Ward, was too easy, Patrick said over his salmon salad and iced tea. It was hard to say how the Galesburg plant could have withstood new Asian competition, the demanding big-box retailers, and the rigors of accelerated product cycles. The pressures on the factory were real; Hake may have felt he had no choice in the matter. Indeed, some Wall Street analysts blamed Hake for not offshoring more and cutting costs deeper and faster.[9] But for Patrick, it all went beyond Hake to the big investors and the board; that's where the major decisions were made. Lester Crown, an influential voice on the board and the company's biggest shareholder (4.1 million shares)—and Obama's first big-money supporter—had pushed for selling Maytag and closing the Galesburg factory, arguing that it wasn't competitive.[10] In his defense, Crown, a Chicago power broker, had been a long-term investor in Maytag and a vocal critic of short-termism and speculation. But it was clear that Hake had been brought in to cut costs, which included shuttering Appliance City and ridding Maytag of its connection to feisty Local 2063. It was part of a plan to sell the company so the big investors—who had seen substantial losses under Ward—could move their fortunes elsewhere.

That's how Patrick saw it. "These people are not interested in what they're building, the company or the name, like they used to be," the former Machinists leader said. "The owners were concerned about the quality, the name, their reputation, and everything. Management then took pride in not laying people off, expanding their business, and hiring people. They were all part of the community. Even Admiral, this was their baby. With these investors, they're off somewhere else making these decisions depending on how much profit we're making. So, yes, I think Maytag could have survived. But with investors, it's how much return on our money do we get? Are we going to settle for 5 percent? If we get 5 percent, will we want 10 percent?" In the end, though,

Maytag's sale to Whirlpool didn't work out for the Crown family, which had seen the value of its Maytag holdings drop by roughly $200 million from the peak under Hadley. The Crowns, however, remained one of Chicago's wealthiest families and a key force behind Obama's political ascent. To some, Obama's populist rhetoric rang hollow given his close relationship to Lester Crown.[11]

As Patrick and I walked out of the Landmark Cafe, it was apparent that some questions about the demise of Appliance City and Maytag would go unanswered.[12] Patrick, however, felt certain there had been a cultural shift among the economic and political elite. He didn't believe those who argued that the investor class deserved tax breaks so they would create more jobs. The short-term speculators at places like Bain Capital, made famous in Mitt Romney's 2012 presidential run and an early suitor of Maytag, extracted their spoils by eliminating jobs, not creating them.[13] "That's been the problem," Patrick said, as mellow and even-tempered as always. "They're not the job-makers anymore, they're the profit-takers. And that's where we're at."

THE OLD MAYTAG headquarters in Newton was sold for $1 in 2012 by a "motivated seller" after its listing in the *Wall Street Journal*.[14] I wondered if Fred Maytag's credo was still in the building's lobby. "Our management," it read, "must maintain a just balance among the interests of customers, employees, shareowners and the public. Although these groups may apparently compete in their short-term goals, their long-range interests coincide, for none can long benefit unless the needs of all are served."[15] The "Grandpas Maytag," as Hadley called them, were not alone, of course. In 1914, Henry Ford announced that he would pay his auto workers an unheard-of $5 a day. It was not just a matter of economic justice, Ford argued, but of growing a class of middle-income consumers through high wage jobs.[16] Communitarian Republican leaders of old would likely decry the narrow bottom-lines and self-serving libertarianism of some of today's titans of industry. But is it nostalgic or naive to think that manufacturing, corporate responsibility, and government investment can lead to another era of shared prosperity like the postwar years?

Some stalwarts of Midwestern manufacturing such as John Deere, Caterpillar, and Harley-Davidson survived the exodus, even if they had outsourced and downsized to do so. All the major appliance manufacturers—Whirlpool, General Electric, Bosch and Siemens, Electrolux, and Haier—have stateside factories. And Patrick reminded me that Whirlpool still makes refrigerators—with Whirlpool, Amana, and Jenn-Air nameplates—just across the Mississippi River in Amana, Iowa.[17] Maytag traditionalists like Krejci and Bevard pointed to Sub-Zero, which makes luxury refrigerators in Madison, Wisconsin. Viking Range Corporation, Dacor, and Thermador also make most of their appliances in the United States. "It's a matter of keeping production here," a Sub-Zero spokesperson said, regarding their resistance to offshoring, "where our quality standards can be more closely monitored."[18]

The Chrysler factory in nearby Belvidere, Illinois, had hung on as well, thanks in part to federal loans. In 2013, 4,198 hourly workers and 1,703 body shop robots produced the Jeep Patriot and Compass and, since 2012, the Dodge Dart, all on the same line. When I visited the immaculate 280-acre, five-million-square-foot facility in June 2013, it was pumping out 1,302 cars a day in nearly unrelenting production. Under UAW signs and amid work stations papered over with spreadsheets, the auto assemblers—sporting casual T-shirts and wearing iPods—aimed to surpass 300,000 cars that year, prodded in no small part by intracompany competition (explicitly encouraged by the company) with Dodge truck-maker Planta Ensamble Saltillo and other Chrysler plants. Chrysler, Caterpillar, and GE—it should be noted—had all aggressively taken advantage of NAFTA and shifted many jobs to Mexico.[19] But for a company whose very existence had recently been in doubt, the bustling Chrysler factory was a remarkable sight.[20]

American manufacturing is far from dying. The United States runs just behind China in manufacturing output and is far ahead of Japan and Germany. And while much of what we buy at Walmart or Target comes from Asia, much else is still produced here. Of all of the goods and services Americans consume, 88.5 percent is home-grown, and only 2.7 percent is "Made in China." Even in "durables," such as cars and refrigerators, Americans spend two out of every three dollars on American-made content. American manufacturing output is at an all-time high, having increased 600 percent since 1940.[21] But there's a rub. In that same period, what on average took 1,000 workers to produce now takes only 175. The U.S. steel industry is incredibly productive; it turns out as much steel as it ever did—with one-tenth of the workers. Whirlpool recently reshored production of its KitchenAid hand mixers to Greenville, Ohio. It only amounted to 25 jobs.[22]

Today there are about 12 million manufacturing jobs in the United States. Of all sectors, manufacturing has by far the highest multiplier, meaning that it supports from three to fifteen jobs in other sectors. "Making things" drives technological change and has virtuous spillover effects, lessens the trade deficit, and creates more value in the American economy per dollar than any other sector.

Dave Bevard put it best. "I don't know of an economy that can survive on the principle of 'You mow my lawn, and I'll wash your dishes,'" Local 2063's last president had said at rallies, to hoots and cheers. "What we have today is people playing the stock market and shifting money here in the morning and there in the afternoon. But what did you make? We're great because we make things."[23]

GENERAL ELECTRIC'S FAMOUS Appliance Park in Louisville, so long in slow decline, has begun to scrape off its rust. In 1973, it was the workplace of 23,000, a vast white-line production complex, big enough to merit its own zip code and a mile-long parking lot. By 2011, it had dwindled to 1,863. Starting in 2009, GE began to invest over $1 billion in American-made appliances, adding dishwasher, washer, and dryer lines, and the GeoSpring hybrid water heater line. The 2012 opening of the cutting-edge facility, the first new manufacturing facility at the park since 1957, was "inspirational" and would begin to "reverse decades of outsourcing," GE Appliances' Chip Blankenship announced. The next month GE announced a new "ecomagination"-inspired French-door refrigerator—a high-tech update of the old Admiral Duplex. The GE refrigerator line came from Celaya, Mexico.[24]

General Electric was an unlikely leader. Jack Welch, its former CEO, was an offshoring pioneer. "Ideally," he said in 1998, "you'd have every plant you own on a barge to move with currencies and changes in the economy."[25] According to manufacturing expert John Shook, Welch led a "herd mentality" into the devastating plant shuttering and offshoring wave of the early 2000s. The big brand-name multinationals cut their U.S. work forces by 2.9 million during the 2000s while increasing overseas employment by 2.4 million, leading to an unprecendented decade of zero net job growth that devastated the middle and working classes.[26]

In recent years, though, the fault-lines of the world economy have begun to shift. Higher oil and shipping costs and higher wages have made China less attractive to business—and have made Mexico the most competitive place to manufacture goods for North America.[27] Lower natural gas prices, more competitive wages, and higher labor productivity have also spurred reshoring in the United States. Current GE CEO Jeffrey Immelt argued in 2012,

"Outsourcing that is based only on labor costs is yesterday's model."[28] Harry
Moser, an MIT-trained engineer and founder of the Reshoring Initiative,
estimated that "about 60 percent of the companies that offshored manufacturing didn't really do the math."[29] One analysis estimated that by 2020, up
to 30 percent of America's imports from China could be U.S.-made. Further,
with a weakened dollar, affordable and productive labor, and its enormous car
market, the United States is again a competitive producer of cars and trucks.
Japanese and German automakers have invested over $44 billion in the past
two decades in the U.S. Midwest and South, resulting in 80,000 jobs.[30]

More than simple math is driving this apparent shift. In "The Insourcing
Boom," *The Atlantic*'s Charles Fishman details the case of the GeoSpring
hybrid water heater. In China, production was a convoluted, ten-hour ordeal.
Cheap labor, though, had hidden the production inefficiencies and kept costs
relatively low. To prepare for the new line in Louisville, a team of design engineers, manufacturing engineers, line workers, and marketing and sales staff
overhauled the water heater's design and manufacturing process. That's when
something amazing happened. In the place once known as "Strike City," the
team trimmed production time per unit from ten to two hours, cut material costs by 25 percent, boosted quality and energy efficiency, and reduced
time-to-market from five weeks to 30 minutes—the time it took to drive the
water heater to a nearby Louisville warehouse. Most amazing, the hybrid
water heater—a leading-edge unit that uses 60 percent less energy than a
typical water heater and can be controlled by iPhone—costs less to make in
Kentucky than in China. The retail price dropped 20 percent.[31]

It was that kind of shop-floor collaboration that made Galesburg's
Appliance City work, according to union man Michael Patrick and factory
superintendent Fred Pickard—rivals and friends for decades. There had been
hands-on, trial-and-error innovation that happened at the intersection of the
thinking and the doing of production. Globalization had broken that link,
putting design and marketing in advanced economies and manufacturing in
far-flung, low-cost places. I wondered if, with the right leadership, a refrigerator like General Electric's $3,099 luxury model now made in Louisville, could
have been made today in Galesburg.

If the appliance-making is gone for good from Galesburg, perhaps there's
something else for the little city in western Illinois. After being hit hard by
free trade, Walla Walla, Washington, turned around with wine-making and

wine tourism. Its comeback centered on a hands-on Enology and Viticulture program at the local community college that's launched 25 wineries and hundreds of skilled workers into the industry. South Bend, Indiana, once home to Studebaker automobiles, is now home to a data center for cloud-based computing, with hopes for a rebirth based on high-tech manufacturing. At West Philadelphia High School, students develop and race hybrid sports cars to develop the skills needed in today's advanced manufacturing. In Greenville, South Carolina, the BMW Scholars Program offers competitive, German-style apprenticeships to develop multiskilled workers in mechanics, electronics, and robotics. Apprenticeship programs that integrate study with hands-on work are a leading explanation for Germany's relatively low youth-unemployment rate and high economic productivity.[32]

Inside Louisville's bright new water heater facility, the assembly lines are short, lean, and efficient. It is a far cry from Michael Patrick's early years, when he would end his workday with a cold bath to soak out fiberglass shards and rub the dried coal tar off his fingers. The new GE jobs are fairly well paid, and they're union. That's where the similarities end. Replacing the sweaty bustle of yesterday is an orderly, automated, and sparsely peopled landscape. And one that demands higher skill levels. Manufacturers say that even amid high unemployment, openings for high-skilled manufacturing jobs—computer-assisted metal cutters, diesel electricians, and machinists—regularly go unfilled.[33] These are "middle-skill" jobs, and where government investment comes in.[34] Middle-skill workers are phlebotomists, nurse technicians, and radiology technicians, like Annette Dennison. They are skilled electricians, plumbers, HVAC experts, and welders, like Mike Smith at John Deere. A key question, then, is whether the public education and community college systems of the United States can provide useful and meaningful career pathways, outside of and in addition to four-year colleges, to match the moment. As George Carney said, "Not everybody is cut out for college." It's not just Carney; 63 percent of American workers do not have a college degree.[35]

THREE HOURS FROM Galesburg's demolition site is the building that used to be known as Maytag Newton Laundry Products Plant #2. Inside, a hundred union men and women fabricate long, sleek steel-and-concrete wind turbine towers. Trinity Structural Towers considered moving to a low-wage site in Mexico but chose instead to invest $21 million to retrofit the historic plant on the north side of this rural Iowa town. A mile away at TPI Composites, 700 men and women, about 30 percent of them former Maytag workers, fabricate 20,000-pound fiberglass wind blades that stretch nearly half a football field in length. There are many fewer jobs than there were before Whirlpool shuttered Maytag's headquarters and factories in Newton. The jobs pay a little less, and some are part-time and nonbenefited. But Newton's effort to remake itself offers a note of hope.[36]

It took a lot of work to bring the 1,000 wind-power jobs to Newton. There were the aggressive city and state tax incentives for Trinity and TPI, and a State of Iowa grant for retrofitting Plant #2. Newton worked hard to market itself as the perfect location for emergent wind-energy producers. It lies in the middle of the expansive Great Plains wind power market, has ready access to rail lines as well as to Interstate 80, and there's an experienced and eager production workforce. Newton fit into Iowa's strategic energy independence and wind-powered economic growth plan. By 2012, Iowa received 20 percent of its electricity from wind (up from 6 percent in 2007) and had reduced its greenhouse gas emissions dramatically. The wind industry has pulled in billions in private investment and created 7,000 wind power-related jobs statewide.[37]

Nationwide, wind farms tripled wind electricity generation from 2008 to 2012.[38] Federal support has been critical in getting the fledgling industry off the ground, especially a tax incentive known as the Production Tax Credit (PTC). In addition, the Commerce Department protected American wind tower makers by levying stiff duties on Chinese manufacturers when they dumped wind towers in the United States at unfairly subsidized prices.[39] At the end of 2013, however, the PTC expired amid congressional partisanship and inaction, leaving the wind industry in doubt about its future. Meanwhile, oil and gas producers continue to enjoy permanent credits.[40] The federal government needs to do better if Newton's emerging green energy industry is to persist in former Laundry Products Plant #2.

For decades the United States has neglected the industrial and social policy that helped make it the dominant producer of the 20th century. The first third of the 20th century unleashed dizzying changes: the Great War, mass immigration, race riots, rapid urbanization, and the rise of Ford and General Motors, electrical power, radio, motion pictures, women's suffrage, and "a whirl of modernisms which almost [passed] belief," according to *Recent Social Trends*, a presidential report from the time.[41] The Roaring Twenties also led to a surge in inequality and an economic collapse. The New Dealers believed the subsequent Depression was a political collapse as much as it was an economic one, and so they sought political renewal after a period of policy "drift" and inaction in the face of challenging times.

Political scientists Jacob S. Hacker and Paul Pierson argue that we live in a similar time today, now decades into an era of growing inequality in which the federal government has failed to respond to new economic realities. They reject the idea that globalization and technological change—and their disproportionate impact on less-educated and lower-skilled workers—explains the growing income gap adequately. Rising inequality is less about education gaps than it is about those at the very top of the income distribution pulling away. Even among the college-educated, for instance, there is enormous inequality. Further, they show that other advanced economies, exposed to the same global pressures and with greater gaps in education and skills, have experienced less growth in inequality. To illustrate this point, they write, "there is more inequality among workers with the *same* level of skills (measured by age, education, and literacy) in the United States than there is among *all workers* in some of the more equal rich nations."[42] Upgrading a society's human capital is essential, of course, but deficits in education and skills in the United States are at most a minor cause of growing income inequality.

Instead, Hacker and Pierson argue, growing inequality is the direct result of politics and public policy. In the late 1970s there was an "unseen revolution" in which organized business interests (e.g., the Business Roundtable, Chamber of Commerce, National Association of Manufacturers) and "conservative idea merchants" (wealthy conservative activists and well-funded think tanks like the Heritage Foundation) grew their influence in Washington. The result was decades of policies beneficial to business—including the rewriting of rules on taxes, financial markets, and executive pay—while policy generally became *less* generous toward the vast majority of Americans and was harmful to labor.[43] With the policymaking playing field tilting in favor of business, the United States entered the rapidly globalizing economy in a way that, on balance, benefited economic elites and hurt workers.

Economic globalization is not the nub of the problem, then; it's how the American political system responded (and failed to respond) to it. European countries, on the other hand, have adopted variations of "flexicurity," a set of taxpayer-funded labor market and social policies that seek to provide employers with flexibility and workers with greater economic security. These policies include portable health insurance; more secure and portable retirement benefits; and expanded unemployment, skills-building, and wage supports. A person with portable health benefits, for example, is better positioned to transition to another job, take a year off for building skills, or take advantage of an entrepreneurial opportunity.[44] Flexicurity policies also help companies hampered by the expense of "legacy costs" in pensions and health care for aging union employees, which is a big reason why U.S. companies sought out nonunionized workforces much more than companies elsewhere did.

Why exactly, though, should we care about inequality? The United States, after all, is still a rich nation. The downward mobility that Tracy Warner has experienced may seem unfair, but she and her son have material comforts that people in poor countries often do not. George Carney is living on much less, but he has a television, a cellphone, and enough food to eat. The kids that Doug Dennison works with may not have the resources of wealthier kids, and they may have a tougher time achieving the American Dream, but they're in school and have a decent place to rest their heads at night. Plus, inequality can even be useful, as economist Gary Becker argued; it can have great "social value." If rewards for education and human capital development are driving inequality, he contended, then that's "good inequality" because then people seek out education and skills and move up the income ladder when they do. However, this perspective misses the changed political context, as Hacker and Pierson suggest, and does little to explain the main driver of inequality in the United States, public policy. In addition, Becker's argument misses inequality's sociological consequences, a theme *Boom, Bust, Exodus* attempts to explore in places across North America.[45]

Equality, it turns out, may be the linchpin of a society's health. In a wide-ranging study of the advanced economies of North America, Europe, and Asia, epidemiologists Kate Pickett and Richard Wilkinson found that higher inequality means more high school drop-outs, more homicides, and more mental illness, and higher rates of imprisonment. Infant mortality and obesity increase. Feelings of isolation, alienation, and anxiety increase. They found that social trust, educational performance, and social mobility decline as well. In unequal, wealthy societies like the United States, Singapore, Portugal, and the United Kingdom, there is a greater consciousness of superiority and inferiority, more feelings of being devalued and disrespected, and more worries about status competition. In poor countries, where people suffer from hunger, ramshackle housing, and stark material deprivation, increasing a nation's income matters a great deal to overall social health. For advanced economies, however, higher overall national wealth does *not* translate to longer, healthier, and happier lives or fewer social problems like teen pregnancy, violence, and addiction. Pickett and Wilkinson find that it is *relative* position, and whether social gaps are growing or shrinking, that really matters in a country like the United States.[46]

After the collapse of the Gilded Age, "it was the government that reinvented American capitalism," Hacker and Pierson write. Later, in the 1930s, the New Deal set in place the economic and political institutions that led to decades of broadly shared prosperity and greater equality. It built a new industrial relations system, detailed regulations of corporations and financial markets, and a network of strategic subsidies. The activist state made enormous investments in education and research like the GI Bill, the National Science Foundation, and the National Institutes of Health in order to foster innovation and a skilled workforce and to drive productivity and growth. The United States would remain a private market economy, but the federal government would play a more assertive role in protecting the public from capitalism's rough edges and reallocate incomes through the tax code and public programs.[47] But the New Deal did more than that. It reinvigorated the long-held American belief that we are all responsible for our fellow citizens.[48]

In the 2013 State of the Union address, President Obama highlighted a recent uptick in manufacturing and the reshoring trend. "Caterpillar is bringing jobs back from Japan," he announced. "Ford is bringing jobs back from Mexico. After locating plants in other countries like China, Intel is opening its most advanced plant right here at home. And this year, Apple will start making Macs in America again."[49]

In July 2013 Obama picked up that message in a major economic speech at Knox College in Galesburg. In the 2012 election, Obama had won Knox County and most of the surrounding counties again, but a little less convincingly than he had in 2008. Some in the area thought he was too close to Wall Street, and that the reshoring trend was just a drop in the bucket, which it was. Tom Buffenbarger, the Machinists president who had shared the stage with Obama at the 2004 Labor Day rally in Galesburg, endorsed Obama in 2012. But the vocal Hillary Clinton supporter hadn't backed away from his scorching criticism from the 2008 Democratic primary, when he called Obama a two-faced "thespian," contending that his support for Maytag workers had been all show and no substance, and criticizing him for his ties to Lester Crown.[50] Progress had indeed been slow; in the 2013 State of the Union speech Obama still had some of the same applause lines that he had used in the 2004 rally, including the one about closing tax loopholes for corporations that take jobs overseas. Nonetheless, the president had been to Galesburg so many times by this point that he was much like an old friend who had made it big, and was doing the best he could. He was received with roaring applause as he walked into the Knox gymnasium to camera flashes and big smiles.

"It is good to be home in Illinois. It is good to be back!"

It wasn't long before Obama got to manufacturing. "For the first time since the 1990s, the number of American manufacturing jobs has actually gone up instead of down," the President said. "But we can do more . . . I'm going to be pushing to open more manufacturing innovation institutes that turn regions left behind by global competition into global centers of cutting-edge jobs . . . I know there's an old site right here in Galesburg, over on Monmouth Boulevard—let's put some folks to work!"[51]

EPILOGUE

THERE WERE ONLY 21.7 seconds left, and his team was up comfortably 65–50. But when a Monmouth-Roseville player committed an ill-advised foul, Doug Dennison darted several feet onto the hardwood court to shout his last in-game lesson of the season. "Play smart. Don't stop the clock. No fouls!" He wore a gray tie, starched white shirt, and dark blue suit pants matching the consolidated school's new blue-and-gray colors. A white towel for dabbing his sweaty forehead hung over his shoulder, having replaced his pinstriped suit jacket.

The small gym was packed, and every spot in the eight rows of bleachers filled by a parent, a student, or a local fan. It was the same gym that the 50-year-old coach had played in a generation before. And it was the same gym in which Doug's father, Bob Dennison, and his buddy, longtime Local 2063 president Mike Patrick, had played in the 1950s. The gym, small as it was, didn't look its age. It was bright with a high ceiling and had a fresh coat of paint that read "Titans" on one side and "Dare to Dream" on the other. Outside the gym entrance, two students were selling raffle tickets to fund the junior prom. Downstairs a gaggle of Girl Scouts and their moms were selling cookies in the concession area. A few people were smoking outside in the cold February night.

That Friday night Dennison's junior varsity squad finished their 2012–2013 season at 19–4, with sole ownership of the West Central Conference title. "I told you in the locker room, if you play defense, I will call you champions at the end of the night," Dennison had said during a timeout when the game was still in doubt. He felt then that the young Titans were losing their edge over the stubborn and physical Sherrard Tigers. Dennison had coached some of these boys since the fourth grade, and he wasn't about to let them finish the season on anything but a high note. He paced nonstop and barked himself hoarse for two hours that night. "I have a blast coaching," he told me later. "It's a dream come true."

Dennison took no time off after the season's last JV game. That Sunday he opened the spring season with his seventh- and eighth-grade "junior Titans." He coached the fundamentals: dribbling and ball control, passing and teamwork, and footwork and tenacious defense. Most of all, he tried to teach his boys the intangibles that would give them an edge in life as in basketball: hard work, sustained focus, and self-discipline. He knew that these Monmouth boys, even if they had these character traits, had a hard road ahead of them after high school—much harder than his own.

A few weeks later, in March, the Monmouth-Roseville High School varsity squad, filled with young men Dennison had coached, drilled, and mentored for years, won four playoff games en route to a sectional win and an appearance in the Elite 8 of the Illinois High School Association's 2A boys basketball tournament.

That fall, Annette left the Peoria hospital where she'd worked since interning there in 2006. The commute, and the job, had worn on her. Though she would continue to do X-rays part-time at the Henry C. Hill Correctional Center, she set off in late 2013 on a second self-reinvention as a conductor for BNSF. "I think she's crazy," Doug said of Annette taking the itinerant, though well-paying job, "but the boys and I will hold down the fort."

On January 19, 2014, Doug posted this on his Facebook page: "Today is a little bitter/sweet for me. I would be celebrating 30 years @ Maytag today had they not sold us out and shut the doors to move production to Mexico. We had a nice 30 and out pension that we had fought hard for and worked hard to earn ... Although I'm still bitter over how things went down, the closing of that door has opened up so many others! I'm getting to do today what I had always dreamed of doing (coaching high school basketball) ... You knocked me down Maytag and CEO Ralph Hake ... BUT I got back up! Today is a beautiful day despite you!" The post got 78 likes.

ED KRUEGER LEFT his Edinburg, Texas, home and headed south in his red, late-model Ford Escort. After crossing the Pharr International Bridge, he headed to a promotora's home in nearby Colonia Unidad Obrera on Reynosa's east side. Most U.S.-side not-for-profits had forbidden their staffs from traveling to the Mexican side of the border in the past few years. Krueger, who had been working the colonias since 1961, now only made it across the border once or twice a week, but he had never considered stopping. "I think it's tragic that too many people have broken those lines of communication," the longtime organizer said. "We need to have more channels of communication across the border. There's so much misunderstanding." Krueger was the only gringo we saw in our 2013 trip to Reynosa.

Krueger and the promotoras gathered in the shade of a Modelo restaurant canopy for a strategy session that Saturday morning. The 82-year-old moved slowly to a white plastic lawn chair, hunched considerably over his cane as he walked. After introductions and small talk, and with caged love birds chirping nearby, the promotoras began talking through their cases as Krueger scribbled messy shorthand into a small spiral notepad. His hands were shaky, and the writing was undecipherable to anyone but Krueger himself.

Laura Flora came to the meeting to get advice from Krueger and the promotoras. Flora had been working at Bana Box, where she folded cardboard into shipping boxes and glued labeling onto packaging for products like cellphones. Her last few months of pay stubs showed that she averaged about 45 hours and 780 pesos ($62.50) take-home pay each week, or about $1.40 an hour.

Flora told Krueger and the promotoras that the Bana Box factory burned down a few weeks earlier in April. Some maquila workers panicked but no one was hurt, Flora said, because it was a shift change and everyone was able to get out quickly. She said the fire alarms only sounded half an hour after the fire started, and the sprinklers never activated. The factory, which was full of combustibles, was reduced to nothing but cinders. The 49-year-old Flora was now, once again in May 2013, looking for work. As Flora told the story, tech-savvy Erika, who was now nearly finished with *secundaria*, showed Krueger a grainy video of the fire on her cellphone.[1]

"Is there a union there?" asked Krueger in slow, methodical Spanish. "Are there union withholdings on the pay stub?"

"It's a *fantasma* [a ghost union], Don Eduardo," one of the promotoras said. "The union belongs to the business."

After more discussion, Flora realized that since she had already accepted a small severance from Bana Box, there was little she could do to take action against the company.

Toward the end of the meeting, Bety, one of the veteran promotoras, shared some memories of Krueger. She recalled when the "gringo loco" walked though her neighborhood as a spry 63-year-old talking to maquiladora workers. For the last two decades, she said, Krueger had helped them to learn labor law, cultivate friendships with other workers (Krueger calls them "clusters"), and run dynamic meetings and role-playing exercises meant to inform and mobilize. Claudia, a younger promotora in a glittery DKNY shirt and with a young boy at her knees, said the work is pretty straightforward. "It's really basic information you share," she said. "Many are, frankly, simple people, people that may have never had a printed paycheck in their lives."

Krueger had outlasted Mike Allen, his old friend and rival from the seminary, who passed away in 2010. In his final years, Allen had hauled in all sorts of recognitions for his ambitious bicultural, trans-border development work at MEDC. He had been named "Border Texan of the Year" in 2006. West Military Highway in McAllen had become, "Mike Allen Boulevard." On the Reynosa side, just a few blocks from the promotoras' meeting, was "Mike Allen Avenue," inaugurated by the Tamaulipas governor in a 2010 ceremony.[2] Mike Allen had felt affection for his longtime rival, but the mere mention of Krueger had always rankled him and his partner Keith Patridge. "Krueger just doesn't get it!" Allen would say. "All of us have to change. If we don't grow or learn, you know, I would be the same as Ed Krueger."

There will likely be no roads, statues, or big public ceremonies for Krueger. Don Eduardo, trudging faithfully into his sixth decade of grassroots work, will be remembered quietly in the poorest corners of Reynosa and Rio Bravo, Tamaulipas, and Hidalgo County, Texas. Many will remember him as a selfless hero who worked to empower the most humble of people on both sides of the border, as they sought to chip away surely, but ever so slowly, at the edifice of oppression. Others, especially those in the halls of power, may take Mike Allen's perspective on Krueger's legacy, remembering an obstinate do-gooder tossing wads of paper at the approaching bulldozer, as someone who "just doesn't get it."

And what about others trying to rescue this border city from its lawless, lopsided prosperity?

Reynosa's human rights crusader, Arturo Solís, died, as did his organization. The captivating social entrepreneur who met with Kofi Annan and Vicente Fox now rests mostly forgotten at a vandalized grave site on a small triangle of land adjacent to the McAllen-Hidalgo-Reynosa Bridge and the Rio Grande.[3]

Once-enterprising local reporters were now also silent. Some had been kidnapped; all had been intimidated. Reynosa had become a "black hole for information," according to Tim Johnson, the Mexico bureau chief for McClatchy Newspapers. Anyone interested in what was really happening in Reynosa had to piece together fragments of news accounts, many from outside the area, and Twitter and Facebook posts.[4]

Teresa Chávez had made Derechos Obreros y Democracia Sindical into a civil association, won some victories, and joined the board of Martha Ojeda's Coalition for Justice in the Maquiladoras. Chávez had accumulated a thick file of papers with official rulings in favor of the workers she had represented.

For the past few years she had been sidelined by major health problems. Chávez had pushed her body too hard working in the maquila while doing the advocacy work. Her daughter, Marina Ferror, though still passionate about the cause, had been too busy with work and her children to take up Chávez's lead. Besides, they said, El Cártel's ubiquitous presence made their door-to-door organizing nearly impossible. Chávez and Ferror claimed the CDG had even infiltrated the CTM, still powerful and still basically the only union in Reynosa, a city of over one million people. Chávez was sure the CDG was behind the 2008 murder of José Piña Ortega, the CTM replacement for Angel "Tito" Rodriguez. Piña, a more worker-friendly leader, was executed gangland style, she said, for challenging the labor status quo and the corrupting influence of El Cártel. There was some evidence to back Chávez's claim. A 2013 lawsuit revealed that the narcos had made regular incursions into a Reynosa maquiladora that made laboratory furniture. Keith Patridge, having taken the helm at MEDC, tried to calm investors' concerns about this and other grim news about the border violence. "That is happening everywhere in the world," Patridge said as part of the MEDC's robust public relations effort at the time.[5]

The once-promising DODS, with some concrete accomplishments in hand, seemed finished. Its membership had splintered. Chávez and Ferror hadn't seen Aneth Delgadillo, the aspiring lawyer, in years. And María de la Luz Potero's cancer had returned, and, this time, it claimed her life. Chávez and Ferror were certain it was the toxins Potero had worked with at Delphi since she was 15 that had poisoned her body, but there wasn't anything they could do but mourn their friend's untimely death. At least the father was apparently doing a fine job raising Potero's three children.

For Krueger, though, there was always hope. The little victories kept him coming across the border every week. Progress was halting and slow, but more companies paid the severances required by law now. More supplied face masks, gloves, and other safety equipment.[6] There was nothing to do but to keep the faith and pursue more small victories—victories that made people's lives better in concrete ways. When asked to reflect on his life's work, Krueger chose to tell a story.

In August 1999 Hurricane Bret hit Reynosa. Management at computer hard drive-producer Seagate said they would shut down production early, and everyone would be paid for the full day. When the paychecks came the following week, though, the hurricane hours were missing. The workers pressed up the chain of managers until they won the pay they were promised, which amounted to about 20 pesos, just a dollar or two. The workers were elated, and, for some, there was a shift in thinking. The small amount of money hadn't been the point, Krueger said, though every peso mattered. It was about those women and men looking those managers in the eyes and standing up for themselves, their peers, and their rights. It was about pushing back against the multinationals and holding them accountable when nobody else was. It was about shifting labor culture in this hot and unforgiving border town. It was about people-centered development and women's empowerment. But most of all, the old man said as he finished the story, "It's about human dignity."

GEORGE CARNEY, HEAD neatly shaved and with a whitening goatee, sat in a burgundy booth at the Welcome Inn in Milan, a little town on the outskirts of Rock Island, Illinois. From behind a plate of pancakes, sausage links, and runny eggs, he slowly lifted his right arm. Carney retracted his lips and clenched his teeth as loud pops and a disquieting grinding sound came from his shoulder. Nearly three years since his injury, he still had debilitating pain and struggled with sleep. Cortisone injections, "some electrode thing," and pain killers had all helped some with the symptoms, but the deep joint and nerve damage now seemed to be a fixture in his life. Carney had recently inquired about getting the arm, which felt like it was squeezed tight in a too-small neoprene sleeve, amputated. The doctor told him the nerve pain would remain even if the arm were removed. He still took a long list of medications. He took Lyrica, Hydrocodone, and Tylenol for the pain. He took Seroquel to sleep. He took Dilantin to prevent seizures. And he took Wellbutrin, Citalopram, and Xanax to address major depression, anxiety, and suicidal ideation. "That's it," Carney said with a sly grin. "That's all I take!"

Carney was required to look for work, and he wanted more than anything to be useful, to not feel discarded. He had recently interviewed with Dish

Network to hand out fliers and solicit new customers in a Quad Cities mall. Or at least that's what Richard and Beth told him. Carney recalled nothing of the interview and little about the entire day other than talking to his mother on the phone. The memory loss had happened once before, and it unnerved him. The doctor said memory loss was not uncommon in his condition.

Carney didn't get the Dish Network job, which was fine with him because the minimum wage job paid considerably less than his weekly $500 workers' compensation check. Plus, there was no way he could stand for a full shift at the mall or anywhere else. The checks came somewhat irregularly, but they would keep coming until he got another job or reached "maximum medical improvement." "The second I clock in at Hy-Vee [a supermarket] or wherever, they're off the hook," Carney said. "They say they'll make up the difference [between the weekly earnings and the workers' comp check], but I don't believe them."

At the Welcome Inn booth, we ran through every possible entry-level retail or service sector job we could think of: cashier or stocker at Hy-Vee, his old bartending job at Milan Lanes, ticket-taker at the movie theater, a desk job or computer work, and distance or local truck driving to name a few. Nothing fit. He wasn't allowed to lift more than 20 pounds. His right hand was too damaged to type well or even to get change out of his pocket. He couldn't stand for long periods, walk steep inclines, or climb ladders. He had memory loss problems, and the threat of another seizure made him nervous about long-range commercial trucking.

"It might be bad for your job if you end up in Chicago when you're supposed to be in Atlanta," Carney said with a laugh. "Hell, I don't even think a McDonald's would hire me. Would you hire me, knowing everything you know about me right now? With the liability you'd be taking on?" Carney poured a generous helping of syrup over his thick pancakes. "I sure wish I had that job back," he said of the Maytag job.

Carney still spent much of his time curled up in his corner of their single-wide in Woodland Mobile Home Park with the curtains closed. He came out a little more often now, though. His brother Richard had recently come home after months in the hospital. That day Richard, still in recovery, tasted his first food in months, some applesauce. He said it tasted great. Richard sat fully stretched out in his recliner, next to a glass case with a shotgun, a few rifles and handguns, and two long Asian swords. "That boy can't get a break," Carney said of his brother.

Carney was still depressed, but he wasn't suicidal anymore. The drugs the psychiatrist had given him had helped with his sleep, the constant chatter in his mind, and his mood somewhat. And it also felt good to help Richard in his recovery and take on some of his chores, like driving their mother to Iowa City for her doctor appointments. And for the last year Carney had been dating again for the first time in years. "Debbie is probably too nice for me," the 53-year-old said. They had fun together on the weekends, typically having a few drinks and shooting pool at Milan Lanes or, on special occasions, heading down to the river for an outdoor concert or some gambling on a riverboat. Carney surprised Debbie on Valentine's Day when, after telling her flowers were a waste of money, he snuck a fresh bouquet into her bedroom while she was at work.

"That has helped a lot," Carney said of having a partner again. "Even though I haven't been able to save a dime since we started dating!" Even after a difficult decade, Carney had never lost his sense of humor.

LAURA FLORA'S DREAM finally came true. Everybody was together, in a way. Four generations of her family gathered at her parents' modest, cinderblock home in Vamos Tamaulipas, a far-flung, perfectly rectangular colonia surrounded by expansive sorghum fields. Flora's father, now a great-grandfather, grilled chicken and beef among the flowering tropical plants of his home's outdoor area. It was Mother's Day.

Flora's family had been fragmented since she left Tierra Blanca, Veracruz, in 2001 with her two oldest children, desperate to find something better. When she came back for her three youngest in 2004, Flora hoped to reunite in central Florida with her parents, her two oldest children, and her new American grandchildren. That second trip failed, forcing her to make do in Reynosa. Even in 2013 Flora had still never seen those grandchildren in person. Recently, though, she and her daughters had taken to *Face* (Facebook) on their low-end smartphones. The breach between Reynosa and Florida, which had seemed so gaping for so long, was now less painful. They could spend Mother's Day together through texts, posts, likes, and dozens of small, blurry photos.

Laura Suarez, Flora's oldest daughter in Reynosa, had two young boys of her own now. So Flora had managed to bring together four generations of her family in the flesh as well. The younger boy caromed around the open-air home in only a diaper and sneakers with orange Cheetos powder sprinkled around his mouth and a matching orange drink in hand. Although Suarez came up a year short of finishing high school, she had made it a year further than her mother. Flora had told her daughter that her education was the only inheritance she could give her, and that she wanted more for her than the unending weariness of parenting while working the maquila. But Flora was hardly disappointed in her 20-year-old daughter. Suarez's two exuberant boys were the love of this proud grandmother's life.

Suarez and her husband, Ignacio ("Nacho") Anduaga, both worked at TRW, an automotive components factory near former Planta Maytag III, which Whirlpool had sold in a deal brokered by Keith Patridge. (The maquila now makes refrigerators for Chinese appliance giant Haier.)[7] Suarez worked quality control, testing the speed and functionality of switches and parts like windshield wipers. After three years at TRW, she was still stuck at the lowest operator level and, she said, there were no opportunities for moving up without more education. As a young parent, she didn't have the time or money. She showed us a recent paycheck indicating she had taken home 1,243 pesos ($100) in just one week with lots of overtime. Because of the Infonavit deduction, Anduaga's paycheck was less, 569 pesos ($45). Without overtime, and without the housing deduction, the young couple each made about $1.55 per hour. They were young, healthy, and resilient, they had each other, and they didn't seem as run down from the maquila work as older workers. For now, though, Suarez was stuck in the same circumstances as Flora before her. She left her children early in the morning to work long weeks at a tedious, dead-end job for not enough money.

A week or so earlier, a family friend named Roge, had returned from the other side and tried to persuade Flora and anyone willing to risk it to sneak across the border to find work. Anduaga wanted to go. The amiable and handsome new father knew he could provide better for his family on the other side, and he trusted Roge to get him there. Suarez and Anduaga talked it over.

"I told him that I supported him," Suarez said. "We could find a way to get the money together, but we decided against it. It's not that we were afraid. It's simply that he's got two and a half years at TRW now, which would make it easier to process a visa. On the other hand, if they capture him, he would lose the chance to go legally for the rest of his life. Our dream for our children is to go to the other side legally."

Flora's daughters will wrestle with the same life-and-death questions Flora had dealt with now for decades. I wondered if Flora's daughters would be able to move beyond their mother's station and thought about the enormous burden Flora had borne for that chance. One thing was certain. Flora's girls had adapted to the rough-and-tumble of border life. They were articulate, confident, and sophisticated. They had taken to cellphones and *Face* like other urban teens and rolled their eyes playfully at their less-than-tech-savvy mom. That fall, Erika would start at Instituto Tamaulipeco de Capacitación para el Empleo, an industry-oriented high school where she planned to study computers and get a technical degree.

There was gratitude on that Mother's Day. Flora looked back at her long years at Maytag—a company that had, in any reckoning, taken much more from her than it had given in return—with generosity. "It was tiring, a real killer," Flora said. She talked about her first two years on the Maytag night shift when she had often felt so exhausted—as if she had a constant hangover—that she couldn't even interact with her three young girls when she got home. "But I see it as a good time because there was a lot of work, a lot of hours."

As Flora spoke, Erika sat on a wood bench hugging her grandfather's arm as he made funny faces at his diapered great-grandson. That day, at least, everything was right.

LATE INTO A Friday afternoon in February 2013, Jackie Cummins sat at her desk, filing papers before heading home for the weekend. Jackie, still strong and wide-shouldered from a couple of decades of physical factory labor, wore a pink "Cottage Rehab" T-shirt over a gray long-sleeve shirt and loose-fitting black sweatpants. A cross necklace, her work keys, and ID card hung from her neck below her dyed blonde hair. Her little office, a converted patient's room with a 19" tube television mounted high on the wall, was tucked back in a far corner of the hospital's third floor. A steady flow of girlfriends, including her new "bestie," Renee, stopped in to say their goodbyes for the weekend as they pulled on their winter coats.

Jackie's stint at Dr. Kandy Sayrs' dental office in 2009 hadn't lasted. But four years later, after starting in a minimum-wage housekeeping job at Galesburg Cottage Hospital, she had found a home among the physical and occupational therapists in the rehabilitation and transitional care units. It was all women, as it always was, that afternoon, and the office was filled with snarky, end-of-shift banter.

Jackie had recently been promoted to $11 an hour as an "administrative assistant." In reality, though, she did it all, a "Jackie-of-all-trades." She cleaned and readied vacated rooms. She helped rehabbing, elderly, and morbidly obese patients walk down the hall with their IV poles in tow. She had learned CPR and had been called to use a hand-pumped ventilator on a couple of occasions. Once she cleaned up vomit and blood after a teenage girl's suicide. She now did the billing and scheduling for rehabilitation specialists and their unit's quarterly reports. Recently she had learned audit reporting for the State of Illinois.

"It seems like every time she comes home, they've added more and more to her job," Shannon said the next morning in the living room of their new home. "And I'm like, my God they expect a lot from her based on what they pay her."

That Saturday Jackie and Shannon showed me the five-bedroom, two-bathroom home they had recently bought on the west side of Abingdon. They rented their other home on Lower Street, which they had purchased for $57,000 well before the Maytag closure. The realtor wanted to list it for $42,000, which was less than what they owed.

The couple was spending every weekend and most nights rehabbing the sizable, boxy home at the corner of Monmouth and Maple. There was still a lot of work to do. Brown water-stains ran down the house's white aluminum siding from the windows. The rickety garage looked as if it should have collapsed months earlier, and the porch required gingerly steps. The couple confessed that many unsightly indoor stains and blemishes from the previous owner were, for now, only covered up until they could afford proper repairs to the ceiling panels, damaged walls, and discolored floorboards.

Jackie had learned about the deceased hoarder's home from a Maytag friend. They bought the dumpster of a home for $8,000 from the owner's son, who had flown in from the East Coast, desperate for a quick sale and eager to unload his father's enormous and odd collection of things, from towering stacks of magazines to a racing lawnmower that could evidently push 60 miles per hour. Jackie and Shannon couldn't get a loan for it so they pieced together every last bit of their Maytag savings and took a chance on the century-old house.

In the past six months they had cleared out the mess, which included mice, a dead bird, and mountains of trash. They installed new water lines and two toilets, which were both in disrepair and had gone unused. On YouTube they learned how to repair light switches and redo electrical wiring. They re-carpeted the upstairs, renovated their kitchen on the cheap, and built a veg-etable box in their side yard.

Slowly they were making a condemnable house into something close to beautiful. They added a dark china cabinet and dining room table that Jackie had received from her Aunt Linda's recent passing. They were given a kitchen island by a friend. They traded some extra cabinets for a newish carpet roll. Jackie salvaged scraps of drywall from a construction site to repair their upstairs hallway ceiling. Just about everything else had come from Jackie's compulsive yard-sale hunting on Saturday mornings.

Twelve years earlier Jackie and Shannon had been making nearly $60,000 together (about $76,000 in 2013 dollars) and had no dependents. Now they earned about $37,000 a year, didn't have health insurance, and had two adoptive children. "Everyone is hustling," Jackie said. It was common now. Many in the area didn't have a choice but to be crafty to make ends meet. "But I always feel like I can make something out of nothing. I never feel stuck." She bought cheap pieces of furniture and repaired, painted, and reupholstered them for her own yard sales. They bartered for a scooter to zip around town and to Galesburg on the side roads. Shannon bred African cichlids as a hobby but also to sell for $5 a pop. They learned how to make their own laundry soap on Pinterest. A couple months earlier, Jackie had done some cleaning for an old woman she had met at the hospital. Jackie just wanted to help out, but the woman insisted, rather peculiarly, that she take some spoons and a couple of five-pound bags of sugar as payment. The spoons were in Jackie and Shannon's silverware drawer.

Shannon had done retraining by the book. She chose computer network-ing, an official government "growth field," and studied hard. She got good grades and finished her associate's degree. She did an extensive job search that spanned western Illinois and eastern Iowa from Peoria to Burlington to Davenport. Nothing came of it.

A decade later, Shannon was in her fifth year at Abingdon High School as a special education aid. A lot of former Maytag folks, especially women, had moved, one way or another, into the lowest rungs of the rural health-care and education systems. These two sectors, heavily reliant on federal and state funding and full of low-paying jobs, were the real growth sectors. Shannon worked mostly with struggling freshmen, modifying their tests, teaching algebra and geometry, and American and Illinois history. "It's an eight-hour test of patience," she said of the $10.51-an-hour job. Shannon just saw her first class graduate, which was, for some of the kids with whom she'd worked, a "miracle." It felt good to be a part of that, she said. For extra money some summers, Shannon worked retail at Goodwill washing, folding, and hanging clothes and stocking shelves.

Of her partner, Jackie said, "You know those people in life that love learning so much that they just want to pass it on, like everybody will enjoy it? Well, Shannon is one of those people. Just the other day she was trying to tell me about some British fort in Vincennes, because I'm from there."

"Yeah, she wasn't very interested," Shannon, the self-confessed "nerd," said. "But I was really excited. I love school. I do!" The kindly and motherly 45-year-old, in wire-rimmed glasses and short, bobbed brown hair, fit the part. It fit her much better than making refrigerators had. She was an educator now—and proud of it.

Jackie had also, finally, found the right place.

"I did *not* want to go work at Cottage," Jackie said. "But I just fit in from the moment I started. More than anything, I love the elderly. And I would have never known that about myself."

"I think Jackie's found her niche," Shannon agreed.

Jordon, now 14-years-old, sat silently in the dark living room as the couple spoke about the steady, meaningful jobs they had finally found. "So many jobs later, so many changes later, and it's really kind of cool, in our forties, to be doing something that's necessary," Jackie said. "But it is sad, and maybe it's kind of socialistic of me to say, but people make so much more money doing silly things that don't add up to much."

Economists talk of the "winners" and "losers" of economic globalization. Jackie and Shannon had fallen hard, but they did not see themselves as victims. And they certainly did not see themselves as "losers." Like other former Maytag workers, they still cared about the displacement and hardship around them, but they had moved on, and they weren't looking for pity. "Would I like to do better? Do I want to win the lottery?" Jackie asked rhetorically. "Well, yes! Who doesn't?"

"But, when you take that last breath," she said, "it was about how you had lived your life. That's how your time on earth is judged in the final analysis. I'm proud of where we're going. At least I can look back and say we did the right thing. We may have issues, and our lives may not be perfect. But we've done the right thing and I feel good. I'm a victor."

NOTES ON METHOD

IN GRADUATE SCHOOL, a friend of mine from New York liked to call me "hay-seed." I objected at first, but I soon embraced the nickname, in part because I knew he was right. My roots were small-town Indiana, playing in a creek or jumping curbs on my red, white, and blue bicentennial-edition Evel Knievel dirt bike. So when I moved to Galesburg in 2001, as a junior faculty member at Knox College, I found a town not unlike Batesville, Indiana, where I spent most of my youth. It was neighborly, laid-back, and unpretentious.

And deeply anxious. From the moment I arrived, it was hard to miss the apprehension that hung in the air. Changes were afoot in Newton, Iowa, Maytag's headquarters, located three hours away. Ralph Hake, a number-crunching finance executive from Whirlpool, had become Maytag's leader that summer, leaving many locals uneasy. Maytag had recently opened a subassembly factory in Reynosa, Mexico, where workers pieced together a labor-intensive part of the Galesburg refrigerator: the water-and-ice dispenser. Maytag had also moved several engineers to their newly acquired refrigeration plant in nearby Amana, Iowa. The venerable factory's tenuous existence seemed to hold the entire town in its thrall.

September 11th of that year only added to local disquiet. People still drove leisurely through town, greeted each other on the streets, and talked amiably to their neighbors. However, there was a sense in this little city of 33,000, a place like many others in the Rust Belt, that something ominous was encroaching. "Why is our country now always in such turmoil?" wondered Maytag assembler Jackie Cummins when I first met her. "Why am I in Middle America having to sweat such big issues?"

When the factory's closing announcement came a year later, in October 2002, the quiet worries turned to loud and public confusion and anger. I thought I understood the magnitude of the announcement until I witnessed the visceral reaction resounding across the area that fall. On November 17, I went to a hastily organized "Americans Against NAFTA" (AAN) rally in the gymnasium at Carl Sandburg, the local community college. Tony Swanson, a third-generation appliance maker, and some fellow workers had started AAN to boycott Maytag and to shame Hake and Maytag into staying.

"How people in his position can sleep at night is beyond me," Swanson had told Galesburg's paper, *The Register-Mail*, the day before the rally. "I mean, how can they knowingly destroy thousands of American citizens' lives and the communities they live in and still look at themselves in the mirror? If that is what wealth does to you, I don't want any part of it." In the newspaper interview Swanson argued the parallel between September 11, 2001, and the strike by "corporate terrorists" from Maytag on October 11, 2002.[1]

At the morning rally, a boy and girl, both about ten, kneeled over white poster board to make homemade signs on the polished basketball court. The boy colored in an American flag, and the girl drew a map of the United States with a big blue star highlighting Washington, DC. Each wrote, "Help Save American Jobs!" in bubble letters and colored them red, white, and blue. People trickled into the Sandburg gymnasium. Swanson and the other organizers seemed discouraged by the turnout. About twenty or thirty people were waiting quietly on the bleachers when the event started. One woman suggested fear of reprisals by Maytag had kept people away. "Lots of people are scared," she said.

The first speaker was a Knox College colleague, an economics professor. He compared the relentless "drive to efficiency" to the nearby Mississippi River. "I don't think there's a way to stop these forces," he said. "They always produce dislocations." He advised against the boycott. He suggested that those being let go embrace the federal retraining assistance while they could. He suggested they figure out how to live with the changes, difficult as they may be. It was, he said, their only choice.

"That's an economics address! If I wanted *that* I would have taken the economics course at Sandburg," yelled an audience member. He dismissed the professor's analysis and pointed to what he saw as the central problem: "I don't have any say in government anymore, not one word."

Added another, "The training programs, the assistance program are all great, but your tax dollars train me for a job that doesn't exist!"

Swanson piled on. "Some say we're protectionist. Well, hell yes I am! Somebody's got to protect American jobs! If you want to pack up and move overseas then you better be ready to pay out of the nose for it. They have a right to make money, but we have rights too."

After the rally a rancorous Internet battle raged about whether to push a boycott of Maytag. The idea proved too controversial; an economic blow could hurt Maytag pensioners. Discouraged by the rally turnout and without the boycott, AAN folded a few weeks later and a palpable sense of impotence set in. It was apparent that this seminal moment in the region's history would be experienced in ways well beyond its impact on local pocketbooks.

I kept thinking about my well-meaning economics colleague and the fuming workers talking past one another. Each seemed utterly baffled by the opaqueness of the other's perspective. Yet they were on the same side. Each cared deeply about Galesburg and the plight of its blue collar workers. Why couldn't the workers understand, the economist must have thought, that this drive to efficiency was not only inevitable but desirable? One has to adapt. The workers at the rally, on the other hand, insisted the problem was political. They wanted to regain the political voice and economic parity they had once had and seen slip away over the years. I couldn't reconcile the two positions; there were no easy answers. The questions these Maytag workers had to ponder went beyond their small city and beyond their nation's borders. I wanted to make sense of it all, if I could. And I wanted to know what would happen to the soon-to-be-displaced workers in my new home.

When I started my research in the fall of 2002, I didn't have well-formulated research questions based in a scholarly literature to which I wanted to contribute. I didn't have any idea how long the project might take. But, as with my dissertation research in Chicago on welfare reform implementation in the late 1990s, I was drawn to a subject that was deeply felt locally, but resonated nationally. As a graduate student, Andrew Abbott, Gerald Suttles, and Richard Taub had inspired me to embrace the lively and eclectic methodologies of the Chicago School of Sociology. Robert Park, the principal architect of the First Chicago School in the 1920s, implored his students to explore the social worlds of Chicago. "One more thing is needful," Park wrote, "first hand observation. Go and sit in the lounges of the luxury hotels and on the doorsteps of the flophouses; sit on the Gold Coast settees and the slum shakedowns; sit in the orchestra hall and in the Star and Garter burlesque. In short, gentlemen, go get the seat of your pants dirty in real research."[2] I decided to bring the urban ethnographic field methods I had learned in Chicago to the western Illinois prairie.

In 2002 I began researching Maytag's and Galesburg's history, tracking developments in the local paper, and talking with Maytag line workers, managers, and union leaders. Being a small town, virtually everyone had some connection to Maytag, and nearly every day counted as research in one way or another. I played in regular pick-up basketball games with a local Maytag manager and Knox alum and chatted across the counter with a Maytag spouse at the Gizmo, a snack bar in the center of the Knox campus. I attended Labor Day parades, several rallies in Galesburg and in Newton, and participated in Rotary Club and Galesburg Public Library events on the topic. I went on a factory tour, then the factory auction, and then several walk-throughs of the emptied giant. I visited Dave Bevard, Doug Dennison, and Aaron Kemp at the Labor Temple on Grand Avenue for informal conversations, sometimes with my classes when political candidates came through town. On several occasions the union leaders would visit my Knox classes to speak to my students. After moving to Chicago in 2006, I visited Galesburg and the outlying small towns regularly and corresponded with former Maytag people on the phone, through email, and over Facebook, which proved to be an enormously valuable research tool.

Over the course of a decade, in addition to the informal interactions, I collected fifty-one transcribed interviews with the fifteen individuals and families that I tracked most closely. I had another fourteen formal interviews with other workers, local and corporate managers, and people working in employment or social services. As the project progressed, I began to focus on a subset of emblematic stories. Michael Patrick's biography, for instance, provided the long view, whereas Tracy Warner's story highlighted the struggles of single parents. A limitation of my research was my inability to track a few of my initial interviewees from 2004. Even though surprisingly few left the area, I often wonder how they fared—and how it might recolor my analysis and presentation. The 2010 Maytag Employees in Transition survey, an undertaking of the Maytag Project led by journalism professor Marilyn Webb at Knox College, provided a window into the post-Maytag experience. The survey randomly sampled 425 of the final 902 workers. One hundred and thirty-three (31 percent) responded.

For historical background, I benefited from Knox College's Special Collections and Archives in beautiful Seymour Library and the Galesburg Public Library's Archives. Dave Bevard shared the International Association of Machinists and Aerospace Workers Local Lodge 2063's official minutes dating back to 1956 and contract agreements going back to 1957, along with several audio cassette recordings of contract presentations. Also, I collected hundreds of articles from *The Register-Mail*, which deserved the awards it garnered for its extensive and in-depth coverage of this story.

A ROBUST AND defensive nationalism permeated the slow two-year death of the factory between 2002 and 2004, and you could hear it in conversations and at every rally, parade, and public discussion—"U-S-A, U-S-A, U-S-A" was the chant outside Maytag's annual shareholders' meeting in Newton in 2003. But the fact that Galesburg's flagship product, the Maytag side-by-side, would be made in Mexico was rarely discussed at these events, which struck me as odd. I soon realized that people in town, including myself, did not have a clue about the new factory in Reynosa, how much the jobs would pay, who the new refrigerator makers would be, why they were there, or how all this looked to them. I realized that my research—a project at its core about economic globalization—would feel incomplete without exploring the other side of this cross-border transaction. Galesburg's story was a global story now, and that was the only way it made sense to tell it.

For the Reynosa story, Josh Walsman—my friend, colleague, and translator—and I did interviews during facility tours; in cars and taxis; in restaurants, diners, and nightclubs; in Reynosa's city hall and meeting rooms on the Texas side; and in front yards and living rooms in the far-flung colonias on the city's edge. Over five visits from 2003 to 2013—ranging from four days to two weeks—we did seventy discrete, recorded interviews with fifty-six individuals, most of them translated and transcribed. The recordings range from an eight-minute conversation with a woman in the bed of a pickup truck to a few three-hour interviews with maquiladora workers. The maquilas, we learned in our initial Reynosa trips, were peopled in extraordinary proportions with Veracruzanos. So in 2007 we extended our fieldwork to several towns in northern Veracruz—Papantla, El Chote, Agua Dulce, Volador, Barra de Cazones, and Naranjos. This third step took us into the orchards of ejidatarios, austere mayors' offices, and a beachfront restaurant. In 2013 Josh and

I traveled to Ramos Arizpe-Saltillo after Whirlpool purchased Maytag and moved side-by-side refrigerator production there.

Many of our richest experiences on the Mexico side (and in McAllen, Texas) were open-ended group discussions: the long afternoon with Emilio and Ismael Fuentes at La Palapa de Kime in Barra de Cazones, the focus group with four maquila workers next to a noisy Reynosa highway, and the two stimulating morning discussions in McAllen, Texas, with Mike Allen and Keith Patridge, to name a few. We recorded and transcribed nineteen group discussions, most of which required translation. Fieldnotes from informal conversations—at the Reynosa human rights office as children ran around, at our friends Arqueles Garcia and Gris Cruz's place on a hot Saturday night, during a tour of a chorizo maquila or the big Dodge truck factory in Saltillo— enriched the Mexico-side documentation as well. For historical background on the South Texas farmworkers' struggle, I consulted with the San Antonio Public Library's Special Collections. With the expert help of photographer David Samuel Stern—also my brother-in-law—I compiled thousands of photographs, which were invaluable in recovering details and a sense of place as I wrote.

IT WAS IMPORTANT to me to be meticulous, and to tell a story that was factual down to the last detail. When I first heard Mike Daisey's infamous monologue on "This American Life" about China's Foxconn factories, I was mesmerized.[3] His first-person account of exploited underage workers, forced overtime, and dreadful living conditions was gripping and exquisitely told. It was also fabricated, a fact that Daisey was appallingly slow to admit, insisting for some time that it spoke to a higher, artistic truth. Some on the Left defended Daisey, claiming that by attacking Daisey's minor transgressions in reporting, the major transgression—the widespread exploitation of young women in China's factories—had been shunted aside.

The facts should always be paramount in any nonfiction storytelling. It is, after all, nonfiction. If one seeks insight and understanding, and perhaps to influence public opinion and public policy, the means to those ends must be unassailable. As such, I have endeavored to use transparent and accountable methods. I have used as a guide Mitchell Duneier's *Sidewalk*, which presents a controversial—at least among sociologists—but principled approach to fieldwork in its Appendix.[4] Like Duneier, I adopted many of the conventions of journalism rather than those of my home discipline, sociology. I used a digital voice recorder, and I use people's exact words—or our best translations in the case of Spanish-speakers—wherever there are quotation marks. Instead of made-up place names and pseudonyms, I've used the real names of places and, with their explicit permission, the real names of people as well. I believe it is important to offer accountability to one's readers and to other researchers.

This standard of fact-check accountability is a basic tenet of journalism and, in my view, ought to be the standard, wherever possible, in the social sciences. The people I met in my fieldwork, in fact—with only one temporary exception—preferred to have their real names used. They often wondered why I'd even asked. Why would they want to be anonymous? They wanted their voices to be heard. And that, perhaps, was the essential point of this whole endeavor: to listen to the voices of some of those bearing the burdens of rapid economic change. There are, of course, cases in which pseudonyms are necessary. In an article I wrote about Reynosa for *The Register-Mail*, for instance, I used a pseudonym to protect a worker's identity from the company for which he was working at the time. Fortunately, there are no cases like that in *Boom, Bust, Exodus*.

Even with my subjects' permission, I am ultimately the one doing the representation of their lives. It is difficult, therefore, for a subject to make an informed decision about having their real names used before they know how they will be represented. With that in mind, I asked the main subjects in the book to read the sections about their lives in order to review the veracity of the facts and my representations. It made me anxious to share these accounts, but I felt it was important to reciprocate the trust people had given to me by offering what I had written about them.

Taking this step can sometimes be a mistake. It can lead to self-censorship during the writing process—the urge not to upset the people who, in many cases, have become friends. I did my best to avoid that pitfall. This step can also lead to editorial requests for significant changes. I was thankful that my subjects did not ask to change depictions and that they helped me make some factual corrections. Readers may see my relationships with my research subjects as an inherent source of bias—and, therefore, a weakness. Perhaps so. But it is also, in my view, a strength. And, frankly, when doing ethnography, I know of no way around developing relationships, and wouldn't want to do it any other way, besides.

WHEN JOSH AND I made our second visit to the McAllen Economic Development Corporation in 2003, Mike Allen and Keith Patridge started our conversation by taking issue with my series about Reynosa that had appeared in *The Register-Mail* a few months earlier. Patridge rejoined his imagined fight with Galesburg workers. "If a person thinks that they should get $20 or $30 an hour to put something together with screws when someone else is willing to do it for 50 cents an hour, guess where it's going to go? I mean, that's economics. The problem is that we get too many people that are too lazy. They think they're owed something." To Patridge, the story of globalization seemed to be partly an Economics 101 tutorial and partly a pull-yourself-up-by-your-bootstraps morality tale. Mike Allen took a different tack. He pointed to one of the main characters in *The Register-Mail* series, Atanacio Martinez, a maquiladora worker whose son had surpassed him in education level, and whose future looked bright. It was a hopeful story, a story of progress, a story of globalization's possibilities. "That's the story you should be telling," the charismatic dealmaker said in a rather insistent tone.

I struggled with what kind of story to tell. There were so many potential storylines and idiosyncratic biographies. Any narrative I put together would necessarily be a simplified and selective reconstruction of a complicated, multilayered set of individual experiences and social and economic phenomena. And I was acutely conscious of my role as the narrative builder, my biases as a middle-class liberal from the Midwest, and my responsibilities to the "subjects" whose lives I would represent.

As the project progressed, I became increasingly committed to presenting people and places—not definitive theoretical assertions or political diatribes (though this book, like any, has a point of view)—at the center of the story. I was attracted to the idea of humanistic sociology. Andrew Abbott argues that a humanist sociologist "starts from the presumption that the other is a version of humanity, to be granted the dignity of being taken seriously on his or her own terms." The humanist sociologist's task is to figure out "how to translate the moral activity of that subject into our own ways of imagining what is happening to him or her in the social process."[5] This perspective recalls C. Wright Mills' "sociological imagination," which seeks to "translate personal troubles into public issues, and public issues into the terms of their human meaning." Effective sociology moves fluidly between the intimate realm of human meaning and its broader context, Mills suggested, in order "to grasp the interplay of man and society, of biography and history, of self and world."[6] Abbott also argues that sociology can be lyrical. Good sociological research is emotionally engaged with the social world, not distant and judgmental. It gives voice to research's subjects, embodies "humane sympathy," and, if done well, paints with Wordsworth's "coloring of the imagination."[7] Whether or not I succeeded, these ideas helped guide my attempt to tell a humane story about people, the places in which they live, and the social forces that swirl around and over them.

Books about industrial capitalism and economic globalization tend to discuss Big Ideas, engage in Big Debates, and make sweeping claims. Many are excellent. I was drawn, though, to the little, local stories that I felt resonated with Mills' "public issues." There was the story of a young and pregnant Sue Wilson's reluctant bravery in the face of discrimination. There was the story of Mike Allen's earth-moving ambition and Ed Krueger's humble personal ministry of social justice, both of which spanned over half a century in the Magic Valley. There was Laura Flora's dogged fight to get her daughters into a safer home and to see her grandchildren in the United States again. There was the red-faced debate between brothers Emilio and Ismael Fuentes about how to be a good man in rural Mexico.

These stories were embedded in the context of economic upheaval—but fundamentally experienced in noneconomic ways. They were about parenting, shifting gender roles, and evolving social identities; pride in production, family, and community; thwarted expectations, anger, and vulnerability; and the persistence of hope, the will to recapture happiness, and, maybe most of all, resilience. It is my hope that the stories in *Boom, Bust, Exodus*, when taken together, offer a view of globalization that the Big Idea books do not—a view grounded in human experience, meaning, and the sociological imagination.

ACKNOWLEDGMENTS

THE LONG, MEANDERING path to this book began in the summer of 2002 when rumors swirled, as they often did, about the fate of the big appliance factory on Galesburg's southwest edge. In those early years at Knox College, Nancy Eberhardt and Jon Wagner in the Department of Anthropology and Sociology and Dean Larry Breitborde were unfailingly supportive in spirit and in coin. I was equally fortunate at the University of Chicago, where Dean of the College John W. Boyer, Master of the Social Sciences Collegiate Division Elisabeth S. Clemens, and Director of the Public Policy Studies program Jim Leitzel offered flexibility, travel funds, and abundant encouragement. My agent at the Gernert Company, Erika Storella, helped me ably through the proposal process and connected me to Tim Bent at Oxford University Press. Tim, himself from Cedar Rapids, Iowa, is an old-fashioned and hands-on editor. I feel so fortunate to have had a book editor who, well, edits—and all the way from punctuation marks to the big ideas. He helped me pare down, enhance, and clarify the manuscript throughout, making me look more intelligent than I am and saving me embarrassment at several turns. I learned a great deal in the process—and it didn't hurt that he made me laugh along the way. Needless to say, the remaining flaws and imperfections are entirely my own.

Along the path I have been so fortunate to have made new friends, many of whom appear in these pages. I was astonished by Mike Patrick's patience and near-photographic memory. Our numerous conversations amounted to tens of thousands of transcribed words and painted for me a vivid picture of the early years of Appliance City in Galesburg. Dave Bevard, another lifer from the old factory, must be relieved that the project—and my hundreds of pestering calls and emails over the past twelve years—has, at long last, wrapped up. I will always cherish the colorful reminiscences and potent analysis that this talented man shared with me in Local 2063's humble offices, in my class-rooms, and over lunches in Chicago's Greektown. I will also always remember and be grateful to Doug and Annette Dennison, Jackie and Shannon Cummins, Tracy Warner, and George Carney who, during trying times, opened their homes to me. This book simply would have been impossible without their generosity—and that of many other fine people from the small cities and towns of western Illinois including Sue Wilson, Fred Pickard, Darin and Tammy Shull, Deb Pendergast, Mark Semande, Mike Smith, Joe Krejci, Kirk King, Mark Good, Aaron Kemp, Leonard Hadley, and many others.

The same goes for the U.S.-Mexico border, where, on both sides, Josh Walsman and I were welcomed by people in social positions both high and low. When we started in 2003, having just walked across the border with our backpacks and only a vague sense of direction, we met Arqueles Garcia and Gris Cruz at a human rights organization. The young couple arranged four interviews for us on our first day and, a decade later, we remain extremely grateful for their continued help and, even more, for their warm friendship. We have also known Ed Krueger for ten years now, and we could not have done the fieldwork that we did without his guidance, wisdom, and rich network of promotoras and maquiladora workers. In that network was Laura Flora Oliveros, one of many maquila workers who so generously shared their stories with Josh and me. Flora, in typical Mexican fashion, even invited us in without hesitation for a long visit and interview during her family's Mother's Day dinner. I also wish to thank Marielena Arizpe, who made our most recent trip to Monterrey, Ramos Arizpe-Saltillo, and Reynosa incredibly rewarding and comfortable. Our one-man driver and security team, Cuberto Mendoza, made the trip safe and fun and shared many insights of his own. Whether it was a colonia in Reynosa, a factory in Saltillo, a rickety mayor's office in Volador, or an ejido in Agua Dulce, Josh and I, without exception, were escorted like honored guests and close friends by people we had only just met. It was extraordinary. I hope this book serves in some way to honor all the women and men we met who make the things we buy and farm the food we eat.

I have also relied considerably on the help of some longtime friends. Robin Ragan, associate professor of modern languages and director of the Center for Global Studies at Knox College, did yeoman's work translating and transcribing early interviews from Mexico. Marilyn Webb, while she was Distinguished Professor of Journalism at Knox College and director of the Knox News Team, spearheaded the Maytag Project, which included the Maytag Employees in Transition survey that provided bigger sample size data on workers' outcomes and perspectives. Rich Stout, professor of economics, guided the data collection and analysis. I am so grateful for my time and friends at Knox; it is a special place. My brother-in-law and talented artist, David Samuel Stern, took stunning photographs in Galesburg, Reynosa, and northern Veracruz and produced some remarkably evocative collages to which I refer often. Old graduate school buddy Michael J. Rosenfeld, a Stanford sociologist, read early drafts of the manuscript and provided expert feedback that made the book much better than it would have been without it.

This project could not have been done without Josh Walsman. Our mothers met while pregnant in 1970, so our friendship goes way back. As such, the encouragement and moral support Josh provided throughout the project was hardly surprising. Josh was the first person I called when I had the idea to follow the Maytag story to Mexico. I remember sitting on my Cherry Street porch in Galesburg talking it through with him on the phone. Josh did more than encourage me, though; he signed on to help. Over a decade later, we were wrapping up our fifth trip to Reynosa. I am so grateful that my best friend also happens to be the perfect intellectual colleague and complement. With a graduate degree in Latin American studies and several years of grassroots development work in El Salvador, Josh is a savvy questioner, conversationalist, and translator. Despite my best efforts, my spoken Spanish remains fairly hopeless so I needed him to make important calls, translate on the fly when I was lost, and, when we returned, review the recordings in detail for rigorous transcriptions. Somehow those trips to Mexico were all remarkably rich and fluid. Much of that we owe to the remarkable hospitality that met us at every turn. In equal measure, though, Josh, a social butterfly in both languages, deserves enormous credit for the success of our fieldwork there. I would be remiss not to thank Josh's wife, Evelyn Diaz, and his mother, Charm Seright, for allowing me to abscond with Josh so many times for so long.

My wife, Mona Dugo, has been there for me at every step of this long— surely too-long—journey. As the project grew in space and time, she was relentlessly patient. It was uncanny and perhaps undeserved support—based on a vague promise that something good would come of it, eventually. I mean anyone can say that they're working on a book and ask to have hours on end to sit in the sick blue-white glow of the study. It's only possible to finish, though, if you have someone who believes in you for the long haul and gives you that time and their support—not to mention cooking lunch for the kids and taking them ice-skating, and, oh, by the way, can you read this chapter? Mona was that someone for me. Whenever I emerged from that study, there she was. I could always count on her and our girls—Haley, Maya, and Olivia—to wrestle me out of the rough patches as I tried to find my way.

NOTES

PROLOGUE

1. Gloria Anzaldúa, *Borderlands: The New Mestiza = La Frontera*, p. 3. San Francisco: Aunt Lute, 1987.
2. Mike Davis, *Planet of Slums*, p. 5. New York: Verso, 2006.
3. E. P. Thompson, "Time, Work-Discipline, and Industrial Capitalism," *Past and Present* 38 (December 1967): 80.
4. Karl Marx, *Capital*. In Vol. 1, Section 4, *The Marx-Engels Reader*. 2d ed. Edited by Robert C. Tucker, pp. 319–329. New York: Norton, 1978. Originally published in 1867.

CHAPTER 1

1. Locally the plant was still known as Midwest Manufacturing, or just "Midwest," as it had been since 1936. It was a wholly-owned subsidiary of Admiral Corporation. It would be called "Appliance City" by some in the 1960s and early 1970s. Admiral used "Appliance City" in some of its company literature.
2. "The Admiral Story: At Midwest Manufacturing Corp. in Galesburg, Illinois," Special Section. *Galesburg Register-Mail*, April 9, 1964.
3. *Report on Carcinogens*, 12th ed. Washington, DC: U.S. Department of Health and Human Services, Public Health Service, Toxicology National Program. June 10, 2011.
4. Much of this chapter, including some dialogue, is based on a series of nine interviews and several telephone and in-person conversations with Michael Patrick. When possible, I verified Patrick's account in interviews with other Maytag workers, including Dave Bevard and Sue Wilson, and with Fred Pickard, a plant superintendent at the Galesburg plant for over thirty-three years. I also consulted the Knox College Special Collections and Archives in Seymour Library, the Galesburg Public Library Archives, and *The Register-Mail* archives for an understanding of the conditions inside the Galesburg factory in the Admiral era.
5. "Factory Labor Rates," pp. 40–50 in "1958–1960 Agreement between Midwest Manufacturing Corporation and Midwest Lodge No. 2063, International Association of Machinists (AFL-CIO) of Galesburg, Illinois." The base rate for an assembler

working over nine months a year was $1.63 and $1.60 for a worker like Patrick who worked six to nine months. Since Admiral was a low base rate, high incentive shop, workers typically earned more than the base rate—usually about 140 percent or 150 percent of their base rate; *Income of Families and Persons in the United States: 1959* (January 5, 1961). Current Population Reports: Consumer Income. Washington, DC: U.S. Department of Commerce, 1961.

6. Tom Wilson, "Admiral Plant Contributed Much," *The Register-Mail* (February 27, 2010);"The Admiral Story: At Midwest Manufacturing Corp. in Galesburg, Illinois," Special Section. *Galesburg Register-Mail*, April 9, 1964; "Welcome to Midwest Manufacturing Corporation's Open House: In Honor of all Employees and their Families," 1961 Admiral Corporation company document in Galesburg Public Library Archives.

7. Maytag Special Section. *The Register-Mail* (September 15, 2004). Population statistics gathered from several sources including the U.S. Census—*1990 Census of Population and Housing Unit Counts United States* and the American FactFinder of the U.S. Census Bureau. "Historic peak" means Galesburg's decennial population peak because a population count or estimate was only conducted every ten years at that time.

8. *Life* (March 12, 1965) (emphasis in original); *Life* (October 7, 1966); the third advertisement is from a catalog of undetermined vintage.

9. "The Admiral Story: At Midwest Manufacturing Corp. in Galesburg, Illinois," Special Section. *Galesburg Register-Mail*, April 9, 1964; Michael E. Porter, *Cases in Successful Business Strategy*, p. 466. New York: The Free Press, 1983, on Admiral television sales.

10. James T. Patterson, *Grand Expectations: The United States, 1945-1974*, pp. 315–316, 323, 348. New York: Oxford University Press, 1996.

11. "Historic Census of Housing Tables." Washington, DC: U.S. Census Bureau, 2011. (http://www.census.gov); Patterson 1996, pp. 312, 314, 333.

12. Lizabeth Cohen, *A Consumers' Republic: The Politics of Mass Consumption in Postwar America*, p. 123. New York: Vintage, 2003. According to Patterson 1996 (p. 70), household appliance consumption jumped fivefold from 1939 to 1948; "A Hard Look at Consumer Credit," *Life* (November 21, 1955).

13. William Safire, "The Cold War's Hot Kitchen," *New York Times* (July 23, 2009); Lizabeth Cohen, *A Consumers' Republic: The Politics of Mass Consumption in Postwar America*, pp. 125, 126. New York: Vintage, 2003.

14. David M. Kennedy, *Freedom from Fear: The American People in Depression and War, 1929-1945*, p. 857. New York: Oxford University Press, 1999; Patterson, 1996, p. 312; U.S. Department of Commerce, Bureau of Economic Analysis (http://www.bea.gov).

15. Kennedy 1999, pp. 856–857.

16. "Historical Data: Midwest Manufacturing Corporation," Knox College Special Collections and Archives, Seymour Library, Galesburg, Illinois (n. d.); "Midwest: Produces for War, Plans for Peace, 1944," Midwest Manufacturing Corporation document in Galesburg Public Library Archives.

17. Patterson 1996, p. 40. Patterson writes that 35.5 percent of the nonagricultural workforce was union.

18. Patterson 1996, p. 315.

19. John Kenneth Galbraith, *The Affluent Society*, pp. 1, 258–259, 260. New York: Mariner Books, 1998. Originally published in 1958.

20. M. Samuels, "Uses and Sources of Electric Power." In *Building the Future City*. Vol. 242 *of Annals of the American Academy of Political and Social Science*. Edited by Robert B. Mitchell, pp. 71–74. Philadelphia: American Academy of Political and Social Science, 1945.

21. The Admiral production estimate comes from Fred Pickard, production superintendent for over thirty-three years. Pickard estimated that at peak production the Admiral plant produced 3,000 units per day in the late 1960s, while the average was between 2,000 and 3,000. At 47 weeks of production per year, subtracting for holidays and summer vacation, his estimate puts refrigerator production between 470,000 and 705,000. His estimate conforms to Michael Patrick's. Jim Eagle, "Admiral Marks 60 Years of Growth," *Prairie Journal* (Spring 1984), cites that in the 1970s "up to 2,750 refrigerators and freezers were produced per shift, in addition to microwaves, air conditioners, and dehumidifiers" (p. 44). In 1960 Midwest produced 250,000 appliances according to Admiral Corporation, "Welcome to Midwest Manufacturing Corporation's Open House: In Honor of all Employees and their Families," 1961. Booklet for an Appliance City open house from Galesburg Public Library Archives.

22. *Statistical Abstract of the United States*, p. 822. Washington, DC: U.S. Bureau of the Census, 1960; *Historical Statistics of the United States: Colonial Times to 1970, Part 2*, p. 694. Washington, DC: U.S. Bureau of the Census, 1975; Rosemary Feurer, *Radical Unionism in the Midwest, 1900–1950: The Dynamic Relationship between Unionism and Radicalism*, p. 87. Urbana: University of Illinois Press, 2006. Michael Patrick estimated that 150 manufacturers were winnowed to "maybe a dozen" in the 1970s; Karl Marx, *Capital*. In Vol. 1, Section 4, *The Marx-Engels Reader*. 2d ed. Edited by Robert C. Tucker, p. 437. New York: Norton, 1978. Originally published in 1867; Maytag Story Archive, *Newton Daily News* (May 10, 2006).

23. In 1964 the International Association of Machinists changed its name to the International Association of Machinists and Aerospace Workers.

24. Anne F. Patterson, "A Memorial to the Life of Ross D. Siragusa," Chicago: The Siragusa Foundation, 1996.

25. *Civilian Labor Force Participation Rates by Sex, 1950 to 2005 and Projected 2010 to 2050*. Office of Publications & Special Studies (http://www.bls.gov/opub). Washington, DC: U.S. Bureau of Labor Statistics, January 2007.

26. "Factory Labor Rates," pp. 53–62 in "1969–1973 Agreement between Midwest Manufacturing Corporation and Midwest Lodge No. 2063, International Association of Machinists and Aerospace Workers (AFL-CIO) of Galesburg, Illinois." This section is based on two interviews with Sue Wilson. Interviews with Michael Patrick and David Bevard corroborated her account of the gender-related changes in factory management and shop-floor culture.

27. Larry Mishel, "The Wedges between Productivity and Median Compensation Growth," p. 2. *Economic Policy Institute*, Issue Brief #330 (April 26, 2012); Lawrence Mishel, Josh Bivens, Elise Gould, and Heidi Shierholz, *The State of Working America*, pp. 58–60. 12th ed. Economic Policy Institute. Ithaca, NY: Cornell University Press, 2012.

28. Jerry M. Flint, "Freezer Demand Exceeds Supply," *New York Times* (October 6, 1973); Maytag Special Section, *The Register-Mail* (September 15, 2004), states that in 1974, "employment exceeds 5,000." Michael Patrick guessed it was more like 4,700 or 4,800. He said for every three workers there was an "indirect" worker on the office side, so nonproduction workers and truck drivers likely exceeded 1,000. "Admiral Corp. Workers Ratify Three-Year Contract," *Wall Street Journal* (April 3, 1973), pins Local 2063 membership at 3,200. "Rockwell International Furloughs 500 Employes [*sic*]," *Wall Street Journal* (December 1974), pins the total at 4,000 near the peak, but doesn't specify who is included in the count. Because the production side probably exceeded 4,000, total employment likely surpassed 5,000 at its peak, an extraordinary figure for a city of 36,000 and a county of 61,000.

29. Tom Nelson, "Changes Ahead for City, Work Force: How Galesburg Becomes after Maytag's Closing Largely Depends on Its People, *The Register-Mail* (October 20, 2002); Gene F. Summers, Sharon Evans, Frank Clemente, Jon Minkoff, and E. M. Beck, Jr., *Industrial Invasion of Nonmetropolitan America*, New York: Praeger, 1976. Patrick stated that the fortunes of Midwest manufacturers ebbed and flowed closely with that of the automobile industry, which, though it would soon face an oil crisis, was humming along. "If the autoworkers were laid off that would affect us," Patrick said. "When they got back going, people would start buying kitchen appliances again and we'd get back to work"; Jeff Faux, "Manufacturing: Key to America's Future." Presentation to Industrial Union Council Legislative Conference, Economic Policy Institute (February 4, 2003); Bureau of Labor Statistics website (http://www.bls.gov); John D. Kasarda, "Urban Industrial Transition and the Underclass." In *The Ghetto Underclass: Social Science Perspectives*. Vol. 501 *of Annals of the American Academy of Political and Social Sciences*. Edited by William Julius Wilson, 26–47. Newbury Park, CA: SAGE, 1989; William Julius Wilson, *The Truly Disadvantaged: The Inner City, the Underclass, and Public Policy*. Chicago: University of Chicago Press, 1987; Dennis Roth, "Thinking about Rural Manufacturing: A Brief History," *Rural America* 15.1 (January 2000): 12–19.

30. Ridgely Hunt, "Galesburg: Rockwell's America," *Chicago Tribune* (May 26, 1974).

CHAPTER 2

1. This scene is drawn from many sources including several interviews with Ed Krueger. The primary sources include the collection of reports and eyewitness accounts from an extensive set of U.S. Senate hearings: *Hearings before the Subcommittee on Migratory Labor of the Committee on Labor and Public Welfare United States Senate*, Ninetieth Congress, First Session, "Migratory Labor Legislation" (Hearings held in 1967). Washington, DC: U.S. Government Printing Office, 1968. Other primary sources include another set of Senate hearings and a district and U.S. Supreme Court case: *Hearings before the Subcommittee on Migratory Labor of the Committee on Labor and Public Welfare United States Senate*, Ninetieth-First Congress, "Migrant and Seasonal Farmworker Powerlessness" (July 21; Hearings held in 1969), Washington, DC: U.S. Government Printing Office, 1970; U.S. District Court for the Southern

District of Texas, Brownsville Division, December 4, 1972, "Francisco Medrano et al., Plaintiffs v. A. Y. Allee et al., Defendants," No. 67-B-36; and Supreme Court of the United States, May 20, 1974, "A. Y. Allee et al., Appellants, v. Francisco Medrano et al.," No. 72-1125. In the June 9, 1967, issue of the *Texas Observer*, Ronnie Dugger and others did remarkably thorough and balanced reporting on the tumultuous events before, during, and after this pivotal night. I used the following sources to corroborate and otherwise detail the account: Alan J. Watt, *Farm Workers and the Churches: The Movement in California and Texas*, pp. 137–161. College Station: Texas A&M University Press, 2010; Timothy Paul Bowman, *Blood Citrus: Citriculture, Colonialism, and the Making of Anglo-American Identity in the Lower Rio Grande Valley Borderlands during the Twentieth Century*, pp. 259–273. Ph.D. dissertation thesis, Southern Methodist University, 2011; John William Weber III, *The Shadow of the Revolution: South Texas, the Mexican Revolution, and the Evolution of Modern American Labor Relations*, pp. 382–387. Ph.D. dissertation thesis, College of William and Mary, August 2008; Julian Samora, Joe Bernal, and Albert Peña, *Gunpowder Justice: A Reassessment of the Texas Rangers*, pp. 131–156. Notre Dame, IN: Notre Dame Press, 1979; Mike Cox, *Time of the Rangers: From 1900 to the Present*, pp. 271–272. New York: Forge, 2009; H. Joaquin Jackson and James L. Haley, *One Ranger Returns*, pp. 8–9. Austin: University of Texas Press, 2008; David R. Jones, "Tension Rises as Rangers Confront Melon Strikers," *New York Times*, May 31, 1967; Kemper Diehl, "Clergyman Charges Texas Rangers Too Rough," *San Antonio Express-News*, May 28, 1967; "Trouble in the Melon Patch," *Newsweek*, June 19, 1967; "Rangers Tell of 'Dimas Incident,'" *San Antonio Express-News*, June 14, 1968; Dennis Farney, "The Texas Rangers: Lawmen Get Their Man, but Their Tactics Are Currently Under Fire," *Wall Street Journal*, September 13, 1967.

2. Douglas E. Kneeland, "Tensions Mount in Texas Melon Country as Striking Field Hands Press for Union Recognition, More Pay," *New York Times*, May 19, 1967; United Farm Workers Organizing Committee, "'La Casita Farms, Inc.'—A Profile of a 'Small Texas Farmer,'" United Farm Workers Organizing Committee 1967 press release.

3. The claim of "poorest in Texas" uses per capita income in 1960: $534. The 1960 census, the best source for county-level data for the 1960s, lists Starr County as the 17th poorest county in the nation in 1960, but that figure likely underestimates poverty in the area considerably given the hard-to-count nature of the impoverished migrant population. By some measures neighboring Hidalgo County is worse off. Specific data on Starr County population, poverty, and farmworker income levels taken from Bowman, *Blood Citrus*, p. 53; *Hearings 1968*, Part 2, p. 359; United Farm Workers Organizing Committee 1967, p. 3; David R. Jones, "Farm Labor: Viva el Picket Sign," *New York Times*, July 30, 1967; Kneeland, "Tensions Mount in Texas Melon Country as Striking Field Hands Press for Union Recognition, More Pay," May 19, 1967. The "internal colony" argument is compellingly put forward in Bowman, *Blood Citrus*. The number of people of Mexican origin in Starr County ranged in reports from 90 percent to 97 percent. Bowman, *Blood Citrus*, p. 271, pins the Starr County average wage at 75 cents an hour; United Farm Workers Organizing Committee 1967, p. 5, claimed a range between 40 and 85 cents. According to Eugene L. Boutilier,

"Legislation: An Answer," *Concern*, August 1–15, 1967, 10, farmworker wages were on par with industrial wages in the early 20th century and in 1966 was the lowest paid occupation in the country. According to Boutilier, the average national farmworker wage was $1.16, but $1.05 in Texas, in 1966. A newspaper account from the time (Nicholas C. Chriss, "Church Council Fires Minister Helping Poor," *Los Angeles Times*, February 21, 1969) pegs the pre-strike wages in South Texas at 50 cents an hour. It is safe to assert that the closer to Mexico, the lower the wages for farmworkers. At the time, the federal government was in the midst of a staged implementation of a minimum wage that included farmworkers; "Texas Jury Calls Farm Strike Illegal," *New York Times*, November 18, 1966. The Starr County sheriff's office put out an aggressively anti-union newspaper. Other references to slanted media coverage: Watt, *Farm Workers and the Churches*, p. 137; Kneeland, "Tensions Mount in Texas Melon Country as Striking Field Hands Press for Union Recognition, More Pay," May 19, 1967; Bowman, *Blood Citrus*, p. 270.

4. National Labor Relations Board, "National Labor Relations Act" (http://www.nlrb. gov/resources/national-labor-relations-act).

5. A detailed account of the arrests and violence directed at the protesters exists in Supreme Court of the United States, May 20, 1974, "A. Y. Allee et al., Appellants, v. Francisco Medrano et al.," No. 72-1125. Also in Weber III, *The Shadow of the Revolution*, pp. 382–387. The insecticide incident is documented in Bowman, *Blood Citrus*, p. 262, and *Hearings* 1968, Part 2, p. 663 (a special reprint of several *Texas Observer* articles from the summer of 1966); United Farm Workers Organizing Committee 1967, p. 5.

6. *Hearings*, 1968, Part 2, p. 661 (a special reprint of several *Texas Observer* articles from the summer of 1966); Kneeland, "Tensions Mount in Texas Melon Country as Striking Field Hands Press for Union Recognition, More Pay," May 19, 1967; United Farm Workers Organizing Committee, 1967, p. 4.

7. La Casita also outmaneuvered the strikers when picketers tried to persuade "green carders" crossing over to recognize the strike and not to work La Casita's fields. Instead of picking up the day laborers at 6 a.m., management went to the Roma international bridge at 2 a.m., loaded two buses full of laborers, and got to work early.

8. United Farm Workers Organizing Committee, 1967, p. 24.

9. The events of this portion of the evening are contested on some details. I drew mainly from the eyewitness accounts in *Hearings*, 1968, Part 2, including extensive accounts by Ed Krueger, Douglass Adair, and Tina Krueger. Their accounts are largely corroborated by the *Texas Observer* accounts and the account of Gary Garrison, an Associated Press reporter. The Rangers claim that they were not rough. Two books sympathetic to the Rangers—Cox 2009 and Jackson and Haley 2008—offer a surprisingly similar account, though they differ on some details and interpretation. I report here only the details that are well established and consistent in multiple accounts. The Rangers accounts of that evening changed in several important ways over time and were consequently suspect. Also the district and Supreme Court decisions and the report of the Texas Advisory Committee to the U.S. Commission on Civil Rights ultimately found the strikers' accounts more credible on that night and generally.

10. Dugger, "Arrests Impede the Picketing," June 9, 1967, 15. The Rangers' cars were marked distinctively with an "RKK" license plate prefix and therefore easy to identify.

11. *Hearings*, 1968, Part 2. Adair's and Ramirez's accounts vary in the exact words but not in content in their eyewitness accounts so I didn't use a direct quotation here but rather a paraphrase of what Allee said. Garrison's account in Dugger, "Arrests Impede the Picketing," June 9, 1967, 18, corroborates their account.

12. *Hearings before the Subcommittee on Migratory Labor of the Committee on Labor and Public Welfare United States Senate*, Ninetieth Congress, First Session, "Migratory Labor Legislation," p. 383. (Hearings held in 1967.) Washington, DC: U.S. Government Printing Office, Part 2, 1968.

13. "Rangers Tell of 'Dimas Incident,' " June 14, 1968.

14. Ronnie Dugger. "The Rangers and La Huelga," *Texas Observer*, June 9, 1967; Dugger, "Arrests Impede the Picketing," June 9, 1967, 15.

15. *Hearings* 1968, Part 2, Medrano's testimony (pp. 404–407); Dugger, "Arrests Impede the Picketing," June 9, 1967, 16–17.

16. *Hearings* 1968, Part 2, Medrano's testimony (pp. 404–407); Dugger, "Arrests Impede the Picketing," June 9, 1967, 16–17. In fact, the protesters had nothing but good things to say about the Mission and Edinburg police, the sheriff of Hidalgo County, and the Mission police, who all had treated them with "courtesy." Other than the fine breakfast for Medrano, though, the federal government had steered clear of the escalating conflict in the isolated valley.

17. Robin Lloyd, "Rio Grande's Farm Labor Drama Depresses Senators: Probe Unit Seen Displeased with Role of Rangers," *Washington Post*, July 9, 1967.

18. *Hearings*, 1968, Part 2, p. 407.

19. *Hearings*, 1968, Part 2, pp. 1, 2.

20. *Hearings*, 1968, Part 1, p. 5.

21. *Hearings before the Subcommittee on Migratory Labor of the Committee on Labor and Public Welfare United States Senate*, Ninetieth-First Congress, "Migrant and Seasonal Farmworker Powerlessness," 1970 (July 21; Hearings held in 1969), pp. 923, 934. Washington, DC: U.S. Government Printing Office, 1970.

22. "Rangers Tell of 'Dimas Incident,' " June 14, 1968; United States District Court for the Southern District of Texas, Brownsville Division, 1972 (December 4), "Francisco Medrano et al., Plaintiffs v. A. Y. Allee et al., Defendants," No. 67-B-36, 14; Ronnie Dugger, "Allee and Garrison Deny the Allegations," *Texas Observer*, June 9, 1967.

23. Robert Draper, "Twilight of the Rangers," *Texas Monthly*, February 1994; Ronnie Dugger, "Conversations with the Captain," *Texas Observer*, June 9, 1967, 23, 20.

24. Draper, "Twilight of the Rangers," February 1994; Ronnie Dugger, "The Dimas Incident," *Texas Observer*, June 9, 1967; Watt, *Farm Workers and the Churches*, p. 153; Oscar J. Martinez, *Border People: Life and Society in the U.S.-Mexico Borderlands*, p. 228. Tucson: University of Arizona Press, 1994. Allee saw Dimas as an outlaw, and by some accounts he was right. Dimas had an extensive criminal record, including a murder. And the fact that Dimas reportedly died in a 1973 bar shootout with the son of a deputy sheriff who had arrested strikebreakers lends some credence to Allee's view. Antonio Orendain recalled a handful of local strikebreakers that resented the

outsiders from California telling them not to be violent. They showed him three rifles and 25 sticks of dried-out dynamite in the trunk of their car.

25. Dugger, "Arrests Impede the Picketing," June 9, 1967, 15.

26. "Boss Signs Agreement: First Victory for the Union in Starr County," *El Malcriado*, June 7, 1967, 17; *Hearings*, 1968, Part 2, pp. 624–625 (reprint of "Farm Workers Sign 1st Agreement," May 17, 1967); *Texas AFL-CIO News; Hearings*, Part 1, p. 174; Jean White, "Rights Group to Probe Texas Farm 'Peonage,' " *Washington Post*, December 13, 1968; Dugger, "Arrests Impede the Picketing," June 9, 1967, 15; Kneeland, "Tensions Mount in Texas Melon Country as Striking Field Hands Press for Union Recognition, More Pay," May 19, 1967.

27. Martinez, *Border People*, p. 230; Sean Gaffney, "Standing Up: Decades-Ago Crusade for Farmworkers by Chavez Contemporary Echoes in Valley," *The Monitor* (McAllen, TX), September 1, 2008; Nicholas C. Chriss, "Church Council Fires Minister Helping Poor," *Los Angeles Times*, February 21, 1969. In *Hearings* 1970, Krueger said, "Anglo-Americans who are involved in the movement or sympathetic to the movement find it increasingly difficult to maintain a relationship, a viable, active relationship with the Mexican-American movement in South Texas" (p. 932).

28. Barry T. Hirsch, David A. Macpherson, and Wayne G. Vroman, "Estimates of Union Density by State," *Monthly Labor Review*, July 2001, 54.

29. The farmworkers' strike did push up wages in the Valley. One reason for this was that farmworkers on the Mexico side had recently won a strike, and their wages moved up to 27 pesos (about $2.50) a day. U.S. growers needed to maintain an enticing-enough wage differential so migrants would still risk crossing the border in droves. Higher wages were tolerable to growers. Collective bargaining, though, was not just an assault on their pocketbook, but also on economic freedom and a treasured way of life. Larry Goodwyn, "How It Is in Texas—A U.S. Farm," *Texas Observer*, June 9, 1967, 16.

30. This profile of Othal Brand is taken from several sources including "Former McAllen Mayor Othal Brand Has Died," *The Monitor*, December 12, 2009; Susan Duffy, "The Last Patrón: McAllen's Mayor Is Used to Getting His Own Way," *Texas Monthly*, July 1981, 84–88; John M. Crewdson, "Mayor Keeps Office in Rio Grande Town," *New York Times*, May 11, 1981.

31. Duffy, "The Last Patrón, July 1981, 84–88; "Videotapes of Beatings Figure in Federal Inquiry of Police Force in Texas," *New York Times*, April 4, 1981.

32. Duffy, "The Last Patrón, July 1981, 84–88; Crewdson, "Mayor Keeps Office in Rio Grande Town," May 11, 1981.

33. Gathered from several sources including U.S. Census, *1990 Census of Population and Housing Unit Counts United States* and the U.S. Census Bureau's FactFinder.

34. Matt Whittaker, "Enjoying the Job: Mike Allen Is Big in, for Valley Business," *McClatchy-Tribune Business News*, February 10, 2006.

CHAPTER 3

1. Winston Williams, "Dogged Rockwell Bets on Reagan," *New York Times*, September 30, 1984, 4.

2. Leonard Wiener, "New Owner Could Sharpen View of Admiral's Future," *Chicago Tribune*, October 28, 1973. The merger was completed in 1974. The purchase was announced in 1973.

3. Williams, "Dogged Rockwell Bets on Reagan," September 30, 1984; David Schwartzman, *The Japanese Television Cartel: A Study Based on Matsushita v. Zenith*. Ann Arbor: University of Michigan Press, 1994; Michael Patrick interviews; "Rockwell International Corporation Annual Report, 1978," *America's Corporate Foundation*; "Rockwell Is Seen Restudying Future of Its Admiral Unit," *Wall Street Journal*, January 19, 1978; "Rockwell International Says Its Admiral Group Plans to Close 2 Plants," *Wall Street Journal*, August 30, 1976; Leonard Wiener, "Rockwell Selling Admiral," *Chicago Tribune*, January 30, 1979; Robert Lindsey, "Builder of the B-1 Bomber," *New York Times*, October 11, 1981.

4. From an issue of *Focus* (n. d.), a Rockwell International company magazine from the late 1970s, Galesburg Public Library Archives.

5. Sherman M. Sweeney, "History of Maytag Galesburg Refrigeration Products," Mississippi Valley Chapter 123. Presented to American Society of Heating, Refrigeration and Air-Conditioning Engineers, Inc., in St. Louis, Missouri, April 1995; Michael Patrick interviews; Maytag Special Section, Galesburg, Illinois, *The Register-Mail*, September 15, 2004. The Admiral acquisition pushed Magic Chef into the Fortune 500 for the first time in 1980—at number 500. Rockwell International was at number 37 and growing (Fortune 500 Rankings: money.cnn.com/magazines/fortune/fortune500_archive/snapshots/1979/1145.html). Under Magic Chef, the Galesburg factory put out the popular "Entertainer" refrigerator, the "a la mode," which made ice cream, and a "Party Ice" machine during the early 1980s, helping Magic Chef anchor itself in the appliance business.

6. James Feyrer, Bruce Sacerdote, and Ariel Dora Stern, "Did the Rust Belt Become Shiny? A Study of Cities and Counties That Lost Steel and Auto Jobs in the 1980s," *Brookings-Wharton Papers on Urban Affairs* 1 (2007): 41–89; Thomas H. Klier, Richard H. Mattoon, and William A. Testa, "Assessing the Midwest Economy: Looking Back for the Future—A Summary," *Chicago Fed Letter*, Federal Reserve Bank of Chicago (June 1997) 118; William A. Testa, Thomas H. Klier, and Richard H. Mattoon, "Challenges and Prospects for Midwest Manufacturing," *Chicago Fed Letter*, Federal Reserve Bank of Chicago (March 2005) 212b.

7. Tom Nelson, "Real Estate Market Will Suffer from Maytag Closure: But to What Extent Open to Debate," *The Register-Mail*, February 23, 2003; David Hotle, "Assessors Disagree on Impact of Maytag Closure," *The Register-Mail*, September 29, 2003; William Mullen and Janet Cawley, "Hard Times on Main Street, U.S.A.," *Chicago Tribune*, March 14 1982; R. C. Longworth, "A Town's Bumpy Road to Recovery," *Chicago Tribune*, December 18, 1983; Timothy D. Schellhardt, "Troubled Town: Galesburg, Ill. Finds Slump and Job Losses Offset Deflation's Boon," *Wall Street Journal*, May 18, 1982.

8. Michael Patrick interviews; Iver Peterson, "Rebound in Appliances Helps Few Ex-Workers," *New York Times*, April 18, 1983; Associated Press, "Tennessee Pickets Routed," *New York Times*, February 25, 1983. Rymer and his band of southern lawyers learned to work with Local 2063 as they continued to fight tooth and nail against

the union effort in Tennessee ("After a Bitter, 7-Month Battle, Magic Chef Appears to Have Soundly Defeated Union," *Wall Street Journal*, August 30, 1983). Ultimately the National Labor Relations Board found against Magic Chef in 1987 in the Cleveland, Tennessee, case. Magic Chef was required to post in its plant an official Notice to Employees that promised: "We will not threaten employees with reprisals if they speak to other employees about the Union" (Magic Chef, Inc. and Dorothy Williamson, Case 10-CA-19683, *Decisions of the National Labor Relations Board*, No. 33, p. 286, September 30, 1987).

9. "So, Who's Dull? Maytag's Top Officer, Expected to Do Little, Surprises His Board—Company Man Hadley Shows That Disparaged No. 2s Can Rise to the Occasion," *Wall Street Journal*, June 23, 1998; Daniel F. Cuff, "Maytag to Acquire Magic Chef for $740 Million," *New York Times*, March 25, 1986; Alex Kotlowitz and Linda Williams, "Maytag Agrees to Acquire Magic Chef in Stock Swap Valued at $750 Million," *Wall Street Journal*, March 25, 1986; "$1 Billion Merger in Appliances," *New York Times*, October 25, 1988; "Admiral Moving from Schaumburg," *Chicago Sun-Times*, July 23, 1987.

10. Laurence D. Ackerman, *Identity Is Destiny: Leadership and the Roots of Value Creation*, p. 178. San Francisco: Berrett-Koehler, 2000; "Appliance City," Maytag Special Section, *The Register-Mail*, September 15, 2004; Vartanig G. Vartan, "Market Place: 2 Appliance Independents," *New York Times*, March 31, 1986; "Maytag Corporation," Funding Universe, available at: http://www.fundinguniverse.com/company-histories/Maytag-Corporation-Company-History.html.

11. Mullen and Cawley, "Hard Times on Main Street, U.S.A.," March 14, 1982; Michael Locin and Tom Franklin, "Thompson Turns Prison Dedication into a Political Event," *Chicago Tribune*, October 18, 1986.

12. Robert Hoover and John Hoover, *An American Quality Legend: How Maytag Saved Our Moms, Vexed the Competition, and Presaged America's Quality Revolution*, p. 216. New York: McGraw-Hill, 1993.

13. John Gorman, "Maytag Builds Success to Last, without Repairs" (cover story), *Chicago Tribune*, September 8, 1986.

14. Funding Universe, "Maytag Corporation," available at: http://www.fundinguniverse.com/company-histories/Maytag-Corporation-Company-History.html.

15. Peter Nulty and Justin Martin, "National Business Hall of Fame," *Fortune* 131.6 (April 3, 1995); Gorman, "Maytag Builds Success to Last, without Repairs," September 8, 1986; Lee M. Maxwell, *Save Women's Lives: History of Washing Machines*, p. 47. Eaton, CO: Oldewash, 2003; A. B. Funk, *Fred L. Maytag: A Biography*, p. 66. Cedar Rapids, IA: The Torch Press, 1936; Ackerman, *Identity Is Destiny: Leadership and the Roots of Value Creation*, p. 180; John N. Ingham, Vol. 2, *Biographical Dictionary of American Business Leaders*, p. 875. Westport, CT: Greenwood, 1983.

16. Funk, *Fred L. Maytag: A Biography*, p. 131.

17. "Gives Workers $130,000: Iowan Marks 70th Birthday by Gifts to 500 Employees," *New York Times*, July 15, 1927; "Obituaries: F. L. Maytag: Maker of Household Aids," *New York Times*, March 27, 1937; Funk, *Fred L. Maytag: A Biography*, p. 195.

18. Funk, *Fred L. Maytag: A Biography*, p. 211.

19. Maytag Collector's Club website: http://www.maytagclub.com/page-12.htm; Funk, *Fred L. Maytag: A Biography*, pp. 92, 93, 208; Hoover and Hoover, *An American Quality Legend*, p. 125.

20. Funk, *Fred L. Maytag: A Biography*, p. 97; Hoover and Hoover, *An American Quality Legend*, p. 127.

21. Funk, *Fred L. Maytag: A Biography*, p. 97.

22. Nulty and Martin, "National Business Hall of Fame," April 3, 1995; Hoover and Hoover, *An American Quality Legend*, pp. 132–133, 134–136.

23. Rosemary Feurer, *Radical Unionism in the Midwest, 1900–1950: The Dynamic Relationship between Unionism and Radicalism*, pp. 87–89, 97. Urbana: University of Illinois Press, 2006; "Maytag Strike," *New York Times* (front page), August 7, 1938.

24. Hoover and Hoover, *An American Quality Legend*, p. 137.

25. "Mr. Maytag: The Big Man of Newton Faces up to His Responsibilities," *Life*, 27.25, (December 19, 1949): 71–79; Hoover and Hoover, *An American Quality Legend*, p. 142.

26. "Fred Maytag Dies: A Manufacturer," *New York Times*, November 5, 1962; Justin G. Longenecker, "Management Priorities and Management Ethics," *Journal of Business Ethics* 4.1 (February 1985): 65–70; Hoover and Hoover, *An American Quality Legend*, p. 153.

27. "Mr. Maytag: The Big Man of Newton Faces up to His Responsibilities," 71–79; "Fred Maytag Dies: A Manufacturer," November 5, 1962, Hoover and Hoover, *An American Quality Legend*, p. 3.

28. "Milestones" section, *Time Magazine*, November 16, 1962.

29. Robert L. Rose, "Maytag's Acquisitions Don't Wear as Well as Washers and Dryers: Company Hears Complaints," *Wall Street Journal*, January 31, 1991.

30. Ackerman, *Identity Is Destiny*, p. 182.

31. Rose, "Maytag's Acquisitions Don't Wear as Well as Washers and Dryers, January 31, 1991.

32. Hoover and Hoover, *An American Quality Legend*, p. 37.

33. Ackerman, *Identity Is Destiny*, p. 190.

34. "So, Who's Dull? Maytag's Top Officer, Expected to Do Little, Surprises His Board," June 23, 1998.

35. Robert F. Hartley, *Management Mistakes and Successes*, p. 285 Hoboken, NJ: Wiley, 2010.

36. "So, Who's Dull? Maytag's Top Officer, Expected to Do Little, Surprises His Board, June 23, 1998; David Leonhardt, "The Saga of Maytag's Lloyd Ward: The Remarkable Journey to Become CEO" (cover story), *BusinessWeek*, August 8, 1999. Also on market share growth: Tom Nelson, "'Competitively Viable' Not Defined: Employees Still Don't Know Why Amana Was Kept over Galesburg," *The Register-Mail*, October 14, 2002.

37. The long, improbable run of the factory alone bears out Bevard's assessment. In the 1990s, Fred Pickard, who sat in on contract negotiations, echoed Bevard's sentiment from the other side of the bargaining table.

38. Maytag Timeline, *The Register-Mail*, October 11, 2002; Steven Greenhouse, "City Feels Early Effects of Plant Closing in 2004," *New York Times*, December 26, 2002; John R. Pulliam, "'Major Blow to City and Region' a Year Ago," *The Register-Mail*,

October 11, 2003; Nelson, "'Competitively Viable' Not Defined," October 14, 2002; Tom Nelson, "Study: Maytag Closing to Have Huge Ripple Effect: Thousands of Other Jobs, in Many Sectors, Will Be Affected," *The Register-Mail*, January 27, 2003.

39. "So, Who's Dull? Maytag's Top Officer, Expected to Do Little, Surprises His Board, June 23, 1998; Leonhardt, "The Saga of Maytag's Lloyd Ward," August 8, 1999; Amey Stone, "Can Maytag's Stock Keep Spinning Faster? Having Soared 150% in Two Years, Beating Expectations Gets Harder and Harder," *BusinessWeek*, July 30, 1999.

CHAPTER 4

1. Marjorie Whigham-Desir, "A Watershed Appointment: Lloyd Ward Assumes Role as CEO at Maytag Corp.," *Black Enterprise*, August 1, 1999; David Leonhardt, "The Saga of Maytag's Lloyd Ward: The Remarkable Journey to Become CEO" (cover story), *BusinessWeek*, August 8, 1999.

2. Carl Quintanilla, "Lloyd Ward Puts a New Spin on Maytag," *Wall Street Journal*, November 26, 1996. Ward's charisma was conveyed time and time again in interviews I did with managers and union leaders who interacted with him.

3. John S. Reed, "John Reed on Big Banks' Power and Influence," *Moyers & Company*, Interview with Bill Moyers, February 1, 2012.

4. Norm Winick, "What's the Motivation for the Restructuring at Maytag?" *The Zephyr* (Galesburg, Illinois), April 5, 2000.

5. Amey Stone, "Can Maytag's Stock Keep Spinning Faster? Having Soared 150% in Two Years, Beating Expectations Gets Harder and Harder," *BusinessWeek*, July 30, 1999; David Barboza, "Maytag Shares Tumble 26% on Concerns over Earnings," *New York Times*, September 11, 1999. Maytag was not on the shadowy path of Enron or WorldCom, but analysts charged that Maytag executives had misled investors and analysts on sales figures and overhead costs.

6. Leonard Hadley, CEO of Maytag, Interviewed by Wilmer Tjossem, *Quaker Life*, September 1999; Quintanilla, "Lloyd Ward Puts a New Spin on Maytag," November 26, 1996; David Leonhardt, "The Saga of Maytag's Lloyd Ward, August 8, 1999; William Ryberg, "Maytag Chief Happy to Call Newton Home," Associated Press, April 11, 2002.

7. Josh Bivens, "Shifting Blame for Manufacturing Job Loss: Effects of Rising Trade Deficits Shouldn't Be Ignored," Economic Policy Institute Briefing Paper 149, April 8, 2004; U.S. Census Bureau, "Trade in Goods with China," (http://www.census.gov).

8. Kelly K. Spors, "World Business, A Special Report; Against the Grain: A Chinese Appliance Maker Has Placed Its Bet on a Counterintuitive Strategy: It's Bringing Jobs to the U.S.," *Wall Street Journal*, October 1, 2004; "Maytag Projects Second Half Results Lower Than Previously Anticipated Primarily Due to Loss of Business at Circuit City and Heilig-Meyers Stores," *PR Newswire*, September 14, 2000.

9. Maytag Corporation, "Executive Severance Agreement," Securities and Exchange Commission filing, December 27, 2000. Dave Bevard said that a $9 million golden parachute would have kicked in if Lloyd Ward had sold the company.

10. "Maytag's Interim CEO Stops Rumors—Almost; Manufacturing: Workers No Longer Worry about a Move or Sale, But Wonder If Ex-Chief Was Asked to Resign," January 26, 2001.

11. Leonard Hadley, phone interview, February 24, 2012.

12. Associated Press, "Lloyd Ward Resigns as Maytag Chairman, CEO; Disagreement? Predecessor Returns from Retirement to Serve in the Interim," *Telegraph-Herald* [Dubuque, Iowa], November 11, 2000; "Maytag's Interim CEO Stops Rumors—Almost," January 26, 2001; Winick, "What's the Motivation for the Restructuring at Maytag?" April 5, 2000.

13. Ward's post-Maytag career lends credence to his critics. Most notably, Ward became CEO of the U.S. Olympic Committee in November 2001, with the apparent effect of making the famously dysfunctional organization even worse off. In January 2003, Ward found himself being grilled by a Senate panel led by John McCain for inept management, misuse of USOC funds, and allegedly steering Olympics business contracts to an energy company controlled by his brother. Afterwards Ward continued to come up short as an effective leader. Ward said iMotors—which failed shortly after he took its helm in 2001—would be a Fortune 500 company. Ward also said he would one day run a Fortune 100 company: "I'm telling you, I will run a Fortune 100 company before my journey is over" (David Barboza, "His Rear-View Mirror Reflects Big Business," *New York Times* [February 7, 2001]). Today, the once "watershed" CEO, one of *Fortune's* "Most Powerful Black Executives in America" and one of *BusinessWeek's* "Top 25 Executives," leads CleanTech Solutions Worldwide, where he and a handful of family members operate a small certified Minority Business Enterprise that offers recycling services. The CEO who said his goal was "to be the best CEO on the planet" passed into infamy. "Breakaway (A Special Report): The Challengers—New Enterprises, Old Values," *Wall Street Journal*, June 18, 2001; Matthew S. Scott, "Lloyd Ward: Victim or Villain?" *Black Enterprise*, January 1, 2004; Richard Sandomir, "Chief of U.S. Olympic Committee Quits Amid a Furor over Ethics," *New York Times*, March 2, 2003; Eric Fisher, "Senate Panel to Push for Reforms in USOC," *Washington Times*, February 14, 2003; Barboza, "His Rear-View Mirror Reflects Big Business," February 7, 2001; Jere Longman, "Professionalism Eludes U.S. Olympic Committee," *New York Times*, January 26, 2003; Amy Shipley, "Embattled CEO Ward Leaves USOC," *Washington Post*, March 2, 2003; Richard Sandomir, "Former Olympic Wrestler Is Running U.S.O.C., for Now," *New York Times*, March 4, 2003; Whigham-Desir, "A Watershed Appointment," August 1, 1999.

14. Selena Roberts, "Sports of the Times; The U.S.O.C. Wanted Class. What It Got Was Crass," *New York Times*, March 2, 2003.

15. James P. Miller, "New Maytag CEO Is Industry Veteran," *Chicago Tribune*, June 20, 2001; Ryberg, "Maytag Chief Happy to Call Newton Home," April 11, 2002.

16. Heesun Wee, "Maytag Is Cleaning Up Its Act," *BusinessWeek*, May 17, 2002; "Maytag Will Buy Amana Appliances for $325 Million," *Wall Street Journal*, June 6, 2001.

17. Admiral Corporation, "Welcome to Midwest Manufacturing Corporation's Open House: In Honor of All Employees and Their Families," 1961. Booklet for an Appliance City open house from Galesburg Public Library Archives.

18. Leonard Hadley, phone interview, February 24, 2012.

19. Tom Nelson, "Maytag Labor Contract Expires This Weekend; Ratification Vote Planned Sunday," *The Register-Mail*, April 5, 2002.

20. This account of the April 7, 2002, contract presentation and vote was compiled from newspaper accounts and interviews with Michael Patrick, Sue Wilson, Dave Bevard, Doug Dennison, Annette Dennison, and Tracy Warner.

21. Jeff Rogers, "The Maytag Vote," *The Register-Mail*, April 9, 2002.

22. Tom Nelson, "Maytag Union Stays on Job; Strike Vote Fails, So Contract Rejected Soundly by Workers Goes into Effect," *The Register-Mail*, April 9, 2002.

23. Rogers, "The Maytag Vote," April 9, 2002.

24. Nelson, "Maytag Union Stays on Job," April 9, 2002.

25. Rogers, "The Maytag Vote," April 9, 2002. The strike vote was 954 to 509 in favor of striking.

26. The next day local management was unprepared to implement the contract, even though it was entirely their contract, with their language. They had planned no workshops on implementing the imminent policy changes, as was the custom after a contract vote. Bevard and Dennison were certain that local management had been assured that there would be a strike.

27. Davide Dukcevich, "Repairing Maytag," Forbes.com (http://www.forbes.com/2002/10/11/1011maytag.html), October 11, 2002.

28. Jim Little, "A Letter to Maytag Employees: From Jim Little, Vice President, Operations, Galesburg Refrigeration Products," *The Register-Mail*, October 11, 2002; Tom Nelson, "Maytag Plant Closing; Production to Begin Winding Down in 2003," *The Register-Mail*, October 11, 2002; David Hotle, "Workers Are Shocked, Angry and Disappointed: Emotions Run the Gamut Friday Morning," *The Register-Mail*, October 12, 2002.

29. Karen S. Lynch, "Ten-Eleven: Inside a Job Loss, Five Years Later," *The Zephyr*, October 18, 2007.

30. David Hotle, "Rank and File See Little They Can Do: Union Reps to Meet on Details of Closure," *The Register-Mail*, October 12, 2002.

31. "Maytag Earnings Up 48% in Quarter," *New York Times*, October 15, 2002.

32. Sherman M. Sweeney, "History of Maytag Galesburg Refrigeration Products," Mississippi Valley Chapter 123. Presented to American Society of Heating, Refrigeration and Air-Conditioning Engineers, Inc., in St. Louis, Missouri, April 1995.

CHAPTER 5

1. Mike Allen's history was taken from two in-person interviews in 2003 at the McAllen Economic Development Corporation (MEDC) and from newspaper sources including: Ana Ley, " 'Padre Mike' Allen Dies at 72," *The Monitor* [McAllen, Texas], August 26, 2010; Enrique Rangel, "Following NAFTA's Calling," *Dallas Morning News* (Monterrey Bureau), December 11, 1994.

2. Lucinda Vargas, "The Maquiladora Industry in Historical Perspective," p. 8, *Business Frontiers*, Issue 4, Federal Reserve Bank of Dallas, El Paso Branch, 1998; James

J. Parsons, "Review of Mexico's Natural Gas: The Beginning of an Industry," *Economic Geography* 45.4 (October 1969): 374–375.

3. Vargas, "The Maquiladora Industry in Historical Perspective," p. 8; Cathy Booth Thomas, "La Nueva Frontera: The Rise of the NAFTA Manager," *Time*, June 11, 2001; John McClintock, "Mexico's Child-Labor Woes Raise Trade-Pact Concerns," *Baltimore Sun*, December 15, 1991; Susana Hayward, "Made in Mexico? Adios, Jobs; Cheap Labor Lures U.S. Firms South," Associated Press in *Chicago Sun Times*, May 25, 1992; Tim Knapp and John Harms, "When the Screen Goes Blank: A Television Plant Closing and Its Impact on Workers," *Sociological Quarterly* 43.4 (Autumn 2002): 611; Joyce Peterson, "Defending Their Dignity: Women Maquiladora Workers Fight Oppression, Squalor," *Austin American Statesman*, December 16, 1990.

4. John J. Dwyer, *The Agrarian Dispute: The Expropriation of American-Owned Rural Land in Postrevolutionary Mexico*, p. 264. Durham: Duke University Press, 2009.

5. Jorge Durand, Douglas S. Massey, and Rene M. Zenteno, "Mexican Immigration to the United States: Continuities and Changes," *Latin American Research Review* 36.1 (2001): 111.

6. Altha J. Cravey, *Women and Work in Mexico's Maquiladoras*. Lanham, MD: Rowman & Littlefield, 1998; Rachel Kamel and Anya Hoffman, *The Maquiladora Reader: Cross-border Organizing since NAFTA*. Philadelphia: Mexico-U.S. Border Program, 1999; Norma Iglesias Prieto, *Beautiful Flowers of the Maquiladora: Life Histories of Women Workers in Tijuana*. (Translated by M. Stone). Austin: University of Texas Press, 1997; Lawrence Douglas Taylor Hansen, "The Origins of the Maquila Industry in Mexico," *Comercio Exterior* 53.11 (November 2003); Joseph Pryweller, "Border Towns Face Growing Pains," *Plastics News*, January 21, 2002.

7. "Border Boom Town: Businesses Targeting McAllen as Trade Soars." *San Antonio Express-News*, October 11, 1992.

8. "Mexican Governor Ends Labor Dispute," *Houston Chronicle*, August 19, 1989; Victoria A. Hirschberg, "The City as Growth Machine: Reynosa, Mexico," Master's thesis, Community and Regional Planning and Master of Arts in Latin American Studies, University of New Mexico, December 2009; Associated Press, "U.S. Eyes Mexican Pact: Americans See New Era in Labor Relations," *Newsday*, September 7, 1989.

9. Edward J. Williams and John T. Passé-Smith, *The Unionization of the Maquiladora Industry: The Tamaulipan Case in National Context*, Institute for Regional Studies of the Californias, San Diego State University, 1992; "Mexican Governor Ends Labor Dispute," August 19, 1989.

10. "Border Boom Town: Businesses Targeting McAllen as Trade Soars." *San Antonio Express-News*, October 11, 1992.

11. Stephen W. Spivey, "McAllen, Texas Businesses Expand Operations in Anticipation of Mexican Growth," *The Monitor*, March 7, 2003; Interview with Stephen W. Spivey, business reporter for *The Monitor*, June 27, 2003.

12. "Border Boom Town: Businesses Targeting McAllen as Trade Soars," October 11, 1992.

13. Leslie Sklair, "Transnationals Across the Border: Mobilizing U.S. Support for the Mexican Maquila Industry," *Journal of American Studies* 24.4 (August 1990): 172; "At Border, Optimism on Trade Accord," *New York Times*, October 17, 1993.

14. Booth Thomas, "La Nueva Frontera," June 11, 2001.

15. Rangel, "Following NAFTA's Calling," December 11, 1994.

16. S. Lynne Walker, "Maytag Plant Expansion in Mexico Takes Hundreds of U.S. Jobs South," Copley News Service, April 12, 2003.

17. "Border Boom Town: Businesses Targeting McAllen as Trade Soars," October 11, 1992.

18. Simon Romero, "Mexican Wealth Give Texas City a New Vitality," *New York Times*, June 14, 2003.

19. Sharyland Plantation website: http://www.sharylandplantation.com/about_history.aspx.

20. Interview with Stephen W. Spivey, June 27, 2003; Stephen H. Lee, "Bicultural Border Boomtown Seen for Texas, Mexico," *Dallas Morning News*, December 10, 1998.

21. William H. Frey, "Population Growth in Metro America since 1980: Putting the Volatile 2000s in Perspective," Brookings Institution, Metropolitan Policy Program (March 2012); U.S. Department of Housing and Urban Development, HUD State of the Cities Data System (SOCDS) (http://www.huduser.org/portal/datasets/socds.html). In a report that included smaller metropolitan areas, McAllen-Edinburg-Mission (48.5 percent) was fourth behind Las Vegas (85.5 percent); Naples, Florida (65.3 percent); and Yuma, Arizona (49.7 percent) in population growth in the 1990s. Marc J. Perry and Paul J. Mackun, "Population Change and Distribution, Census 2000 Brief," U.S. Census Bureau (April 2001).

22. Bonnie Pfiste, "Bucking the Statewide Trend: Border Sees Job Growth, McAllen Leads State with 5,100 Positions Created in Past Year," *San Antonio Express-News*, November 19, 2002.

23. Romero, "Mexican Wealth Give Texas City a New Vitality," June 14, 2003.

24. U.S. Census Bureau's FactFinder (Census Tract 020402) (http://factfinder2.census.gov/faces/nav/jsf/pages/index.xhtml).

25. Romero, "Mexican Wealth Give Texas City a New Vitality," June 14, 2003; U.S. Census Bureau's FactFinder.

26. Chad Richardson and José A. Pagán, "Human and Social Aspects of Cross-Border Development in the McAllen/Reynosa Area," Working Paper 2002-9, Center of Border Economic Studies, The University of Texas-Pan American, October 2002; Roanoke Valley-Alleghany Regional Commission, "National Ranking from the 2000 United States Census Bureau: A Demographic Comparison between the Roanoke Valley Alleghany Region and Other Counties and Cities in the United States," 2005. There were 331 Metropolitan Statistical Areas (MSAs) in the 2000 census. The McAllen MSA had the second highest ranking in percent youth, average household size, and percent minority, and the fourth highest ranking in percent noncitizen.

27. Attorney General of Texas website: https://maps.oag.state.tx.us/colgeog/colgeog_online.html#; John Henneberger, Kristin Carlisle, and Karen Paup, "Housing in Texas Colonias," *The Colonias Reader: Economy, Housing, and Public Health in U.S.-Mexico Border Colonias*. Edited by Angela J. Donelson and Adrian X. Esparza, p. 102. Tucson: University of Arizona Press, 2010; Angela J. Donelson and Adrian X. Esparza, "Introduction," *The Colonias Reader: Economy, Housing, and Public Health*

in U.S.-Mexico Border Colonias. Edited by Angela J. Donelson and Adrian X. Esparza, p. 4. Tucson: University of Arizona Press, 2010; Federal Reserve Bank of Dallas, "Texas Colonias: A Thumbnail Sketch of the Conditions, Issues, Challenges and Opportunities," Community Affairs Office of the Federal Reserve Bank of Dallas, January 1997; Richardson and Pagán, "Human and Social Aspects of Cross-Border Development in the McAllen/Reynosa Area," October 2002; Leda Perez and Jacqueline Martinez, "Community Health Workers: Social Justice and Policy Advocates for Community Health and Well-Being," *American Journal of Public Health* 98 (2008): 11–14.

28. Jorge Chapa and David J. Eaton, *Colonia Housing and Infrastructure.* Austin: University of Texas, LBJ School of Public Affairs, 1997. Interestingly, the MSA statistical rankings mentioned above do not rank the McAllen MSA highly in the percentage of people that have moved into the area in the past five years. Roanoke Valley-Alleghany Regional Commission, 2005, "National Ranking from the 2000 United States Census Bureau," 2005.

29. Richardson and Pagán, "Human and Social Aspects of Cross-Border Development in the McAllen/Reynosa Area," October 2002. Families here are generally of mixed immigration status. Between couples and within families are U.S. citizens, legal residents, quasi-legal "guests," and the undocumented. Although many are officially unemployed, one survey found that in actuality very few are "mainly unemployed."

30. Richardson and Pagán, "Human and Social Aspects of Cross-Border Development in the McAllen/Reynosa Area," pp. 18–19, October 2002.

31. Karl Marx and Friedrich Engels, "Manifesto of the Communist Party," *The Marx-Engels Reader.* 2nd ed. Edited by Robert C. Tucker, p. 476. New York: Norton, 1978. Originally published in 1848.

CHAPTER 6

1. Of the final 900 Maytag workers laid off in 2004, 45 percent were women.

2. David Hotle, "Union President Calls for Maytag Boycott," *The Register-Mail*, May 8, 2003.

3. Tom Nelson, "Maytag Workers Union Plans Rally at Shareholders Meeting," *The Register-Mail*, April 24, 2003. Illinois Governor Rod Blagojevich was invited but did not attend.

4. Tom Nelson and David Hotle, "Other Maytag Locales Wonder, Who's Next? Amana, Newton, Herrin Workers Are Concerned," *The Register-Mail*, May 10, 2003.

5. Tom Nelson, "Closing Arguments" and "Hake's Take: Workers Not at Fault for GRP's Faults; Maytag CEO Says Design Platform Created Quality Concerns," *The Register-Mail*, May 9, 2003.

6. David Hotle, "Union Rallyers: Work's Just the Beginning," *The Register-Mail*, May 9, 2003.

7. Jessica L. Aberle, "Bomb Threats by Disgruntled Ex-Butler Worker," *Copley News Service*, November 19, 2003; John Pulliam, "Butler Lays Off Another 72 Workers: No

More Layoffs Scheduled Now, Plant Manager Says," *The Register-Mail*, November 24, 2003; Tammy Bould, "Maytag Worker Arrested after Chase: Man Had Unloaded Weapon in His Car," *The Register-Mail*, November 19, 2002; Tammy Bould, "Maytag Worker's Gun Was Loaded: Police Report Says Five Rounds Were Found in Weapon," *The Register-Mail*, November 20, 2002.

8. Joe Krejci's perspectives come from interviews in 2004 and 2011.

9. Tom Nelson, "Study: Maytag Closing to Have Huge Ripple Effect: Thousands of Other Jobs, in Many Sectors, Will Be Affected," *The Register-Mail*, January 27, 2003. Maytag payroll was $61 million. The study said the appliance industry accounted for 7.7 percent of employment in Knox County and 12.2 percent of total value-added. In addition to 1,600 Maytag workers, there would be 575 "indirect" job losses—when Maytag stopped buying goods and services locally—and 1,475 "induced" job losses, or "ripple effect," causalities. When modeled against the boom year of 1999 when Maytag CEO Hadley left, the region would face a predicted total loss of 5,617 jobs. Knox County, population 56,427, would endure the brunt of this impact.

10. Michael V. Copeland, "Stuck in the Spin Cycle: Maytag, the All-American Appliance Icon, Is Learning a Dangerous Lesson: You Can't Manage a Turnaround Just by Managing Costs," *Business 2.0 Magazine*, CNNMoney.com [http://money.cnn.com/magazines/business2/business2_archive/2005/05/01/8259675/] May 1, 2005; Don Durfee, "The Top Spot: Why More Companies Are Tapping Their Finance Chief for CEO," *CFO Magazine*, October 2005; Don Cooper, "Maytag CEO Doesn't Deserve Golden Parachute," *The Register-Mail*, April 5, 2006. Hake's inability to inspire was a weakness that Whirlpool's board had perhaps seen when it passed over Hake for the Whirlpool CEO position. When Maytag tapped Hake two years later, it joined a trend wherein Chief Financial Officers were increasingly assuming CEO chairs in major corporations because of their experience talking to Wall Street and their emphasis on shareholder value and return on investment.

11. This account, including all quotations, was constructed from observations, informal interviews at the event, transcribed audio recordings of the speeches, and two newspaper accounts: David Hotle, "Labor Rally Stirs Hope for Future," *The Register-Mail*, September 5, 2004; Tammy Bould, "Hundreds Attend Rally," *The Register-Mail*, September 5, 2004. See "Notes on Method" for more on methodology.

12. Tom Nelson, "Maytag Threatens Herrin, Amana Jobs: Wants IAM President to Back Down on Boycott Call," *The Register-Mail*, June 8, 2003.

13. David Brooks, PBS coverage of the 2004 Democratic National Convention, July 27, 2004.

14. Hotle, "Labor Rally Stirs Hope for Future," September 5, 2004.

CHAPTER 7

1. Laura Flora's story, including all quotations in this and subsequent chapters, was constructed from several conversations in both 2007 and 2013, all of which were translated and transcribed. In 2013 we established a Facebook connection that was helpful

in checking facts and providing further details. See "Notes on Method" for more on methodology.

2. Virgilio Partida Bush and Miguel Ángel Martínez Herrera, "Migración Interna," *La Situación Demográfica de México 2006,"* p. 181. México, D.F.: Consejo Nacional de Población, December 2006. The claim that the Veracruz-Tamaulipas flow is strongest is true if we exclude interstate movement between the states comprising the Mexico City megapolis (Distrito Federal and Estado de México). The population in Veracruz was partly replenished by 192,599 immigrants *into* Veracruz in the decade after NAFTA. Still, Veracruz had the highest net out-migration rate (again, other than Distrito Federal, which lost people to suburban and exurban states on its immediate periphery).

3. Jorge Durand, Douglas S. Massey, and Rene M. Zenteno, "Mexican Immigration to the United States: Continuities and Changes," *Latin American Research Review* 36.1 (2001): 108; Tessie Borden and Sergio Bustos, "Hurt by NAFTA, Mexican Farmers Head North," *The Arizona Republic,* July 27, 2003; Raúl Romo Viramontes, Leticia Ruiz Guzmán, and Mónica Velázquez Isidro, "El Papel de la Migración en el Crecimiento de la Población: Análisis de Los Componentes de la Dinámica Demográfica a Nivel Entidad Federativa, 2000-2010," in *La Situación Demográfica de México 2011,* pp. 195, 198. México, D.F.: Consejo Nacional de Población, November 2011; *Perfil Sociodemográfico de Veracruz de Ignacio de la Llave,* p. 47. Instituto Nacional de Estadística, Geografía e Informática, 2008.

4. David Spener and Kathleen Staudt, "The View from the Frontier: Theoretical Perspectives Undisciplined," *The U.S.-Mexico Border: Transcending Divisions, Contesting Identities.* Edited by David Spener and Kathleen Staudt, p. 3. Boulder, CO: Lynne Rienner, 1998.

5. Our visit to the Papantla region of northern Veracruz took place in the summer of 2007. I was accompanied by Josh Walsman (translator) and David Samuel Stern (photographer). See "Notes on Method" for a detailed account of the Mexico-side fieldwork.

6. "Plan Municipal de Desarrollo, 2011-2013," p. 24. Papantla H. Ayuntamiento Constitucional, 2011-2013.

7. Among states with the highest rural populations—Veracruz, Chiapas, Oaxaca, Puebla, Guanjuanto, Guerrero, and others—Veracruzanos were now the most likely to live in a depopulating area. *Vecinos* (neighbors) from the nearby state of Puebla replenished some of the working-age deserters. But in recent years in Agua Dulce, maintained Mayor Gonzalez, many more had left than entered. Jorge Durand, Douglas S. Massey, and Rene M. Zenteno, "Mexican Immigration to the United States: Continuities and Changes," p. 108; Dolores Acevedo and Thomas J. Espenshade, "Implications of a North American Free Trade Agreement for Mexican Migration into the United States," *Population and Development Review* 18.4 (December 1992): 732; Octavio Mojarro and Germán Benítez, "El Despoblamiento de los Municipios Rurales de México, 2000-2005." *La Situación Demográfica de México 2010,* pp. 189–191. Consejo Nacional de Población, November 2010.

8. Alejandro Nadal, "The Environmental and Social Impacts of Economic Liberalization on Corn Production in Mexico," p. 27. A Study Commissioned by Oxfam GB and

WWF International, September 2000; Karen Hansen-Kuhn, "Making U.S. Trade Policy Serve Global Food Security Goals," *Sustainable Development Law & Policy* 11.3 (Spring 2011); "May 10 'Deal' Does not Alter Peru and Panama FTA NAFTA-style Agriculture Rules that Promote Hunger, Destruction of Legal Rural Livelihoods and Displacement," *Public Citizen*, May 10, 2007: http://www.citizen.org/publications/index.cfm.

9. Since the early 1990s, crop insurance, guaranteed prices, technical and marketing support, subsidies for electricity and fertilizer, and credit for small farmers had been reduced or eliminated. In Volador, another village in the Papantla municipality, a field laborer said that there were some supports for housing and roofing but there is a cost for the materials—despite the fact that local officials got them for free. In parts of rural Mexico, the administration of these state supports was notoriously corrupt, but they were supports nonetheless. Gerardo Otero, "Review: Neoliberal Reform in Rural Mexico: Social Structural and Political Dimensions," *Latin American Research Review* 35.1 (2000): 187–207; Thomas J. Kelly, "Neoliberal Reforms and Rural Poverty," *Latin American Perspectives* 28.3 (May 2001): 90; Marilyn Gates, "Debt Crisis and Economic Restructuring: Prospects for Mexican Agriculture," *Neoliberalism Revisited: Economic Restructuring and Mexico's Political Future*. Edited by Gerardo Otero, pp. 43–68. Boulder, CO: Westview, 1996; Interview with René de la Cruz, Rural Development, translated by Cecilia Chapa, course material available at: https://courses.cit.cornell.edu/iard4010/topic4/index.html.

10. Timothy A. Wise, "Agricultural Dumping Under NAFTA: Estimating the Costs of U.S. Agricultural Policies to Mexican Producers," pp. 19–24. Washington, DC: Woodrow Wilson International Center for Scholars, Mexican Rural Development Research Reports, Report 7, 2010. The U.S. $99 per hectare figure represents the average income losses for a corn farmer as a result of the "dumping margin," the difference between the export price and its cost of production. The average dumping margin for U.S. corn in Mexico was 19 percent from 1997 to 2005 (meaning U.S. farmers sold corn for, on average, 19 percent less than it cost them to produce it). Wise estimates this dumping margin cost Mexican producers as a whole $6.6 billion over that time period.

11. Gisele Henriques and Raj Patel, "NAFTA, Corn, and Mexico's Agricultural Trade Liberalization," Americas Program. Silver City, NM: Interhemispheric Resource Center, January 28, 2004; Nadal, "The Environmental and Social Impacts of Economic Liberalization on Corn Production in Mexico," pp. 8–11, September 2000. According to Nadal, over 80 percent of corn cultivation is rain-fed rather than irrigated and 40 percent of corn producers are subsistence farmers that produce no surplus. Small farmers with less than five hectares make up 45 percent of corn growers in Mexico. Further, 60 percent of all cultivated land in Mexico was for corn production.

12. Wise, "Agricultural Dumping Under NAFTA," p. 19; Oxfam International, "Dumping without Borders: How U.S. Agricultural Policies Are Destroying the Livelihoods of Mexican Corn Farmers," p. 20. Oxfam Briefing Paper, August, 2003; Marceline White, "Look FIRST from a Gender Perspective: NAFTA and the FTAA," *Gender and Development* 12.2 (2004): 49; Acevedo and Espenshade, "Implications of a North American Free Trade Agreement for Mexican Migration into the United States," p. 732.

13. Wise, "Agricultural Dumping Under NAFTA."

14. Alejandro Nadal, "Corn in NAFTA: Eight Years After." Science, Technology and Development Program, El Colegio de México, Research Report for the North American Commission for Environmental Cooperation, May 2002; Henriques and Patel, "NAFTA, Corn, and Mexico's Agricultural Trade Liberalization," January 28, 2004; Amanda King, "Ten Years with NAFTA: A Review of the Literature and an Analysis of Farmer Responses in Sonora and Veracruz, Mexico," pp. 4, 33, CIMMYT (International Maize and Wheat Improvement Center) Special Report 06-01 with the Congressional Hunger Center, 2006; Steven Zahniser, "NAFTA at 13: Implementation Nears Completion," p. 13, Economic Research Service, U.S. Department of Agriculture, March 2007; Ana de Ita, "Fourteen Years of NAFTA and the Tortilla Crisis," Americas Program Special Report, January 10, 2008.

15. Aslihan Arslan and J. Edward Taylor, "Farmers' Subjective Valuation of Subsistence Crops: The Case of Traditional Maize in Mexico," *American Journal of Agricultural Economics* 91.4 (November 2009): 956–972.

16. Nadal, "The Environmental and Social Impacts of Economic Liberalization on Corn Production in Mexico," p. 41. This figure does not include those indirectly tied to corn production like those in storage, transportation, trade, tortilla making, and more. Nadal's estimate simply multiples the 3 million-plus corn-producing units times the average rural household size (six) to get 18 million.

17. Arslan and Taylor, "Farmers' Subjective Valuation of Subsistence Crops," 956–972; Claire Hope Cummings, "Risking Corn, Risking Culture," World Watch Magazine, November/December 2002.

18. King, "Ten Years with NAFTA," p. 40. According to King, Zona Totonaca encompasses Papantla del Orlarte and ten other, smaller surrounding municipalities. In addition to Totonacos, there are Huastecos, Tepehuas, Otomíes, Popolucas, Mixtecos, Zapotecos, Mixes, Nahuas, Chinatecos, Mazatecos, and Zoques in the area.

19. Steven Zahniser and Andrew Roe, "NAFTA at 17: Full Implementation Leads to Increased Trade and Integration," p. 32. Economic Research Service, U.S. Department of Agriculture, March 2011.

20. Eight hectares was the average parcel size in Agua Dulce's ejido, one of 29,942 ejidos covering over half of Mexico's agricultural lands. "Mexico, NAFTA, and Agriculture: A Snapshot," p. 12. U.S. Department of Agriculture, Global Agriculture Information Network (GAIN) Report, 2006.

21. Thomas H. Spreen, Mark G. Brown, and Jonq-Ying Lee, "The Impact of NAFTA on U.S. Imports of Mexican Orange Juice," p. 3. Paper presented at the Tri-National Research Symposium, San Antonio, Texas, November 1996; Dulce Flores, "Annual Citrus Report 1995," pp. 4, 7. USDA Foreign Agricultural Service, American Embassy, Mexico City, Mexico, Report MX5072, November 13, 1995.

22. Dulce Flores and Mark Ford, "Mexico Citrus, Citrus Report 2008," p. 11. USDA Foreign Agricultural Service, American Embassy, Mexico City, Mexico, Report MX8078, November 25, 2008. The Foreign Agricultural Service GAIN (Global Agriculture Information Network) reports of the USDA of citrus production in Mexico, starting in 1995, provide producer prices, labor costs, input costs,

average yields by region, and other information germane to making these estimates.

23. Mongabay Commodity Prices: http://data.mongabay.com/commodities/category/3-Pr../11-Prices/490-Oranges/60-Producer+Price+%28USD%7Ct onne%29/138-Mexico. Gonzalez and Cruz's estimates—along with those of Volador's mayor, Aaron Barrera—were consistent with these commodity prices.

24. Flores and Ford, "Mexico Citrus, Citrus Report 2008," p. 10; Dulce Flores and Gabriel Hernandez, "Mexico Citrus, Citrus Report 2002," p. 13. USDA Foreign Agricultural Service, American Embassy, Mexico City, Mexico, Report MX2162, November 27, 2002; Dulce Flores, "Mexico Citrus, Citrus Report 1998," p. 2. USDA Foreign Agricultural Service, American Embassy, Mexico City, Mexico, Report MX8139, November 16, 1998.

25. Flores and Ford, "Mexico Citrus, Citrus Report 2008," p. 11.

26. Cruz said that for a month or two at harvest time, if workers could fill twenty or thirty 25-kilogram boxes of limes in a day, they could make good money. At 20 pesos ($1.80) for each box, an efficient harvester could earn 400 ($36) per day.

27. Mexico imported about as many oranges from the United States as it exported to the United States. Flores and Ford, "Mexico Citrus, Citrus Report 2008," p. 8; Richard Beilock, Ramon Espinel, and Sikavas Naampang, "The Non-event of Produce and NAFTA," The Estey Centre Journal of International Law and Trade Policy 3.1 (2002): 155; Julie V. Stanton, "Potential Entry of Chile into NAFTA: Are There Lessons from U.S./Mexican Fruit and Vegetable Trade?" *Review of Agricultural Economics* 21.1 (Spring/Summer 1999): 114.

28. King, "Ten Years with NAFTA," p. 29. Citrus had a 15-year import tariff phase-out to protect U.S. citrus growers and a snapback provision, which reinstated tariffs under certain price and trade volume conditions.

29. Ibid.

30. Louis Uchitelle, "Nafta Should Have Stopped Illegal Immigration, Right?" *New York Times*, February 18, 2007.

31. David Williams and Gabriel Hernandez, "Mexico Agricultural Situation: Mexico, NAFTA, and Agriculture, A Snapshot," p. 5. USDA Foreign Agricultural Service, American Embassy, Mexico City, Mexico, Report MX6060, July 27, 2006; Timothy A. Wise, "Small-Scale Farmers and Development: Assume a Different Economic Model." Global Development and Environment Institute, Globalization Commentaries, September 27, 2010.

32. Stanton, "Potential Entry of Chile into NAFTA," p. 114. Also, low production volumes made small-scale farm unattractive for investment because of high transaction costs. One ejido-based producers' group developed a citrus-processing project (for making orange juice) so that orange growers could avoid the problem of market gluts and low orange prices (King, "Ten Years with NAFTA," p. 29).

33. Uchitelle, "Nafta Should Have Stopped Illegal Immigration, Right?" February 18, 2007.

34. Interview with Everardo Elizondo, May 10, 2013.

35. D'Vera Cohn, Ana Gonzalez-Barrera, and Danielle Cuddington, "Remittances to Latin America Recover—But Not to Mexico," p. 4. Pew Research Center, Washington, DC, November 15, 2013; Jesus Cañas, Roberto Coronado, and Pia M. Orrenius, "Explaining the Increase in Remittances to Mexico," Federal Reserve of Dallas, Southwest Economy, July/August 2007.

36. For more on this topic, refer to David Fitzgerald, *A Nation of Emigrants: How Mexico Manages Its Migration.* Berkeley: University of California Press, 2008.

37. Peter S. Goodman, "In Mexico, 'People Do Really Want to Stay': Chicken Farmers Fear U.S. Exports Will Send More Workers North for Jobs," *Washington Post,* January 14, 2007.

38. Among ejidatarios, 41 percent sell something to meet liquidity needs. De Ita, "Fourteen Years of NAFTA and the Tortilla Crisis," January 10, 2008.

CHAPTER 8

1. Dave Carpenter, "Sharp Jobs Declines Hammers State: More than 150,000 Illinois Manufacturing Jobs Lost since June 2000," *Peoria Journal Star* (Associated Press), November 30, 2003; Neil Irwin, "Aughts Were a Lost Decade for U.S. Economy, Workers," *Washington Post,* January 2, 2010. Over a longer time period, from June 1998 to February 2005, Illinois lost 224,000 manufacturing jobs. Other Rust Belt states that lost over 20 percent of their manufacturing jobs include Michigan, Ohio, and Pennsylvania. Some non–Rust Belt states, such as Washington, Mississippi, Oklahoma, and Virginia, lost over 20 percent as well. It was a devastating period for manufacturing across the country ("The State Crisis: Manufacturing Jobs Lost," AFL-CIO graphic, 2005).

2. Kylee Norville, "Former Maytag Workers Mourn a Loss of Community," Knox News Team in *The Register-Mail,* March 13, 2011. According to the article, former Maytag employees had very strong social ties in the factory: "82 percent of those who responded answered that they strongly identified with their co-workers and that they were almost like family. Similarly, 85 percent of respondents said they miss or really miss their former co-workers. Only 12 percent said they hardly miss former co-workers and a mere 2 percent said they didn't miss their former co-workers at all." These statistics are from the 2010 Maytag Employees in Transition survey conducted as part of the Maytag Project at Knox College led by Marilyn Webb.

3. David Hotle, "Factory Falls Silent Thursday: Workers Prepare for the Next Phase," *The Register-Mail,* September 17, 2004.

4. Galesburg Public Library, "Galesburg Coulter Disc Company," archival photograph and captions, c. 1910; Galesburg Public Library, "Galesburg Coulter Disc Company day crew," archival photograph and captions, August 20, 1929; Sherman M. Sweeney, "History of Maytag Galesburg Refrigeration Products," Mississippi Valley Chapter 123, Presented to American Society of Heating, Refrigeration and Air-Conditioning Engineers, Inc. in St. Louis, Missouri, April 1995. Available at: http://www.mississippivalleyashrae.org/history/maytag.pdf.

5. In 1950, when Admiral purchased the factory, refrigeration engineers and technicians were brought to Galesburg. Prior to that, Midwest Manufacturing made only the cabinets and sent them elsewhere for final assembly.

6. Mike Kroll, "Property Tax Problems Looming Yet Again: Maytag Strikes Again," *The Zephyr*, February 2005; David Hotle, "Maytag Will Get Property Tax Refund: Assessment Appeal Settled; Taxing Bodies Will Lose Funds This Year," *The Register-Mail*, February 13, 2003; Tom Nelson, "Maytag Exit Cuts Tax Revenue: City, County, Schools All Will Be Getting Less as a Result," *The Register-Mail*, November 10, 2002.

7. A. B. Funk, *Fred L. Maytag: A Biography*, p. 94. Cedar Rapids, IA: The Torch Press, 1936.

8. International Association of Machinists and Aerospace Workers Local 2063, Meeting Notes, September 9, 2003 to February 8, 2005.

9. Elizabeth Becker, "04 Trade Deficit Sets Record, $617 Billion," *New York Times*, February 11, 2005; Hollie Shaw, "Wal-Mart Closes First Union Store in Quebec Store: Cites Lack of Profit," *National Post*, February 10, 2005.

10. Angela Barnes, "The Maytag Repairman Sure Has His Work Cut Out; Appliance Maker's Bleak Outlook Have Some Wondering about Its Viability," *The Globe and Mail* (Canada), April 26, 2005; Don Cooper, "Maytag CEO's Bountiful Severance Package Awaits," *The Register-Mail*, October 4, 2005; David Barboza, "From China, a New Bid for Maytag and Status," *New York Times*, June 22, 2005; David Marcus, "A Sale to Stop the Bleeding," *Corporate Control Alert*, August 2005; Mark Tatge, "Maytag's Repairman," February 19, 2003 (http://www.forbes.com/2003/02/19/cz_mt_0219maytag.html); Michael V. Copeland, "Stuck in the Spin Cycle: Maytag, the All-American Appliance Icon, Is Learning a Dangerous Lesson: You Can't Manage a Turnaround Just by Managing Costs," *Business 2.0 Magazine*, CNNMoney.com, May 1, 2005.

11. *Yellen v. Hake*, Case 4:05-cv-00388-RP-TJS, District Court for the Southern District of Iowa Central Division, filed July 7, 2006; Associated Press, "Maytag Faces Lawsuit; 2 Executives Allegedly Misled the Public about the Company's Business Outlook," *Telegraph–Herald*, Dubuque, Iowa, July 7, 2005; David Pitt, "Judge Dismisses Lawsuit against Former Maytag CEO Ralph Hake, Others," Associated Press, July 11, 2006; Jennifer Reingold, "CEO See-Ya!" *Fast Company*, August 2005.

12. Barboza, "From China, A New Bid for Maytag and Status," June 22, 2005.

13. Kelly Spors, "Against the Grain: A Chinese Appliance Maker Has Placed Its Bet on a Counterintuitive Strategy: It's Bringing Jobs to the U.S." *Wall Street Journal*, World Business (A Special Report), October 1, 2004.

14. International Association of Machinists and Aerospace Workers website: http://www.goiam.org/index.php/headquarters/history-of-the-iam.

15. Bruce Nissen, "Wage Losses and Union Decline: 1980s through the Early 2000s," *Encyclopedia of United States Labor and Working-Class History*. Edited by Eric Arnesen, pp. 1471–1479. New York: Routledge, 2007. The IAMAW was down from over one million in the late 1970s to 610,605 in 2004. UAW membership declined from 1.4 million in the 1970s to 654,657 in 2004. The USWA was down from over one million to 535,461 in 2004.

16. Barry T. Hirsch and David A. Macpherson, "Union Membership, Coverage, Density, and Employment among Public Sector Workers, 1973–2010," Union Membership and Coverage Database from the CPS (http://www.unionstats.com/); Barry T. Hirsch, David A. Macpherson, and Wayne G. Vroman, 2011, "State Union Membership Density, 1964-2010," Union Membership and Coverage Database from the CPS (http://www.unionstats.com).

17. U.S. Bureau of Labor Statistics, "Union Members Summary," Economic News Release, January 24, 2014.

18. Robert D. Putnam, *Bowling Alone: The Collapse and Revival of American Community.* New York: Simon and Schuster 2000.

19. Costas Panagopoulos and Peter L. Francia, "The Polls—Trends: Labor Unions in the United States," *Public Opinion Quarterly* 72.1 (2008): 139.

20. Megan Thee, "Poll: Record High for Wrong-Track Rating," *New York Times*, October 14, 2008, *The Caucus: The Politics and Government Blog of The Times.*

CHAPTER 9

1. Consejo Nacional de Evaluación de la Política de Desarrollo Social, "Informe de Evaluacion de la Politica de Desarrollo Social en México 2008," pp. 14, 18. México, D.F.: Consejo Nacional de Población, 2008.

2. Tim Knapp and John Harms, "When the Screen Goes Blank: A Television Plant Closing and Its Impact on Workers," *Sociological Quarterly* 43.2 (Autumn 2002): 611; Victoria A. Hirschberg, "The City as a Growth Machine: Reynosa, Mexico," p. 38. Master's thesis, The University of New Mexico, December 2009; Susana Hayward, "Made in Mexico? Adios, Jobs; Cheap Labor Lures U.S. Firms South," Associated Press in the *Chicago Sun-Times*, May 25, 1992; "U.S. Firms Descend on Mexico," *Las Vegas Review-Journal*, May 18, 1992; Sam Quiñones, "In Living Color," *Latin Trade* 11.1 (January 2003): 50; INEGI (Instituto Nacional de Estadística y Geografía), Banco de Información Economica, http://www.inegi.org.mx/sistemas/bie/. Overall maquila employment evened between men and women in 2001.

3. Knapp and Harms, "When the Screen Goes Blank," p. 611.

4. Jesús Cañas, Roberto A. Coronado, Robert W. Gilmer, and Eduardo Saucedo, "The Impact of the Maquiladora Industry on U.S. Border Cities," Working Paper 1107, p. 24. Federal Reserve Bank of Dallas, Research Department, May 17, 2011.

5. INEGI (Instituto Nacional de Estadística y Geografía): http://www.inegi.org.mx. The maquiladora during this period became a fixture of the Mexican economy. The percentage of Mexican manufacturing represented by the maquilas had grown from 7 percent in 1985 to 35 percent in 2000 (John H. Christman, Global Insight, "Mexico's Maquiladora Industry Outlook, 2004–2009." Presented at "Framing the Future: Tomorrow's Border Economy," Federal Reserve Bank of Dallas—El Paso and San Antonio Branches, December 3, 2004).

6. John Sargent, "Charter Evolution in Maquiladoras: A Case Study of Reynosa, Tamaulipas," Working Paper 2003-16, Center of Border Economic Studies, The University of Texas-Pan American, January 2003; Bonnie Pfister, "Bucking the Statewide Trend, Border Sees Job Growth, McAllen Leads State with 5,100 Positions Created in Past Year," *San Antonio Express-News*, November 19, 2002; "Texas Border Economy," Presentation by Robert W. Gilmer, Vice President and Senior Economist, Federal Reserve Bank of Dallas, 2009.

7. Cañas, et al., "The Impact of the Maquiladora Industry on U.S. Border Cities," May 17, 2011.

8. Sergio Peña, "Recent Developments in Urban Marginality along Mexico's Northern Border," Habitat International 29 (2005): 285–301; Christman, "Mexico's Maquiladora Industry Outlook, 2004–2009," December 3, 2004; S. Lynne Walker, "With Mexico Venture, Maytag Goes with the Flow," Copley News Service, April 13, 2003.

9. Portions of this paragraph originally appeared in Chad Broughton, "The World at the U.S.-Mexican Border," *Contexts* (Winter 2010).

10. All of the pay estimates in this section are based on several itemized paystubs given to us by Maytag workers. Other sources on pay, including a CFO report, Ed Krueger, Herber Ramírez and several other interviews, confirmed that the amounts in the paystubs were typical of maquila paystubs throughout the sector.

11. Two examples: S. Lynne Walker, "Maytag Plant Expansion in Mexico Takes Hundreds of U.S. Jobs South," Copley News Service, April 12, 2003; Steven Greenhouse, "City Feels Early Effects of Plant Closing in 2004," *New York Times*, December 26, 2004. This sort of reporting (hourly wage in the United States compared to a benefits-loaded and otherwise exaggerated wage in Mexico) understates the wage gap—and how much it drives immigration—significantly.

12. Steve Ingham was interviewed by John David, reporter for WQAD-8 (Moline, Illinois), as part of our collaborative excursion to Reynosa in December 2004.

13. I originally published Pablo Lara Sanchez's story in Chad Broughton, "Maytag Refrigerators Roll out of Mexico," *The Register-Mail*, February 6, 2005, using the pseudonym "Diego Sanchez." At the time Lara was concerned about repercussions from Maytag.

14. Regarding the claim about flat wages in Mexico see Figure 9.4; "Maquiladora Industry: Past, Present, and Future," El Paso Business Frontier, Issue 2 (2002), Federal Reserve Bank of Dallas (El Paso Branch); and Nacha Cattan and Eric Martin, "Stagnant Wages May Decide Mexico's Election," Bloomberg BusinessWeek, June 21, 2012.

15. Consejo Nacional de Evaluación de la Política de Desarrollo Social, "Informe de Evaluacion de la Politica de Desarrollo Social en México 2008," p. 14. For peso to dollar conversions I used the 2004 exchange rate of 1 peso = .09 dollars and rounded to nearest 25-cent increment.

16. Steve Ingham was interviewed by John David, reporter for WQAD-8 (Moline, Illinois) as part of our collaborative excursion to Reynosa in December 2004; Jeri Penn, phone interview, December, 2004.

17. Other, non-maquila manufacturing workers in Mexico fared even worse. Their wages actually bought less in 2002 than in 1980. "Maquiladora Industry: Past, Present, and Future," *El Paso Business Frontier*, Issue 2 (2002). Federal Reserve Bank of Dallas (El Paso Branch).

18. INEGI (Instituto Nacional de Estadística y Geografía): http://www.inegi.org.mx. In this monthly data series, INEGI reported average wages earned in a month in pesos in Tamaulipas, adjusting the series to 2002 pesos to account for inflation. The wage data includes total received in earnings such as regular and overtime pay, in-kind payments such as food stamps and transportation stipends, and benefits such as housing support and vacation pay. Over this period, a maquila worker's hourly take-home earnings could be considerably less. To get the hourly wage in dollars, I took the average of each year's monthly wages, converted to dollars, converted the monthly rate to the weekly rate, and then divided by 48 hours. INEGI stopped this data series in early 2007.

19. Comité Fronterizo de Obreras, "Six Years of NAFTA: A View from Inside the Maquiladoras," October 1999. Issued by the CFO in cooperation with the U.S.-Mexico Border Program of the American Friends Service Committee.

I originally published María Elena García's perspectives in the newspaper series, Chad Broughton, "Reynosa: City of Promise and Poverty," *The Register-Mail*, September 26–29, 2003, using the pseudonym "Rosa Nuñez."

20. Chad Broughton, "The Cost of Living in Reynosa," *The Register-Mail*, September 28, 2003.

21. The currency conversion rates I use changes based on year of fieldwork from which I report.

22. Comité Fronterizo de Obreras, "Los Trabajadores y Maytag," February 17, 2005, http://www.cfomaquiladoras.org/trabajadoresymaytag.es.html.

23. INEGI (Instituto Nacional de Estadística y Geografía), Banco de Información INEGI, http://www3.inegi.org.mx/sistemas/biinegi/default.aspx. From 1990 to 2005 the official population grew from 282,667 to 526,888, an average of 16,281 per year, or 44.6 per day.

24. Ibid. The population dispute may have been, in part, political posturing between rival political parties (PRI in Reynosa and PAN in Mexico City), but it was very difficult to settle satisfactorily. Although the official count stood at 526,888 in 2005, municipal officials in Reynosa pointed to the IMSS (social security) database to make a population estimate exceeding 1.5 million in the late 2000s. Those officials argue, in our interviews and in the Mexican press, that the federal government purposefully underestimates border populations to lessen the federal fiscal responsibility for the massive infrastructure needs (Marco Esquivel, "INEGI contó mal en Reynosa: Alcalde," *Hoy Tamaulipas*, December 4, 2011).

25. José A Tijerina and Antonio Medellín, "Fortalecimiento de los ingresos de los gobiernos estatales en México," Centro de Análisis y Difusión Económica, Documento de Investigación No. 3 (December). Monterrey: Centro de Análisis y Difusión Económica, 1998.

26. Infrastructure development is arguably *the* essential ingredient for leveraging economic integration and broadening its benefits. One study found that infrastructure deficits accounted for a third of the difference in productivity between Latin America and East Asia (Luis Serven and William E. Easterly, eds. *The Limits of Stabilization: Infrastructure, Public Deficits and Growth in Latin America*. Palo Alto, CA: Stanford University Press, 2003). Another study shows how "infrastructure disadvantages in these states [in Mexico's south] were amplified by the move from import substitution industrialization to trade openness in Mexico." That is, structural disadvantages are amplified, not flattened in a free trade, free market regime (Marcela González Rivas, "Trade Openness, Infrastructure, and the Wellbeing of Mexico's South," *Mexican Studies/Estudios Mexicanos* 27.2 (Summer 2011): 407–429).

27. INEGI (Instituto Nacional de Estadística y Geografía), Banco de Información INEGI, http://www3.inegi.org.mx/sistemas/biinegi/default.aspx. Official population growth from 2000 to 2005 in Reynosa was 420,483 to 526,888, or 21,281 per year. Using Cantú's estimate of 4,000 to 5,000 housing units per year yields a growth-to-housing rate of between 4.26 and 5.32 to 1.

28. Chad Richardson and José A. Pagán, "Human and Social Aspects of Cross-Border Development in the McAllen/Reynosa Area," Working Paper 2002-9, pp. 67. Center of Border Economic Studies, The University of Texas-Pan American, October 2002.

29. Kylee Norville, "Former Maytag Workers Mourn a Loss of Community," Knox News Team in *The Register-Mail*, March 13, 2011. Michael Patrick noted that the enormous Maytag family picnics were supported by a tax on vending machines inside Appliance City and planned by a committee of union and management employees.

30. Interview with María Prieto, Director of Industrial Development in Reynosa, July 1, 2003. Freelance garbage collectors are also called *pepenadores*, although this term refers to waste recyclers that work garbage dumps. Lynn Brezosky, "Reynosa Hasn't Found Matamoros Success," *San Antonio Express-News*, January 13, 2008; Angela Orlando, "Mexico," Vol. 1, *Encyclopedia of Consumption and Waste: The Social Science of Garbage*. Edited by Carl A. Zimring, general editor, and William L. Rathje, consulting editor, pp. 535–536. Thousand Oaks, CA: SAGE, 2012.

CHAPTER 10

1. The quotation is from Fuentes' 1971 collection of essays, *Tiempo Mexicano*. Quotation from Julia Preston and Samuel Dillon, *Opening Mexico: The Making of a Democracy*, p. 33. New York: Farrar, Straus and Giroux, 2005.

2. One person said that white missionaries had been to the town a few decades earlier.

3. The verb Lucia used was "regalar" (to give or gift). Lucia said they sold the chiles for 80 pesos (about $7.25) a kilo, and the middlemen would turn around and sell them for $200 to $300 pesos (around $18 to $27). Barrera had slightly different estimates, but both suggested massive profits for coyotes.

4. Robert D. Putnam, *Bowling Alone: The Collapse and Revival of American Community*, p. 294. New York: Simon and Schuster, 2000.

5. "Plan Municipal de Desarrollo, 2011-2013," p. 24. Papantla H. Ayuntamiento Constitucional, 2011–2013.

6. Jonathan Fox, "How Does Civil Society Thicken? The Political Construction of Social Capital in Rural Mexico," *World Development* 24.6 (1996): 1091.

7. Elizabeth Fitting, "Importing Corn, Exporting Labor: The Neoliberal Corn Regime, GMOs, and the Erosion of Mexican Biodiversity," *Agriculture and Human Values* 23 (2006): 16; Christy Getz, "Social Capital, Organic Agriculture, and Sustainable Livelihood Security: Rethinking Agrarian Change in Mexico," *Rural Sociology* 73.4 (2008): 556, 559; Amanda King, "Ten Years with NAFTA: A Review of the Literature and an Analysis of Farmer Response in Sonora and Veracruz, Mexico," p. 31. CIMMYT (International Maize and Wheat Improvement Center) Special Report 06-01 with the Congressional Hunger Center, 2006.

8. Used in this context, "coyotes" refers to migration agents rather than market middlemen.

9. This account of the Papantla, Veracruz region's history is taken from Emilio Kourí, *A Pueblo Divided: Business, Property, and Community in Papantla, Mexico*. Stanford, CA: Stanford University Press, 2004.

10. Kourí cites Juan de Carrión, *Descripción del Pueblo de Gueytlalpan (Zacatlán, Juxupango, Matlaltan y Chila, Papantla), 30 de mayo de 1581 (Relación de Papantla)*. Edited by José García Payón. Xalapa, Mexico: Universidad Veracruzana, 1965.

11. Kourí, *Pueblo Divided*, pp. 111, 114–116, 120, 206.

12. Global trade, especially with the United States, and the pursuit of profit drove "progress" for the "backward" locals, not liberal ideology or the changes in the law. In 1897, a year after the Papantla rebellion, a local official spoke at a privatization ceremony. He told the assembled Indians, "You were ignorant of the inestimable good that the government through its wise laws wanted to do you, and, advised in bad faith by people who exploited your ignorance, you were led to embrace those fears and induced to commit the gravest crime of all, which is to rebel against a legitimate government. . . . Stay close to the government and you will never again have family tragedies or material losses to lament." Kourí, *Pueblo Divided*, pp. 275–276.

13. Willem Assies, "Land Tenure and Tenure Regimes in Mexico: An Overview," *Journal of Agrarian Change* 8.1 (2008): 38; John Mason Hart, *Revolutionary Mexico: The Coming and Process of the Mexican Revolution*, pp. 106–107. Berkeley: University of California Press, 1987.

14. John Foran, "Reinventing the Mexican Revolution: The Competing Paradigms of Alan Knight and John Mason Hart," *Latin American Perspectives* 23.4 (1996): 120.

15. Hart, *Revolutionary Mexico*, pp. 92, 160. Two land policies during the Porfiriato—the Decree on Colonization and Demarcation Companies of 1883 and the Law on the Occupation and Alienation of Barren Lands of 1894—encouraged U.S. involvement and land concentration. U.S. demarcation companies were employed by the Mexican government to identify land that could be sold to private parties. In payment for the 59 million hectares these companies demarcated, they received 20 million hectares, over 10 percent of Mexico's territory. The remaining 40 million hectares were acquired by wealthy landowners and mining and railway interests (Assies, "Land Tenure and Tenure Regimes in Mexico," p. 38).

16. Ana de Ita, "Land Concentration in Mexico after PROCEDE," *Promised Land: Competing Visions of Agrarian Reform*. Edited by Peter Rosset, Raj Patel, and Michael Courville, pp. 148–149. Institute for Food and Development Policy. Oakland, CA: Food First Books, 2006; Steven E. Sanderson, *Agrarian Populism and the Mexican State: The Struggle for Land in Sonora*, p. 43. Berkeley: University of California Press, 1981. Sanderson also notes that wages for the landless, mostly agricultural workers, dropped by 15 percent to 30 percent from 1877 to 1911. Friedrich Katz lecture on the Mexican Revolution at the University of Chicago, October 13, 2009; U.S. State Department Archive, "Punitive Expedition 1916–1917" (http://2001-2009.state.gov/r/pa/ho/time/wwi/108653.htm).

17. Alan Knight, "Land and Society in Revolutionary Mexico: The Destruction of the Great Haciendas," *Mexican Studies/Estudios Mexicanos* 7.1 (Winter 1991): 73–104.

18. U.S. Department of Agriculture, "Mexico, NAFTA, and Agriculture: A Snapshot," p. 12. Global Agriculture Information Network Report, 2006.

19. Raúl L. Madrid, *Retiring the State: The Politics of Pension Privatization in Latin America and Beyond*, pp. 71–72. Stanford, CA: Stanford University Press, 2003; David Harvey, *A Brief History of Neoliberalism*, pp. 99–100. Oxford: Oxford University Press, 2006; Nora Lustig, *Mexico: The Remaking of an Economy*, p. 120. Washington, DC: Brookings Institution Press, 1992. During de la Madrid's presidency, the proportion of protected, domestically manufactured products dropped from 93 percent in 1982 to 23 percent in 1988.

20. During his *sexenio* (six-year term), Salinas reduced subsidies, credits, and price controls in the rural sector. Salinas came into power in 1988 as a privileged, intelligent, and energetic *técnico* possessed of a strong desire to make his mark on Mexican history. Salinas had joined the de la Madrid administration as minister of planning and the budget. Echoing exiting U.S. president Ronald Reagan's famous, era-defining assertion that "government is the problem," Salinas said, "The reality is that in Mexico, more government meant less response to the social needs of our people." Salinas and other Mexico City technocrats discounted popular support for small-scale agriculture as backward thinking. Supporting campesinos was well intentioned but part of an age-old problem in Mexico—and it weighed down the country's ascendance as a modern, global power. The statist economy needed to be pared to the bone. To integrate into the global agricultural market, Mexican farmers in rural states like Veracruz would have to go big and shift to export crops. As anthropologist John Gledhill writes, "It rapidly became clear that Salinas was willing to sacrifice the interests of the agricultural sector to get NAFTA through Congress." John Gledhill, "Fantasy and Reality in Restructuring Mexico's Land Reform," p. 7. Paper presented at the Society for Latin American Studies meeting, St. Andrews University, 1997; Julia Preston and Samuel Dillon, *Opening Mexico: The Making of a Democracy*, p. 184. New York: Farrar, Straus and Giroux, 2005.

21. PROCEDE, the name of the legal process to identify and title land, titled 55 percent of ejido land by 2006. Since ejidos covered over half of Mexico's territory, this was no small feat. This second wave of land privatization did not lead to a wholesale dismantling of ejidos, however. Nor did PROCEDE lead to a dynamic land market or more productive farming, as urban technocrats envisaged. U.S. Department of Agriculture, "Mexico, NAFTA, and Agriculture: A Snapshot," p. 12.

22. de Ita, "Land Concentration in Mexico after PROCEDE," p. 160; Sarah Hamilton, Billie R. DeWalt, and David Barkin, "Household Welfare in Four Rural Mexican Communities: The Economic and Social Dynamics of Surviving National Crises," *Mexican Studies/Estudios Mexicanos* 19.2 (Summer 2003): 434.

CHAPTER 11

1. Fred Whittlesey, "Maytag CEO Ralph Hake: The Poster Child for What's Wrong with CEO Pay," *Pay and Performance: The Compensation Blog*, January 29, 2006; Richard Gibson, "Maytag Chairman, CEO Ralph Hake Announces Plans to Resign," Dow Jones News Service, April 3, 2006; "Maytag CEO Ralph Hake Announces Departure," Associated Press, April 3, 2006; Karen S. Lynch, "Pension Perils: What You May Not Know about an American Icon," *The Zephyr* (n.d.); Maytag Corporation, "Maytag Corporation: Change of Control Agreement," April 1, 2002. Hake's golden parachute also included numerous multiyear health and retirement benefits.

2. Monica Davey, "With Loss of Maytag, Town Faces the Loss of Its Identity," *New York Times*, June 7, 2006; Associated Press, "Whirlpool to Cut 4,500 Jobs, Close Plants," *USA Today*, May 10, 2006; David Pitt, "Judge Dismisses Lawsuit against Former Maytag CEO Ralph Hake, Others," Associated Press, July 11, 2006.

3. Whittlesey, "Maytag CEO Ralph Hake: The Poster Child for What's Wrong with CEO Pay," January 29, 2006; Don Cooper, "Maytag CEO's Bountiful Severance Package Awaits," *The Register-Mail*, October 4, 2005; "Maytag CEO Ralph Hake Announces Departure," Associated Press, April 3, 2003.

4. Health Systems Research at the University of Illinois College of Medicine at Rockford, "Knox County Healthy Community 2010: Community Analysis," p. 66. Prepared for the Knox County Health Department, March 20, 2010. Medicaid does not cover dental care. More than half of the children in Knox County did not have dental care. Knox County Health Department, "Knox County Community Health Improvement Plan," A Product of the Healthy Communities Project: 2005–2006, September 14, 2006.

5. Jenn Lloyd, "Well-Paid Factory Jobs a Thing of the Past, Education Key for Future Generations," Knox News Team in *The Register-Mail*, March 11, 2011.

6. Louis Jacobson, Robert J. Lalonde, and Daniel Sullivan ("The Impact of Community College Retraining on Older Displaced Workers: Should We Teach Old Dogs New Tricks?" *Industrial and Labor Relations Review* 58.3 [April 2005]: 398–415) found that the income benefit for older men was 7 percent; for women, it was significantly higher: 10 percent per year attended. Diana Furchtgott-Roth, Louis Jacobson, and Christine Mokher ("Strengthening Community Colleges' Influence on Economic Mobility," October 2009. A Publication of the Economic Mobility Project, an Initiative of the Pew Charitable Trusts) found the benefit per year was between 4 percent and 6 percent, about the same benefit as a four-year college. Thomas J. Kane and Cecilia E. Rouse ("Labor Market Returns to Two-and Four-Year Colleges: Is a Credit a Credit and Do Degrees Matter?" Working Paper 4268, National Bureau of Economic Research, Cambridge, MA, 1993) found a benefit of 5 percent to 8 percent. Duane E. Leigh and Andrew M. Gill ("Labor Market Returns to Community College: Evidence for Returning Students," *Journal of Human Resources* 32.2 [Spring 1997]: 334–353) found a similar effect as Kane and Rouse (1993) but noted that returning male students enrolled in short training programs did especially well, on average.

7 James Lardner, "The Specter Haunting Your Office," *New York Review of Books* 54.10 (June 14, 2007): 3.

8. Andrea Houlihan, "No Quick Fix for Lost Maytag Jobs," Knox News Team in *The Register-Mail*, March 13, 2011. This result came from the 2010 Maytag Employees in Transition survey conducted as part of the Maytag Project at Knox College led by Marilyn Webb. The survey randomly sampled 425 of the final 902 Machinists at the factory. One hundred and thirty-three responded. The survey found that 52 percent in the sample retrained. Their sample tilted toward more senior workers, who tended to have slightly lower rates of retraining, so the number may have been slightly higher among the 1,600 laid-off production workers. David Lindstrom estimated that "700 to 800 people went through training pretty successfully from Maytag and Butler," which is consistent with the 50 percent estimate.

9. Nathan Williams, "Which Former Employees Fare Better? Men or Women?" Knox News Team in *The Register-Mail*, March 11, 2011.

10. This fact was calculated by the author using Knox College's Maytag Project data about the final 902 laid-off workers. Of women, 29.7 percent reported attending Carl Sandburg College, whereas 15.6 percent of men did. Although Sandburg was the main destination, displaced workers attended a wide variety of schools and certification programs in the region. The gendered educational differences reflect a cleavage throughout the country. Women, on average, get higher grades in high school than men, regardless of ethnic or racial group. Further, among men and women with comparable GPAs in high school, women have higher rates of college enrollment (Furchtgott-Roth, Jacobson, and Mokher, "Strengthening Community Colleges' Influence on Economic Mobility," October 2009). This study was based on data on Florida students.

11. Houlihan, "No Quick Fix for Lost Maytag Jobs," March 13, 2011; Williams, "Which Former Employees Fare Better? Men or Women?" March 11, 2011. The responses of men and women differed, for instance, on the question, "We have to invent our own personal futures." Seventy-two percent of women, compared to 58 percent of men, agreed or strongly agreed.

12. Health Systems Research at the University of Illinois College of Medicine at Rockford, "Knox County Healthy Community 2010: Community Analysis," p. 51; John R. Pulliam, "Galesburg BNSF Yards See It All," *The Register-Mail*, October 20, 2008.

13. Eric Timmons, "BNSF to Add 87 Railroad Jobs in Galesburg This Year: Railroad Plans Projects to Improve Traffic Flow," *The Register-Mail*, April 20, 2011.

14. Jennifer DeWitt and Thomas Geyer, "Deere Lays Off 367 at Harvester Works," *Quad-City Times*, September 10, 2009; Deborah Solomon and Greg Hitt, "A Globalization Winner Joins in Trade Backlash," *Wall Street Journal*, November 21, 2007; Deere & Company, "Feet on the Ground, Eyes on the Horizon," Deere & Company Annual Report 2013 (http://www.deere.com/en_US/docs/Corporate/investor_relations/pdf/financialdata/reports/2014/2013_annual_report.pdf).

15. Houlihan, "No Quick Fix for Lost Maytag Jobs," March 13, 2011. It is likely that survey respondents had, on average, higher education levels to begin with and had done better after the layoffs than nonrespondents.

16. Henry S. Farber, "Job Loss in the Great Recession: Historical Perspectives from the Displaced Workers Survey, 1984–2010," Working Paper 17040, p. 40. National Bureau of Economic Research, May 2011. These figures include survey takers that went from full-time to part-time jobs. The post-displacement wages are particularly low for older workers with a lot of seniority at their previous job.

17. Houlihan, "No Quick Fix for Lost Maytag Jobs," March 13, 2011.

18. Ryan Sweikert, "What the Future Holds for the Aging Ex-Maytag Worker," Knox News Team in *The Register-Mail*, March 11, 2011.

CHAPTER 12

1. Ann Cass of Proyecto Azteca as quoted in Carolyn C. Cavaness, "It's not about winning, it's about being faithful. . . ." *Union in Dialogue Blog*, Union Theological Seminary

in the City of New York (June 28, 2010), http://unionindialogue.org/2010/06/28/its-not-about-winning-its-about-being-faithful/.

2. Infonavit stands for the Instituto del Fondo Nacional de la Vivienda para los Trabajadores, or the National Housing Fund for Workers Institute: http://www.infonavit.gob.mx/.

3. Habitation for the Planet: http://www.habitationfortheplanet.org/blog/2012/03/base-of-the-pyramid-housing-mexico-infonavit/.

4. Jorge G. Castañeda, *Mañana Forever? Mexico and the Mexicans*, pp. 56–57. New York: Knopf, 2011.

5. Angel "Tito" Rodriguez headed Sindicato Industrial Autónomo de Operarios en General de Maquiladoras, a union affiliated with the CTM, which represented 10,000 workers in 65 plants.

6. "Charro," or "cowboy," became synonymous with corrupt union bosses in the 1940s—the modern version of the *cacique*. Jaime Pensado, *Political Violence and Student Culture in Mexico: The Consolidation of Porrismo during the 1950s and 1960s*, p. 210. Ph.D. dissertation, University of Chicago, 2008.

7. Comité Fronterizo de Obreras, "Los trabajadores y Maytag," February 17, 2005: http://www.cfomaquiladoras.org/trabajadoresymaytag.es.html.

8. Jefferson Cowie, *Capital Moves: RCA's Seventy-Year Quest for Cheap Labor*, p. 155. Ithaca, NY: Cornell University Press, 1999; Interviews with María Prieto, director of industrial development in Reynosa, July 1 and December 12, 2003.

9. John Kenneth Galbraith, *American Capitalism: The Concept of Countervailing Power*. Boston: Houghton Mifflin, 1952. Charles Debner further developed this idea in *Corporation Nation: How Corporations Are Taking over Our Lives and What We Can Do about It* (New York: St. Martin's Press, 1998).

10. Interview with Benjamin Davis, Mexico Country Program Director, Solidarity Center, AFL-CIO, December 7, 2004; Jessica Rocha, "Maquiladora Jobs, Pay Decline: Plant Workers Struggling to Make Ends Meet," *Valley Morning Star*, April 18, 2004.

11. Chad Richardson and José A. Pagán, "Human and Social Aspects of Cross-Border Development in the McAllen/Reynosa Area," Working Paper 2002-9, p. 10. Center of Border Economic Studies, The University of Texas-Pan American, October 2002.

12. McAllen Economic Development Corporation, http://www.mcallenedc.org, accessed September 2003. The website no longer mentions labor unions.

13. This account comes from two interviews with Teresa Chávez and is supplemented by Tyche Hendricks, *The Wind Doesn't Need a Passport: Stories from the U.S.-Mexico Borderlands*. Berkeley: University of California Press, 2010.

14. Sam Dillon, "A 20-Year G.M. Parts Migration to Mexico," *New York Times*, June 24, 1998.

15. Kristin Petros, "Motherhood, Mobility and the Maquiladora in Mexico: Women's Migration from Veracruz to Reynosa," Summer Funds Research Report, Center for Latin American Social Policy, Lozano Long Institute of Latin American Studies, The University of Texas at Austin, September 4, 2006; Kristin Petros, "Women on the Border: Gender, Migration, and the Making of 'Reynosa, Veracruz, Mexico,'" XXVII ILASSA Student Conference Research Paper, The University of Texas at Austin, February 1, 2007.

16. E. P. Thompson, "Time, Work-Discipline, and Industrial Capitalism," *Past and Present* 38 (December 1967): 91. Thompson writes about assimilation to time and

work-discipline through the generations for industrial workers: "The first generation of factory workers were taught by their masters the importance of time; the second generation formed their short time committees in the ten-hour movement; the third generation struck for overtime or time-and-a-half. They had accepted the categories of their employers and learn to fight back within them. They had learned their lesson, that time is money, only too well" (p. 86).

17. Comité de Apoyo, "Financial Summary," 2003. Unpublished accounting report.

18. Associated Press, "2 More Leave Delphi; Financial Restatement on Track," *USA Today*, June 9, 2005; Gretchen Morgenson, "Justifying Monster Pay Packages at Delphi," *New York Times*, November 13, 2005.

19. McAllen Economic Development Corporation, "People Make the Difference," in "Maquiladora: An Advertising Supplement to *The Monitor*," May 31, 2003.

20. Cass, *Union in Dialogue Blog* (June 28, 2010). Union Theological Seminary in the City of New York, http://unionindialogue.org/2010/06/28/its-not-about-winning-its-ab out-being-faithful/.

21. John R. Pulliam, "They Did It Again! Whirlpool Closing Reynosa Plant; Mexico City That Took 1,600 Jobs from Galesburg Will Lose 750 Jobs," *The Register-Mail*, February 1, 2008.

22. "Union Leader Killed in Reynosa," *Valley Central*, December 18, 2008.

23. Federal Reserve Bank of Dallas, "Maquiladora Industry Update," 2006, slide presentation, http://www.dallasfed.org/research.cfm; Federal Reserve Bank of Dallas, "New Data Confirm Pickup in Juárez Factory Jobs," 2010 (second quarter), *SouthWest Economy*, p. 14; United Nations, "Integration of the Human Rights of Women and a Gender Perspective: Violence against Women," Report of the Special Rapporteur on Violence against Women, Its Causes and Consequences, Yakin Ertürk, Mission to Mexico, January 13, 2006 (English summary); Damien Cave, "Wave of Violence Swallows More Women in Juárez," *New York Times*, June 23, 2012; INEGI (Instituto Nacional de Estadística y Geografía), Banco de Información Económica, http://www.inegi.org.mx/sistemas/bie/; Benjamin Davis, "Workers' Freedom of Association Under Attack in Mexico," Solidarity Center Policy Brief, August 2008: http://www.solidaritycenter.org.

24. Lynn Brezosky, "Reynosa Hasn't Found Matamoros Success," *San Antonio Express-News*, January 13, 2008.

25. Davis, "Workers' Freedom of Association under Attack in Mexico," August 2008.

26. "Editorial: Shoring Up NAFTA: Finding the Promised Jobs That Never Turned Up," *McClatchy-Tribune Business News*, July 11, 2007. NAFTA was seen by many as a shortcut to the hard work of strategic convergence and job creation. This negligence was notable in U.S. immigration policy, which has a profound impact on economic development in Mexico. As Patricia Fernández-Kelly and Douglas S. Massey note, "NAFTA's silence with respect to labor rights and worker mobility is comprehensible in the observation that, contrary to the basic precepts of the European Union and its project of political and economic integration, the overarching goal of the treaty was to advance the economic interests of a new bi-national class of investors, not the fortunes of citizens in general" (Patricia Fernández-Kelly and Douglas S. Massey, "Borders for Whom? The Role of NAFTA in Mexico-U.S. Migration," *Annals of the American Academy of Political and Social Science* 610 [March 2007]: 115). Further,

as Raul Rodriguez writes, NAFTA was "never meant to be a sufficient condition. Narrowing income gaps between countries, lifting standards of living, and bolstering competitiveness should be at the core of . . . a new partnership that goes beyond NAFTA" (Raul Rodriguez, "Parameters of Partnership in U.S.-Mexico Relations, Challenges in Competitiveness: Infrastructure Development," p. 14. The Woodrow Wilson Center's Mexico Institute, January 2005). These commentators contend that immigration reform that promotes legal, circular movement of labor—following the European Union's example—would benefit both economies, and it would better fit the spirit of free and fair economic integration.

CHAPTER 13

1. Sections of this chapter were also used in Chad Broughton, "Migration as Engendered Practice: Mexican Men, Masculinity and Northward Migration," *Gender & Society* 22.5 (October 2008): 568–589.
2. U.S. Department of the Army, http://countrystudies.us/mexico/76.htm.
3. All of the conversations and quotations used in this chapter were recorded, translated, and transcribed from Spanish by Josh Walsman and the author. Please see "Notes on Method" for details concerning methodology.
4. Michael Hoefer, Nancy Rytina, and Bryan Baker, "Estimates of the Unauthorized Immigrant Population Residing in the United States: January 2011," p. 3. U.S. Department of Homeland Security, Office of Immigration Statistics, March 2012; Jeffrey S. Passel, D'Vera Cohn, and Ana Gonzalez-Barrera, "Population Decline of Unauthorized Immigrants Stalls, May Have Reversed," p. 6. Pew Research Center, Washington, DC, September 23, 2013.
5. Gordon H. Hanson and Craig McIntosh, "The Great Mexican Emigration," Working Paper 13675, National Bureau of Economic Research, 2007.
6. Despite the appeal of these apparently high wages, it's important to note that since the mid-1960s, the time of the farmworker strikes in the lower Rio Grande Valley, average wages of Mexican-born immigrants in the United States, somewhat astonishingly, have been flat, even as their education level has risen (Douglas S. Massey and Julia Gelatt, "What Happened to the Wages of Mexican Immigrants? Trends and Interpretations," *Latino Studies* 8.3 [2010]: 328–354).
7. Daniel Carroll, Annie Georges, and Russell Saltz, "Changing Characteristics of U.S. Farm Workers: 21 Years of Findings from the National Agricultural Workers Survey," p. 29. Presented at the Immigration Reform and Agriculture Conference: Implications for Farmers, Farm Workers, and Communities, University of California, D.C. Campus, May 12, 2011.
8. In an email, Daniel Carroll of the Office of Policy Development and Research at the U.S. Department of Labor wrote that figuring out the number of migrant and seasonal farmworkers is a fairly daunting task. The best estimate, he said, was Philip Martin's, based on the National Agricultural Workers Survey. Martin estimated that there were 1.4 million crop workers and 429,000 livestock workers in 2007 (an estimated 1.1 million were unauthorized). Philip Martin, "AgJOBS: Provisions, Eligibility,"

Rural Migration News 15 (July 2009): 3. Carroll also noted the U.S. Department of Agriculture's Census of Agriculture estimate puts *total* "hired farm labor" at around 2.6 million. The USDA's estimate for *average* annual employment of farmworkers is a little over one million. Carroll noted that, in agriculture, average employment is usually doubled to get total employment because of high rates of turnover.

9. Steven Greenhouse, "Growers' Group Signs the First Union Contract for Guest Workers," *New York Times*, September 17, 2004; David Bacon, *The Right to Stay Home: How U.S. Policy Drives Mexican Migration*, p. 24. Boston: Beacon Press, 2013.

10. Dana P. Goldman, James P. Smith, and Neeraj Sood, "Immigrants and the Cost of Medical Care," *Health Affairs* 25.6 (2006): 1700–1711.

11. Kevin Sack, "Illegal Farm Workers Get Health Care in Shadows," *New York Times*, May 10, 2008.

12. U.S. Department of Labor, "Findings from the National Agricultural Workers Survey (NAWS) 2001–2002: A Demographic and Unemployment Profile of United States Farm Workers," p. 39. Research Report 5, 2005.

13. Sarah Varney, "Health Law Adds New Expense for Farmers: Insurance for Field Workers," *Kaiser Health News*, August 21, 2013.

14. Farm Labor Organizing Committee, "Successes of CBA between FLOC/NCGA during 2005 Season," 2006. Farm Labor Organizing Committee, AFL-CIO.

15. David Bacon, "Guest Workers and a Union for Tobacco Workers," *TruthOut Report*, October 29, 2012. The total farmworker figure includes crop workers but not livestock workers (see note above). Martin, "AgJOBS: Provisions, Eligibility," p. 3; PBS Frontline, "Rape in the Fields," June 25, 2013.

16. Robert Smith, *Mexican New York: Transnational Lives of New Immigrants*, p. 50. Berkeley: University of California Press, 2006.

CHAPTER 14

1. I took my Knox College students to Farmland Foods in Monmouth on five occasions in the mid-2000s. The factory tours included interviews with safety manager Patrick Anderson, other staff members, and brief interactions with workers.

2. Chad Broughton, "Bringing the Organization Back In: The Role of Bureaucratic Churning in Early TANF Caseload Declines in Illinois," *Journal of Sociology & Social Welfare* 37.3 (September 2010): 155–182; Lawrence M. Mead, "The Reauthorization of TANF," Testimony before the Committee on Finance, U.S. Senate, April 2002.

3. Administration for Children & Families (ACF), "TANF Recipients, August 1996 to June 2007," Department of Health & Human Services, http://www.acf.hhs.gov; Pamela J. Loprest, "How Has the TANF Caseload Changed over Time?" p. 3. Urban Institute, Temporary Assistance to Needy Families Program, Research Synthesis Brief Series, Brief 08, March 2012.

4. U.S. Census Bureau, "Income, Poverty, and Health Insurance Coverage in the United States: 2007," p. 45. Washington, DC: Bureau of the Census, 2008.

5. Richard Gibson, "Maytag Chairman, CEO Ralph Hake Announces Plans to Resign," Dow Jones News Service, April 3, 2006; "Maytag CEO Ralph Hake Announces

Departure," Associated Press, April 3, 2006; Karen S. Lynch, "Pension Perils: What You May Not Know about an American Icon," *The Zephyr* (n.d.).

6. Personal interview, DHS Family Community Resource Center in Warren County, September 8, 2010. The caseworker wished to remain anonymous.

7. Administration for Children & Families (ACF), "Archives: Caseload Data 2000–2008," Department of Health & Human Services, http://archive.acf.hhs.gov/programs/ofa/data-reports/caseload/caseload_recent.html.

8. U.S. Census, 2010, American FactFinder, factfinder2.census.gov.

9. Adam Smith, "Of the Wages of Labour," in *An Inquiry into the Nature and Causes of the Wealth of Nations*, Book 1, Chapter 8. By Adam Smith, p. 86. Dublin: Messrs. Whitestone et al., 1776.

10. U.S. Census Bureau, "Income, Poverty, and Health Insurance Coverage in the United States: 2008," p. 43. Washington, DC: Bureau of the Census, 2009.

11. Alemayehu Bishaw, "Poverty: 2009 and 2010," American Community Survey Briefs, ACSBR/10-01, October 2011. Washington, DC: U.S. Census Bureau, 2011. McAllen Edinburg-Mission, Texas, ranked first in the nation by a large margin among metropolitan areas.

12. Health Systems Research at the University of Illinois College of Medicine at Rockford, "Knox County Healthy Community 2010: Community Analysis," p. 58. Prepared for the Knox County Health Department, March 2010.

13. U.S. Census, 2010, American FactFinder, factfinder2.census.gov. Avon's population in 2000 was 917; in 2010, it was 799, a 12.9 percent drop.

CHAPTER 15

1. This account is taken from fieldwork in Agua Dulce, including interviews with Gonzalez and Cruz, and is corroborated in detail in Amanda King, "Ten Years with NAFTA: A Review of the Literature and an Analysis of Farmer Responses in Sonora and Veracruz, Mexico," pp. 40–43. CIMMYT (International Maize and Wheat Improvement Center) Special Report 06-01 with the Congressional Hunger Center, 2006, and Amanda King, "Trade and Totomoxtle: Livelihood Strategies in the Totonacan Region of Veracruz, Mexico," *Agriculture and Human Values* 24 (2007): 29–40.

2. King, "Ten Years with NAFTA," p. 43.

3. The blackberry case study is based primarily on Donna L. Chollett's research: Donna L. Chollett, "From Sugar to Blackberries: Restructuring Agro-export Production in Michoacán, Mexico," *Latin American Perspectives*, Issue 166, 36.3 (2009): 79–92, and Donna L. Chollett, "Renegotiating Gender and Class in the Berry Fields of Michoacán, Mexico," *Dialectical Anthropology* 35 (2011): 147–169. On *cañeros* and the sugar industry I referenced Robert Knapp, "Mexico and Sugar: Historical Perspective," Foreign Agricultural Service Horticultural and Tropical Products Division, USDA. Washington, DC: Foreign Agricultural Service, 2004; Elizabeth Malkin, "In Mexico, Sugar vs. U.S. Corn Syrup," *New York Times*, June 9, 2004; and Katherine Scaife, "Inadequate Institutions and Inefficient Outcomes in Mexico's Sugar Industry," M.A. Thesis, Tufts University, The Fletcher School, March 7, 2010.

4. B. C. Strik and C. E. Finn, "Blackberry Production Systems—A Worldwide Perspective," *Acta Hort* (ISHS) 946 (2012): 341–347, http://www.actahort.org/books/946/946_56.htm.

5. Ana de Ita, "Fourteen Years of NAFTA and the Tortilla Crisis," Americas Program Special Report, January 10, 2008.

6. Chollett, "From Sugar to Blackberries," p. 83; Steven Zahniser and Zachary Crago, "NAFTA at 15: Building on Free Trade," pp. 9, 11, 28. Economic Research Service, U.S. Department of Agriculture, 2009.

7. Chollett, "From Sugar to Blackberries," pp. 79–92; David Bacon, "Guest Workers and a Union for Tobacco Workers," *TruthOut Report*, October 29, 2012. Chollett notes that Los Reyes growers formed a cooperative to enhance their leverage with buyers. Soon after, the fledgling organization was co-opted by the companies and abandoned.

8. U.S. Department of Agriculture, "Mexico, NAFTA, and Agriculture: A Snapshot," pp. 12, 15. Global Agriculture Information Network Report, 2006. The Secretariat of Agrarian Reform noted that 500,000 women held title to ejidal land in 2006.

9. Chollett, "From Sugar to Blackberries," p. 86.

10. Donna L. Chollett, "Renegotiating Gender and Class in the Berry Fields of Michoacán, Mexico," p. 167; Ros Krasny and Chris Prentice, "4-U.S. groups accuse Mexico of dumping sugar as sweetener tensions build," Reuters, March 29, 2014.

11. Manuela Angelucci, "Love on the Rocks: Alcohol Abuse and Domestic Violence in Rural Mexico," IZA Discussion Papers 2706, Institute for the Study of Labor (IZA), 2007; Sarah Hamilton, "Neoliberalism, Gender, and Property Rights in Rural Mexico, *Latin American Research Review* 37.1 (2002): 119–143; Sarah Hamilton, Billie R. DeWalt, and David Barkin, "Household Welfare in Four Rural Mexican Communities: The Economic and Social Dynamics of Surviving National Crises," *Mexican Studies/Estudios Mexicanos* 19.2 (Summer 2003): 433–462.

12. David Karp, "At Last, Sweet Blackberries Stay the Course," *New York Times*, July 25, 2007.

13. Zahniser and Crago, "NAFTA at 15," p. 28.

14. Jaime E. Málaga and Gary W. Williams, "Mexican Agricultural and Food Export Competitiveness," pp. 6–7, 34–35. TAMRC International Market Research Report No. IM-01-06, February 2006; Zahniser and Crago, " NAFTA at 15," pp. 49, 50.

15. Gisele Henriques and Raj Patel, "NAFTA, Corn, and Mexico's Agricultural Trade Liberalization," p. 2. Americas Program. Silver City, NM: Interhemispheric Resource Center, January 28, 2004; de Ita, "Fourteen Years of NAFTA and the Tortilla Crisis," January 10, 2008. Fruits accounted for 6 percent of arable land and vegetables accounted for 3 percent.

16. Despite the political rhetoric on both sides of the border, the displacement of rural communities in Mexico was not unforeseen among scholars and politicians. It was generally accepted by leading migration scholars and policymakers that free trade in the short term produces a "migration hump," but that in the long term there is less migration than without it. Philip L. Martin and J. Edward Taylor, "The Anatomy of a Migration Hump," in *Development Strategy, Employment, and Migration: Insights from Models*. Edited by J. Edward Taylor, p. 45. Paris: OECD, Development Centre,

1996. Two leading economic scholars of NAFTA, Gary Clyde Hufbauer and Jeffrey J. Schott, argued that it was inevitable that, as Mexico industrializes, agriculture would require fewer hands, and that rural Mexicans would bear the "adjustment costs." Gary Clyde Hufbauer and Jeffrey J. Schott, *NAFTA Revisited: Achievements and Challenges*, p. 286. Washington, DC: Institute for International Economics, 2005.

17. Eduardo Zepeda, Timothy A. Wise, and Kevin P. Gallagher, *Rethinking Trade Policy for Development: Lessons from Mexico under NAFTA*. Policy Outlook, pp. 12–13. Washington, DC: Carnegie Endowment for International Peace, 2009; Philip Martin and J. Edward Taylor, "Ripe with Change: Evolving Farm Labor Markets in the United States, Mexico, and Central America," p. 18. Washington, DC: Migration Policy Institute, 2013. From 1991 to 2003, the number of campesinos in Mexico, most of them corn farmers, declined from 4.3 million to 2.7 million. U.S. Department of Agriculture, "Mexico, NAFTA, and Agriculture: A Snapshot," p. 10. By other numbers, those involved in agricultural economic activity dropped from 10.6 million to 8.6 million from 1991 to 2007 (Mark Weisbrot, Stephan Lefebvre, and Joseph Sammut, "Did NAFTA Help Mexico? An Assessment After 20 Years," Washington, DC: Center for Economic and Policy Research, February 2014, p. 13).

18. Alexandra G. Ponette-González and Matthew Fry, "Pig Pandemic: Industrial Hog Farming in Eastern Mexico," *Land Use Policy* 27 (2010): 1108; David Bacon, "How U.S. Policies Fueled Mexico's Great Migration," *The Nation*, January 4, 2012; Granjas Carroll de México website (http://www.granjascarroll.mx/ing_gcm_somos.php), accessed 1/20/14.

19. Timothy A. Wise and Betsy Rakocy, "Hogging the Gains from Trade: The Real Winners from U.S. Trade and Agricultural Policies," GDAE Policy Brief 10-01, p. 3. Environment Institute, Tufts University, January 2010. To take one example, no longer could the Mexican government mandate local hiring and training to stimulate economic development in a place like Tierra Blanca or Perote. By contrast, Chapter 11 of NAFTA set out supranational legal protections and investment rights for foreign companies like Smithfield. Multinationals could use Chapter 11 not simply as a shield against government seizures of property but as a way to attack regulatory policies and government functions. "NAFTA Chapter 11 Investor-State Cases: Lessons for the Central America Free Trade Agreement," p. 79. *Public Citizen*, 2005; Patricia Fernández-Kelly and Douglas S. Massey, "Borders for Whom? The Role of NAFTA in Mexico-U.S. Migration," *Annals of the American Academy of Political and Social Science* 610 (March 2007): 103.

20. Jeff Tietz, "Boss Hog," *Rolling Stone*, Issue 1015, December 14, 2006; Vesilind, "NAFTA's Trojan Horse & the Demise of the Mexican Hog Industry," 2011. More recently, there has been a push toward "crate-free" pork and movement in both industry and policy realms away from the use of gestation crates. The Humane Society of the United States, "An HSUS Report: Welfare Issues with Gestation Crates for Pregnant Sows," February 2013.

21. Ponette-González and Fry, "Pig Pandemic: Industrial Hog Farming in Eastern Mexico," p. 1107.

22. Tietz, "Boss Hog," December 14, 2006.

23. Vesilind, "NAFTA's Trojan Horse & the Demise of the Mexican Hog Industry," pp. 21–22.

24. Wise and Rakocy, "Hogging the Gains from Trade," January 2010. Wise and Rakocy note that the U.S. Farm Bill of 1996 was a brief experiment in getting the U.S. government out of agricultural commodity markets. The immediate crisis that followed led policymakers back into subsidizing row crops like soybeans and corn—a practice, of course, that runs counter to U.S. rhetoric promoting free and fair trade.

25. Vesilind, "NAFTA's Trojan Horse & the Demise of the Mexican Hog Industry," p. 11. Smaller, diversified farmers who grew their own corn, soy, and other fodder faced a competitive disadvantage in the new regime as well. Wise and Rakocy, "Hogging the Gains from Trade," p. 2.

26. Wise and Rakocy, "Hogging the Gains from Trade," p. 3.

27. Ginger Thompson, "NAFTA to Open Floodgates, Engulfing Rural Mexico," New York Times, December 19, 2002.

28. Bacon, "How U.S. Policies Fueled Mexico's Great Migration," January 4, 2012.

29. Wise and Rakocy, "Hogging the Gains from Trade," p. 3.

30. Robert Manning, "Five Years after NAFTA: Rhetoric and Reality of Mexican Immigration in the 21st Century," p. 3. Washington, DC: Center for Immigration Studies, 2000.

31. Bacon, "How U.S. Policies Fueled Mexico's Great Migration," January 4, 2012.

32. Wise and Rakocy, "Hogging the Gains from Trade," p. 4.

33. Bacon, "How U.S. Policies Fueled Mexico's Great Migration," January 4, 2012. As if the irony of former hog farmers working in hog slaughterhouses was not enough, both American and Mexican taxpayers found themselves subsidizing "free trade" and the scaling-up of corporate-led, industrialized agriculture. U.S. taxpayers pay $20 billion a year in farm subsidies. Mexican taxpayers pay for PROCAMPO, an income-support program used in part to help make up for the big losses in corn, soybeans, wheat, rice, cotton, beef, pork, and poultry—all subsidized heavily by U.S. taxpayers. Timothy A. Wise, "Agricultural Dumping under NAFTA: Estimating the Costs of U.S. Agricultural Policies to Mexican Producers," Mexican Rural Development Research Reports, Report 7, pp. 7–8. Woodrow Wilson International Center for Scholars, 2010.

34. Bacon, "How U.S. Policies Fueled Mexico's Great Migration," January 4, 2012; Ponette-González and Fry, "Pig Pandemic: Industrial Hog Farming in Eastern Mexico," p. 1109; Tietz, "Boss Hog," December 14, 2006.

35. Donald G. McNeil, Jr., "In New Theory, Swine Flu Started in Asia, Not Mexico," New York Times, June 23, 2009; Centers for Disease Control and Prevention, "What People Who Raise Pigs Need to Know about Influenza (Flu)," January 2012; Ponette-González and Fry, "Pig Pandemic: Industrial Hog Farming in Eastern Mexico," p. 1108; Lauren Etter and Ana Campony, "The Swine-Flu Outbreak: Expert Says Farm Isn't Flu Origin," Wall Street Journal, April 30, 2009; Gabriele Neumann, Takeshi Noda, and Yoshihiro Kawaoka, "Emergence and Pandemic Potential of Swine-Origin H1N1 Influenza Virus," Nature 459 (June 18, 2009): 931–939; Rebecca J. Garten, et al., "Antigenic and Genetic Characteristics of Swine-Origin 2009 A(H1N1) Influenza Viruses Circulating in Humans," Science 325 (July 10, 2009): 197–201; Jon Cohen, "Swine Flu Outbreak: New Details on Virus's Promiscuous Past,"

Science 324 (May 29, 2009): 1127; Centers for Disease Control and Prevention, "Origin of 2009 H1N1 Flu (Swine Flu): Questions and Answers," November 25, 2009; Vesilind, "NAFTA's Trojan Horse & the Demise of the Mexican Hog Industry," 2011.

36. Vesilind, "NAFTA's Trojan Horse & the Demise of the Mexican Hog Industry," 2011.
37. Tietz, "Boss Hog," December 14, 2006.
38. Bacon, "How U.S. Policies Fueled Mexico's Great Migration," January 4, 2012.
39. Manuel Roig-Franzia, "A Culinary and Cultural Staple in Crisis: Mexico Grapples with Soaring Prices for Corn—and Tortillas," *Washington Post*, January 27, 2007; Tom Philpott, "Tortilla Spat: How Mexico's Iconic Flatbread Went Industrial and Lost Its Flavor," *Grist Magazine*, September 13, 2006.
40. Anthony DePalma, "How a Tortilla Empire Was Built on Favoritism," *New York Times*, February 15, 1996.
41. Roig-Franzia, "A Culinary and Cultural Staple in Crisis," January 27, 2007. Raul Salinas was effectively the head of CONASUPO, the corn and commodities distribution program of the Mexican government, from which Maseca bought most of its corn.
42. DePalma, "How a Tortilla Empire Was Built on Favoritism," February 15, 1996.
43. Stephen D. Morris, "Corruption and the Mexican Political System: Continuity and Change, *Third World Quarterly* 20.3 (June 1999): 630; Julia Preston and Samuel Dillon, *Opening Mexico: The Making of a Democracy,* p 481. New York: Farrar, Straus and Giroux, 2004.
44. Janet M. Tanski and Dan W. French, "Capital Concentration and Market Power in Mexico's Manufacturing Industry: Has Liberalization Made a Difference?" *Journal of Economic Issues* 35.3 (September 2001): 675–711.
45. Thompson, "NAFTA to Open Floodgates, Engulfing Rural Mexico," December 19, 2002. BIMBO, the world's biggest baking company and Mexico biggest food company, benefited from cheap grain imports as well. Its brand catalog would grow to include Sara Lee, Earthgrains, Boboli, and Entenmann's in the United States and many others around the world.
46. Marla Dickerson, "Tortilla Makers Try Not to Get Flattened," *Los Angeles Times*, October 28, 2003; Geri Smith, "Wrapping the Globe in Tortillas," *Bloomberg Businessweek*, February 25, 2007.
47. Public Citizen, "NAFTA Truth and Consequences: Corn," accessed on January 15, 2014 (http://www.citizen.org/trade/article_redirect.cfm?ID=11330). Public Citizen states on their website, "In the years immediately following NAFTA's introduction for example, buyers that contracted with U.S. exporters had access to loans through the U.S. Commodity Credit Corporation at 7 percent for 3 years. Interest rates from Mexican lenders ran between 25 and 30 percent at that time."
48. Alexandra Spieldoch, "NAFTA: Fueling Market Concentration in Agriculture," Institute for Agriculture and Trade Policy, March 2010; Oxfam International, "Dumping without Borders: How U.S. Agricultural Policies Are Destroying the Livelihoods of Mexican Corn Farmers," p. 19. Oxfam Briefing Paper, August 2003; Public Citizen, "NAFTA Truth and Consequences: Corn," (http://www.citizen.org/trade/article_redirect.cfm?ID=11330). Monsanto and Novartis/Syngenta are two examples. Large Mexican and American companies continued to dictate agricultural

policy under the pro–big-business governments of Vicente Fox and Felipe Calderón in the 2000s.

49. Public Citizen, "Down on the Farm: NAFTA's Seven-Years War on Farmers and Ranchers in the U.S., Canada and Mexico," p. 19. Public Citizen's Global Trade Watch, June 26, 2001.

50. Ibid., p. 15.

51. Evangelina Hernández E Ignacio Alvarado, "Sagarpa Benefició a Cargill con 500 mdp," *El Universal*, February 17, 2010; Javier Valdez Cárdenas, "Compra de Maíz Sudafricano, duro Golpe al Agro Nacional: Campesinos," p. 31. *La Jornada*, May 6, 2012; de Ita, "Fourteen Years of NAFTA and the Tortilla Crisis," January 10, 2008; Kristin Appendini, "Tracing the Maize-Tortilla Chain," *UN Chronicle* 45.2–3 (2008).

52. Thompson, "NAFTA to Open Floodgates, Engulfing Rural Mexico," December 19, 2001; NPR News, "Imported Corn from the US Makes It Hard for Mexican Farmers to Make a Profit," Anchor Bob Edwards and reporter Gerry Hadden, July 1, 2003; Tina Rosenberg, "Why Poor Farmers in Mexico Go Hungry," *International Herald Tribune*, March 5, 2003.

53. Nadal, "The Environmental and Social Impacts of Economic Liberalization on Corn Production in Mexico," p. 8.

54. The *canasta básica* (basic food basket), a measure used by a Mexican government social development organization and including corn, grain, milk, beans, eggs, and other essentials, rose faster than overall inflation. From December 1993 to April 2007, overall inflation was 357 percent. The price of the *canasta básica* rose 421 percent. Humberto González Chávez and Alejandro Macías Macías "Vulnerabilidad Alimentaria y Política Agroalimentaria en México," *Desacatos: Revista de Antropología Social* 25 (September–December 2007): 67. Mexico scholar Darcy Victor Tetreault writes, "A handful of TNCs have come to dominate the agricultural-inputs markets, food processing, and supermarket chains . . . there has been a sensational rise in the cost of fertilizers and seeds. Food prices have also skyrocketed, driven by a host of factors, including increased interest in biofuels, rising demand for beef and cereals in developing countries, and market speculation. The result is a global food crisis" (p. 90). Darcy Victor Tetreault, "Alternative Pathways out of Rural Poverty in Mexico," *European Review of Latin American and Caribbean Studies* 88 (April 2010): 77–94. Food hunger and child malnutrition remained at high levels as well. Coneval, "Porcentaje de Personas en Pobreza por la Dimension de Ingreso, 1992–2010," (http://web.coneval.gob.mx/Informes/Pobreza%20por%20ingresos%20 2010/grafico02_ingresos_2010.jpg); Laura Carlsen, "NAFTA Is Starving Mexico," October 20, 2011, *Foreign Policy in Focus* (blog post).

55. Roig-Franzia, "A Culinary and Cultural Staple in Crisis," January 27, 2007; de Ita, "Fourteen Years of NAFTA and the Tortilla Crisis," January 10, 2008. Timothy A. Wise argues that the biofuel-induced price increases in corn were "a large net loss" to Mexico. The crises strained Mexico's trade balance, used scarce hard currency, raised consumer food prices, and drove up the cost of government safety net programs. Timothy A. Wise, "The Cost to Mexico of U.S. Corn Ethanol Expansion," Working Paper No. 12-01, p. 11. Global Development and Environment Institute, May 2012.

56. Wise, "Agricultural Dumping under NAFTA," p. 19.
57. Appendini, "Tracing the Maize-Tortilla Chain," 2008.
58. Eric Schlosser, *Fast Food Nation: The Dark Side of the All-American Meal*, p. 120. New York: Houghton Mifflin, 2001.

CHAPTER 16

1. This is Tracy Warner's version of events.
2. Illinois State Board of Education, eReport Card Public Site, (http://webprod.isbe. net/ereportcard/publicsite/getSearchCriteria.aspx). The state average of "low-income" students also increased, but not as rapidly, from 37.5 percent in 2002 to 49.9 percent in 2013. The child poverty rate for Galesburg, according to the 2008–2012 five-year estimates of American Community Survey data at the American FactFinder, (http://factfinder2.census.gov/faces/nav/jsf/pages/index.xhtml) was 35.4 percent; GREDA, "2011 Community Profile," p. 3, http://greda.org.
3. "Income, Poverty, and Health Insurance Coverage in the United States: 2010," p. 61. Washington, DC: U.S. Census Bureau, 2011.
4. Neil Irwin, "Aughts Were a Lost Decade for U.S. Economy, Workers," *Washington Post*, January 1, 2010; Economic Policy Institute, *State of Working America* website (http:// stateofworkingamerica.org/chart/swa-income-figure-2a-real-median-family).
5. Lawrence Mishel and Josh Bivens, "Occupy Wall Streeters Are Right about Skewed Economic Rewards in the United States," Economic Policy Institute Briefing Paper 331, 2011. While the top one percent of households took nearly 60 percent of the gains from 1979 to 2007, only 8.6 percent of growth went to the bottom 90 percent. The top 0.1 percent took 36 percent of gains, an even more disproportionate share.
6. Author's calculations based on data from Lawrence Mishel, Josh Bivens, Elise Gould, and Heidi Shierholz, *The State of Working America*. 12th ed. Ithaca, NY: Cornell University Press, 2012 (http://stateofworkingamerica.org/data/); Lawrence Mishel, "The Wedges between Productivity and Median Compensation Growth," p. 2. Economic Policy Institute Issue Brief No. 330, April 26, 2012.
7. Isabel V. Sawhill and John E. Morton, "Economic Mobility: Is the American Dream Alive and Well?" p. 11. Washington, DC: Economic Mobility Project: An Initiative of the Pew Charitable Trusts, May 2007. Median personal income for men in 1974 was $40,210 and $35,010 in 2004, adjusted for inflation.
8. Illinois School Report Card, Mercer County Junior High, 2011.
9. Susan DeMar Lafferty, "Schools Flunk? That's Bunk, Southland Educators Say," *Chicago Sun-Times*, October 30, 2011.
10. Illinois School Report Card, Mercer County Junior High, 2011.
11. Sean F. Reardon, "The Widening Academic Achievement Gap between the Rich and the Poor: New Evidence and Possible Explanations," pp. 91–115 in *Whither Opportunity? Rising Inequality, Schools, and Children's Life Chances*. New York: Russell Sage Foundation, 2011.
12. Sabrina Tavernise, "Education Gap Grows between Rich and Poor, Studies Say," *New York Times*, February 9, 2012.

13. Sean F. Reardon, "The Widening Academic Achievement Gap between the Rich and the Poor," p. 111.

14. John Ermisch, Markus Jäntti, and Timothy M. Smeeding, eds. *From Parents to Children: The Intergenerational Transmission of Advantage.* p. 18. New York: Russell Sage Foundation, 2012; "Does America Promote Mobility As Well As Other Nations?" November 2011. Economic Mobility Project, The Pew Charitable Trusts.

15. Thurston Domina, "Brain Drain and Brain Gain: Rising Educational Segregation in the United States, 1940–2000," *City and Community* 5.4 (2006): 403.

16. Thurston Domina, "Brain Drain and Brain Gain: Rising Educational Segregation in the United States, 1940–2000," *City and Community* 5.4 (2006): 387–407; Douglas S. Massey and Nancy A. Denton, *American Apartheid: Segregation and the Making of the U.S. Underclass.* Cambridge, MA: Harvard University Press, 1993; Thurston Domina, "What Clean Break? Education and Nonmetropolitan Migration Patterns, 1989–2004," *Rural Sociology* 7.3 (2006): 373–398; Patrick J. Carr and Maria J. Kefalas, *Hollowing Out the Middle: The Rural Brain Drain and What It Means for America.* New York: Beacon Press, 2009.

17. U.S. Census Bureau, "Total Population in Occupied Units by Tenure by Units in Structure," 2006–2010 American Community Survey 5-Year Estimates. Washington, DC: Bureau of the Census, 2012.

18. Lance George and Jann Yankausas, "Preserving Affordable Manufactured Home Communities in Rural America: A Case Study." Washington, DC: Housing Assistance Council, March 2011; Lance George and Milana Barr, "Moving Home: Manufactured Housing in Rural America," Washington, DC: Housing Assistance Council, December 2005.

19. U.S. Census Bureau, "Percent of Housing Units That Are Mobile Homes, United States: Urban/Rural and Inside/Outside Metropolitan and Micropolitan Area," 2006–2010 American Community Survey 5-Year Estimates. Washington, DC: Bureau of the Census, 2012.

20. Lance George and Milana Barr, "Moving Home: Manufactured Housing in Rural America," December 2005.

21. Isabel V. Sawhill and John E. Morton, "Economic Mobility: Is the American Dream Alive and Well?" p. 10. Washington, DC: Economic Mobility Project: An Initiative of The Pew Charitable Trusts, May 2007.

22. U.S. Department of Labor, "Charting the U.S. Labor Market in 2005," "Chart 5–9. The Change in Real Earnings since 1979 Has Been More Favorable for Women than for Men at All Levels of Education," Bureau of Labor Statistics, http://www.bls.gov/cps/labor2005/chartbook.pdf.

23. Paul A. Tiffin, Mark Pearce, Carole Kaplan, Trian Fundudis, and Louise Parker, "The Impact of Socio-economic Status and Mobility on Perceived Family Functioning," *Journal of Family and Economic Issues* 28 (September 2007): 653–667.

24. Paul Krugman, "Medicaid on the Ballot," *New York Times*, October 28, 2012; Chapin White and James D. Reschovsky, "Great Recession Accelerated Long-Term Decline of Employer Health Coverage," National Institute for Health Care Reform, Research Brief No. 8, March 2012.

25. David Hotle, "Workers Are Shocked, Angry and Disappointed: Emotions Run the Gamut Friday Morning," *The Register-Mail*, October 11, 2002; David Hotle, "Rank

and File See Little They Can Do: Union Reps to Meet on Details of Closure," *The Register-Mail*, October 12, 2002.

26. Jenneke Adriana Oostman, "The Pursuit of Happiness: A Third of Former Maytag Workers More Satisfied Now," Knox News Team in *The Register-Mail*, March 13, 2011; Rebecca Beno, "What Happened to Last 902 to Work at Galesburg Plant?" Knox News Team in *The Register-Mail*, March 13, 2011.

27. Jenneke Adriana Oostman, "The Pursuit of Happiness," March 13, 2011.

28. Daniel Gilbert, *Stumbling on Happiness*, pp. 137–138. New York: Vintage, 2007. What made the layoffs particularly upsetting was the prospect of downward mobility. "Indeed, people hate pay cuts," Gilbert writes, "but research suggests that the reason they hate pay cuts has very little to do with the pay part and everything to do with the cut part . . . We think losses are more powerful than equal-sized gains" (pp. 151, 160). Human beings, Gilbert argues, are hardwired to think in relative rather than absolute terms so what the layoff victim focuses on is the imminent loss. The mind looks to the starting point—say a $15-an-hour wage like Maytag's—and "prefeels" the $10-an-hour wage they'll earn in the future.

29. Daniel T. Gilbert, Matthew D. Lieberman, Carey K. Morewedge, and Timothy D. Wilson, "The Peculiar Longevity of Things Not So Bad," *Psychological Science* 15.1 (2004): 18.

30. Timothy D. Wilson and Daniel T. Gilbert, "Affective Forecasting: Knowing What to Want," *Current Directions in Psychological Science* 14.3 (2005): 131–134.

31. Adam Smith, *The Theory of Moral Sentiments*. Part III, Chapter III: Of the Influence and Authority of Conscience. New York: Penguin Books, 2009. Originally published in 1759.

32. Sarah Juist, "Former Maytag Workers Feel Betrayed by the 'American Dream,'" Knox News Team in *The Register-Mail*, March 13, 2011. Eighty-four percent believed that the American Dream is out of reach for manufacturing workers, whereas 57 percent believed that it is out of reach for them. Psychologists call this the "attribution paradox." Timothy D. Wilson and Daniel T. Gilbert, "Affective Forecasting: Knowing What to Want," *Current Directions in Psychological Science* 14.3 (2005): 131–134; Shelley E. Taylor, "Adjustment to Threatening Events: A Theory of Cognitive Adaptation," *American Psychologist* 38.11 (November 1983): 1161–1173.

33. Max Haller and Markus Hadler, "How Social Relations and Structures Can Produce Happiness and Unhappiness: An International Comparative Analysis," *Social Indicators Research* 75 (2006): 169.

CHAPTER 17

1. Our guide at Planta Ensamble Saltillo, senior manufacturing planner Juan Arellano Gomez, said that union rules prohibited women from line work in the Dodge truck factory. There were, however, women in management, security, and technical professions both inside and outside the production areas.

2. The economic, political, and cultural dynamics of this regime are well described by David Harvey as "flexible accumulation" in his important 1990 book, *The Condition of Postmodernity: An Enquiry in the Origins of Cultural Change*, Blackwell: Malden, MA.

3. There are several reasons why Whirlpool and other companies chose Ramos Arizpe-Saltillo. The Saltillo area is a stronghold of Tereso Medina Ramírez of the CTM. Opponents call Medina a *charro* leader, a power broker who works to maintain labor peace and control for companies rather than advocate for workers (Judith Rosenberg, *The Rhetoric of Globalization: Can the Maquiladora Worker Speak?* Ph.D. dissertation thesis, University of Texas at Austin, May 2006). The Saltillo area is also fairly unique in that it is home to competing railway lines, which is an enormous advantage for exporters and rare in a country in which most regions are served by one provider.

4. "Nearshoring" refers to "moving a business function to a country that is closer via geography, time zone, cultural characteristics, or economic structure to the company's home country as a means of cutting costs and improving services" (Graebel Companies, "Offshoring? Reshoring? Nearshoring?" p. 3. September 2012).

5. INEGI (Instituto Nacional de Estadística y Geografía), Banco de Información Economica, "Estadística Integral del Programa de la Industria Manufacturera, Maquiladora y de Servicios de Exportación (IMMEX)" http://www.inegi.org.mx/sistemas/bie/. Mexico ended publication of separate maquiladora data in March 2007. Since March 2008, the Mexican government has used a more inclusive category, IMMEX (Manufacturing, Maquila and Export Service Industry), which includes maquiladoras and other export-oriented manufacturing. IMMEX employment figures, therefore, are higher than the discontinued maquiladora data.

6. Mike Allen and Keith Patridge also sought out higher-tech and leading-edge industries for the McAllen-Reynosa area as they indicated in their interviews and as John Sargent writes (John Sargent, "Charter Evolution in Maquiladoras: A Case Study of Reynosa, Tamaulipas," Working Paper 2003-16, Center of Border Economic Studies, The University of Texas-Pan American, January 2003). Sargent found that companies did not locate higher complexity operations in Reynosa because of a shortage of highly skilled professionals, deficient infrastructure, government corruption, excessive bureaucracy, and a "one size fits all" approach to maquila investment.

7. The most rigorous economic analysis of Coahuila's handling of globalization is filled with praise for Montemayor's development efforts (Leendert Andrew de Bell, *Globalization, Regional Development and Local Response: The Impact of Economic Restructuring in Coahuila, Mexico*. Amsterdam: Dutch University Press, 2005). After his six-year term as governor, Montemayor became director general of PEMEX, where he was implicated in a scandal. The charges against him were later dismissed, and he was fully exonerated of all charges.

8. Laura Flora showed us her severance payment from Maytag in 2008 (by then owned by Whirlpool). Flora received 29,707 pesos ($2,675), an enormous payout worth between half and a full year's regular pay. Holding multinational maquila operators accountable for legally required severance payments has been a major goal of grassroots organizers at the border. Flora's payout is emblematic of how far that effort had come, though Ed Krueger says there is still far to go on that front.

9. Hannah Strange, "Profile: the Brutal Cartel Boss Who Took Sadistic Killing to New Levels," *The Telegraph*, July 16, 2013; *Global Post*, "Mexican Authorities Arrest Mayor

for Helping a Drug Gang Extort City Council Members," April 16, 2014; Richard Fausset, "Mexican Towns, Once Frozen with Fear, Now Frozen in Time," *Los Angeles Times*, February 26. 2013; Tracy Wilkinson, "Mexico Creates Task Force to Search for the Missing," *Los Angeles Times*, May 27, 2013; United Nations, "Integration of the Human Rights of Women and a Gender Perspective: Violence against Women," Report of the Special Rapporteur on Violence against Women, Its Causes and Consequences, Yakin Ertürk, Mission to Mexico, January 13, 2006 (English summary).

10. Celina B. Realuyo, "It's All about the Money: Advancing Anti-money Laundrying Efforts in the U.S. and Mexico to Combat Transnational Organized Crime," Washington, DC: Woodrow Wilson International Center for Scholars, Mexico Institute, pp. 6–7, May 2012; National Drug Intelligence Center, "National Drug Threat Assessment 2009." U.S. Department of Justice.

11. National Drug Intelligence Center, "South Texas High Intensity Drug Trafficking Area: Drug Market Analysis 2011," pp. 9–10. U.S. Department of Justice; Richardson and Pagán, "Human and Social Aspects of Cross-Border Development in the McAllen/Reynosa Area," p. 23.

12. Phone interview with Martha Ojeda, Executive Director of the Coalition for Justice in the Maquiladoras, June 13, 2012.

13. Daniel Borunda, "El Paso Rankings: Safest, Best Places for Families, Least Hipster," *El Paso Times*, January 14, 2014 (http://www.elpasotimes.com/news/ci_24865165/el-paso-rankings-safest-best-places-families-and).

14. Todd Bensman, "Investigation: US Retailers Fuel Mexico's Drug Wars: U.S. Officials Visit Texas in Hopes of Clamping Down on the Cross-Border Weapons Pipeline," *GlobalPost*, April 3, 2009.

15. Melissa del Bosque, "Navigating Chaos," *The Texas Observer*, September 29, 2010.

16. Tracy Wilkinson, "Caught behind Enemy Lines," *Los Angeles Times*, November 6, 2010.

17. Tony Judt, "The Wrecking Ball of Innovation," Review of Robert B. Reich's *Supercapitalism: The Transformation of Business, Democracy, and Everyday Life*, *New York Review of Books* 54.19 (December 6, 2007).

18. Ed Vullimay, "Day of the Dead," *The Observer Magazine* (England), December 7, 2008. Drug lords had even purchased some maquila companies as fronts and infiltrated others. Abetted by bank privatizations, they had also joined bank boards to help with laundering money. Chad Richardson and José A. Pagán, "Human and Social Aspects of Cross-Border Development in the McAllen/Reynosa Area," pp. 23–25. Working Paper 2002-9, Center of Border Economic Studies, The University of Texas-Pan American, October 2002; Ildefonso Ortiz, "At Reynosa Factory, Claims of Regular Gulf Cartel Visits," *The Monitor*, May 18, 2013.

19. Juan Alberto Cedillo, "Ex-militar que busca a familiares desaparecidos ataca sede de gobierno de Coahuila," *Proceso*, May 9, 2013.

20. *El Universal*, "Ataque a Palacio, Sin Nexos con el Crimen: gobernador," May 11, 2013.

21. The Coca-Cola Company, 2012 Annual Review and Online per Capita Consumption Chart, April 1, 2013 (http://www.coca-colacompany.com/annual-review/2012/pdf/2012-per-capita-consumption.pdf).

22. Sarah E. Clark, Corinna Hawkes, Sophia M. E. Murphy, Karen A. Hansen-Kuhn, and David Wallinga, "Exporting Obesity: U.S. Farm and Trade Policy and the Transformation of the Mexican Consumer Food Environment," *International Journal of Occupational and Environmental Health* 18.1 (March 2012); Javier Valdez Cárdenas, "Compra de Maíz Sudafricano, duro Golpe al Agro Nacional: Campesinos," *La Jornada*, May 6, 2012.

23. "Walmart's Mexican Morass," *The Economist*, April 28, 2012; Sarah E. Clark, et al., "Exporting Obesity" (March 2012). Many of the pawn shops and cash advance places in Reynosa are big, national chains.

24. Jason Cohen, "Rio Grande Valley Tops List of 'America's Poorest Cities,'" *Texas Monthly*, October 9, 2012; Peter Linneman and Albert Saiz, "Forecasting 2020 U.S. County and MSA Populations." University of Pennsylvania Working Paper, April 2006.

25. Elizabeth Weil, "Heavy Questions," *New York Times Magazine*, January 2, 2005.

26. Karen A. Hansen-Kuhn, Sophia M. E. Murphy, and David Wallinga, "Exporting Obesity: How U.S. Farm and Trade Policy Is Transforming the Mexican Food Environment," Institute for Agricultural and Trade Policy, April 2012 (adapted from Clark et al., "Exporting Obesity" [March 2012]).

27. Mark Weisbrot, Stephan Lefebvre, and Joseph Sammut, "Did NAFTA Help Mexico? An Assessment After 20 Years," Washington, DC: Center for Economic and Policy Research, February 2014, pp. 4–10.

28. Jeffrey S. Passel, D'Vera Cohn, and Ana Gonzalez-Barrera, "Net Migration from Mexico Falls to Zero—and Perhaps Less," p. 6. Pew Research Center, Washington, DC, April 23, 2012.

29. Richardson and Pagán, "Human and Social Aspects of Cross-Border Development in the McAllen/Reynosa Area," October 2002, p. 25.

30. "La Banda de Sicarios Los Zetas 'Te Quiere a ti, Militar o ex Militar,'" *El País*, April 15, 2008; Brenda Fiegel, "The Recruitment of Assassins by Mexican Drug Cartels," Foreign Military Studies Office/Joint Reserve Intelligence Center, Border Security Team Fort Leavenworth, Kansas, February 3, 2009.

31. INEGI (Instituto Nacional de Estadística y Geografía), Banco de Información Economica, http://www.inegi.org.mx/sistemas/bie/.

CHAPTER 18

1. Joe Ward, "Owners Demolishing Part of Old Maytag Plant," *The Register-Mail*, August 31, 2012.

2. Amey Stone, "Can Maytag's Stock Keep Spinning Faster? Having Soared 150% in Two Years, Beating Expectations Gets Harder and Harder," *BusinessWeek*, July 30, 1999.

3. Leonard Hadley, phone interview, February 24, 2012.

4. Bob Lutz, *Car Guys vs. Bean Counters: The Battle for the Soul of American Business*, pp. x-xii, 73. New York: Penguin, 2011.

5. Michael V. Copeland, "Stuck in the Spin Cycle: Maytag, the All-American Appliance Icon, Is Learning a Dangerous Lesson: You Can't Manage a Turnaround Just by

Managing Costs," *Business 2.0 Magazine*, May 1, 2005. CNNMoney.com (http://money.cnn.com/magazines/business2/business2_archive/2005/05/01/8259675/).

6. Angela Barnes, "The Maytag Repairman Sure Has His Work Cut Out; Appliance Maker's Bleak Outlook Have Some Wondering about Its Viability," *Globe and Mail* [Canada], April 26, 2005; Don Cooper, "Maytag CEO's Bountiful Severance Package Awaits," *The Register-Mail*, October 4, 2005; David Barboza, "From China, a New Bid for Maytag and Status," *New York Times*, June 22, 2005; David Marcus, "A Sale to Stop the Bleeding," *Corporate Control Alert*, August 2005.

7. Copeland, "Stuck in the Spin Cycle," May 1, 2005.

8. Peter Hussmann, "Newton Couple Sues Ralph Hake, Contractor over Problems Found at Home Former Maytag CEO Built in 2002," *Newton Independent*, March 28, 2011.

9. James P. Miller, "A Fall from Grace: Maytag's Woes Tied to U.S. Focus, Size," *Chicago Tribune*, May 29, 2005.

10. In 2004, when Barack Obama was running for Senate and campaigning with Dave Bevard and Doug Dennison in union halls across Illinois, the Crown family was one of Obama's biggest, if not his biggest, financial backer. Lester Crown, whose family had an enormous financial stake in Maytag Corporation, said to the *Chicago Tribune* that the plant "had not been competitive for years." In the end, it was Crown's assessment that likely mattered most, Patrick said. Lester Crown, chair of the Chicago Council on Global Affairs and philanthropist to the Chicago Lyric Opera, was, at age 87 and retired, still the twelfth most powerful person in Chicago in 2013, according to *Chicago Magazine*—just ahead of his ally, Senator Dick Durbin. Part of that influence was tied to his longtime relationship with Barack Obama. The Crown family gave at least $128,000 to Obama in his 2004 senatorial campaign and were major bundlers for Obama in his two presidential runs. Obama's chief strategist, David Axelrod, said that Obama did not know of the Crown family's holdings in Maytag when he mentioned the Galesburg plant closing in his electrifying DNC speech or during his Labor Day campaign stop in Galesburg in 2004. Axelrod also argued that candidates and donors needn't share perspectives on everything, which is reflected in the *Tribune* exposé of the Crown-Obama connection in which Crown criticizes Obama's stance on the plant closing. The Crown family made their fortune at weapons giant General Dynamics, manufacturer of the F-16, the Trident submarine, and the Abrams tank. Crown was also involved in a bribery scandal in the 1970s and 1980s, and several sources claim that General Dynamics has benefited substantially from what amounts to the "legal bribery" of more recent years. The balance of the evidence, however, suggests that Crown invested in Maytag for the long haul, at least at first, when Chicago Pacific Corporation (owner of Hoover) merged with Maytag. Along with John C. Bogle and Warren Buffett, Lester Crown worked on a high-profile Aspen Institute panel on the social responsibilities of business after the financial crisis. The report, "Overcoming Short-termism," suggested sweeping changes to executive compensation, investment practices, and business ethics. "I don't think Crown started that way," Dave Bevard said, "but he has to do business with the sharks." And to win office in Illinois, Obama had to swim with the sharks as well—all while barnstorming the union halls of Illinois.

"100 Most Powerful Chicagoans," edited by Cassie Walker Burke, *Chicago Magazine* 62.3 (March 2013); Bob Secter, "Obama's Fundraising, Rhetoric Collide," *Chicago Tribune*, February 1, 2008; Peter Hussman, "Lester Crown Resigns from Maytag's Board of Directors," *Newton Daily News*, September 1, 2005; Kate Ryan, "Crowns' Big Maytag Stake Gets Soaked," *Crain's Chicago Business*, April 30, 2005; Nicolas J. S. Davies, "The Crown Family: Investing in Weapons, War, and Obama," *Z Magazine* (May 2012); Douglas Frantz, "Lester Crown Keeps Top-Secret Clearance," *Chicago Tribune*, August 2, 1986; The Aspen Institute, "Overcoming Short-termism: A Call for a More Responsible Approach to Investment and Business Management," Business and Society Program, September 9, 2009; Steven Pearlstein, "Wall Street's Mania for Short-Term Results Hurts Economy," *Washington Post*, September 11, 2009.

11. Kate Ryan, "Crowns' Big Maytag Stake Gets Soaked," *Crain's Chicago Business*, April 30, 2005. In 2005 the Crowns held 4.1 million shares, which were worth upwards of $300 million when shares were trading in the $70 range in July 1999 (when it was likely overvalued). The *Crain's* article shows that in 2005 those shares were worth roughly $40 million. When Whirlpool acquired Maytag in 2006, Whirlpool purchased Maytag for $10.50 a share (earning the Crowns about $43 million, assuming 4.1 million shares) and 0.1193 of a share in Whirlpool stock ($92.773 at the time, or about $45 million for the Crowns).

12. People in Galesburg and in Local 2063 could only speculate on what happened in the upper reaches of the post-Hadley Maytag Corporation. From all accounts, it had devolved into a poorly run, unprofitable, and nontransparent company that refused to speak with its workers, the union, and local, state, and federal representatives. In the vacuum of information came plenty of conspiracy theories, some of them, perhaps, not far from the mark. Some believed Hake's failure at Maytag wasn't, in fact, a failure at all. Doug Dennison said he couldn't prove anything, but the entire Hake saga was incredibly fishy. "He was the bean counter at Whirlpool and for some reason Maytag snatched him up. And within a few years we're gone and now all of a sudden Whirlpool owns Maytag. It's awful coincidental. Somebody was asleep at the wheel." Dave Bevard was convinced, and had some evidence to back his claims, that Hake ran the company into the ground to make it "ripe for the picking."

13. Matt Taibbi, "Greed and Debt: The True Story of Mitt Romney and Bain Capital," *Rolling Stone*, August 29, 2012.

14. Peter Hussmann, "Sale of Maytag Headquarters Campus Complete; $1 as Advertised," *Newton Independent*, April 17, 2012. This was the second sale of the old headquarters. The first was in 2007 to Iowa Telecom for $1.5 million.

15. "Fred Maytag Dies: A Manufacturer," *New York Times*, November 5, 1962; Robert Hoover and John Hoover, *An American Quality Legend: How Maytag Saved Our Moms, Vexed the Competition, and Presaged America's Quality Revolution*, p. 3. New York: McGraw-Hill, 1993.

16. Hedrick Smith, "When Capitalists Cared," *New York Times*, September 2, 2012.

17. Workers at the Amana plant had a union contract, although only half of the workforce paid dues to the Machinists because Iowa is a right-to-work state.

18. Gian Trotta, "Which Appliances Are Still American-made?" *Consumer Reports*, April 19, 2011.

19. David E. Bonior, "Obama's Free-Trade Conundrum," *New York Times*, January 29, 2014.

20. The Belvidere plant manager, Eric Schimmel, praised Chrysler's new working relationship with Fiat. Fiat, he said, emphasizes transparency and technology transfer both ways. It also emphasizes extensive worker input across its manufacturing facilities. Plant officials also praised the UAW and the government for their critical roles in one of the greatest turnaround stories of recent years.

21. Ro Khanna, "Five Myths about Manufacturing Jobs," *Washington Post*, February 18, 2013; Marc Levinson, "U.S. Manufacturing in International Perspective," Washington, DC, Congressional Research Service, February 20, 2014; Galina Hale and Bart Hobijn, "The U.S. Content of 'Made in China,'" Federal Reserve Bank of San Francisco Economic Letter 2011-25, A Pacific Basin Note, August 8, 2011. Khanna notes that American manufacturing workers are nearly six times as productive as Chinese factory workers and 1.5 times more productive than Japanese and German workers. This claim, however, is problematic according to the detailed analysis of Michael Mandel ("The Myth of American Productivity," *Washington Monthly*, January/February 2012).

22. William Strauss, "Is U.S. Manufacturing Disappearing?" Federal Reserve Bank of Chicago, August 19, 2010; Richard Longworth, "Company Towns, After the Company Leaves Town," Transcript from *Talk of the Nation*, National Public Radio, anchored by John Donvan, November 14, 2011; James R. Hagerty, "Remade in the USA: Once Made in China: Jobs Trickle Back to U.S. Plants," *Wall Street Journal*, May 21, 2012.

23. President's Council of Advisors on Science and Technology, *Report to the President on Capturing Domestic Competitive Advantage in Advanced Manufacturing*, pp. 1, 7. AMP (Advanced Manufacturing Partnership) Steering Committee Report, July 2012.

24. GE Appliances, "GE Opens First New Manufacturing Operation in Louisville, Ky. in Over 50 Years," Press release, February 10, 2012; GE Appliances, "GE Unveils French Door Refrigerator Factory in Louisville's Appliance Park," Press release, March 20, 2012; Charles Fishman, "The Insourcing Boom," *The Atlantic*, December 2012; Gian Trotta, "Which Appliances Are Still American-made?" *Consumer Reports*, April 19, 2011.

25. "Welcome Home: The Outsourcing of Jobs to Faraway Places Is on the Wane. But This Will Not Solve the West's Employment Woes," *The Economist*, January 19, 2013.

26. Charles Fishman, "The Insourcing Boom," December 2012. Fishman quotes John Shook, CEO of the Lean Enterprise Institute and a manufacturing expert here. David Wessel, "Big U.S. Firms Shift Hiring Abroad: Work Forces Shrink at Home, Sharpening Debate on Economic Impact of Globalization," *Wall Street Journal*, April 19, 2011. By contrast, those big companies expanded U.S. jobs by 4.4 million and added 2.7 million overseas in the 1990s. Neil Irwin, "Aughts Were a Lost Decade for U.S. Economy, Workers," *Washington Post*, January 1, 2010; Economic Policy Institute, *State of Working America* website (http://stateofworkingamerica.org/chart/swa-income-figure-2a-real-median-family).

27. Damien Cave, "As Ties With China Unravel, U.S. Companies Head to Mexico," *New York Times*, May 31, 2014.

28. Charles Fishman, "The Insourcing Boom," December 2012.

29. Jeffrey R. Immelt, "The CEO of General Electric on Sparking an American Manufacturing Renewal," *Harvard Business Review*, March 1, 2012. It should be noted that Immelt attempted to sell off GE Appliances in 2008 before adopting the insourcing approach.

30. Charles Fishman, "The Insourcing Boom," December 2012; Paul Markillie, "Manufacturing the Future: New Technologies Like 3D Printing Will Transform the Assembly Line," *The Economist*, November 21, 2012; America Revealed, "Made in the USA," PBS Video (http://video.pbs.org/video/2227791872/).

31. Charles Fishman, "The Insourcing Boom," December 2012. Fishman discusses a case where GE workers helped eliminate 35 percent of the labor that went into making a dishwasher but were guaranteed by the company that it would not cost them their jobs. "Increasingly," *The Economist* wrote of the reshoring surge, "product innovation will go hand-in-hand with production breakthroughs, so more companies will want their research and development teams close to their factories" (*The Economist*, "Additive Manufacturing: Print Me a Jet Engine," November 22, 2012). With advanced manufacturing, there's more proprietary technology to keep close to home and a need for greater control over the supply chain. Compressed product cycles (a refrigerator now has to be refreshed every two or three years instead of seven) makes "the alchemy among engineers, marketers, and factory workers all the more important," Fishman writes.

32. "Training Students for Jobs in Washington's Wine Industry," PBS NewsHour, September 10, 2012 (http://video.pbs.org/video/2277619791); Sonari Glinton, "A Company Town Reinvents Itself in South Bend, Ind.," National Public Radio, June 28, 2012; Aisha Labi, " Apprenticeships Make a Comeback in the United States," *Chronicle of Higher Education*, November 26, 2012; "Philadelphia High School Students Design Car of the Future," National Public Radio, June 9, 2010; "Fast Times at West Philly High," PBS Frontline, July 17, 2012.

33. Anthony Brino, "Some Manufacturing Jobs Go Begging," *Evanston Now*, February 13, 2012; Ben Casselman, "Help Wanted: In Unexpected Twist, Some Skilled Jobs Go Begging," *Wall Street Journal*, November 26, 2011; Britton Lombardi and William A. Testa, "Why Are Manufacturers Struggling to Hire High-Skilled Workers?" *Chicago FedLetter* 289, Federal Reserve Bank of Chicago, August 2011. Three of four manufacturers say there is a "skills gap" that has impeded their ability to expand. President's Council of Advisors on Science and Technology, *Report to the President on Capturing Domestic Competitive Advantage in Advanced Manufacturing*, p. 29.

34. David H. Autor, "The 'Task Approach' to Labor Markets: An Overview," National Bureau of Economic Research, Working Paper No. 18711, January 2013.

35. David E. Bonior, "Obama's Free-Trade Conundrum," *New York Times*, January 29, 2014.

36. Stephen Lacey, "Romney's Opposition to Wind Tax Credit May Become a Political Liability in Iowa: 'This Is a Very Big Deal for Us,'" *Think Progress*, August 23, 2012; Thomas Fitzgerald, "In a Former Factory Town, Clean-Energy Jobs Bring Hope,"

Philadelphia Inquirer, July 19, 2009; Environment Protection Agency, "Former Maytag Appliance Plant, Newton, Iowa Success Story: Small Town Redevelops as Wind Energy Manufacturing Hub," RE-Powering America's Land: Siting Renewable Energy on Potentially Contaminated Land and Mine Sites, *EPA Newsletter*, March 2009; Dan Kelley, "Only Look Forward from This Point on," *Newton Daily News*, February 15, 2013; James Glade, "Iowa Jobs Depend on Wind Power Manufacturing," *Eyes on Iowa*, Drake University School of Journalism and Mass Communication, December 5, 2012; CNN, "Iowa's Turnaround Town," *CNNMoney*, January 3, 2012; David Pitt, "Obama Returns to Newton to Seek Wind Tax Credits," Associated Press, May 25, 2012; Mike Mendenhall, "TPI Composites' Newton Facility Settles Class Action Labor Lawsuit," *Newton Daily News*, September 11, 2012; Mike Mendenhall, "TPI Workers Weigh Idea of Unionization with IBEW Local 347," *Newton Daily News*, May 1, 2012.

37. Stephen Lacey, "Romney's Opposition to Wind Tax Credit May Become a Political Liability in Iowa," August 23, 2012; David Pitt, "Obama Returns to Newton to Seek Wind Tax Credits," May 25, 2012; Environment Protection Agency, "Former Maytag Appliance Plant, Newton, Iowa Success Story," March 2009.

38. Dan Kelley, "Only Look Forward from This Point on," *Newton Daily News*, February 15, 2013.

39. Matthew L. Wald, "U.S. Imposes Duties on Chinese Wind Tower Makers," *New York Times*, May 31, 2012. The International Trade Commission sided with the United States in the trade dispute (Cassandra Sweet, "U.S. Agency Backs Antidumping Tariffs on Chinese Wind-Tower Producers," *Wall Street Journal*, January 18, 2013).

40. Stephen Lacey, "Romney's Opposition to Wind Tax Credit May Become a Political Liability in Iowa," August 23, 2012.

41. David M. Kennedy, *Freedom from Fear: The American People in Depression and War, 1929–1945*, p. 13. New York: Oxford University Press, 1999. Kennedy quotes the President's Research Committee on Social Trends, *Recent Social Trends in the United States*, pp. xii, 1. Westport, CT: Greenwood, 1970.

42. Jacob S. Hacker and Paul Pierson, *Winner-Take-All Politics: How Washington Made the Rich Richer—and Turned Its Back on the Middle Class*, pp. 34–37. New York: Simon & Schuster, 2010. They reject the "skills-biased technological change" (SBTC) argument that higher rewards for formal education and advanced skills have driven the income inequality gap. "Inequality is dramatically higher in the United States not because of greater skill gaps or greater returns to education, but because within-group inequality is greater than it is in other rich nations," they write.

43. Hacker and Pierson, pp. 41–72. Emphasis in original.

44. Arne L. Kalleberg, *Good Jobs, Bad Jobs: The Rise of Polarized and Precarious Employment Systems in the United States, 1970s to 2000s*, pp. 183, 187. New York: Russell Sage Foundation, 2011; Arne L. Kalleberg, "The Social Contract in the Era of Precarious Work," *Pathways*, Fall 2012. Kalleberg adds "representation security," or a right to collective representation, which forces employers into long-term, rational

planning, and "skill reproduction security" to round out the three pillars of a new social contract for a new era.

45. Gary S. Becker, "How Can Inequality Be Good?" Hoover Digest No. 3, The Economy, July 13, 2011.

46. Kate Pickett and Richard Wilkinson, *The Spirit Level: Why Greater Equality Makes Societies Stronger*. New York: Bloomsbury, 2009. One innovative epidemiological study found that income inequality accounted for more than 100 deaths per 100,000 in each income quartile, suggesting inequality has a negative impact across the income distribution. John W. Lynch, George A. Kaplan, Elsie R. Pamuk, Richard D. Cohen, Katherine E. Heck, Jennifer L. Balfour, Irene H. Yen, "Income Inequality and Mortality in Metropolitan Areas of the United States," *American Journal of Public Health* 88.7 (1998): 1074–80.

47. Hacker and Pierson, *Winner-Take-All Politics: How Washington Made the Rich Richer*, pp. 55–56.

48. Jeff Faux, *The Servant Economy: Where America's Elite Is Sending the Middle Class*, p. 6. Hoboken, NJ: John Wiley & Sons, Inc., 2012.

49. The White House, "President Barack Obama's State of the Union Address–As Prepared for Delivery," February 12, 2013. One Mac line and a $100 million investment was for cash-rich Apple Computer just a toe in the water, but it was a start. "The consumer electronics world was really never here," Apple CEO Tim Cook said. "It's a matter of starting it here" (Ronnie Polidoro, "Apple CEO Tim Cook Announces Plans to Manufacture Mac Computers in USA," Rock Center with Brian Williams, December 6, 2012.)

50. Bob Secter, "Obama's Fundraising, Rhetoric Collide," *Chicago Tribune*, February 1, 2008; John M. Broder, "Warming Up for Clinton, Taking Aim at Obama," *New York Times*, February 19, 2008, The Caucus: *The Politics and Government Blog of The Times*.

51. The White House, "Remarks by the President on the Economy—Knox College, Galesburg, IL," July 24, 2013. Office of the Press Secretary (http://www. whitehouse.gov/the-press-office/2013/07/24/remarks-president-economy-k nox-college-galesburg-il).

EPILOGUE

1. Flora's account matched that in David Silva, "Infierno en Reynosa: Fuego devora maquiladora," *El Mañana*, April 23, 2013.

2. Dave Hendriks, "McAllen Renames Military Highway to Honor Allen," *McClatchy-Tribune Business News*, February 23, 2011; Martha L. Hernandez, "BRIEF: Reynosa Christens Mike Allen Avenue," *McClatchy-Tribune Business News*, December 28, 2010; Ana Ley, "'Padre Mike' Allen dies at 72," *The Monitor* [McAllen, Texas], August 26, 2010; Matt Whittaker, "McAllen Business Trailblazer Named Border Texan of Year," *McClatchy-Tribune Business News*, January 18, 2006.

3. "Monumento al migrante y de Arturo Solís abandonado," *La Prensa*, April 25, 2011.

4. Tim Johnson, "What's Going on in Reynosa?" Mexico Unmasked blog, *McClatchy Newspapers*, March 14, 2013; Dawn Paley, "Off the Map in Mexico: In the Wake of a

Militarized Drug War, the Power of Cartels Is More Pervasive Than Ever," *The Nation*,
May 23, 2011; Matt Rivers, "KSAT Investigates Information Blackout in Reynosa,
Mexico: Blackout Keeps Residents in Dark about Drug War," KSAT Television, San
Antonio, April 25, 2013; Raymundo Pérez Arellano, "We Got out of Tamaulipas Alive,"
translated testimony published in *Borderland Beat*, March 23, 2013; John Rosman,
"No Official Death Count from Long Gun Fight in Reynosa," *Fronteras Desk*, March
27, 2013; "Gunmen Open Fire on Reynosa Newspaper," *The Monitor*, May 7, 2012.

5. "Union Leader Killed in Reynosa," *Valley Central*, December 18, 2008; Ildefonso
Ortiz, "At Reynosa Factory, Claims of Regular Gulf Cartel Visits," *The Monitor*, May
18, 2013. Two other promotoras with whom we spoke did not think that the CDG
was involved with the CTM but agreed that it had been much more difficult to move
around the colonias, especially at night.

6. Maquiladora operators were still slack about following ergonomic, safety, and other
regulations, the promotoras said. Local managers would present a safe plant to
inspectors and foreign visitors only to return to standard practice later.

7. Patridge became CEO of MEDC in 2006 as Mike Allen's health declined. He brokered Whirlpool's 2008 sale of former Planta Maytag III to Fisher & Paykel, an appliance company from New Zealand. In 2012 Haier purchased Fisher & Paykel.

NOTES ON METHOD

1. "Q&A with Tony Swanson," *The Register-Mail*, November 16, 2002.

2. Robert C. Prus, *Symbolic Interaction and Ethnographic Research: Intersubjectivity and
the Study of Human Lived Experience*, p. 119. Albany: State University of New York
Press, 1996.

3. This American Life, "Mr. Daisey and the Apple Factory," WBEZ Chicago, January 6,
2012. The story has been retracted and is unavailable.

4. Mitchell Duneier, *Sidewalk*. New York: Farrar, Straus, and Giroux, 1999.

5. Andrew Abbott, "For Humanist Sociology," in *Public Sociology: Fifteen Eminent
Sociologists Debate Politics and the Profession in the Twenty-first Century*. Edited by Dan
Clawson, et al., pp. 203–204. Berkeley: University of California Press, 2007.

6. C. Wright Mills, *The Sociological Imagination*, pp. 4, 187. New York: Oxford University
Press, 2000. Originally published in 1959.

7. Andrew Abbott, "Against Narrative: A Preface to Lyrical Sociology," *Sociological
Theory* 25.1 (March 2007): 71, 94.

INDEX